Islam and Science provides the necessary background for understanding the contemporary relationship between Islam and modern science. Presenting an authentic discourse on the Islamic understanding of the physical cosmos, Muzaffar Iqbal explores God's relationship to the created world and the historical and cultural forces that have shaped and defined Muslim attitudes towards science. What was Islamic in the Islamic scientific tradition? How was it rooted in the Qur'ānic worldview and whatever happened to it? These are some of the facets of this rich and fascinating account of a tradition that spans eight centuries and covers a vast geographical region.

Written from within, this ground-breaking exploration of some of the most fundamental questions in the Islam and science discourse, explores the process of appropriation and transformation of the Islamic scientific tradition in Europe during the three centuries leading up to the Scientific Revolution.

Ashgate Science and Religion Series

Series Editors:

Roger Trigg, *Department of Philosophy, University of Warwick, UK*
J. Wentzel van Huyssteen, *James I. McCord Professor of Theology and Science, Princeton Theological Seminary, USA*

Science and religion have often been thought to be at loggerheads but much contemporary work in this flourishing interdisciplinary field suggests this is far from the case. The Ashgate Science and Religion series presents exciting new work to advance interdisciplinary study, research and debate across key themes in science and religion, exploring the philosophical relations between the physical and social sciences on the one hand and religious belief on the other. Contemporary issues in philosophy and theology are debated, as are prevailing cultural assumptions arising from the 'post-modernist' distaste for many forms of reasoning. The series enables leading international authors from a range of different disciplinary perspectives to apply the insights of the various sciences, theology and philosophy and look at the relations between the different disciplines and the rational connections that can be made between them. These accessible, stimulating new contributions to key topics across science and religion will appeal particularly to individual academics and researchers, graduates, postgraduates and upper-undergraduate students.

Other titles published in this series:

Scientism
Science, ethics and religion
Mikael Stenmark
0 7546 0445 4 (HBK)
0 7546 0446 2 (PBK)

Theology and Psychology
Fraser Watts
0 7546 1672 X (HBK)
0 7546 1673 8 (PBK)

Science, Theology, and Ethics
Ted Peters
0 7546 0824 7 (HBK)
0 7546 0825 5 (PBK)

Islam and Science

MUZAFFAR IQBAL
Center for Islam and Science (CIS), Canada

ASHGATE

Published by
Ashgate Publishing Limited
Gower House
Croft Road
Aldershot
Hampshire GU11 3HR
England

Ashgate Publishing Company
Suite 420
101 Cherry Street
Burlington, VT 05401-4405 USA

Ashgate website: http://www.ashgate.com

British Library Cataloguing in Publication Data
Iqbal, Muzaffar
Islam and science. - (Ashgate science and religion series)
1. Islam and science
I. Title
297.2'65

Library of Congress Cataloging-in-Publication Data
Iqbal, Muzaffar.
Islam and science / Muzaffar Iqbal.
p. cm. -- (Ashgate science and religion series)
Includes bibliographical references.
ISBN 0-7546-0799-2 (alk. paper) -- ISBN 0-7546-0800-X (pbk. : alk. paper)
1. Islam and science. 2. Religion and science. I. Title. II. Series.

BP190.5.S3 I67 2002
297.2'65--dc21

2002066449

ISBN 0 7546 0799 2 (HBK)
ISBN 0 7546 0800 X (PBK)

Printed and bound in Great Britain by MPG Books Ltd, Bodmin, Cornwall

وَمِنْ آيَاتِهِ

خَلْقُ السَّمَاوَاتِ وَالأَرْضِ

وَاخْتِلَافُ أَلْسِنَتِكُمْ وَأَلْوَانِكُمْ

إِنَّ فِي ذَلِكَ لَآيَاتٍ لِلْعَالِمِينَ ۞

(الرُّوم: ٢٢)

And of His Signs
is the creation of the heavens and the earth,
and the diversity of your languages and colors;
indeed, there are Signs in this, for those who know.
(Q. 30:22)

For Basit Kareem Iqbal—
My son and companion in spirit

Contents

Acknowledgments *ix*
Transliteration and Dates *xi*
Abbreviations *xiii*
Introduction *xv*

1 The Beginning 1
2 And these are the Signs 29
3 Making of the Tradition 39
4 Islam and Science Nexus 71
5 Withering of the Tradition 125
6 Transmission and Transformation 171
7 Winds of Change 201
8 The Colonial Cut 213
9 The Colonized Discourse 241
10 The Scientific Exegesis 279
11 The New Nexus 293

Bibliography 315
Index 335

Acknowledgments

It is impossible to repay the debt one accumulates while writing a book. It is not even possible to enumerate the names of all those who contribute in the writing of a book, directly and indirectly. Such is the nature of this enterprise. And yet, one can take comfort in the fact that once published, the book does not remain the property of its author; it assumes a life of its own and repays those who help in its emergence, in its own currency. However, not withstanding this impossibility of acknowledging all sources, I wish to thank a few without whose involvement this book would have not come into existence.

The book owes a great deal to the painstaking work of a small group of historians of science who have brought to light numerous manuscripts and treatises dealing with various aspects of the Islamic scientific tradition. Their work has just begun to reconstruct the contours of the Islamic scientific tradition. With thousands of manuscripts still waiting to be studied, it is still a long way before we can have any definite idea of the nature of this tradition that lasted longer than the Greek, Persian or even the modern scientific traditions. While historians of science are painstakingly reconstructing information, it is important that their findings be placed in the larger context of the Islamic tradition of learning of which the scientific tradition was merely one part. This is a task that historians of science leave to the general historians who in turn leave it to the specialists. Hence, the cultural matrix which gave birth to the Islamic scientific tradition has not received attention it deserves. Likewise, the factors that contributed to the decline and eventual disappearance of the Islamic scientific tradition still remain a mystery. This book attempts to construct a coherent account of the larger religious and cultural background in which the Islamic scientific tradition came into existence; it also explores—though without final conclusions—the vexingly complex issue of decline. I am aware that my conclusions, however tentative, might not be shared by certain historians of science whose work forms the building blocks for these conclusions. But I have attempted to remain faithful to historical facts.

I am grateful to my friend Dr. Zafar Ishaq Ansari who read the whole manuscript. He read the manuscript at a time when numerous other matters demanded his attention. His painstaking attention to details has been most helpful in standardizing the transliterated text. I am also thankful to him for pointing out certain crucial conceptual issues which needed clarification or elaboration.

The book would not have come into existence without the kindness and love of my immediate family. Their involvement in the project was not only through their generous acceptance of my physical, emotional and mental absence from family life while the work was in progress, but also through direct participation. I particularly cherish the memories of our excitement that each finished chapter brought to the household. The delightful face of my daughter Noor upon seeing me coming out of my study with a finished chapter in hand, the warm reception that generally followed and the discussions we had on the chapter not only rejuvenated me by somehow obliterating the effects of long and solitary labor but also brought a happiness that is almost impossible to express. Elma, my wife, proofread the whole manuscript several times, helped in the compilation of bibliography and the index. Her involvement in the project was, however, much more than this and it remains a cherished memory. Likewise, the book owes a great deal to the love and support of my son Basit, to whom the book is affectionately dedicated.

Needless to say that only I am responsible for all the flaws and shortcomings that remain. A work of this nature can never be a finished work. The Islamic scientific tradition was so intimately connected with the worldview created by Islam and so thoroughly rooted in the Qur'ān that its study encompasses much more than a single book can hope to do. The study of this relationship is, however, essential for any understanding of the contemporary dilemmas faced by the Muslim world. I hope this work contributes to this wider understanding in some small way.

Wuddistan
Rajab 1423 AH
September 2002

Transliteration and Dates

Transliteration of Arabic, Persian, and Urdu follows the convention of the *Encyclopaedia of Islam* with the following modifications: j is used for *jīm*; q for *qāf* and no letter is underlined. The Arabic guttural consonants *hamza* and *ʿayn* are represented as ʾ and ʿ, respectively; *hamzat al-waṣl* is also represented by ʾ. Certain well-known place names have been left in their familiar form which may present occasional anomalies but the benefit of writing Baghdad and Nishapur, rather than Baghdād and Nishābūr, are obvious. Likewise, Makkah and Madinah; and not Makka and Madīna. However, there are exceptions, dictated by usage or need to distinguish between certain letters; thus, Baṣra and not Basra. Personal names have only been transliterated for the pre-nineteenth century period; thus Ibn Sīnā and not Ibn Sina but Muhammad Iqbal and not Muḥammad Iqbāl. There are a few exceptions to this practice where less common names from the post-nineteenth century era have been transliterated.

The Qurʾānic passages are cited in italics without quotation marks; this distinguishes the Qurʾānic text from the rest without excessive quotation marks. All translations are mine. References to Ḥadīth (sayings of the Prophet) are cited as: compiler/book number/hadīth number.

Double dates have been used for the pre-nineteenth century period when discussing events or persons in the Islamic tradition. This helps the reader to quickly place the developments within the Islamic Hijra Calendar as well as in the Common Era (CE); it also provides a comparative time scale. The Hijra Calendar uses the event of the *Hijra* (migration) of Prophet Muḥammad from Makkah to Madinah in 622 CE as its starting date. The 1st of Muḥarram, 1 after the Hijra of the Prophet corresponds to Friday, July 16th, 622 of the Julian Calendar. The Muslim year is almost ten days shorter than the solar year; hence the two overlap in an irregular manner, with the hijra year (AH) often spanning two years in the Common Era. Common Era date can be calculated as: $\text{CE} = 622 + \text{H} - (\text{H} \div 33)$.

Abbreviations

DSB	*Dictionary of Scientific Biography*
EI	*Encyclopaedia of Islam, new edition*
Fihrist	*al-Fihrist*
GAL	*Geschichte der arabischen Litteratur*
GAS	*Geschichte des arabischen Schrifttums*
Iḥyāʾ	*Iḥyāʾ ʿUlūm al-Dīn*
Q.	*al-Qurʾān*
Wafayāt	*Wafayāt al-Aʿyān wa Anbāʾ Abnāʾ al-Zamān*

Introduction

We live in a world that has been transformed by a unique event: the rise of modern science in Europe in the seventeenth century. From its origin in the tiny part of Western Europe, this singular phenomenon has spread to all parts of the world during the last three centuries. Its transforming force has changed many aspects of how we live, die, communicate, marry, give birth to children, produce food, clothing, housing and conduct the other thousand and one daily routines of our lives.

Modern science is also the only part of the Western civilization that is unquestionably welcomed in all cultures. It is definitely in high demand in the Muslim world. From political leadership to reformers and from the common man in the street to the opinion leaders, everyone seems to agree that the Muslim world needs to catch up with the West in science and technology. The resolutions adopted by the Organization of Islamic Conference at its regular summits, the mantra of the political leadership in countries as far apart as Morocco and Pakistan and the writings of various leaders throughout the Muslim world—all incessantly demand more and more science. It is another matter that in their blissful innocence, they often confuse technology with science and even when they mean science, they usually only mean the applied sciences. Thus, it is not surprising that in public discourse about science in the Muslim world, the phrase most often used is "science and technology" in one breath, without a pause.

Since the time of the nineteenth century modernist reformers, the general opinion in the Muslim world has been that the West was able to advance and colonize almost the entire Muslim world because of its science and technology, both spoken of as if they are one. This has given birth to the "catching up syndrome"—the idea that as soon as the Muslim world acquires science and technology, it will catch up with the West. This has been articulated by such a large cross-section of leadership and with such regularity that it has become the gospel of contemporary development strategies.

Considering the impact of modern science on the modern world, perhaps it is not unwarranted that Muslims should be so enthralled by it. In addition, there are the essential needs of the contemporary Muslim societies which dictate a reliance on modern science and its products. These range from genetically altered seeds to telecommunication, from defense needs to pharmaceuticals and from consumer goods to essential chemicals.

In fact, for all practical purposes, the Muslim world, comprising one quarter of human beings now living on planet earth, is utterly dependent on the modern science and technologies based on it. This dependency is not merely the artificial dependency of the elite for consumer goods; rather, this is a fundamental dependence in almost all areas of life—from commodities of daily use to airplanes that transport millions of Muslims around the world every year. And this dependence is increasing. In this, the Muslim world shares its predicament with other non-Western countries. Perhaps it would not be wrong to say that science is the only product of Western civilization which has produced an unquenchable hunger in all other civilizations.

In its triumphal march during the last three centuries, modern science has obliterated all other ways of exploring nature, at least in a practical sense. One does not need years of research to verify this claim: from Islamabad to Jeddah and from Beijing to Niamey, contemporary scientific research is conducted on the same foundations as it is in any university or research laboratory in a non-Muslim country. It is obvious that a nuclear magnetic resonance spectrometer that has been installed in Makkah does not produce Islamic spectrographs; likewise thousands of Muslim scientists who work in European and North American laboratories do not produce Islamic science just because they are Muslims. They are workers in a vineyard that is deeply rooted in a civilization other than Islamic, the erroneous notion of universality and neutrality of modern science notwithstanding.

What is extraordinary in modern science is its global reach, not the illusion of its conformity with the metaphysical principles of all civilizations. This global reach also means a transforming power; it is these two aspects—the global reach and the transforming power—that have made it an unprecedented phenomenon in human history. What is without parallel in modern science is not any profound metaphysical or spiritual foundation; it is the sheer magnitude of its reach, its ability to penetrate cultures as different as Islamic and Hindu, Chinese and those of the North American aboriginal people. Emerging in a small part of Europe in the seventeenth century, through a complex process of appropriation, transformation and assimilation of Greek and Islamic scientific traditions, modern science soon broke away from both the Greek and the Islamic traditions in many fundamental ways. In time, it not only attempted to describe and explain nature, it also formulated its own "theology of nature". It gave birth to its own language and culture. During the course of the last three centuries, it has produced a community of scientists who belong to different races and religions but who share ideas and theories in a language made up of symbols and notations. They can discuss the origin and evolution of the cosmos and life on the basis of shared symbols and notations; they can interact through equations. The fact that electrons, atoms and molecules on the one hand, and gears, levers and beams on the other, have become universally accepted words in which contemporary scientists, engineers as well as the ordinary citizens of various nation-states communicate and conduct their daily business all over the world is indicative of the vast reach of the scientific enterprise.

This global penetration of modern science is a *fait accompli*, whether one likes it or not. If history can be our guide, it does not seem possible that we will return to a concept of matter—and ultimately of the whole universe—which is built upon the pre-seventeenth century notions of matter, space and time. Whatever judgment we may choose to pass on modern science, there is no escape from it. Even in the domain of non-Western medicine, where results of alternate philosophies of the human body and its maladies and treatments have been effectively demonstrated, modern Western medicine has been rapidly replacing traditional practices, thus causing an irreparable loss for the whole human race.

In the West, the rise of modern science has been accompanied by struggles with religious authorities as well as theological reflection on the new science and its products. These inner tensions and dynamics have produced an impressive amount of literature that deals with issues related to various aspects of Christianity and science. From Augustine to Newton, every major philosopher and scientist has reflected on the implications of scientific discoveries on their faith. There has been a surging interest in the science-religion discourse during the last quarter of the twentieth century. Briefly stated, the defining questions of contemporary science and religion discourse in the West revolve around a central core that include questions related to the origin of the cosmos, life and the notion of human person. These questions have arisen through advances in cosmology, quantum physics, neuroscience, evolutionary biology and other related disciplines which have made it possible for these sciences to provide purely "scientific answers" to some of the oldest and most fundamental questions humans have ever asked: What is life? When and how did it begin? What is the nature of nature? Is nature merely a huge coagulation of purposeless matter that has somehow emerged on the cosmic plane? Or is there any teleology observable in natural phenomena? Does God act in the physical world? Or are natural causes sufficient to explain everything—from thunderstorms to the formation of galaxies? Traditionally, it has been the prerogative of religions to provide answers to these questions. Now science makes the same attempt. This encroachment of science in a territory held by religions for centuries has generated several new facets of age-old science-religion discourse. The new religion and science discourse seeks to build bridges between science and Christian theology.

In the non-Christian traditions, the situation is rather different. In the case of Islam, the contemporary science-religion discourse is something of an historical anomaly. Islamic tradition has never faced a situation like the one it faces today. There are historical reasons for this. Modern science came to the Muslim world at a time when most of the traditional Muslim lands were under direct colonial rule. By then, the Islamic scientific tradition had withered. The great centers of learning that had sustained a continuous flow of scholars and scientists for centuries had all been hollowed out. And this had happened, not due to the devastation caused by the Mongol armies, as it is normally assumed, but in three apparently powerful and rich empires that had emerged following the Mongol invasion. Historical data clearly show that the Muslim world had recovered rather quickly from the Mongol disaster and within a short time, a large-scale realignment had produced three new empires: the Ottoman (1290-1924), the Ṣafavī (1501-1722), and the Indian Timūrī (1526-1857). During this later period, cities like Iṣfahān, Delhi and Istanbul were much more magnificent than Baghdad and Baṣra of the ʿAbbāsid era. Adorned with public parks, palaces, great open squares, impressive mosques, hospitals, schools, extensive irrigation works, and caravanserais, these cities supported artisans and craftsmen at a scale never before witnessed in the Islamic civilization. These three empires were not lacking in wealth and splendor, yet the Islamic scientific tradition withered in this era of riches. Why? This remains one of the most enigmatic questions of the history of science. Chapter five explores this question in some detail.

But regardless of the causes, the Muslim world did experience a profound loss of its most enduring tradition and eventually paid the heavy price through subjugation by the European powers which arrived in the traditional Muslim lands with armies carrying superior arms, built through advances in science and technology. Thus, for the Muslim world, the experience of colonization marks the watershed between the two eras: their colonization not only transformed the most basic institutional structures in the traditional Muslim lands, it also transfigured the tradition that had given birth to these administrative, educational and research institutions. When the direct colonial rule ended, not only the geographical boundaries were re-drawn but a new intellectual tradition was also enacted. It is this new intellectual tradition that has produced a cultural schizophrenia in the contemporary Muslim world. Seen from the perspective of the colonized, it was the sheer force of modern science and technology that had made it possible for England and France to colonize a large part of the world. This self-diagnosis then gave birth to the "catching up syndrome" and produced an insatiable hunger for modern science.

But this is in retrospect. For the late nineteenth century Muslim reformers, no such luxury existed. They had no time to ask serious questions about the relationship between Islam and modern science. Their concerns demanded immediate attention and practical responses; their survival was at stake. Faced with the task of survival, they postulated that the reason for their colonization was that they had fallen behind in developing modern science and the remedy was, therefore, to acquire it, as fast as possible. As a result, they saw modern science and technology as the most desirable aspect of Western civilization and implored their people to acquire it at all costs. In order to provide religious support to their agenda, an Islam and science discourse was construed on the basis of proving that no disharmony could exist between the "Work of God" and the "Word of God". This misconstrued discourse has, by now, produced mountains of literature that attempts to find evidence of every modern scientific discovery in the Qur'ān. This apologetic literature also attempts to show that the Qur'ān is, in fact, the word of God because it contains scientific theories and facts which modern science has only recently discovered.

Seen from the perspective of the Islamic tradition, such constructions are rather odd. During the centuries when science was an actively pursued discipline within the bosom of Islamic civilization, its relationship with Islamic worldview was never even a question: the Islamic scientific tradition had emerged from the same ethos which had given birth to all other branches of knowledge and it was fully integrated into the hierarchy of Islamic thought. Ibn Sīnā would have thought it absurd to conceive of "Islam" and "science" as two separate entities which had to be somehow related to each other. Al-Ghazālī would have considered the very idea of "Work of God" and "Word of God" appalling. Mullā Ṣadrā would think that such a division is a product of an unhealthy mind. During the time when the Islamic scientific tradition was a living entity, no such division was perceivable. Even when foreign currents were introduced into the Islamic tradition, they were quickly assimilated through an organic process of transformation. That which could not become Islamic remained outside the domain of Islamic polity as a foreign entity.

This is no more the case. The emergence of the contemporary Muslim nation-states was not accompanied by a renewed link with the Islamic tradition of learning that had produced monumental works of science, philosophy, religious thought, and literature. During the colonial era, that tradition was transfigured. In the meanwhile, the world had also changed drastically and a vast body of new knowledge had been produced. This new body of scientific knowledge demanded careful scrutiny, appropriation and assimilation. But all of this could only happen if the severed ties to the Islamic tradition of learning were re-established. But these ties could only be re-established if there were some "breathing space" for the task of reconstruction—a breathing space that could allow a large number of Muslim scholars and scientists to reclaim their tradition. But such a generation of scholars could only be produced if they were educated and trained in an organic and living Islamic tradition that was capable of appropriating and naturalizing new knowledge, as it did in the ninth to eleventh centuries. Thus, the daunting task of revival became hostage to a vicious circle and remains unfinished.

In reference to the framework of inquiry, it is important to realize that whereas in the West, it is theology that has been poised as a counterweight in the Christianity and science discourse, the same cannot be the case for Islam. For a meaningful discourse between Islam and modern science, Islamic theology cannot be expected to play the same role because in the Islamic tradition, theology deals with a different subject matter and its status is not like that which it has in the Christian tradition. In fact, it can be said with enough justification that just as there are no councils, synods, or ecclesiastical institutions in Islam, there is no theology as the term is understood in the Western religious tradition. The representatives of the Islamic tradition chose another name for their "theology": *uṣūl al-dīn,* "the principles or foundations of religion". In doing so, they also established an analogy with the term *uṣūl al-fiqh,* "the principles or foundations of jurisprudence". It must be stressed that this difference is much more than semantic; these two terms insist that they, respectively, refer to a "theology" and a jurisprudence based on the sacred scripture of Islam, the Qur'ān, and the *Sunna* (*lit.* the "Way") of the Prophet of Islam. And while there were, and still are, various schools of law in Islam, all believers agree on these two primary sources of Islam. And though Kalām is recognized as a distinct branch of philosophy, the traditionalists have clearly distinguished their discourse from Kalām, which was based on rationalist inspiration. But even Kalām cannot be said to be "theology" in the strict sense of the term as it is used in the Christian tradition. The subject matter of Kalām includes many aspects of philosophy rather than theology, embracing, for example, logic, epistemology, and cosmology. The practitioners of Kalām, *mutakallimūn*, regarded their discipline to be a philosophical metaphysics and considered themselves to be the rivals of the *falāsifa* (philosophers), the practitioners of *falsafa* (philosophy).

Thus, for a creative exploration of the relationship between Islam and modern science, one needs to examine modern science from the perspective of the Islamic concept of nature taken as a whole and within its own matrix which is based on the revealed text, the Qur'ān, and supplemented by the Sunna of the Prophet of Islam. This is not an easy task because as soon as one brings the revealed text into the contemporary discourse, there appears to be a hardening of attitudes and closing of doors because the science-religion discourse in the West is construed in the framework of theology and science and not in terms of the Bible and science, at least not in the mainstream. But perhaps the worst impediment is the parallel that is more likely to be drawn between such a stance and the presence of an extremist strand in the West which posits the Bible as a counterweight in the science-religion discourse, a strand that is despised in the academic world. However, notwithstanding this difficulty, one cannot think of a genuine Islam and science discourse which is not rooted in the Qur'ān.

It must also be recognized that as a transplant, modern science raises a different set of questions for the Islamic tradition from that which forms the core of discourse between Christianity and modern science, though there is bound to be some overlap. These questions are also different from those which arose naturally within the Islamic scientific tradition during the centuries when it was a living tradition. These new questions require a new methodology and a new language of discourse. This book attempts to examine and answer some of these questions. It builds upon the work of a small number of scholars in the vanguard who share an awareness of loss and a consciousness of the need to recover and revive the Islamic intellectual tradition which had given birth to Islamic scientific tradition.

Islam and science discourse cannot attain any degree of authenticity without its roots going back to the Islamic scientific tradition. What was Islamic in Islamic scientific tradition? How was this tradition rooted in the

Qur'ānic worldview and whatever happened to it? How does modern science differ from the Islamic scientific tradition? Equally important are the epistemological considerations concerning the status of the Qur'ān in relation to modern science and the nature and meaning of the so-called scientific verses of the Qur'ān. Similarly, the Islamic understanding of the physical cosmos, God's relationship to the created beings and the Islamic concept of life and its purpose are essential to any meaningful discourse on Islam and science.

It will not be an overstatement to say that this is an essential task which needs to be undertaken by a large number of Muslim scientists who are deeply rooted in various Islamic sciences. But contemporary Muslim scientists are a product of secular institutions. They do not receive any formal training in Islamic sciences and their knowledge of Islam's formidable tradition of learning is, by and large, fragmentary. Islamic scholars, on the other hand, generally remain oblivious to modern science. They have neither the academic training nor the technical skills to discuss the relationship between Islam and science. As a result, the Islam and science discourse has remained underdeveloped. It is not even taken seriously, though considering the impact of modern science on the Islamic civilization, a serious interaction with modern science at this level is not merely an academic exercise; it is an essential imperative. Modern science also attempts to redefine the very notions on which the relationship between humanity and its natural habitat is built. It has created several strands of its own pseudo theology and has opened many new domains of ethical and moral concerns through advances in such fields as genetics and neuroscience. But above all, it is the triumphant force of modern science that seeks to replace all worldviews other than its own which needs an urgent and creative response by all religious traditions, most of all from Islam which remains anchored in the Divine Word, the Qur'ān, as it has always been.

CHAPTER ONE

The Beginning

By the time science emerged as an organized activity in the Muslim world, the Islamic civilization had already experienced two profound revolutions. The first was an intellectual revolution of the first order, the second, a social revolution which brought three advanced civilizations into mutual contact in the Muslim world through a language that was to become the *lingua franca* of Muslim learning: Arabic. Both of these revolutions had far reaching consequences for the emerging Islamic scientific tradition.

The intellectual revolution was brought about by an intense meditation on the Qur'ān by the companions of the Prophet of Islam. In the course of one generation, the Qur'ān had transformed the entire range of human experience for the Arabs—from the rules of their language to the most mundane matters of daily life. Revealed to the "unlettered Prophet"[1] in "clear Arabic"[2] during the course of twenty-three years (610-32),[3] the Qur'ān not only contained a moral code and the fundamentals of faith, it also had an advanced technical vocabulary. This rich repository of technical terms, which revolves around the Qur'ānic concepts of life, death, resurrection, prophethood and the moral response of the two sentient beings[4] to its message, provided the first conceptual framework for the Islamic tradition of learning.

The first to emerge in Islam were the religious sciences. During the life of the Prophet, the nascent Muslim community had recourse to him for all their spiritual needs. But after his death, the foremost problem faced by the community of believers was to know how to know God. The path to this knowledge, outlined in the Qur'ān, had to be elucidated. The person most

1. *Nabīyun ummīyun*, Q. 7:7.
2. *'arabīyun mubīn*, Q. 16:103.
3. The exact date of the first revelation is almost impossible to ascertain. Many historians favor 21st day of the month of Ramaḍān, 13 years before the Hijra, when Prophet Muḥammad was 40 years, six months and 12 days old (39 years, three months and 22 days according to lunar calendar). This is based upon the reports that the first revelation came on a Monday, in the month of Ramaḍān. This corresponds to August 20, 610 CE. Other reports suggest the 7th or the 17th day of the same Ramaḍān.
4. Humans and *Jinns*, see Q. 6:128, 130; 51:56; 72:1.

eminently qualified to do this was the Prophet himself but after his death, this responsiblity had to be shared by those who were the most learned. The work of these men and women gave rise to the emergence of the sciences of the Qur'ān (*ʿulūm al-Qur'ān*), which included, among others, the science of its recitation (*ʿilm al-qirā'at*), exegesis (*ʿilm al-tafsīr*), and jurisprudence (*fiqh*)—the queen of Islamic sciences.

This was followed by the emergence of various sciences related to the preservation of the sayings and deeds of the Prophet, Ḥadīth: *ʿilm al-rijāl*, (science of biographies), *ʿilm al-ansāb* (science of genealogy) and *ʿilm al-tārīkh* (science of history). These religious sciences provided the intellectual context and some elements of the methodology that was later used by natural sciences. The key elements of this methodology were an uncompromising adherence to truth and objectivity, a respect for corroborated empirical evidence, an eye for detail and a refined taste for proper categorization and classification of data. It was only after the Qur'ānic sciences had been firmly established and earliest collections of Ḥadīth had been compiled that the Islamic scientific tradition emerged. But more than the mere chronology, what is important here is the fact that the scientific tradition that was to remain the most advanced scientific tradition anywhere in the world for the next eight centuries, arose from the bosom of a tradition of learning that had been grounded in the very heart of the primary sources of Islam: the Qur'ān and Ḥadīth.

The Intellectual Milieu

Before the advent of Islam, Arabs had no science except for the traditional Bedouin knowledge of astronomy and medicine. There were only a few among them who could read and write. But they excelled in poetry and their memory was legendary. Arabic was already a sophisticated language but it did not have scientific technical vocabulary. The rules for Arabic grammar were first formulated by Abū'l Aswad al-Du'ālī (d. 70/688-9), who flourished at Baṣra. According to the legend, it was ʿAlī ibn Abī Ṭālib, the cousin, and later, the son-in-law of the Prophet and the fourth and the last of the four rightly guided caliphs (r. 36-41/656-661) who is said to have told al-Du'ālī to write a treatise on Arabic grammar based on the tripartite principle that the parts of speech are three: the noun, the verb and the particle.[5] This he did and Arabic grammar later developed on the basis of

5. There are different opinions about Abū'l Aswad's name, geneology and *nisba* but all sources agree that he was an eminent *Tābiʿī*, a partisan of

this principle, initially in Madinah, Kūfa and Baṣra—the three earliest centers of intellectual activity in Islam.

Arabs viewed the level of civilization of a person or a nation on the basis of linguistic skills. The purest Arabic was spoken by the Bedouins of the desert and initially it was the extraordinary power of the Arabic of the Qur'ān that baffled the Makkan contemporaries of the Prophet; the Qur'ānic Arabic was beyond anything they had ever heard. Its rhythm, its evocative power, its tremendous force and its unearthly syntax was so enchanting that even those who did not believe in its message used to go where it was being recited, merely to listen to its extraordinary discourse in a language that used the alphabet of their own language but that transcended its bounds by a mysterious mechanism.[6]

But more than the sheer linguistic power of the Qur'ān, it was its urgent invitation to act that provided the earliest stimulus for reflection on nature. The Qur'ān contained a large number of verses that called attention to the harmony, symmetry and order present in the natural world. It drew attention to the regularities of the planetary motion, it asked its readers to reflect on the watercycle, on the alteration of the day and the night, on the way certain trees bifurcate and others do not, though they are rooted in the same soil and receive the same nutrients. It asked the faithful as well as the non-believers pointed and enigmatic questions: What was there behind this astonishing order in the universe? Who was responsible for the functioning of such a grand system? Who had established the order that allowed them to benefit from various processes present in the natural world?

This invitation to reflect on nature was such an insistent theme of the Qur'ān that no one could ignore it, not even those who did not believe in its message. One cannot over-emphasize in a work of this kind the central position that the Qur'ān holds in the development of the Islamic scientific tradition. In fact, every doctrine or every branch of knowledge that appeared in the Islamic polity traces its roots back to the Qur'ān. It would not be wrong to state that the Qur'ān is the foundation upon which everything Islamic is built. This revealed text is the primary source, the

ʿAlī ibn Abī Ṭālib, under whose command he fought at the battle of Ṣiffīn. *Wafayāt*, vol. 2, pp. 535-9; *Fihrist*, pp. 87-90.

6. For example, the reaction of ʿUmar ibn al-Khaṭṭāb and Walīd b. al-Mughīra, two Makkans who knew how to read and write and who had a very developed literary sensibility; both felt utterly powerless against the power of the Qur'ān. The former accepted the message of the Qur'ān, the latter called it magic and sorcery.

essential textbook, not only of the religious sciences but also of all other branches of knowledge that emerged in the Islamic civilization. It is the secret spring of the Islamic Weltanschauung, the very heart of the civilization inspired by this faith which made its first appearance in a remote desert, far from the main currents of other civilizations. We will see how the Qur'ān linked the events occurring in nature to its central message in the next chapter; for now, let us briefly reconstruct the intellectual milieu of the early Muslim era and place the emergence of the Islamic scientific tradition in a broader historical context.

The technical terminology that came into existence as a result of a fervent and profound meditation on the message of the Qur'ān by the first generation of Muslims was employed in the *tafsīr* (exegesis) literature. This was an attempt to understand the precise and multi-layered prose of the Qur'ān. In this process, the new technical terminology was defined in minute details. Grammar, rhetoric and the study of the pre-Islamic Arabic poetry also developed primarily as linguistic aids to the interpretation of the Qur'ān. Thus, before the emergence of the Islamic scientific tradition, certain fundamental concepts, which had direct relation to the study of nature, had already been defined from the Qur'ānic perspective. This included the very notion of knowledge (*al-ʿilm*) and its related concepts—gnosis (*māʿrifa*) and comprehension (*idrāk*).

But the Qur'ān could not be interpreted merely on the basis of linguistics; it required an inspired heart, a profound faithfulness to its main function (guidance), an indefatigable fidelity to the Law (*Sharīʿa*) and a detailed and comprehensive understanding of the life and sayings of its first bearer and interpreter—the Prophet of Islam. Thus it became necessary to recall, recollect and use the sayings and actions of the Prophet for a better understanding of the message of the Qur'ān. The greatest scholars of Islam during this early period were primarily linguists, exegetes and jurisconsults (*fuqahā'*) who dedicated their lives to the patient study and interpretation of the Qur'ān and the Traditions of the Prophet (Ḥadīth) for the urgent needs of the Muslim community. They shaped the emerging intellectual milieu of the Muslim world in such a manner that the vision of Islam could be translated into a tradition of learning that was accessible to all and that could absorb new branches as it grew.

Not surprisingly, at the heart of this tradition of learning was the Qur'ān. Committed to memory in childhood, the Qur'ān regulated every event in the life of the Muslim community; it provided maxims to reflect upon, it nourished the hearts of the believers, it guided the scholars in their search but it also guided those who could not even read the text by a method that directly affected the spirit. This initial flowering of the Qur'ānic sciences created the foundations of Islamic tradition of learning upon which was built the study of nature.

The Qur'ānic Data

The resources available to the emerging Islamic scientific tradition were not laboratories and instruments but a grand metaphysics of nature, a framework for inquiry and a language equipped with the technical terms needed to express the results. The Qur'ān restored to the Arabic words their true character by stripping all illusions produced by the fantasy of pagan poets. Thus consecrated, the Arabic of the Qur'ān referred everything back to the direct and sovereign divine influence. The Qur'ānic name, *ism*, conferred to the thing its reality (*ḥaqīqa*) according to the divine knowledge, its objective existence (*kawn*) in creation and its legal value (*ḥukm*) amongst created beings. This minting of the name (*waḍ*ʿ) simultaneously placed the thing so named in its proper domain among things and established its ontological dependence on the Creator.

When the scientific tradition emerged in the Islamic civilization, its initial technical terms came from the Qur'ān and they referred back to the Qur'ānic usage, establishing a fundamental congruity between their scientific usage and their Qur'ānic meaning. The astonishing fixedness of the Arabic roots helped to identify the radicals of the Arabic verbs even in their most derivative form. In all fifteen verb forms, the verbs remain perpetually connected to their living source of fundamental meaning derived from the consonants. This not only helped in the compilation of Arabic dictionaries on a scientific basis but also established a semantic link between the technical terms and the language of revelation.

The conceptual framework that emerged during the early years of Islamic scientific tradition also used the resources of the Arabic language which were first developed for the study the Qur'ān. Arabic morphology had investigated different aspects of each root word as actualization of divine action. It had granted maximum energy to the imperative mood of the verb. All verbal forms were analyzed in composition, classified in their respective logical order (*taqdīm wa tā'khīr*), and examined in their reciprocal situations with respect to the one who utters them (*al-mutakallim*, the first person), the one upon whom they call (*al-mukhāṭib*, the second person) and the absent one of whom they speak (*al-ghā'ib*, the third). They were evaluated in respect to their degree of actualization in time: *māḍī*, the perfect, the action perfectly decided, realized and *muḍāriʿ*, the aorist.

This structure of language was affected by the Qur'ānic usage of words through the very process of ordering of ideas. This had a direct relevance to the terminology that was used in the Islamic scientific tradition. For example, reflecting on the fourteen consonants that are spelled like isolated letters (*al-ḥurūf al-muqaṭiʿāt*) which appear at the beginning of twenty-nine chapters (*sūwār*, sing., *sūra*) of the Qur'ān,[7] early commentators and grammarians established the basis for the emergence of the doctrine of *ishtiqāq al-akbar*, "superior semantic", codified by Abū ʿAlī al-Ḥasan b. ʿAlī al-Fārisī (d. before 370/980-81).[8] This bold etymological leap was an attempt to fix, outside of time, the idea-type of which such and such a phenomenon should remain constantly a sign. These isolated consonants were also the inspiration for the emergence of the science of the philosophical alphabet (*jafr*) that the sixth Imam, Jāʿfar al-Ṣādiq (d.147/765), is said to have been the first to apply to the Arabic alphabet. Jābir ibn Ḥayyān (d. *ca.* 160/777), one of the first major figures of Islamic scientific tradition whose works have survived, and its most celebrated alchemist, was to make ample use of these resources of the Arabic language in his "Theory of Balances", as we shall see toward the end of this chapter.

The Social Revolution

The social revolution which was to affect the emerging Islamic scientific tradition in a decisive way was brought about by the rapid expansion of the Muslim world into the regions held by three advanced civilizations: the Persian, the Egyptian and the Byzantine. This expansion started soon after the death of the Prophet of Islam in 11/632 and, over the next century and a half, produced a phenomenal intermixing of a large number of people of different races and religions in an ever-expanding geographical state. The swiftness of this expansion, its cosmopolitan nature and its sustained force was to transform the social relations and give birth to a creative energy that would transform all spheres of human activity. This social revolution also helped the nascent Islamic scientific tradition to incorporate into its body almost all extant works of the Persian and Hellenic science during the

7. These 29 *sūwār* are: 2, 3, 7, 10 to 15, 19, 20, 26 to 32, 36, 38, 40 to 46, 50 and 68. The 14 "disjointed letters" (*a, l, m, ṣ, r, k, h, y, ʿ, ṭ, s, ḥ, q, n*) come in 14 combinations of either one, two, three, four or five letters.

8. His advance grammar, *Kitāb ʾabyāt al-Iʾrāb* and its commentary, *Kitāb Sharaḥ ʾabyāt al-Īḍāḥ*, influenced all subsequent works of Arabic grammar. See *Fihrist*, pp. 139-40.

course of three centuries through one of the most startling translation movements in history. This movement, which began in the middle of the eighth century and ended in the middle of the eleventh century, was patronized by a large number of individuals and institutions.

The expansion of the geographical boundaries of the Muslim world was to continue for at least eight centuries but its first two phases stand out as two rapid waves that brought a large area under Muslim dominion. The first took place during an eighteen-year period between 11/632 and 29/649; the second between 74/693 and 102/720. Both of these expansions are important for placing the Islamic scientific tradition in its social context. During the first wave of rapid expansion, which started in the very year of the death of Prophet Muḥammad, first to be conquered was southern Mesopotamia (12/633); two years later Damascus was under Muslim control (14/635); the same year Persians were defeated at Qādisiyya (14/635). The following year (15/637), Byzantines were defeated on the River Yarmūk; in 16/638 Persians were again routed at Jalūla and Ctesiphon, the Sassanian capital was conquered. During the same year, Kūfa and Baṣra were established as garrison bases (*amsār*); both cities would become intellectual centers of the early Muslim centuries. Jerusalem was conquered in 17/638; this brought a large influx of Jews and Christians into the Islamic milieu. By 19/640, all of Persia had been conquered; Egypt fell in 19/640; the same year Armenia was attacked; the next year (20/641), a companion of the Prophet, ʿAmr b. al-ʿĀṣ, conquered Babylon. In 22/643, Fusṭāṭ was founded on the east bank of the river Nile, alongside the ancient Greco-Coptic township of Babylon.[9] In the following year (23/643), Tripoli was conquered; in 26/646 Alexandria was finally captured (it was previously besieged in 22/642 and 24/645); in 29/649 Muslims had a powerful navy which was fighting against Byzantines; the same year Cyprus was conquered.

The second wave of expansion between 74/693 and 102/720 stretched the boundaries of the Muslim world into the very heart of Europe. In 74/693, the Muslim army defeated Justinian II at Sebastopolis, Cilicia; the next year Armenia was conquered; in 78/697 Muslims were in Carthage. In

9. Traces of Babylon are still preserved in the ramparts of the Qaṣr al-Shamʿ. A bridge of boats linked it to the city of Giza (al-Jīza) on the west bank of the Nile. The name, al-Fusṭāṭ (*lit.* the tent) was given to the city because it was founded on the spot where ʿAmr b. al-ʿĀṣ had pitched his tent during the siege of Babylon. The remains of both al-Fusṭāṭ and Babylon are now part of Old Cairo.

92/710, four hundred Muslim soldiers had landed at the southern most tip of the Iberian Peninsula under the command of Ṭāriq b. Ziyād; two years later, all of Spain, except for a strip of territory in the northwest of the peninsula, had been conquered. By 94/712, Muslims had established permanent rule in Sindh and Samarqand, the latter was to become an excellent center of Islamic science. In 99/717, a vanguard of the Muslim army had crossed the Pyrenees into France, seizing Narbonne; by 102/720, Muslims were well settled in Sardinia.

For our purpose, the significance of this rapid expansion lies in the fact that the newly conquered lands brought Muslims in direct contact with the most ancient centers of learning in the midst of a social revolution that involved large-scale displacements and resettlements of a large number of people, conversions and mixing of races and faiths along with the establishment of new garrison cities. The development of new relations between people of different races and religions played a key role in the direction taken by the Islamic scientific tradition during its early days. The newly established contacts between Muslims and the Syriac-speaking Christians on the one hand and between Muslims and the Zoroastrians on the other were instrumental in the emergence of a translation movement that would bring a large number of Persian and Greek scientific texts into the Islamic scientific tradition. We will explore the impact of the translation movement in the third chapter.

It is useful to situate the emerging Islamic tradition of learning in its proper social context; after all, we are dealing with real men and women who lived their lives in relation to others and in a given time and place. We have already mentioned the two powerful conquest waves that swept through the ancient centers of learning, but what does it really mean? How could small armies of Muslims, originating in the city of Madinah, hold a territory so vast, belonging to so many races, cultures and religions? And what were the means of transfer of knowledge from the ancient centers of learning to the nascent Islamic tradition?

Most narratives of Islamic history ignore the remarkable process of social revolution that accompanied this conquest. They record the heroic deeds of individuals, details of battles and encounters of generals but they fail to bring into focus hundreds of thousands of men and women who lived in Ray, Khurāsān, Samarqand, Bukhāra, Córdoba and hundreds of other cities and villages; real human beings who could not be conquered overnight. Armies came and went but these men and women who lived out their lives in their localities did not come into the fold of Islam just because a famous general, having defeated the army of their general, had passed through their town on his way to the next campaign. In order to have a glimpse of the social revolution that accompanied this conquest, we must perceive these changes at a local scale, in very ordinary terms. True, we cannot leave out the heroic deeds and the high drama altogether for that is the stuff of history, but in order to understand the emergence of a new tradition, we must concentrate on a much smaller section of the bigger picture.

The post-conquest Muslim world during the first century of Islam was made up of geographically dispersed and racially diverse communities in which the Arab Muslims constituted the ruling stratum of a multilingual, multi-ethnic but overwhelmingly non-Muslim population. A vast majority of this overwhelmingly non-Muslim population lived in villages, some of which were in such remote areas that the news of the Muslim conquest could only reach there months or even years after the capture of main cities. Hence, whereas the conquest of land was a rapid process, the process of conversion to Islam was not; it took place gradually and naturally.

On the scale on which we wish to construct this picture, we must see this social revolution in small details. What did the Arab armies see when they arrived in new areas? They saw animals, birds and insects which they had never seen before. They saw new methods of irrigation, the use of new fertilizers, new crops and new fruits. They met with new warfare techniques, they encountered new technological devices, they saw bridges, dams, roads, they faced new manners of fortification and new methods of military communications. They saw beautiful ceramics, inks, pigments and embroidered artifacts. Most of these diverse things varied from country to country: what Samaqand offered was different from Egypt and what they found in Sardinia was different from what awaited them in Merv.

In the course of a century, all of these diverse and varied crops, methods and techniques became part of the Islamic civilization which spread over the newly conquered lands. The diffusion of new crops— such as rice, sorghum, hard wheat, sugar cane, cotton, watermelons, eggplants, spinach and many others—in various parts of that large empire meant that new techniques had to be developed for their cultivation in areas where these crops had never been cultivated. This also meant that thousands of men and women learned the use of new cultivation methods, they used new manures, they developed new irrigation systems, they increased their number of crops, making use of the seasons during which time the land had traditionally laid fallow. This meant a completely new rhythm of life which affected their work hours, their family and social relations and their sources of income.

This social revolution also facilitated mobility of people of different racial backgrounds at a scale never witnessed before. It was accompanied by a massive transfer of seeds, pigments and hundreds of other items over a large area. A process of urbanization also accompanied this social revolution. The new urban centers produced by this social revolution had to be provided with civic facilities, water, food, vegetables and sundry other things. This meant building of new dams, water channels, roads and a system of communication.

Throughout this period of unusual creative energy, there was one unifying thing: the Qur'ān, its text having been given a definitive orthographic form during the reign of the third caliph, ʿUthmān b. ʿAffān (r.24-36/644-656). These rapid demographic and social changes also created new challenges of diverse nature. Most of the people in the newly conquered lands did not speak Arabic. How were they going to understand the message of Islam? With the rapid expansion and intermixing of races, new juridical and doctrinal issues arose which could not be settled on the basis of precedence found in the practice of the Prophet or on the textual basis found in the Qūr'ān. It was during this early period of the ever-expanding caliphate when its administrative center moved from Madinah to Damascus in 41/661 that the legal schools started to take definite form. The first of the four major legal schools into which Muslim jurisprudence eventually crystallized was that of Abū Ḥanīfa who used deductive extension of jurisprudence by means of analogy (*qiyās*) and insisted upon the right of preference (*istiḥsān*) of a ruling suited to local needs. The other three legal schools were founded by al-Shāfiʿī (d. 205/820), Mālik b. Anas (d. 179/795) and Aḥmad b. Ḥanbal (d. 241/855).

Nor was this newly emerging social milieu a cohesive entity, and this, too, had profound consequences for the Islamic scientific tradition. The Islamic community was founded on the basis of a series of conditional contractual allegiances (*bayʿa*, *lit.* the squeezing of hands). First, there were the two ʿAqaba contracts, which formed the political and social foundation for the Prophet's migration to Yathrib (later to be called Madinah). Then there is the *Ṣaḥīfa Madinah,* in 48 articles, which is considered to be the first written constitution of the Islamic state. In both, the Prophet appears only as an overseer of the affairs of the Community of Believers, *umma*, without any legislative authority, the legislative magisterium (*amr*) being reserved for the Qur'ān alone. The executive power (*ḥukm*), an imperium, canonical and civil, belonged only to God; the role of the Prophet being only that of a facilitator. "I have received the command to wage war against men until they proclaim publicly: 'there is no deity except God'," he said, "once they announce this, their blood and their possessions become sacred to me by virtue of belief and their judgment belongs to God."[10] It was not up to him to probe the hearts of others; he had only come as a "warner and as a bearer of glad tidings".[11]

The prophetic authority was, thus, entrusted to Prophet Muḥammad by God, in the service of the Qur'ānic Law and his political role was based on a formal contract with the community of believers, through their contractual allegiance literally performed on the hands of the Prophet by their representatives. After the death of the Prophet, this contractual oath was made with the first Caliph, Abū Bakr, by the leaders of various tribes at the gathering held at Saqīfā Banū Sā'da on the day of the death of the Prophet. Abū Bakr received this authority as *Khalīfa tul Rasūl*, the vice-regent of the Prophet. At the death of Abū Bakr in 13/634, the choice fell on 'Umar b. al-Khaṭṭāb, allegiance was sworn on his hands as *Amīr ul-Mu'minīn*, the leader of the believers. On 26 Dhū'l-Ḥijja 23/3 November 644, as he was leading the morning prayer, Abū Lū'lū'a, a Christian slave of al-Mughīra b. Shu'ba, then governor of Baṣra, attacked him with a poisoned knife.[12] On his deathbed, 'Umar constituted a *shūrā* (council) to choose his successor. Three days later, he died on the first day of the new Hijra year 24/644. Through the consultative process, the choice of leadership fell on 'Uthmān and, once again, the leaders of various tribes swore allegiance to him.

But the choice of the leadership of the community became an issue in 36/656, at the time of the assassination of 'Uthmān—a schism from which Muslim polity never really recovered. It was this deep chasm that resulted in shedding of blood of Muslims by Muslims and that raised a fundamental question for which no simple answer could be found: Who was qualified to lead the community? The tension was heightened in 37/657 when two Muslim forces stood against each other at Ṣiffīn. The contest for the caliphate between 'Alī, son-in-law of the Prophet and Mu'āwiya, the governor of Damascus and later the founder of the Umayyad dynasty, had

10. *Bukhārī*/40/34.
11. *Bashīr wa nadhīr*, *cf.* Q. 5:19; 7:188; repeated many times.
12. Abū Lū'lū'a, whose first name was Fīroze, had complained to him about a tax against him and 'Umar had not complied with his request for a waiver, which he thought was not justified.

become a complex affair in which most of the prominent Muslims took sides with one or the other contestant. Swords were drawn but when ʿAlī restrained himself and consented to arbitration, a section of his army mutinied, alleging that his consent to arbitration meant that his claims to caliphate had not been legitimate. The mutineers, who became known as the *Khawārij* (Khārijites or Secessionists), raised fundamental questions about the basis, limits and qualifications for the political authority. Their extreme views set them apart from other Muslims. They held that a Muslim who committed a grave sin (*kabīra*) would cease to be a Muslim and if he were the caliph, his blood would become lawful.

The *Shīʿa*,[13] who had pledged ʿAlī their unquestioning support because they recognized his right to caliphate on the basis of his kinship to the Prophet, challenged this view, as did the *Murjiʿa*,[14] who disagreed with the Khārijite criteria for judging the belief of another Muslim on the basis of outward conformity to Law. They stressed that the submission and love of God was the foundation of belief, not the acts of piety. Should a believer commit one of the grave sins, but still believe, it would not impair his or her faith. They stressed that the ultimate verdict should be left to God; political authority should not be questioned on theological grounds because, in the final analysis, it belongs to God alone to determine the nature of the faith of every Muslim. They agreed with the Khāijites that any pious Muslim chosen by the community could become a caliph, whether or not he descended from Quraysh, the Prophet's tribe. This was unacceptable to the Shīʿa. They vested the right of caliphate and indeed, the right to interpret the Law, in the *Imām*, the rightful heir of the Prophet, who must, by definition, be from his progeny. The Imāmite contended that in addition to the birthright to authority, it was indispensable for the Imām to have received a personal investiture, designating him as endowed with a supernatural privilege: *ʿiṣma*, impeccability, an arbitrary infallibility, guaranteeing him immunity in relation to God and freedom from accountability before men.

Between these extremes, the majority of Muslims followed the middle way. They were called *Ahl al-Sunna waʾl-Jamāʿ*, the people of the Way of the

---

13. The name is derived from *shīʿat ʿAlī*, the partisans of ʿAlī.
14. The term literally means "the upholders of *irjāʿ*" and is derived from the Qurʾānic usage of the verb *arjā* (in non-Qurʾānic usage *arjāʿ*), meaning "to defer judgment", *cf.* Q. 9:106. *Murjiʿa* identified faith (*imān*) with belief, or confession of belief to the exclusion of acts. See "Murjiʿa", *EI*, vol. vii, pp. 605-7.

Prophet (*sunnites*). They maintained that since all actual power comes from God, one must obey any non-apostate Muslim leader, go to prayers and to war under his order without probing too much about his virtues and vices, provided he publicly honors, respects and practices the basic tenets of Islam.

It was during these political and social upheavals that the first major theological controversies arose in Islam; these gave birth to various systematic schools of thought. One of the first such controversies hinged upon the nature of human freedom which had fundamental implications for the political situation of the time. Freedom meant responsibility; it meant that the caliph could not absolve himself from his deeds by invoking an inexorable decree of God. Predestination, on the other hand, meant the opposite. This is how a third group of scholars, the *mutakallimūn*, arose in Islam. They are sometimes regarded as being competitors to the other two groups of scholars, the jurists (*fuqahā'*) and the traditionalists (*muḥaddithūn*), but their area of interest was well-defined and different from the others. Initially, the mutakallimūn were mainly interested in the questions related to free will and predestination, nature of divine justice, hell and heaven and divine attributes. They also formulated a physical theory which was to have important implications for the Islamic scientific tradition; it is briefly discussed in a subsequent section of this chapter.

The Beginning of the Islamic Scientific Tradition

Our knowledge about the origin of the Islamic scientific tradition is still very fragmentary. Most of the primary texts have been either lost or remain unstudied. This is especially true for the period before Jābir ibn Ḥayyān who is said to have died in 160/777. What is certain, however, is the presence of early medical and astronomical traditions that go back to the days of the Prophet. Soon after his migration to Madinah, the Prophet had established a school in his mosque where ʿAbd Allāh b. Saʿīd b. al-ʿĀṣ taught the art of writing.[15] We also know that one form of ransom for the Makkan prisoners of war in the battle of Badr (2/624) was teaching of children for a fixed duration. There are also reports about the existence of

15. On these early developments, see Azmi, Mohammad Mustafa (1978), *Studies in Early Hadith Literature*, American Trust Publications, Indianpolis, pp. 1-5, wherein he quotes some of the earliest sources in support of his claim that the educational policy of the Prophet had established schools in Madinah where reading and writing was taught.

public libraries as early as the middle of the first century of Hijra.[16]

At any rate, the Umayyad prince Khālid b. Yazīd b. Muʿāwiya, the Ḥakīm (philosopher) of the family of Marwān, who flourished in Egypt (d. 85/704 or 90/708) did have a library and is said to have encouraged the first translations from Greek into Arabic. He was interested in medicine, astrology and alchemy. He also made the first contacts with the Alexandrian scholars. But we do not know much about his own works, though legend ascribes a large number of alchemical works to him. We also have a critical edition of the small book that appeared in Paris in 1559 with a rather dramatic title, *Booklet of Morienus Romanus, of the Old Hermit of Jerusalem, on the Transfiguration of the Metals and the Whole of the Ancient Philosophers' Occult Arts, Never Before Published*. This small volume, which set afloat the Latin Morienus, is considered to be the first alchemical work to have reached the West.[17] This text undoubtedly establishes Khālid's diligent search for the genuine practitioner of the art of alchemy as well as his interest in translations of ancient scientific texts into Arabic. Of course, flourish and legend have been added to the Latin text, but the "entire Latin tradition of the Morienus appears to derive from a single source, which was certainly a translation from Arabic."[18] No Arabic original is known but a number of identical passages can be found in various Arabic works, including the thirteenth century work of Abū'l Qāsim Muḥammad ibn Aḥmad al-Irāqī, *Book of Knowledge Acquired Concerning the Cultivation of Gold*.[19] Al-Irāqī also quotes a number of alchemical verses of Khālid. Ibn al-Nadīm tells us in his *Fihrist* that he had himself seen four books by Khalid: *Kitāb al-Hararat, Kitāb al-Ṣahīfatul Kabīr; Kitāb al-Ṣahīfatul Ṣaghīr* and *Kitāb Waṣīyya il'l Ibnuhu fī'l Ṣanʿa*.[20]

The sixth Shīʿī Imām, Jaʿfar al-Ṣādiq (80-147/700-765), who is said to be

16. For example, the library of ʿAbd al-Ḥakam b. ʿAmr al-Jumāḥī contained *kurrāṣāt* (books) for public use, Azmi (1978), p. 5.
17. The Latin text was entitled Morieni Romani, Quondam Eremitae Hierosolymitani, de transfiguratione metallorum, & occulta, summaque antiquorum Philosophorum medicina, Libellus, nusquam hactenus in lucem editus. Paris, apud Gulielmum Guillard, in via Iacobaea, sub diuae Barbarae signo, 1559. An English edition was published in 1974 as A Testament of Alchemy, edited and translated by Lee Stavenhagen (1974), The University Press of New England, Hanover, New Hampshire.
18. Stavenhagen (1974), p. 60.
19. Kitab al-ʿilm al-maktasab fi ziraʿat adh-dhahab (Book of Knowledge Acquired Concerning the Cultivation of Gold), edited and translated by E. J. Holmyard (1923), Paris.
20. *Fihrist*, p. 434.

the teacher and master of Jābir ibn Hayyān, is also credited with some scientific works. His *Book of the Epistle of Jaʿfar al-Ṣādiq on the Science of the Art and the Noble Stone* has been published by Julius Ruska with a German translation.[21] Before proceeding further, let us place this emerging tradition in its social and historic context.

The Social Milieu

At the close of the first Islamic century (August 718), the Islamic tradition of learning had firmly established its roots in the newly emerged centers of learning, especially at Madinah, Kūfa and Baṣra. The social revolution that had accompanied the conquests had set in motion a vast chain reaction, political struggles had fractured the unity of the society and scholars; two civil wars had been fought, several new cities had been founded;[22] Islamic coinage had been minted and the Umayyads had passed the zenith of their rule.

While the earliest scientific works were being composed, a revolt against the Umayyads was taking shape in the newly conquered Iranian cities, especially in Merv. By Ramaḍān 129/747, this resurgent movement in favor of the ʿAbbāsids had gathered enough momentum for a westward march under the leadership of Abū Muslim; thus began the third civil war in Islam. By 132/749, ʿAbbāsid troops had taken control of Kūfa; on 13 Rabīʿ I, 132/750, Abū'l ʿAbbās (posthumously called al-Saffāḥ) was proclaimed caliph at Kūfa; two months later, the Umayyads were decisively defeated at the battle of Greater Zāb and in June of the same year, most of them were massacred but ʿAbd al-Raḥmān I escaped to Spain where he established the Umayyad rule (138-423/755-1031).[23]

---

21. *Kitāb Risāla Jaʿfar al-Ṣādiq fī'l-ʿilm al-Ṣanʿa wal-Ḥajar al-Mukarram*, *Isis*, vol. 7, pp. 119-21.
22. These were initially garrison cities, later they became centers of learning and sciences. They include Kūfa, Baṣra, Fusṭāṭ (now Old Cairo) and Wāsiṭ.
23. ʿAbd al-Raḥmān b. Muʿāwiya b. Hishām (b. 113/731) had lost his father as a child. His mother was from the Berber tribe of Nafza. When the Umayyad state fell, he was living in the village of Ruṣāfa, on the banks of the Euphrates River. As the ʿAbbāsid soldiers surrounded his house, he and his younger brother took flight. They swam across the river; his brother was killed but he made it to the other side. After hiding in various places and traveling in disguise, he reached his mother's tribe and took refuge with his maternal uncles in the coastal city of Nakūr. From here he approached the Umayyad clients in al-Andalus. He entered Córdoba after defeating a local ruler 139/July 756 and was

These were uncertain times. The caliphate of Abū'l ʿAbbās was challenged, he had to fight wars with new contenders and the four years and eight months of his reign could hardly be described as a stable period. When he died in Dhū'l Hijjah, 136/753, his brother Abū Jaʿfar was in Makkah. He rushed back to Kūfa where his caliphate was proclaimed. But he also had to fight with other contenders of caliphate. In 145/762, Abū'l Jaʿfar decided to move his capital to a safer place. He himself went out to find a suitable place and chose Baghdad because of its pleasant climate and the two rivers, Euphrates and Tigris. The city was planned as a circular city with sixteen gates; it was called *Madinatul Islam*, the city of peace. A Persian astrologer and engineer, al-Naubakht (d. c.160/776-77) and Māshāllāh,[24] an Egyptian (?) Jew (d. *ca*. 199/815 or 204/820), made the measurements prior to the construction of the city. The construction was supervised by a Persian, Khālid ibn Barmak.

With the construction of Baghdad, we arrive at the dawn of the Islamic scientific tradition. From this point onwards, it becomes progressively easier to reconstruct the contours of the tradition. Our sources become increasingly more reliable and there is an exponential increase in the available texts. The accounts of the construction of the city tell us about the presence of a large number of specialists in various fields—engineers, astrologers, astronomers, medicine men—Muslims as well as non-Muslims, Arabs as well as non-Arabs, who took part in numerous projects. This establishes the fact that by then, there was already a flourishing tradition of interaction between scholars and scientists belonging to different religions and races. In time, Baghdad would provide a perfect meeting place for an enormously wide range of scientists and scholars; it would also become one of the main centers of a translation movement of unprecedented scope and proportions. We will discuss the relationship between this translation movement and the Islamic scientific tradition in the next chapter.

The fifty year period between 134/750 and 184/800 saw the rule of five

---

proclaimed the *amīr* (ruler). He contented himself with this title, rather than claiming the Caliphate. Nevertheless, he ruled independently and the ʿAbbāsid caliphs let him be. It was not until 316/929, that the Umayyads in al-Andalus proclaimed their caliphate, and that too, only after a Shīʿite caliphate had been established in North Africa. For al-Andalus, see the excellent two volume work, Jayyusi, Salma Khadra (ed., 1994), *The Legacy of Muslim Spain*, 2 vols. E. J. Brill, Leiden.

24. His real name was probably Manasseh (Mīshā in Arabic), most Latin translators named him Messahala with variants such as Macellama and Macelarama.

ʿAbbasīd caliphs.[25] It was during this period that the second legal school (*madhhab*) emerged in Islam. This was based on the works of a number of scholars but was crystallized by the work of Mālik ibn Anas, the compiler of *Kitāb al-Muwaṭṭāʾ*,[26] one of the earliest collections of the Prophetic traditions. The first, or at least one of the earliest legal treatises on taxation, *Kitāb al-Kharāj*, was also written during this period by the able student of Abū Ḥanīfa (d. 151/768), Qāḍī Abū Yūsuf (113-183/731-799),[27] the first supreme judge (*Qāḍī ʾl-Quḍāʾ*) in Islam. All of these developments had deep social, political and religious causes. The Arabic grammar was also systematized during this period. This was to provide a fundamental structure for the emergence of precise definitions of technical terms that were used by the scientific tradition. One of the first books of Arabic grammar, simply called *al-Kitāb* (*The Book*), was written by Abū Bishr (or Abū'l Ḥasan) ʿAmr ibn ʿUthmān ibn Qanbar (d. *ca.* 179/795),[28] a Persian student of al-Khalīl ibn Aḥmad (d. *ca.* 175/791), the founder of the science of Arabic metrics. The first astrolabes were constructed in the Muslim world.[29] The first members of the illustrious Nestorian family of physicians, the Bakhtyashū, arrived in Baghdad and the first translations of Persian medical works were made into Arabic.

This background makes it easier to see, at the outset of this tradition, that it was intimately linked to the religious, cultural, political and social

25. Abū'l ʿAbbās al-Saffāḥ (750-754); Abū Jaʿfar al-Manṣūr (754-775); al-Mahdī (775-785); al-Hādī (785-786) and Hārūn al-Rashīd (786-809).

26. *Lit. The Book of the Beaten Road* or *The Book of the Smooth Path*, containing about 1700 juridical traditions arranged according to the subject, with remarks on the *Ijmāʿ* of Madinah. 15 recensions are known; two have survived in their entirety; numerous contemporary editions exist along with many commentaries, *cf. GAL* vol. 1, p. 176 and 297-9; also *GAS*, vol. 1, pp. 457-84.

27. Arabic edition (Būlāq, 1302/1884), French translation with notes by Fagnan: *Le Livre de l'imôt foncier*, Paris, 1921, also see *Isis*, vol. 4, p. 579; *GAL* vol. 1, p. 171.

28. *GAL*, vol. I, p. 101; also, Derenbourg, Hartwig (1881-89), *Le livre de Sibawaihi*, 2 vols, Paris, German translation based on Derenbourg's text, with extracts from the commentaries of Sīrāfī (d. 368/978-9) and others by Jahn, G. (1894-1900), 2 vols. in 3, Berlin; cited from Sarton, George (1931-48), *Introduction to the History of Science*, 3 vols. The Williams & Wilking Company, Baltimore, vol. 1, part 1, p. 542.

29. One of the first to do so was Abū Isḥāq Ibrāhīm ibn Ḥabīb ibn Sulaimān ibn Samura ibn Jundab (d. *ca.* 161/777); he also wrote some of the earliest works on astrolabe, on the armillary spheres and on the calendar; he is also credited with a *qaṣīda* in praise of astrology.

fabric of the society. The intellectual tradition that emerged from this milieu was more Persian than Arab in many aspects, though its language of expression was Arabic. The message of Islam had made a profound impact on the Persians. Their love of the Prophet and his family, their lofty artistic aspirations, their sense of justice and their urbanity—all played a decisive role in their contribution to the tradition. The ʿAbbāsids had moved westward from Persia, their staunch allies were mostly new Persian Muslims who accepted their claim to authority because of their kinship to the Prophet. Thus, it is not surprising that the first generation of Muslim scientists and scholars who were patronized by the ʿAbbāsids were mostly non-Arabs and some of the most important thinkers of Islam would come from Persia: Ibn Sīnā (370-428/980-1037), Abū Bakr Muḥammad b. Zakariyyā al-Rāzī (*ca.* 250-313/854-925) and Abū Ḥāmid Muḥammad b. Muḥammad al-Ṭūsī al-Ghazālī (450-505/1058-1111).

The Arab contact with Iran was not a mere accident. Mention has already been made of the impact of Islam on the Persians. But the impact was not just unidirectional. The Persianization of the emerging Islamic intellectual tradition is equally important. It was through Iran that the Arabs would find access to some of the most important sources of ancient texts. Iran had remained open to diverse influences for centuries. These include the Greek, Christian, Indian, Zoroastrian and Mānī influences. Located almost half-way between the Arab hinterland and the vast central Asian steppes of various Turkish tribes, it not only provided the necessary link for Islam's inevitable arrival beyond the river Oxus, it also became a conduit for the intellectual links with the Greeks, Byzantines and the Indians.

The paucity of resources does not allow us to reconstruct the early history of the Islamic scientific tradition but this social and political background does explain—at least to some extent—the "sudden" appearance of an intellectual activity that was already mature at birth. Note that by the middle of the second century of Islam, the core Islamic sciences had been firmly established and it had matured to encounter foreign currents and ideas. But what is more important for our purpose is the fact that some of the most important questions to be addressed by the Islamic scientific tradition in those early decades had already surfaced in the context of religious sciences.

Reflecting on the nature of relationship between God and the created beings, a number of mutakallimūn, mystics and thinkers had formulated theories about the nature of the universe, the human body, soul and their mutual relationship. For example, the already mentioned crucial question of free will raised by the Khārijites in legal terms had such grave consequences that it could not be taken lightly by any school of thought: If humans are free in their actions, would a person who committed one of the grave sins (*kabā'ir*) still be a Muslim? The Khārijites had answered it with a firm negative, the Murjī'ites had remained non-committal, al-Ḥasan al-Baṣrī had withheld judgment but his student, Wāṣil b. 'Aṭā' (d. 131/748), disagreed with his master and asserted that a grave sinner must be placed in an intermediary position (*manzila bayna manzilatayn*) between infidelity (*kufr*) and faith (*īmān*). After making his statement, he withdrew from the circle to another pillar in the mosque and was followed by 'Amr ibn 'Ubayd and others. Al-Ḥasan then remarked, "Wāṣil has withdrawn (*i'tazala*) from us,"[30] This was the beginning of a new school of thought in Islam—the Mu'tazila. Wāṣil's contemporary Jahm b. Ṣafwān (d. 128/746), the founder of the Jahmite school, believed in an uncompromising divine omnipotence and, consequently, absolute determination of all human actions by God. Those who shared this view were called the Jabrites (Determinists). In addition to this crucial question, the other problems that arose in these early years included the following: Was the Qūr'ān created in time or was it eternal? Was God's essence identical with His attributes? What was the nature of hell and heaven?

Both the Jabarites and the Mu'tazila believed in the creation of the Qur'ān, they also shared the belief that God's attributes were identical with His essence, but whereas Jahm believed in the ultimate destruction of heaven and hell, together with their inhabitants, the Mu'tazila believed in the eternity of punishment and reward and hence that of hell and heaven. These questions took center stage because of their legal, social and political importance. The earliest scholars to discuss these issues included Ma'bad al-Juhanī (d. 80/699), al-Ḥasan al-Baṣrī (d. 110/728), Ghaylān al-Dimashqī (d. before 126/743), Wāṣil b. 'Aṭā' (d. 132/748) and 'Amr b. 'Ubayd (d. 145/762). In time, the Kalām tradition solidified into two major schools: the Mu'tazila and the Ash'aria.

The mutakallimūn were also interested in cosmological doctrines and,

30. This standard account, quoted by many scholars including Watt, Montgomery W. (1973), *The Formative Period of Islamic Thought*, Edinburgh University, Edinburgh, pp. 209-17, is not without problems; also see van Ess "Mu'tazilah" in Eliade, M. (ed., 1987), *Encyclopedia of Religion*, Macmillan, New York and London, vol. x, pp. 220-1.

more importantly, in formulating a comprehensive physical theory that deals with many aspects of space, void and matter. This physical theory evolved from the works of the first generation of mutakallimūn; by the third/ninth century, it had achieved a remarkable degree of sophistication and it blossomed in the works of the fourth-fifth/tenth-eleventh century mutakallimūn.

Kalām Physical Theory

What are the ultimate constituents (*dhawāt*) which make up the world? What are their attributes and properties? Are these "properties" separate from the "things" they define or are they inseparable from the "things"? These were some of the major questions addressed by the Kalām physical theory.[31] Three basic postulates of the Kalām Physical Theory are: (i) "things" are only constituted out of accidents; (ii) "things" are constituted out of interpenetrating corporeal bodies, and (iii) "things" are constituted out of atoms and inherent accidents. According to the first doctrine, held by Ḥafṣ al-Fard (*fl. ca.* 195/810), Ḍirār ibn ʿAmr (d. 200/815), and al-Ḥusayn al-Najjār (d. *ca.* 220-230/835-845), the world consisted of only accidents (*aʿrāḍ*, sing. *ʿarḍ*) and therefore all attributes and properties of the objects of the world are defined by these accidents. Those who held the second doctrine, such as Hishām ibn al-Ḥakam (d. 179/795), al-Aṣamm (d. *ca.* 200/815), Ibrāhīm ibn Sayyār al-Naẓẓām (d. *ca.* 220-230/835-845) and his followers, believed that the created world consisted of bodies. The last doctrine, which became the dominant Kalām position in the later periods, held that the created world consisted of corporeal atoms and incorporeal accidents which inhere in atoms. This doctrine defined the properties of objects as an aggregate arising from the intrinsic nature of the atoms that constitute them, the accidents which inhere in them, and from the combination of these atoms with their inherent accidents to form larger units. This atomistic doctrine was a totally independent development in the Islamic intellectual thought, without any links to the Greek Atomism for there is no mention of any Greek texts having been translated

31. For an outline and detailed discussion of Kalām physical theory, see Dhanani, Alnoor (1994), *The Physical Theory of Kalām*, E. J. Brill, Leiden, pp. 6-7 and *passim*. Also see Dhanani, Alnoor, "Kalām atoms and Epicurean Minimal Parts" in Ragep, Jamil F. and Ragep, Sally P. (eds., 1996) *Tradition, Transmission, Transformation,* E. J. Brill, Leiden, pp. 157-71.

at this early stage.[32]

These questions were invariably bound with the epistemological considerations: how do we know what we know? This was recognized by all and thus, epistemological considerations formed an integral part of the Kalām physical theories. The dominant view, held by most Muʿtazilīs, was that the "ultimate constituents of the world are real and concrete (and not ideal and theoretical) entities...[and that] it is possible for us to have true knowledge of these constituent entities and their properties."[33] This was a realist epistemology which pitted the mutakallimūn against the skeptics who believed that knowledge of objects, as they are in themselves, is impossible.

In their technical lexicon, the mutakallimūn referred to atom as *jawhar* and distinguished this term from its usage by the falāsifa, who used it to denote the peripatetic view of substance. In their definition, atom (*jawhar*) was explicitly defined as "that which occupies space" (*mutaḥayyiz*). Thus in the very conception of the most fundamental constituent of matter, atom, the mutakallimūn had a built-in notion of space; it was impossible to conceive the atom without, at the same time, conceiving space because, atom, by definition, was a space-occupying thing. A related question was whether the intervening space between the two atoms was empty or not. In other words, could void exist? Or, to put it in yet another way, was the universe a plenum or not? Thus a discussion of atom simultaneously involved the discussion of space and void. Mutakalimūn defined void as being of two kinds: the intercosmic void (spaces between the particles which constitute the cosmos), and the extracosmic void which exists beyond the bounds of the finite universe. Note that for the Greek Atomists, the question of the extracosmic void did not arise because their universe was infinite, containing infinite cosmoi.

The falāsifa also addressed this question. Yaʿqūb ibn Isḥāq al-Kindī (d. 256/870) defined void as a place without any spatial object in it, whereas Muḥammad ibn Zakariyyā al-Rāzī (d. 313/925), one of the most important

32. Dhanani notes that "the question of the origins of *Kalām* atomism and its links with Greek Atomism has been the primary focus of most twentieth century research into *Kalām* physical theory. This narrow focus has limited the examination of *Kalām* atomism to the early period of the development of *Kalām*. Such a research program is beset by several methodological difficulties, the most challenging of which is the paucity of sympathetic accounts of early *Kalām* atomism." Dhanani (1994), p. 6; also note 13.

33. Dhanani (1994), p. 21.

Muslim scientists and philosophers, held the radical concept of absolute space in which material objects are embedded. In his metaphysics, this absolute space or void was one of five eternals, the others being God, soul, matter, and absolute time.[34]

Although a discussion of al-Rāzī's views is premature at this stage, it is important to point out that he stands somewhat alone in his commanding position as a scientist and a philosopher. His fierce independence, his brisk, almost arrogant, rejection of all those whose views he contested, his careful reconstruction of fundamental concepts, and his reliance on meticulous experimental details—all contribute toward making him a towering figure in the history of Islamic tradition. In his view,

> the reality of existence of an infinite three-dimensional space independent of bodies is proven by the fact that men whose judgment has not been corrupted by scholarly quibbles are certain of its existence. The same applies to the concept of time, considering as a flowing substance existing independently of motion. Thus, in a way which *mutatis mutandis* may remind us of Descartes' method of philosophizing, the certitude which attached in the human mind to these concepts was a proof of their external reality.[35]

Another important distinction made by Rāzī between absolute and relative space led him to postulate that the former was not subject to measurements whereas the latter was measured by means of the number of revolutions of the heavenly spheres. Thus, in Rāzī's view, the cosmos was not a primary datum, absolute space and time were more fundamental than the cosmos. Likewise, he held that matter had an atomic structure and subsisted before bodies were formed in a state of dispersion. "The cosmos characterized by the order prevailing in it was thus something derivative and not self-sufficient.... It was created and would in the fullness of time be dissolved."[36] In order to account for the divine, al-Rāzī would, perhaps late in his life, postulate his famous five eternals (God, soul, matter, absolute space and time), in whose existence the universe was a mere interlude.

We will discuss al-Rāzī in due time; however, for now, let us return to the

34. Dhanani (1994), pp. 71-72.
35. Pines, Shlomo (1986), "What was original in Arabic science" in *Studies in Arabic Versions of Greek Texts and in Medieval Science,* The Magnes Press, The Hebrew University, Jerusalem, p. 193.
36. Ibid.

story of the Islamic scientific tradition. While the mutakallimūn were busy in their discussions, there arose a small body of literature, rather quietly, in an entirely different realm—this was the first flowering of the Islamic scientific tradition.

The First Flowering

The first few decades of the Islamic scientific tradition are still shrouded in the dim pre-dawn light. The paucity of information makes it rather difficult to draw a clear picture with confidence. The sudden appearance of a small group of scientists and scholars who are dealing with rather advanced theories does not let us traverse the earlier terrain; it brings us right into the full exposure of the scientific activity in the second half of the second/eighth century. This small group includes Persians, Jews, Muslims, Christians and Nestorians who speak and understand Syriac, Sanskrit, Hebrew and Greek, though they write mostly in Arabic. The meeting place is Baghdad. Their subject areas are mathematics, astronomy, alchemy, natural history and medicine. They already know something about the Greek, Persian and the Indian scientific traditions; they comment on this body of knowledge, they adopt it according to their needs, they reject part of it, they produce critique of this literature, they coin new terms in Arabic to grasp the ideas contained in non-Arabic works. But what is most important for our study is the fact that rather than being mere scientists dealing with experimental data and procedures, they are also theoreticians.

Equally important are the questions they ask, themes that attract them and theories they propose. But it is precisely this that defies classification, for all of them were much more than astronomers, chemists and mathematicians; they were immersed in an all-embracing tradition of learning. Most of them wrote on a wide range of subjects—from anatomy to the intricacies of Arabic grammar and from the construction of astrolabes to the poetry of the pre-Islamic poets.

Let us also note that the Islamic scientific tradition preceded the translation movement that would bring the Greek, Persian and Indian scientific texts into this emerging tradition. Even our meager resources amply prove this. Astronomy, medicine and mathematics were already established fields of study before any major translations were made into Arabic. Translations were done to enrich the tradition, not to give birth to it, as some Orientalists have claimed. In the field of astronomy, for example, George Saliba has conclusively shown that the first generation of astronomers which included Ya'qūb b. Ṭāriq[37] and others were working "before the time of the great translation movement which produced Arabic versions of such Greek scientific masterpieces as the *Almagest* and the *Elements*."[38] He also shows how this early astronomical tradition was related to the Qur'ānic cosmology. The pre-Islamic astronomy which predicted and explained seasonal changes based on the rising and setting of fixed stars (known as *anwā'*) was a subject of interest for the Qur'ānic exegetes as well as for the early lexicographers who produced an extensive literature on the *anwā'* and *manāzil* (lunar mansions) concepts.

> The cosmological tradition of the Quranic text would later produce a separate type of astronomical literature usually referred to as *al-hay'a al-sunnyīa*. The use of the term *hay'a* to describe this tradition as well is of special significance, for it indicates the direction from which this tradition had developed. It is not a coincidence that the mathematical astronomical tradition which dealt with the theoretical foundations of astronomy also defined itself as a *hay'a* tradition, even though it rarely touched upon the Quranic references to the cosmological doctrines.[39]

The towering figure among this early group of scientists is, of course, that of Jābir ibn Ḥayyān. But the fact that the Jābirian corpus contains a large number of highly sophisticated works of an enormously wide scope, indicates that there must have been a flourishing scientific tradition much before Jābir's time because such mature works could not have come into existence within the life time of one person. Dating of Jābir's vast corpus and even its authorship has remained controversial for centuries. In recent times, Paul Kraus has added the weight of his considerable authority to this

---

37. The author of *Maḥlūl fi'l-Sindhind li Daraja Daraja* (*Astronomical Tables in the Sindhind Resolved for Every Degree*), *Tarkīb al-Aflāk* (*Composition of the Spheres*), and *Kitāb al-'illal* (*The Book of Causes*), *fl.* Baghdad in the second half of the 8th century; he is most closely associated with al-Fazārī; see Pingree, David "Ya'qūb ibn Ṭāriq" in DSB, vol. 14, p. 546; "Fragments of the Works of Ya'qūb ibn Ṭāriq" in *Journal of Near Eastern Studies*, vol. 27, pp. 97-125; and Kennedy, E. S. (1967), "The Lunar Visibility Theory of Ya'qūb ibn Ṭāriq" in *Journal of Near Eastern Studies*, vol. 27, pp. 126-32.
38. Saliba, George (1994), *A History of Arabic Astronomy*, New York University Press, New York and London, p. 16.
39. Saliba (1994), p. 17.

controversy; he attributed the *Corpus Jābirianum* to a group of authors of the tenth century. His work, which assembled a large collection of manuscripts, was important for several reasons: it placed these texts in a comprehensive historical setting, it classified them and gave them a manageable format. But Kraus did not have all the texts or historical material at his disposal and he died before he could finish his work on Jābir. Following Kraus rather uncritically, most of the modern scholars continued the same line of thought. They refined the parameters, edited more texts and studied more carefully those that had been edited by Kraus, but they did not question the basic framework of inquiry and its most fundamental premise: the dating and the authorship of the corpus. This dogmatic acceptance of dating and authorship led many historians of science to make false comparisons between Jābarian corpus and later works such as the *Rasāʾil* (*Epistles*) of the Ikhwān al-Ṣafāʾ (Brethren of Purity, *ca.* 373/983); this is also the main cause of many other historically incorrect theories which have been formulated on the ideas first postulated by Kraus.[40]

This situation changed in 1994 with the publication of *Names, Natures and Things* by Syed Nomanul Haq.[41] This book is a veritable storehouse of ideas, painstakingly researched information, hundreds of cross-referenced citations, and a coherent synthesis of various strands that run through Jābirian corpus. It has conclusively shown that there was, in fact, a man by the name of Jābir, the son of Ḥayyān, who had a personal relationship with the sixth Shīʿī Imām, Jaʿfar al-Ṣādiq. Jābir's patronymic name (*kunya*) is variously given as Abū Mūsa and Abū ʿAbd Allāh, with the epithet al-Ṣūfī, his tribal name (*nisba*) is given as al-Azdī and he was either from Kūfa or Ṭūs; hence called al-Kūfī or al-Ṭūsī. Ibn Khallikān calls him Jābir ibn Ḥayyān of Tarsūs[42] meaning that he was from Tarsūs. Ibn al-Nadīm says, "...the Shīʿa have said that he was one of their great men and one of their *abwāb* (doors). They claim that he was a companion of Jaʿfar al-Ṣādiq (may

40. For later studies, see, for example, the facsimile of the Arabic text of the *Poison Book* (Kraus no. 2145), published in 1958 by A. Siggel with a German translation and the 1950 French translation of *Livre du glorieux* (Kraus no. 706) by Henry Corbin. For erroneous synthesis, see the review on Marquet, Y. (1998), *La Philosophie des alchimistes et l'alchimie des philosophes: Jābir ibn Ḥayyān et les "Frères de la Pureté"*, Paris by Haq, S.N. (1992), *Isis*, vol. 83, pp. 120.

41. Haq, Syed Nomanul (1994), *Names, Natures and Things*, Kluwer Academic Publishers, Dordrecht, Boston, London. I have drawn heavily on this work for the construction of my arguments in this section.

42. *Wafayāt*, vol. 1, p. 327.

Allah be pleased with him)....The man is authentic, his case is most apparent and well known, his compositions are important and numerous…it is said that his origins was Khurāsān."[43]

Jābir's enormous corpus contains "theory and practice of chemical processes and procedures, classification of substances, medicine, pharmacology, astrology, theurgy, magic, the doctrine of specific property of things (*ʿilm al-Khawāṣṣ*), and the artificial generation of living beings,"[44] as well as discourses on the occultation of the Imām. In its sweeping breadth, the corpus contains references to diverse sources, ranging from Hermes to Aristotle and Balīnās (Apollonius of Tyana). An important aspect related to the proper dating of Jābirian corpus is the comparison made by Haq between Jābir's quotations from Greek works with those of third/ninth century Arabic translations. Haq has shown that though Jābir refers to his Greek predecessors throughout his corpus, in a vast majority of instances he either paraphrases their writings, or simply explains their doctrines in his own words; this indicates that he lived before the formal translation movement began. But it is on the basis of direct translations found in Jābir's *Aḥjār* that Haq has established his irrefutable evidence. These direct quotations are translated in an archaic style and the terminology is not as refined and consistent as the one found in the mature translations of Isḥāq ibn Ḥunayn.[45]

In any case, our main concern here is with the doctrinal part of Jābir's corpus and especially with his "Science of Balance". Jābir's theory of qualities is at the heart of his whole scientific system. In an attempt to explain the natural world, he constructs a grand system based on four qualities [hot, cold, moist and dry] which are not the four Empedoclean elements which his Greek predecessors had hypostasized; rather Jābir accords this position to the qualities. And this means that qualities, and not the Empedoclean primary bodies, were the true elements of his system. Thus, as far as Jābir is concerned, in the intelligible world existed not some "absolute Fire," but the "incorporeal hot." Jābir does not even designate his four qualities with Aristotelian appellations, *dunamis (quwā,* sing. *Quwwa)* or *poiotês (kayfiyyāt,* sing. *kayfiyya);* rather, he variously calls them 'principles' (*uṣūl,* sing. *aṣl),* 'bases' (*arkān,* sing. *rukn),* 'first simples,' 'first elements and, often, 'natures' (*ṭabāʾiʿ,* sing. *ṭabʿ).* At times, he explicitly distinguishes them

43. *Fihrist,* p. 435.
44. Haq (1994), p. 5.
45. Haq (1994), pp. 25-30.

from *kayfiyyāt*. "The appellation 'nature' was never used by Aristotle in this sense," Haq notes, "here we have, then, a case of a profound conceptual and terminological difference.[46]

Through this independence and corporeality, Jābir's four qualities become true elements, which are, in the natural world, corporeal, subject to a wide range of quantitative manipulations. The intensities of qualities in a body are, therefore, measurable and Jābir proposes an extended scheme of elaborate subdivisions, using units borrowed from ancient astronomy, thus attempting to "elevate the practice of medicine to the infallibility of an exact science"[47] All of this leads one to the question of intensities of qualities and to Jābir's most important contribution: the Science of Balance (*ʿilm al-Mizān*) which he thought was "a divine science (*ʿilm lāhūtī*) whose aim was to reduce all facts of human knowledge to a system of quantity and measure. However, the scope of this science was not limited merely to the measurement of qualitative potencies of drugs—in fact, 'all things fall under the [principle of] Balance,' and 'it is by means of this principle that man is able to make sense of the world'."[48] It is this "Theory of Balance" that is the foundation upon which Jābir constructs his whole system which is characteristically Islamic; it recalls, celebrates and builds upon the central concept of Islam, the Unicity of God, *al-Tawḥīd*, in such a seamless way that there remains no need for any artificial imposition of the Qurʾānic doctrine of a well-balanced and well-proportioned creation on Jābirian system; the system is borne out of this central Qurʾānic notion. Jābir's doctrine encompasses both the sub-lunar world of generation and corruption as well as that which is beyond the Sphere (*al-Falak*). As a methodological thesis,

> Jābir's Balance was the 'way' (*ṭarīq*) through which one understood, made sense of, and, above all, measured and manipulated the objects and the processes of the universe. And since the universe was diverse, so were the Balances. Thus there are Balances of the Intelligence, of the Soul, of Nature, Form and the Sphere of the stars; there are Balances of the four natures, animals, plants and minerals—these are all useful Balances. But, finally, there is the Balance of Letters: and this is the most perfect of all.[49]

---

46. Haq (1994), pp. 59-60.
47. Haq (1994), p. 67.
48. Ibid.
49. Haq (1994), p. 81.

This best of all Balances—variably called the Balance of Letters (*Mizān al-Ḥurūf*), the Balance of Articulation (*Mizān al-Hijjā'*) and the Balance of Utterance (*Mizān al-Lafẓī*)—is elucidated, defended and justified in a systematic way. This enables Jābir to build a comprehensive theory of knowledge, language and music. But Jābir is not merely interested in the formulation of a theory, he is attempting something far greater. He is attempting to construct a philosophical system on the basis of his central principle, *Mīzān al-Ḥurūf*, to systematically explain harmony and balance that exist in the world of nature.

After formulating his "Theory of Balance" in a coherent manner, Jābir then develops an ontological equivalence between the four natures and the Arabic alphabet. He submits all change to the exactness of mathematical laws and calls it the Supreme Principle (*Qā'ida 'uẓmā*) of the world which governs everything—from the distances and movements of the celestial bodies to the specific, immutable and noble proportions of the four qualities that all bodies contain. He even goes to the extent of showing that this proportion was exactly 1:3:5:8 whose sum, 17, was the foundation (*Qā'ida*) of the entire "Science of Balance". By discovering this quantitative structure of all things, an alchemist can learn how to change one thing into another—even inanimate objects into living things—by reconfiguring the qualities. He devotes an entire collection of texts, called *Kutub al-Mawāzīn* (Books of Balances), to the development of these ideas. Recalling the Qur'ānic theme of balance and order in the created universe, affirmed with a particular force throughout the text of the Qur'ān, one begins to understand the foundational links between the Qur'ān and the scientific tradition that was emerging in the Islamic milieu at this early stage. The Qur'ān declares that everything has been created in due proportion and in pairs (Q. 22:5; 26:7; 25:2; 31:10; 50:7; 54:49) and the Creator has established balance (55:7). In Jābir, then, we have a scientist of the first rank, who is attempting to develop a whole system in which one can clearly discern the reverberations of the Qur'ānic doctrine of balance.

By the end of the second century of Islam (August 815 CE), the Islamic scientific tradition had taken firm roots in the newly established intellectual centers of the Muslim world. It had also found ample support and patronage. During the next six centuries, it was to witness an unprecedented expansion, both geographically as well as intellectually. But before tracing further developments, let us see how this tradition was rooted in the Qur'ān.

CHAPTER TWO

And these are the Signs

The Qur᾿ān and the Order of Nature

Islam shares its cosmos with the other two monotheistic religions; in all three Abrahamic faiths, God is the originator of everything that exists. In Islam, this creative act of God, through a simple command, *Kun* (*Be*),[1] became the subject matter of Islamic cosmogony which elucidates the modalities of creation. The Qur᾿ānic creation theme, let us note, includes the physical as well as non-physical worlds—all ontologically linked and existentially dependent upon God.[2] This intrinsic nexus between various levels of existence transforms the multiplicity of appearances into a unity. The ultimate foundation of their interrelatedness at the level of cosmic existence is their ontological dependence on God. Hence the world of nature is related to all other levels of creation. This common ontological foundation made it possible for the Islamic scientific tradition to forge links and share a language of discourse with other disciplines of knowledge which were all arranged in a hierarchy.

The unity of existence is a recurrent theme of the Qur᾿ān which relates it to its central concept of *Tawḥīd*, the Unicity of God. Thus linked ontologically with the realm of the divine, the realm of nature becomes more than the mere physical entity that it is; it becomes a sign (*āya*, pl. *āyāt*), pointing to a transcendent reality beyond itself. This transcendence is semantically linked to the verses of the Qur᾿ān which are also called *āyāt*. But this elegant nexus between the world of nature and the word of God is much more than mere semantics; it is an essential feature of the Qur᾿ānic metaphysics of nature which establishes an inalienable link between various levels of created things by relating them to an All-Encompassing (*al-Muḥīṭ*) and All-Knowing (*al-ʿalīm*) God who is above and beyond all human conceptions; His transcendence can only be defined *via negativa*, by erasing

1. Q. 36:81.
2. The Qur᾿ān speaks of God as being the Sustainer (*Rabb*) and Owner (*Mālik*) of all the Worlds. Q. 1:1; 2:131; 5:28; 6:45; 6:162; 7:54, 61, 67, 104, 121; 10:10, 37; 26:16, 23, 47, 77, 98, 109, 127, 145, 164, 180, 192; 27:8, 44; 28:30; 32:2; 37:87, 182; 39:75; 40:64 to 66; 41:9; 43:46; 45:36; 56:80; 59:16; 69:43; 81:29; 83:6.

from the mind any impurity foreign to the idea of pure divinity (*ulūhīya*). It is through this intense and systematic weeding out of every description, adjective (*ṣiffa*), and image (*ṣūra*) suspected of directing our understanding (*maʿrifa*) or imagination (*wahm*) to a created object (*shay'*, pl. *ashyā'*) other than God that we can arrive at the Qur'ānic conception of the Creator: He is not like anything,[3] neither engendering nor engendered.[4] All that God has us know positively about Himself is His singular uniqueness, His extreme remoteness from everything else.

Since all things exist through and because of God, their ontological dependence on the Creator simultaneously ennobles them by raising their status from being mere things to signs (*āyāt*) of a transcendent Real (*al-Ḥaqq*), who, nevertheless, remains beyond them. Thus rather than being mere dialectical utterances, the "sign verses"[5] of the Qur'ān have an irresistible urgency which draws our attention to that which lies beyond the phenomena being mentioned. It is this ennoblement that makes the rhythmic alteration of the day and the night[6] and the regularities in the movement of the sun, which *traverses its course by the decree of the All-Knowing; and the moon—[for which God] has made stations [to traverse], till it becomes like an old [and withered] stalk of date-palm.*[7] The Qur'ān asserts that commonly observable natural phenomena, such as the orderly movement of the planets, are, in fact, due to the design of the Creator. It draws the attention of its readers to the fact that *the sun does not catch up to the moon and the night cannot outstrip the day; [rather] each revolve in their own orbit,*[8] and asserts that this is not merely the result of certain laws of nature, rather these are "signs" for those who reflect. In fact, the concept of "Laws of Nature", independent of a Law-Giver, is essentially a secular concept because it makes "nature" a law-giver; in Islam, the authority to make laws rests with God alone.

Thus seen from within the Islamic tradition, sciences which explore various aspects of the natural world actually explore one aspect of the

---

3. Q. 42:11: *Laisa ka-mithlihī shay'un* (*Nothing is like unto Him*).
4. Sūra 112 of the Qur'ān contains, in a highly condensed form, this definition *via negativa*: *Say: He is Allah, the One; Allah—the Everlasting (ṣamad); neither endgendering nor engendered; and none is His equal.*
5. So called because of a refrain that occurs in these verses in various forms such as: *And in this is the sign for those who reflect* (Q. 16:11), or *And in this is the sign for those who listen* (Q. 16:65).
6. Q. 2:164.
7. Q. 33:38-9.
8. Q. 33:40.

Qur'ānic cosmos. This cosmos is made up of both the physical as well as non-physical beings according to a grand scheme, conceived and executed by the Creator. The ultimate destination of this created cosmos is a secret that God shares with none. However, the Qur'ān insists that humans discover the modalities through which nature works. It draws attention to the regularities, beneficence and design of various observable natural processes through concrete examples drawn from the world of nature. These processes fall in the domain of various scientific disciplines such as astronomy, physics, mathematics, geology and botany. But when studied in their proper metaphysical context, these processes become means to gain knowledge of that which lies beyond the laws that govern them. This Qur'ānic invitation to reflect on these natural processes is repeated with such urgency that the spatiotemporal plane which contains the world of nature seems to form the very background of the Qur'ānic universe.[9]

These intrinsic links make the high drama of creation, existence and the moral response to revelation out of human volition an integrated whole uniquely anchored in the metaphysical realm though operating in a historical setting. But it must be understood that this varied data—ranging from the natural to the historical—that the Qur'ān presents to its faithful reader is not without an internal plan. This concentrated disposition of material permits the directing thought to shine forth from behind the broad narrative at every instance, from the implicit to the explicit; it emerges by itself, like a design in the midst of the weave; this was one of the most immediate facts recognized by the first Arabs who heard this unearthly text which was neither poetry nor prose but which transcended both. It was this narrative par excellence that would provide pattern to the theologians for fashioning their dialectical process (*ṭarīqa jadalīyya*) which starts with a positive hierarchy, established *a priori* between the two facts considered (*taqaddum, afḍaliyya*). It passes from the "trunk" to the "branch" (*far*ʿ), and concludes *a fortiori*. And it brings back the solution of new question to that of the general problem thus resolved (*radd al-ghā'ib ilā al-*

9. These so-called scientific verses of the Qur'ān have been the subject of a large number of modern scientific commentaries. The Egyptian exegete Ṭantāwī Jawharī (1862-1940) claimed to have counted all the verses which refer to natural phenomena; he fixed this number at 750 (with many others having indirect relevance to the physical universe). He also compared this number to the verses pertaining to legal matters which were "no more than 150". This is, however, highly problematic. See chapter ten for more details.

shāhid). This method, so poignantly used by the Qur'ān,[10] was taken as a standard and employed by al-Shāfʿī, (*burhān innī, istidlāl,* deduction), Ibn Ḥanbal and others who showed that the meaning (*maʿnā*) of the root (*aṣl*) had to coincide in every way with the meaning of the branch, so that the deduction might be valid. These linkages become immediately apparent when the sign verses are seen in the context of the creation theme of the Qur'ān—a context that provides us a fundamental framework of inquiry for what Nasr has called the religious order of nature.[11]

Creation and the Order of Nature

One of the names of God, The Originator (*al-Badīʿ*), is derived from verse 117 of the second sūra of the Qur'ān, "The Cow": *He is the Originator* (Badīʿ) *of the heavens and the earth. Whenever He wishes a matter, He merely says 'Be' and it becomes*. This is *creatio ex nihilo*, a concept that Islam shares with the other two monotheistic faiths. But how did the universe come into being? Through what modalities? What is it made of? When did it come into existence? What are the laws that govern it? These, and similar questions formed the core of Islamic cosmogony which we will explore in the next chapter.

The creation theme of the Qur'ān is one of the simplest in the sense that it relies on self-evident fundamental facts. The modalities of creation are not explained anywhere in the Qur'ān. It simply states the basic facts: the creation of the seven heavens, placed one above the other, in perfect order, the lowest of these adorned and bejeweled and placed above our earth which is the chosen place for human habitat. Then there is the sun, the celestial spheres, the mountains, the stars and a small number of named plants, animals and even insects—all uniquely and seamlessly blended into a whole that springs forth from the same Divine source which gave birth to the first human being. The cosmos (*ʿālam*) came into existence as a sign (*ʿālāma*). The order of nature is, therefore, an evidence and a pointer for that which lies beyond nature: the very source of that order. *Verily, in the creation of the heavens and the earth; in the alternation of the night*

10. For example, Q. 14:24: *Hast not thou seen how Allah sets forth a parable that a good word is like a good tree, whose roots are firm and its branches [extend] to the sky; it brings forth its fruits all the time, by its Sustainer's leave; Allah sets this parable for people that perchance they may be mindful.*
11. This subject was the central theme of Nasr's 1994 Cadbury Lectures at the University of Birmingham. Published in 1996 as *Religion and the Order of Nature*, Oxford University Press, New York.

and the day; in the ships that sail in the ocean with what profits humankind; and in the water which Allah sends down from the skies, giving life therewith to the earth after it had been lifeless and in the beasts of all kind that He disperses on earth; and in the change of the winds and the clouds which are driven between heaven and earth—surely in these are signs for people who understand.[12]

The Qur'ān also makes specific mention of the bee which received revelation (Q. 16:68-9); the spider whose "house" is described as the "frailest of all" in a parable narrating the state of those who take protectors other than God (Q. 29:41); Solomon's hoopoe who carried his message to the Queen of Sheba (Q. 27:28); the raven who taught Qābīl how to bury his brother whom he had slain (Q. 5:31); the she-camel who was a sign to the people of Thamūd (Q. 91:13); the ant who told her fellow ants to protect themselves from the army of Solomon (Q. 27:18); Jonah's fish (Q. 37:142); the wolf that did not eat Joseph (Q. 12:16); the donkey whose braying is the worst of sounds (Q. 31:19); the fly that the false gods could not create (22:73); the frogs, lice, and locusts that appeared in the plagues of Egypt (Q. 7:133); and the mosquito that God does not hesitate to cite as a parable (Q. 2:26). Among the plants and fruits mentioned by the Qur'ān are the olive tree, which is blessed (Q. 95:1), dates, grapes, and pomegranate (Q. 55:68).[13]

This physical cosmos observes a Divine Law just as humans are supposed to. Thus, the Qur'ān tells us about the revelation sent to the bee (Q. 16:68); it mentions the submission of the heavens and the earth to God (Q. 41:11); it celebrates the glorification of God by all that exists in nature (Q. 59:1; 61:1; 62:1; 64:1); it unifies the whole of creation in a grand order and establishes the source and origin of that order and then, in a sweeping manner, states that all of this is destined to exist merely for a short duration after which all will perish—that is, all except God. This emphasis on the transient nature of the created world reverberates throughout the Qur'ānic text as a reminder that none other than God is to be worshipped, for all except Him are mere creatures who owe their existence to His Will.

Within this broad creation theme, the sign verses of the Qur'ān establish a nexus between the physical cosmos and the metaphysical realm by making the physical entity a projection of the unseen wherein resides its sustaining and governing principle. A fundamental characteristic of these verses is that they do not *always* refer to the natural phenomena; historical

12. Q. 2:164.
13. The list is not exhaustive.

events are also spoken of as signs with the same rhetorical embellishment and with the same urgency that is characteristic of those verses which mention natural phenomenon.[14] This establishes a further link, this time with the temporal realm and completes the spatiotemporal domain that is the necessary condition of existence.

Thus the natural world is placed in a created order in space and time. But then these verses make a metaphysical leap into the very heart of the Qur'ānic message: the unique Oneness of the Creator: *Is He not the One who made the earth a stable abode and created rivers flowing through it,* the Qur'ān asks rhetorically, *[the One who] created the mountains therein and created a barrier between the two seas? Is there, then, another god than Allah? Yet, most of them do not know.*[15] In addition, in the general sweep of its narrative, the Qur'ān mentions the rain-bearing clouds and vegetation kingdom; it specifically cites the case of "dead earth" which is revived by God after it has been dead.[16]

The Qur'ānic creation theme specifies the Divine realms and then unites all forms and levels of existence into one organic whole. This unity is then projected on to the human intellect (*fahm, ʿaql*) which is endowed with the power to comprehend that which lies beyond the realm of the five internal senses: *hiss mushtrik* (the sense that gathers all impresssions); *khayāl* (knowledge of the sensient kind); *wāhima* (perception of particular significations: evaluative, estimative); *ḥāfiẓa* (sensitive memory) and *mutakhayyila* (intellective reason).[17] This characteristic is what distinguishes humans (*ins,* sing. *insān*) from other created beings—an ability acquired through the knowledge given to Adam, the first human being.

This knowledge was bestowed upon Adam by none other than the Creator Himself, by teaching him names, *asmā'*. Created on the best of

14. For example Q. 2:248 (the example of the Ark); 2:252 (the case of Jālūt); 2:259 (the case of the man with a donkey who was put to sleep for a hundred years and then brought to life) and many more.
15. Q. 27:61.
16. Q. 36: 35: *A Sign for them is the earth that is dead; We give it life, and produce grain therefrom of which ye eat; and We caused to grow in it gardens of palms and vines, and We caused springs to gush forth therein; that they might eat fruits; although it is not their hands that wrought this; will they not, then, give thanks?*
17. For a useful table of concordance between the principles of Kalām and the philosophical principles borrowed from the Imāmites and the Hellenists before the fourth century Hijra, see Massignon, L. (1982), vol. 3, p. 70.

patterns (*fī aḥsan al-taqwīm*),[18] from a clot of blood,[19] externally a body (*jism*), a weak vessel made of clay, infused with spirit (*ruḥ*), endowed with an inner organ, heart (*qalb*), which is a regular oscillation in the central inner void (*jawf*), the secret and hidden place of conscience (*sirr*) whose secrets will be laid bare at the Judgment, this created being also has a soul, (*nafs*), an aggregate of sensations and actions, an incoherent and obscure mass—thoughts, illusions, desires, feelings—flowing through the body, the principle (*aṣl*) which unites the reprehensible qualities.[20]

The Qur'ān seizes human beings in the very act of their creation, ennobles them through an eternal covenant (*mithāq*) and knowledge bestowed upon them by God. It raises humanity above all other creation because of the trust placed on the humankind by the Creator and because among all the created beings, it was only man who chose to bear the supernatural trust (*amāna*) which was refused by the heavens, the earth and the mountains as being too heavy a burden.[21] The re-discovery of this covenant through remembrance (*dhikr*) acts like a flash of lightening which removes the veils from the *nafs*, unifies and transfigures it, makes it coherent and tranquil. It is this tranquil self, *al-nafs al-muṭma'inna,* to which is said, *O soul at peace, return to thy Lord, well pleased, well pleasing.*[22] It is this unified self which can understand signs spread throughout the cosmos and within its own being: *We shall show them Our signs in the utmost horizons and in themselves, so that it will become clear unto them that this [Qur'ān] is, indeed, the truth; is it not enough that thy Sustainer is witness unto everything?*[23]

The Qur'ān treats as given the basic enigmas of life: birth (described as an embryogeny in several stages (Q. 23:12-14; 40:69); death, resurrection and life after death. It gives humans (and *jinns*) the moral choice of accepting or rejecting its message,[24] prescribes the legal limits of human activity and gives humans the freedom to choose between the two paths.[25] The Qur'ān also does not treat of abstract essences or types; it mentions particular, concrete and singular things and efficient names, *asmā'* (sing. *ism*) such as the All Powerful (*al-Qadīr*), the Irresistible (*al-Jabbār*), the

18. Q. 95:4.
19. Q. 96:2.
20. See the excellent explanation of the four terms, *al-qalb, al-ʿaql, al-rūḥ, al-nafs* in *Kitāb Sharḥ ʿAjā'ib al-Qalb,* in Book XXI of al-Ghazālī's *Iḥyā'*.
21. Q. 33:72.
22. Q. 89:27-8.
23. Q. 41:53.
24. Q. 2:256: *Lā ikrā'ha fī'l-dīn* (*There is no compulsion in religion*).
25. Q. 90: 10: *Wa hadaina hun najdain* (*And guided him about the two paths*).

Owner (*al-Mālik*).

It was left to the Kalām tradition to formulate, in precise terms, the mode of existence of things. And it was the function of the Islamic cosmological sciences to explain how these things came into existence and how they were related to each other as well as to the whole. The mutakallimūn, the philosophers (*filāsifa*) and the mystics (*sufis*) formulated various cosmogonies to elucidate modes of existence. Because all of these traditional cosmogonies addressed the same questions, though from different vantage points, they are all valid within the framework of the Qur'ānic revelation; this is the basis of the existence of multiple cosmogonies in the Islamic tradition; they all sought to explain the cosmos in the light of revelation, in particular, in the light of the doctrine of *al-Tawḥīd*, the Unicity of God, which made it impossible for two cosmic orders to co-exist.

This fundamental principle acted as a prism through which all theories were passed in order to test their validity. It was this powerful doctrine, situated at the very heart of the Qur'ānic message, that made it possible for the Muslim scientists and scholars to transform those Greek theories about nature which conflicted with revelation. But it was not an arbitrary act of faith; rather, it was a consistent operative factor that derived its primary kinetic energy from the Qur'ān and then branched out in various spheres. It was through the inherent power, simplicity and uniformity of this principle that was operative in all realms of knowledge that a coherent Islamic worldview appeared. Through this operation, even the *materia prima* could be appropriated into the Islamic cosmogonies. Abū Isḥāq Ibrāhīm b. Sayyār bin Hāni' al-Naẓẓām (d. between 220/835 and 230/845), for example, reconstructed the problem of the *materia prima* by proposing that "God created all of the primary elements (*ashyā'*) at once, with knowledge; all individual beings which appear progressively (*ẓuhūr*) existed in this beginning in potentiality (*kumūn*)".[26]

---

26. In order to elucidate the hierarchical order of this *meteria prima,* various schools of thought formulated various theories: The Emanationists construed their answer in terms of the five eternal principles of Plotinus (*ca.* 205-70) and of the Harrānians: the creator, the reason (*ʿaql*), the soul (*nafs,* or *hayūla, matter*), the void, the plenum; the Hellenistic solutions were produced by dividing and subdividing the five principles into three aspects, three worlds: the horizons (*āfāq*), interlocking spiritual spheres of influence, the material world and the five senses placed between the two; al-Fārābī (b. *ca.* 258-339/870-950) regarded the four logical causes as typifying the order of self-

The Qur'ān and Science Nexus

It is also noteworthy that the Islamic scientific works, profoundly influenced by the Qur'ānic worldview as they were, seldom mention the so-called scientific verses of the Qur'ān in any direct sense. Numerous examples can be cited. For instance, the *Algebra* of al-Khwārazmī (*ca.* 184-236/800-850), the pioneering work in its field,[27] neither refers to any Qur'ānic verse in the text of the book, nor uses a verse like *God set all things in numbers*[28] as invocation at the beginning of the book; its purpose is purely practical. Even in Ibn Sīnā's *magnus opus, al-Qānūn fi'l Ṭibb,* known to the Latin West as *The Canon,* where one would expect such direct references, they are remarkably absent. In the "Preface" (*Khuṭba tul Kitāb*) of the book, Ibn Sīnā simply seeks Divine help in the task of writing the book, as was customary, and starts the book.[29] The same is true for a vast majority of other scientific works from the classical period of Islam. However, when the purpose of the book was different, there was a free use of the Qur'ānic material. A case in point is al-Bīrūnī's *Kitāb al-Jamāhir fi Ma'rifat al-Jawāhir* (*The Most Comprehensive Book on the Knowledge of Precious Stones*) which frequently quotes the Qur'ānic verses in relation to the various stones and minerals. But this work is not merely a scientific treatise on stones, as its title suggests. Rather, it is an amazing collection of scientific facts, ancient poetry, historical anecdotes, meditations and critique of various theories then current. It is also a repository of the author's life-long observations on the state of human beings and matter.

---

generating beings: substantial cause (*hayūlā*), formal cause (*ṣūra*), efficient cause (*'illa fā'ila*), and the final cause (*tamām*), arranged in three worlds: *rubūbīya, amr* and *khalq*. For a more detailed discussion on this, see Massignon (1982), vol. 3, p. 122.

27. The full title of al-Khwārazmī's work is *Kitāb al-Mukhtaṣar fi Ḥisāb al-Jabr wa'l Muqābla;* original Arabic text has been published with the poorly translated 1831 English version of Frederic Rosen by Pakistan Hijra Council (Islamabad, 1409/1989). In spite of its reliance on Rosen's inaccurate translation, this is still a useful book because it contains the original Arabic text, a long "Introduction" by the Turkish historian of science Aydin Sayili, and enrichments and some corrections to Rosen's notes by Malek Dosay. See note 37 to Sayili's introduction where he mentions Julius Ruska's critique of Rosen's translation; also see Rashed, Roshdie, "L'idée de l'Algébra selon Al-Khwārazmī", *Fundamenta Scientiae,* vol. 4, no. 1, p. 95.
28. Q. 71:28.
29. This *khuṭbā* is merely a page and a half long. See *al-Qānūn fi'l Ṭibb* (1999), ed. by Sa'īd 'l-Laḥḥām, Dār al-Fikr, Beirut.

Likewise, during the entire period of Islamic scientific activity which lasted well into the fifteenth century, we see no evidence of any scientific research program directly motivated by the desire to "prove" the scientific verses of the Qur'ān through science. There is no record of such profane uses of the Divine Book. This is so because the cultural milieu that gave birth to the Islamic scientific tradition was so thoroughly infused with the Qur'ānic worldview and the cosmologies based on its message that there was no need for any artificial and external imposition of the Qur'ānic verses on the scientific works. When al-Ghazālī mentions various natural sciences in relation to the Qur'ān, his method, context and purpose is entirely different from the twentieth century extraneous and ornamental use of the Qur'ān as a way of Islamization of modern science, as we will see in more detail in chapter ten. Suffice it to say here that the birth of the scientific exegesis (*al-tafsīr al-ʿilmī*) of the Qur'ān is a purely twentieth century phenomena. No one thought of writing such an exegesis during the time when scientific activity was at its peak in the Islamic civilization; the roots of scientific *tafsīr* should be traced in the Muslim encounter with the modern West. Since the last quarter of the twentieth century, the Qur'ānic verses which refer to various natural phenomena have become popular departure points for proving that the Qur'ān is, in fact, the word of God because modern science has established the accuracy of certain verses, or because it contains "scientific truths" which were unknown at the time of its revelation. This approach is inherently flawed for it stretches the meanings of the verses to superimpose them on various scientific theories now current, or it merely attempts to prove a revealed Book through human endeavor which itself remains under constant revision. In both cases, there is little to be gained; it amounts to a gross injustice to both the Qur'ān and science. We will return to this subject in more detail in chapter ten.

CHAPTER THREE

Making of the Tradition

The Islamic scientific tradition came into existence amidst a rich flow of diverse cultural, philosophical and scientific currents. Built on the metaphysical foundations provided by the Qur'ān and rooted in the very heart of Islamic revelation, it received the first flow of intellectual currents from the Kalām discourse that reflected on the Qur'ānic description of God and sought ways to comprehend the Divine in human terms. Then came a torrent from the ancient centers of learning—philosophical ideas, religious beliefs, scientific facts and theories. Amidst this influx of diverse crosscurrents, the emerging tradition matured in quick order.

The flow of scientific information and philosophical ideas from Indian, Persian and Greek sources into Islamic thought was a long, sustained and enormously complex phenomenon. Let us note that neither the Indian nor the Greek thought arrived in its original form; both had been transformed during the preceding centuries. The former went through a major transformation in the Persian milieu and the latter in both the Iranian and the Hellenized academies of Syria, notably those of Edessa, Nisibis, Baalbek and Homs. Thus in view of the extent of mutual blending, borrowing and modification of Indian, Persian and Greek traditions during the pre-Islamic era in the large geographical area that eventually became part of the Muslim world, it is perhaps best to describe the material that came into Islamic thought as a complex hybrid that had Indo-Perso-Greek characteristics, intractably blended.

We have a rare inside account of the way in which Ardashīr ibn Bābak, the founder of the Sassanian dynasty (226-651 CE), cultivated learning in his kingdom by acquiring books from India and China. "He sent to India and China for books in those directions," reports Abū Sahl al-Faḍl ibn Nawbakht (*fl.* 2nd/8th century) in Ibn al-Nadīm's well-known *Fihrist*, "and also to the Greeks. He copied whatever was safeguarded with them, even seeking for the little that remained in al-ʿIrāq. Thus he collected what was scattered, gathering together the things dispersed."[1]

1. *Fihrist*, p. 297.

This was neither an isolated incident nor a transitory event. Shāpūr I (241-272 CE), the able son of Ardashīr, followed his father's example "so that there were transcribed into Persian all of those books, such as the ones of Hermes the Babylonian, who ruled Egypt; Dorotheus the Syrian; Phaedrus the Greek from the city of Athens, famous for learning; Ptolemy [Ptolemaeus Alexandrinus]; and Farmāsib the Indian."[2] After these two rulers, we are told, "there appeared Chosroes Anūshriwān (531-687 CE) who collected, edited, and worked over these [books] because of his interest in learning and his love for it."[3] It was during Chosroes' time that the physician Burzōe is said to have traveled to India in search of an herb that revivified the dead. But upon arrival in India, Burzōe found out that "the herb in question was of the *genus allegoricum*: 'the restorer of the dead' was, in fact, a collection of fables known in the Old Sanskrit as the *Pañčatantra*."[4] This collection was translated into Pahlavī by Burzōe with an autobiographical preface which gives us an indication of the kind of intellectual humanism that prevailed at the court. Passing from Burzōe's Pahlavī into Syriac, and then to Arabic through a translation of Ibn al-Muqaffaʿ (*ca.* 102-139/720-756), the collection became an Arabic classic, *Kalīla wa Dimna*, which is still widely read.[5]

In addition to the Indian and Chinese works, Greek texts had also directly influenced both the Indian and the Persian thought. When Yazdajird III, the last Sassanian ruler, died in 31/651 and the whole of Persia came within the ever-expanding fold of Islam, the nascent Islamic scientific tradition was brought in direct contact with the important hospital and academy at Jundishāpūr in Khūzistān, southern Persia.[6] The academy at Jundishāpūr had become the most important center of learning in Persia during the reign of Anūshīrvān. It was further enriched by the influx of fleeing Nestorian scholars after Emperor Zeno closed the academy of Edessa in 489 CE. These Nestorian scholars not only found a

2. Ibid.
3. Ibid.
4. Peters, F.E. (1968), *Aristotle and the Arabs*, New York University Press, New York, p. 48.
5. For a short history of the original text and its various translations see Brockelmann, C., "Kalīla wa-Dimna" in *EI*, vol. vi, pp. 503-6.
6. Variants: Jundaysābūr, Bayt Lāpāt in Syriac; founded by Shāpūr I who made it the home of his Greek prisoners, marked by present day ruins of Shāhābād, taken by Muslims in 17/738, after the occupation of Tustar, during the caliphate of ʿUmar by Abū Mūsā al-Ashʿri. See Huart, CL. "Gondeshāpūr" in *EI*, vol. ii, pp. 1119-20.

new home in Jundishāpūr, they were also greatly respected and honored by Anūshīrvān. When the Neoplatonic school at Athens was closed in 529 CE by a decree of Emperor Justinian, the Athenian scholars also came to Jundishāpūr, making it the intellectual center of the empire—a place that hosted Persian, Greek, Roman, Syrian and Indian scholars and encouraged cross-cultural exchange of ideas.

Thus, it is not surprising that it was from Jundishāpūr that the second ʿAbāssid Caliph, al-Manṣūr (r.136-37/753-754), summoned Jūrjīs b. Bakhtīshūʿ, a Syrian Christian physician, to his court in 147-148/764-765. Jūrjīs, let us note, was the head of the hospital at Jundishāpūr and the Bakhtīshūʿ family had long been associated with the tradition of learning. His arrival in Baghdad established a Baghdad-Jundishāpūr axis that was to remain active for several generations. Jūrjīs was made court physician and he was succeeded by his family members.

It is noteworthy that the Indian and the Persian scientific traditions were still alive at the time of their transmission to the Muslim world and Muslims had recourse to their living representatives whereas the Greek tradition was practically dead at the time of its transmission. Thus, Muslim scientists and translators had to rely entirely on the written texts and their own insights to master the received material.

Translation Movement

The Greek texts that came into the Islamic thought had been modified during their pre-Islamic sojourn in Persian and Syrian milieus. The Syriac-speaking communities of Edessa, Nisibis, Kinnersrin, Homs and Baalbek came into the fold of Islam along with their academies, texts and scholars. The Syriac Christianity was ascetic in its practices. After Jovian's cession of the trans-Tigrine provinces of the Roman Empire to the Sassanians in 363 CE, it had lived outside the borders of the Empire, independent of the ecclesiastical control of Antioch as well as Constantinople. One important effect of this independence expressed itself in the dogmatic difference of these satellite communities with the mainstream Christianity on the nature of the person of Christ. Ultimately, this difference can be traced back to two Constantinopolitan churchmen, Nestorius (d. *ca.* 451 CE), the Patriarch of Constantinople (428-431) who emphasized the humanity of Christ and Eutychius, who placed emphasis on the divinity. Nestorius was condemned at the Council of Ephesus in 431 and in the following years the partisans of

Eutychius, the Monophysites,[7] were able to expel the Nestorian teachers from the Syriac schools. They fled to Nisibis under the able leadership of Barsauma and started to teach there. A second wave followed in 489 CE when the Emperor Zeno closed the Edessan school. The situation became even more complex when the Monophysite position was also condemned at the Council of Chalcedon (451 CE), producing two Syrian Churches: the Nestorian Church of Persia and the Jocobite Church of the Monophysites; the former was doctrinally as well as administratively independent of the Emperor and the latter was subjected to constant persecutions from the Byzantine state.

In retrospect, it seems that the fifth century Christology was shaped around a war of definitions and terms amidst the high noon of patristic scholasticism. It was under these circumstances that the *Organon* entered the scene, providing syllogistic techniques to both camps. The first Syriac translations of Aristotle were produced by churchmen from *ca.* 450 CE until well after the Muslim conquest; these had a strong theological underlay. When Muslims came into contact with this body of literature, it had already developed a technical Aristotelianism, as well as a strong peripateticism. The Syrian churchmen were also interested in grammar. A Syrian monk, ʿEnanishuʿ (*fl. ca.* 650 CE), had composed a grammatical lexicon of consonantly identical Syriac-Greek words, a glossary of difficult terms and a book of definitions of philosophical terms. A Syrio-Greek lexicon is also attributed to Ḥunyan ibn Isḥāq (192-260/808-873), one of the major translators of Greek and Syriac texts into Arabic.

Let us also note that, in addition to the academies of Syriac learning, Muslims had also incorporated Ḥarrān into their realm during the Caliphate of ʿUmar in 19/640. Situated on the small river Jullāb, at the intersection of important caravan routes to Asia Minor, Syria and Mesopotamia, the town is believed to have been the birthplace of Abraham. According to al-Bīrūnī, the town resembled the shape of the moon and it was a community of star worshippers; Ibn Abī Uṣaybiʿa tells us that the Umayyad Caliph ʿUmar II (r. 99-101/717-720) had transferred a school of medicine from Alexandria to Ḥarrān.[8]

---

7. Those who maintain that Christ has one nature, partly divine and partly human; *cf.* Dyophysites, those who maintain that Christ has two natures, one divine and the other human.
8. See Fehervari, G. "Ḥarrān" in *EI*, vol. iii, pp. 227-30. The reference to Ibn Abī Uṣaybiʿa is from his well-known *ʿUyūn al-anbāʾ fī ṭabaqāt al-aṭibbāʾ*, quoted by Fehervari.

The Arabic translations from the Pahlavī, Sanskrit and Syrian texts preceded the translations from the Greek. Most of these early translations are lost, though references to their existence and content survive in numerous later Arabic sources. This translation activity quickly gained momentum and by the time of al-Mā'mūn (r. 198-218/813-833), the internal dynamics of the Islamic tradition of learning had clearly displayed a need for a more systematic, organized and large-scale translation movement. Al-Mā'mūn and several influential personage of his court responded positively to this need and established the famous "House of Wisdom" (*Bayt al-Ḥikma*) which became the hub of one of the most fascinating cross-cultural movements of transmission of knowledge.[9]

This translation movement passed through three distinct phases. The first began before the middle of the second century of Islam, during the reign of al-Manṣūr (r. 136-158/754-775). Major translators of this first phase were Ibn al-Muqaffaʿ(d.139/756) and his son, Ibn Nāʿima (*fl.* 2nd/8th century), Theodore Abū Qurra (d. *ca.* 211/826), the disciple of John of Damascus (d. 749) who held a secretarial post under the Umayyad Caliphs, Thābit ibn Qurrah (d.289/901), the Sabian mathematician,[10] Eustathius (*fl.* 3rd/9th century),[11] and Ibn al-Biṭrīq (263-328/877-944) who was the member of the circle of the Caliph al-Mā'mūn whose accession marks the beginning of the second phase of the translation movement. This second phase of the translation movement brought a host of new translators who worked under the able guidance of Ḥunayn ibn Isḥāq. It was during this period that more polished translations of the previously translated material were produced. In addition, this activity now covered a whole range of ancient texts—from Aristotle to Galen. The third and the final phase of the translation movement marks the appearance of revised versions of older translations and a vast corpus of commentary. This period, which extended from 288 to 411 AH (900 to 1020 CE) also witnessed the emergence of textual criticisms and mastery of the translated texts.

By the middle of the eleventh century, the three-hundred-year-old translation movement had reached its end. During the preceding centuries, it not only brought a large number of Greek, Persian and Indian texts into Arabic, it also tried to graft many new concepts, systems of thought and ways of studying nature onto the Islamic intellectual tradition. Some of

9. See Sourdel, D. "Bayt" in *EI*, vol. i, p. 1141.
10. *Fihrist*, p. 272.
11. *Fihrist*, p. 304; both of them translated for al-Kindī.

these concepts—such as the eternity of the world—were not in harmony with Islamic doctrines. This created a tension that finally produced one of the most startling cases of appropriation and transformation in the history of ideas. This was a slow and deliberate process that examined, classified, sorted, and retained what it needed from the received material. It was the ordering of ideas in the light of revelation; a sublimation of the received material—an act which required generations to complete and which created schism, debates, disagreements, polemics, even indictments and judgments. This inner struggle of a tradition in the making against the foreign currents that were coming into its folds also produced a wide range of philosophers and scientists—some of whom aligned themselves with philosophy; some wrote against philosophy and philosophers. And between these two extremes were a host of others who tried to harmonize Islam's revelatory data with philosophy. The end result of this long process was the appearance of a tradition of learning that examined, explored and synthesized its own unique perspectives on nature and the human condition—perspectives that were distinctly Islamic, though not monolithic.

The Contours of the Tradition

This brief account of the translation movement helps us to construct the environment in which the Islamic scientific tradition began to take shape. Our sources clearly suggest that the Islamic scientific tradition was built on the metaphysical doctrines found in the Qur'ān. It received its kinetic flow from the reflection on nature and the human condition by the early Qur'ān exegetes and, starting in the middle of the eighth century, it came upon a rich harvest of scientific texts, concepts, theories and techniques from the Greek, Persian and Indian sources. What came into the body of Islamic thought from outside was neither accidental, nor marginal. It was a sustained, deliberate and systematic effort that actively sought manuscripts, books and personage to satiate its internal needs. Those who helped in this effort of acquisition of knowledge from other civilizations were initially non-Muslim citizens of an expanding empire who were amply supported and rewarded by their patrons who were part of an urban elite that had come into existence in the new cities.

This flow of Greek, Persian and Indian thought into the Islamic scientific tradition has received ample attention by historians of science whose opinions range from "reductionism to precursorism"—two explanatory terms used by A. I. Sabra in 1987.[12] Reductionism, in this context, refers to the "view that the achievements of Islamic scientists were merely a reflection, sometimes faded, sometimes bright, or more or less altered, of earlier (mostly Greek) examples; Precursorism, on the other hand, reads the future into the past, with a sense of elation".[13] In the final analysis, it may be said that the historians of science are still not able to reconstruct with confidence a complete mosaic of all the currents of thought, scientific facts and theories that came into the Islamic civilization through the highly complex phenomena of cross-cultural transmission but they are certainly able to assert that this was not a passive reception of material into one civilization from another. Rather, it was an enormously complex but creative process that transformed the material in the very act of appropriation. The case for appropriation, rather than reception, has been well established and we will not repeat those arguments.[14] What is of interest to us is this very act of appropriation that defined the relationship between Islam and the science it inspired. But let us note in passing that it was not only the Islamic scientific tradition that was affected by the influx

12. See Sabra, A. I. (1987), "The Appropriation and Subsequent Naturalization of Greek Science in Medieval Islam: A Preliminary Statement" in *History of Science*, vol. 25, pp. 223-43; reprinted with other papers in a collection, Sabra, A. I. (1994), *Optics, Astronomy and Logic: Studies in Arabic Science and Philosophy*, Variorum, Aldershot; all references are to this collection of papers which retains the pagination of the original publications.
13. Sabra (1994), pp. 223-4.
14. In addition to the aforementioned work, the case for originality of Islamic science has been convincingly made by a number of historians of science. See, for example, Pines, Shlomo (1986), "What was Original in Arabic Science" in his *Studies in Arabic Versions of Greek Texts and in Mediaeval Science*, E. J. Brill, Leiden, pp. 181-205; also see various studies on Islamic astronomy by David King, E. S. Kennedy and David Pingree. An interesting example is to be found in the Persian manuscript by the fifteenth century Iranian scientist Jamshīd ibn Masʿūd ibn Maḥmūd Ghiyāth al-Dīn al-Kāshī (or Kāshānī). The discovery of this manuscript has also helped to push the date of the "decline of Islamic science" well past the generally assumed period of 12th or the 13th century. This has been edited and translated by Kennedy, E. S. (1960), Princeton University Press, Princeton. A more recent account of the discovery of two world maps is also important; see King, David (1999), *World-Maps for Finding the Direction and Distance to Mecca*, E. J. Brill, Leiden; also of interest is King, David (1987), *Islamic Astronomical Instruments*, Variorum Reprints, London.

of new currents; the material from other civilizations had a profound impact on the whole range of Islamic thought and some of it came to be regarded as dangerous, extraneous and foreign; this last category is sometimes used to draw the reductionist conclusion that the scientific tradition in Islam was nothing but a "foreign" entity that somehow survived despite the opposition it faced and then died as soon as the religious sciences were able to gain an upper hand. This view has been succinctly called "the marginality thesis" and its validity has been challenged on sound historical evidence.[15]

A brief look at what was translated will allow us to build the structure of the Islamic scientific tradition during its formative period. But before we explore this rich reservoir, let us reconstruct those concepts and theories that emerged in the Islamic civilization prior to these translations; this will enable us to prepare ground for the comparative study of the concepts and theories as well as help in understanding the nature of transformation that followed the translations.

Historical Background of Transformation

As mentioned previously (chapter one), the initial Kalām debates in Islam were mainly concerned with the question of free will and predestination. The Qadrites held that the individual believer had *qudra* (power) over his or her actions. More extreme among them held that God did not have knowledge of the particulars; this allowed them to formulate their doctrine of complete human freedom. On the other extreme were the Jabrites who held that human beings were under compulsion to the extent that God creates all actions—good as well as bad—leaving the individual no choice and freedom; this notion was also shared by some other groups. These early theological debates took place in the shadow of the great social crisis which marked the evolution of Islamic polity between the death of ʿUthmān (d.36/656) and ʿAlī (d. 41/661). This schism was neither the result of a forgetfulness of the Qur'ānic text nor a product of misunderstanding of its central message. The Islamic polity was suffering from a much deeper malady—the disunity of the hearts. This malady gave rise to the appearance of various sects in Islam such as the Shīʿa, the Khārijites and the Murji'ites—all of which ultimately sought legitimacy in the only source available to them: the Qur'ān. And ultimately, in many cases, it was the question of stress on certain Qur'ānic notions that determined a particular dogmatic position. The Khārijites, for example, took an extreme position in

15. Sabra (1994), p. 229-30.

reference to the status of the believer who commits a grave sin (*al-kabīra*); they considered him an infidel (*kāfir*), to be condemned to hellfire forever. The Murji'ites, on the other hand, held the other extreme view: such a sinner not only remains a believer, his or her faith remains untarnished because, they held that action is not part of faith. Amidst these debates, a majority of Muslims followed the middle path and were called the people of the Way of the Prophet and consensus (*Ahl al-Sunna wa'l Jamāʿa*).

A deeper reflection on these early issues enlarged discussion to include such fundamental concepts as the very nature of God and His Word, the Qur'ān. What is the nature of Divine Attributes? How could they be understood in relation to God's essence? How could such explicit references in the Qur'ān as to the possibility of seeing God (Q.75:22) or His face (55:27) or His "sitting upon the throne" (7:54 and 20:5) be interpreted? Was the Qur'ān created in time or did it exist eternally with God?

The ever-increasing realm of Kalām slowly embraced all central questions—including those concerned with eschatology and the fate of sinners—which were being vigorously discussed in various circles in the intellectual centers of the Muslim world, especially in Baṣra and Kūfa. These questions were not merely theoretical discussions of a small group of theologians in their drawing rooms. Rather, these were questions upon which one's faith rested and an incongruous position entailed grave consequences.

It has become customary to summarily represent these developments of the second century Islam in the form of two dominant schools of thought: the Muʿtazilites and the Ashaʿrites. But this simplistic representation is misleading, to say the least. The two schools did not come into existence as two distinct and completely separated modes of thinking; intellectual discourse never lends itself to such neat categories. In reality what happened in the mosques and madāris of the second century Muslim world was a vigorous but quiet precipitation of various formulations; a process that took its own time to crystallize and that went through several intermediate positions before it took its distinct shape. These intermediate steps remain important links between various schools and even though we can now talk of the position of the Muʿtazilites and the Ashʿarites on various issues in somewhat static formulations, in reality, they were never watertight and separate domains of thought. Many so-called distinct schools of thought actually emerged from common grounds. We have, for example, a vivid account of a particular incident that took place in the circle of al-Ḥasan al-Baṣrī (d.110/728)—one of the most accomplished spiritual and intellectual Sufis of Islam—which sheds light on the hybrid nature of discourse at this time.

There exist at least three early accounts of this incident but the main story can be confidently reconstructed, at least in its bare minimum form.[16] This is what we know for sure: a man came and asked al-Ḥasan al-Baṣrī whether they should regard the grave sinner as a believer or an unbeliever. While al-Ḥasan hesitated, one of those in his circle abruptly answered that the grave sinner was neither, but was in an intermediate position (*manzila bayn al-manzilatayn*), literally, his "position is between the two positions". According to the standard version of this account, it was Wāṣil ibn ʿAṭāʾ who thus answered; he then withdrew to another pillar in the mosque whereupon al-Ḥasan remarked that Wāṣil has withdrawn (*iʿtazala*) from us; a remark which became the basis for the term Muʿtazila. This standard version of a famous incident is not without problems as elaborated in subsequent accounts but for our purpose, these problems are not important.[17]

Wāṣil's initial reaction could not have been so drastic as to cause a total split in the circle on all issues. We know for sure that Jahm b. Ṣafwān (d.128/745), the founder of the rival Jahmite school, shared with the Muʿtazila the doctrine of the creation of the Qur'ān; Jahm also shared with the Muʿtazila the opinion that God's attributes are identical with His essence. Jahm, however, disagreed with the Muʿtazila on many other essential issues. For instance, he denied free will and shared with the school of Jabrites (Determinists) his notion of pre-determination of all actions. But more radical was his belief that ultimately both heaven and hell—along with their occupants—will be destroyed. He formulated this view on the basis of the Qur'ānic verses that speak of God as being "the First and the Last" (Q. 57:3) and of the perishing of everything "save His face" (Q. 55:27). This was in sharp contrast to the Muʿtazila belief in the eternal punishment and reward and consequently the eternity of heaven and hell. In time, the Muʿtazila came to be associated with two central beliefs:

---

16. Most histories of Islamic tradition report this story. These include al-Baghdādī's *al-Farq bayn al-firaq,* al-Sharastani's *Kitāb al-milal wa'l niḥal,* Ibn al-Nadīm's *al-Fihrist.*
17. For example, some versions omit al-Ḥasan's statement and attribute the decisive words to others or replace Wāṣil with another person. For details and for a synthetic recasting, see Watt, Montgomery, W. (1973), *The Formative Period of Islamic Thought,* OneWorld, Oxford, pp. 209-17.

absolute divine justice and unity. It was their notion of divine justice that led the Muʿtazila to resolve rationally the apparent problems raised by the Qurʾānic emphasis on God's unlimited sovereignty. The Qurʾān is emphatic about divine justice but it also mentions God's guidance and His misguidance (Q. 3:154; 7:178; 16:21, 24; 32:13) and of His "sealing of the hearts" (Q. 2:5,6; 6:125; 16:95; 61:5), the book of fate (Q. 69:17, 27) and difference in provisions (*arzāq*, sing. *rizq*) given to humans (Q.16:71; 17:30).

The Muʿtazila tried to "vindicate" God through rational means, without repudiating the Qurʾānic doctrines. They contended that good and evil are not arbitrary concepts whose validity is rooted in God's dictates; rather, they are rational categories which can be established through reason, unaided by scripture. Because they held that God was absolutely just, He could not enjoin upon His creatures what was contrary to reason because that would compromise His justice and wisdom. In other words, an omnipotent God could not act in total violation of all the precepts of justice and torture the innocent or demand of His creation the impossible. They also held that humans were free to act in the world. Further developments led to refinement of these concepts. For instance, al-Naẓẓām argued that every activity in the world takes place through secondary natural agents but it must be referred to God in an ultimate sense. He formulated these ideas through his concepts of inherent nature (*ṭabʿ*) of things and that of God's initial creation of the latent properties of things (*kumūn*) that subsequently manifest externally (*ẓuhūr*).[18]

It was in the midst of such debates that the translation movement began and it soon provided new tools—such as logic and syllogism—which could be used to demonstrate one's position. In addition, the translation movement also brought a large body of scientific data and theories into Islamic thought. It is this infusion of information and new ideas that concerns us here. How did this new material affect the Islamic scientific tradition? How was it translated? By whom? How was it used and, eventually, transformed? These, and similar, questions form the framework of our inquiry for they were fundamental factors which determined the contours of the Islamic scientific tradition.

18. For a summary of various positions, see chapter 2 in Fakhry, Majid (1970 and 1983), *A History of Islamic Philosophy*, Columbia University Press, chapter II and Kamal, Mohammad (1993), *Heterodoxy in Islam: A Philosophical Study*, Royal Book Company, Karachi.

It has already been mentioned that the Greek, Persian and Indian texts that came into the Islamic tradition had gone through a complex process of hybridization during the pre-Islamic era. In particular, the Aristotelian and the Platonic traditions had witnessed a profound transformation in attempts to harmonize the two schools of thought. Plotinus (d. *ca.* 260), for example, had transformed Aristotle's Unmoved Mover to the One (*to hen*), the supreme hypostasis beyond world, in his hierarchical scheme of emanation that eventually produced Matter (*hulê*). This large body of literature did not barge upon the Islamic tradition at once; it came in stages and though the first translations were made from whatever manuscripts were available, in time, there appeared a critical control reminiscent of the process of collection and authentication of the Ḥadīth material. Often, more than one translation of the same text was made, various versions were collated and commentaries were written on the differences.[19] Nor was the translation activity a static phenomenon that gave birth to the Arabic versions of Greek, Syriac and Pahlavī texts and having done this, disappeared. It was an organic process that brought material from these traditions into the living body of a tradition that had emerged on the basis of a revealed text. And although the translation movement did come to its logical end in the eleventh century, the process of sorting of the received material, its assimilation and transformation did not stop. Even the translated texts remained under scrutiny, as the fourteenth century philologist and biographer al-Ṣafadī (696-764/1297-1363)—who commented on the two methods of translation used by early translators—tells us. He criticizes the literal method of Yuḥannā ibn Biṭrīq, Ibn al-Nāʿima al-Himsi and others which produced word by word translations, often without regard to the syntactic peculiarities and constructions and he praises the method of Ḥunayn ibn Isḥāq, al-Jawhari and others in their group for translating the message, rather than the words of the texts which they brought into Arabic.[20]

19. For example, Ibn Rushd often cites variants where they have bearing on the interpretation. A case in point is his *Great Commentary* on the *De anima* where he uses an unidentified translation as the basis for his comment, and cites the variants from Isḥāq's version in the body of the *lectio.* Likewise, the text of the *Metaphysica* for his *Great Commentary* is sewn together from a whole series of versions, from the *veteres* to the school of Ḥunayn to the Peripatetic *recentioers.*
20. Ṣalāḥ al-Dīn Khalīl al-Ṣafadī (696-764/1297-1363) makes such comments in many places in his vast corpus. His concern with linguistic problems is evident from such works as his monumental *Taṣḥīḥ al-Taṣḥīf wa*

It is also important to note that whatever was translated, was translated into a living language that was rapidly expanding. Thus, the transformation of the received material was also accompanied by a linguistic transformation. At times, the first translators used the Greek terms for want of exact Arabic equivalents but the latter translators or commentators coined new Arabic terms. This is how a rich repository of technical terms, with precise definitions and explanations, came into Arabic.

In time, there arose an internal need to classify the received material. This gave rise to an extensive tradition of classification of knowledge. This was such an important activity that most Muslim thinkers felt compelled to write their schemes of classification. While these schemes differ from one another, sometimes in substantial ways, they are all hierarchical. They also share a common trait of distinguishing between the revealed knowledge and that which is acquired from other sources. Those sciences which dealt with the former were often called *al-ʿulūm al-naqliyya,* the "transmitted sciences", while the latter were called *al-ʿulūm al-ʿaqliyya*, the "intellectual sciences". The traditional sciences dealt with the Qur'ān, Ḥadīth and subjects related to them and relied upon the transmission of the text through an elaborate process which depended upon an oral tradition going all the way back to the Prophet himself, the recipient of divine revelation. This oral tradition, which was eventually written, remains to this day a uniquely Islamic pedagogical methodology and the authoritative source of authentication. It rests on the intermediatory chain (*isnād*) of transmitters each of whom receives his or her material from the previous authority in the chain orally along with a notarized attestation that the student has heard, received and mastered the text in question and has been given permission (*ijāza*) to transmit it.

This method was based on the notion of authority. The revealed text of the Qur'ān ultimately traces its authority to none other than God who Himself vouchsafed its transmission to his Prophet.[21] From the Prophet, the text traveled to its recipients through a chain of transmitters. The same applied to the actions and utterances of the Prophet (Ḥadīth), in which

---

Taḥrīr al-Taḥrīf which deals with misspellings and misreadings. His biographical collections, notably the massive *al-Wāfī bi'l Wafayāt* and *Aʿyān al-ʿaṣr wa'l-Aʿwān al-Naṣr* (which deal with the lives of his contemporaries) also contain valuable information about the translated texts. See Rosenthal, F. "al-Ṣafadī" in *EI,* vol. xiii, pp. 759-60.

21. Q. 13:37; 17:105.

case the first transmitter heard it from the Prophet. Naturally, there arose a serious need for an elaborate apparatus of authentication of the *isnād*. This also produced in Islam the tradition of *ṭabaqāt* literature—a monumental feast that would guarantee a perpetual dynamic status to the lives of thousands of scholars.[22]

This pedagogic methodology was naturally not suitable for the study of the translated texts that brought Greek, Indian and Persian legacies to Islam. These texts were acquired and studied through a different method. There was no authority behind these texts; they were obtained in written form and they were meant to be comprehended—rather than transmitted—for the sake of one's own understanding. But, it is interesting to note that although medicine, astronomy, mathematics, geometry, alchemy and other natural sciences could be studied from texts alone, they were often studied with a teacher who had mastered them, though there were notable exceptions to this. For instance, Ibn Sīnā (370-428/980-1037) tells us that he mastered the logical, natural and mathematical sciences on his own but he could not comprehend the contents of Aristotle's *Metaphsics* "even when I had gone back and read it forty times and had got to the point where I had memorized it" until he came upon al-Fārābi's commentary.[23] Al-Fārābi himself is known to have studied *Analytica posteriora* with Yūḥannā ibn Ḥaylān. Thus, philosophy (*falsafa*) was often studied with a teacher but on the basis of a text that was subject to textual criticism as well as comment; this tradition is still alive, especially in contemporary Iran.

But the pedagogical methodology alone cannot explain the emergence of a rich and integrated process of examination of the received material. There is virtually no important translated text that did not receive a thorough treatment by subsequent generations. Many texts were re-translated by more able translators who also understood their subject matter. Sometimes, the newer translations affected the whole field. We know, for example, that the transmission of Greek geometrical and

---

22. Lit. *ṭabaqāt* means categories. This literature classified the narrators into various categories, examined their affiliations, teachers, students as well as intellectual developments. A good example of this critical apparatus is al-Ṭabari's monumental commentary on the Qur'ān which cites no less than 24,502 chains of transmitters of which 11,364 are unique. The same is true for the transmission of Ḥadīth literature.
23. This first person account can be found in Gohlman, William, E. (1974), *The Life of Ibn Sina: A Critical Edition and Annotated Translation,* State University of New York Press, Albany, p. 33.

mathematical texts into Arabic began around 174/790 at Baghdad. Among the first to be translated was Ptolemy's *Almagest* and Euclid's *Elements*. The first translation of the *Almagest* was made for the wazir Yaḥyā ibn Khālid ibn Barmak (121-190/738-805) and al-Hajjāj b. Yūsuf b. Maṭṭar al-Ḥāsib (*fl.* late 2nd century) translated *Elements* of Euclid and *Astronomy* of Ptolemy for Caliph Hārūn al-Rashid (170-194/786-809); the latter was called *Kitāb al-Majisṭī* and was completed in 212/827.[24] *Elements* was re-translated by Isḥāq ibn Ḥunayn; this translation was corrected by Thābit ibn Qurra. The *Almagest* was translated at least three times.

Sometimes, the translated texts had to wait a long time before they were "understood", as Ibn al-Nadīm tells us in his *Fihrist*. He states that the two books *On the Determinate Section* of Apollonius were translated into Arabic by an anonymous translator; the first book was corrected by Thābit ibn Qurra but the second book was not "understood". However, a recently published correspondence between the late tenth-century geometer al-Kūhī and his friend al-Ṣābī shows how they tried to make sense of the contents of Book II.[25]

Another interesting example is that of *Conics* of Apollonius which came into the hands of three ninth century mathematicians, the well-known sons of Mūsā: Muḥammad, Aḥmad and al-Ḥasan (*fl.* before 260/873). At first the Banū Mūsā only possessed Books I-VII of the *Conics*, which were, moreover, riddled with scribal errors. In the process of understanding this difficult text, al-Ḥasan ibn Mūsā worked out a theory for plane sections of a cylinder and wrote a treatise on the subject. After his death, his brother Aḥmad found another manuscript of the *Conics* in Syria containing the first four books as well as commentaries by Eutocius of Ascalon (*ca.* 500 CE). By means of this new manuscript and through a judicial use of his brother's treatise, Aḥmad was able to understand the whole of *Conics*. He then had the first four books translated by Hilāl ibn Abī Hilāl al-Ḥimsī and the last three by Thābit ibn Qurra; he himself made corrections and added many cross references. In the process, he developed many purely Arabic technical terms for the theory of conic sections.[26]

---

24. *GAL*, vol. 1, pp. 203.
25. Berggren, J. L. (1983), "The Correspondence of Abū Sahl al-Kūhī and Abū Isḥāq al-Ṣābī: A Translation with Commentaries" in *Journal for the History of Arabic Science*, vol. 7, pp. 39-124.
26. For a more detailed account of this fascinating story see Toomer, Gerald J. (1990), *Apollonius Conics Books V to VII: The Arabic Translation of the Lost Greek Original in the Version of the Banū Mūsā*, 2 vols. Sources in

Roots, Branches and Connections

Another facet of the Islamic scientific tradition was its ability to sustain interest in various scientific problems—a feature it shares with modern science. This meant that sometimes one problem was carried over to the next generation; at others, solutions came several generations later. In any case, there exists conclusive historical evidence that the Islamic scientific tradition was not a small-scale activity sustained by a few individuals who were working in isolation from each other or from the rest of the intellectual currents of their times. Rather, it was a social activity with well-developed mechanisms for transmission of results over the entire geographical spread of the Muslim world. Considering the distances involved, it was really a remarkable feat. In spite of the loss of hundreds of medieval texts, we can still reconstruct the broad outline of this activity. For instance, the solution of the cubic equations by means of conic sections was a branch of mathematics that was solely developed by the Muslim mathematicians without any outside influence. It started as a result of a "gap" in the transmission of the Greek texts. In *On the Sphere and Cylinder* II: 4, Archimedes had assumed that on a given segment AB, a point X can be constructed such that $AX:a=b^2:XB^2$, for given segments a and b.[27] Archimedes never explained this construction, though he promised to do so at the end of his treatise, or he may have, but it was already missing in antiquity. In his commentary, Eutocius of Ascalon (*ca.* 500 CE) provided several constructions of his own. The text of Archimedes and the commentary of Eutocius were both translated into Arabic but at different times and several Muslim geometers had either one or the other but not both; this made it necessary for them to provide their own constructions. Abū ʿAbd Allāh Muḥammad Ibn ʿIsā al-Māhānī (*ca.* 236/850) provided an algebraic solution of the Archimedean problem of dividing a sphere by a plane into segments the volumes of which are in a given ration. Al-Māhānī expressed this problem in a cubic equation of the form $x^3+a=cx^2$, but he

---

History of Mathematics and Physical Sciences 9, Springer-Verlag, New York.

27. In reconstructing this example, I am using modern notations, following Hogendijk who first brought this interesting case to light. See Hogendijk, Jan P. (1996), "Transmission, Transformation, and Originality: The Relation of Arabic to Greek Geometry" in Ragep, Jamil, F. and Ragep, Sally P. (ed.) *Tradition, Transmission, Transformation, Proceedings of Two Conferences on Pre-modern Science held at the University of Oklahoma*, E. J. Brill, Leiden, pp. 33-4.

could not proceed further. The problem was thought unsolvable until Abū Ja'far al-Khāzin (*ca.*318/930) solved the cubic equation by means of conic sections.[28] This was the beginning of the new field of the solution of cubic equations by means of conic sections. Al-Māhānī also wrote commentaries on Books I, V, X and XIII of Euclid's *Elements*. In his treatise on ratio (Book V), al-Māhānī refers to Thābit ibn Qurra.

Likewise, a correspondence between Ibn Sīnā and Abū Rayḥān al-Bīrūnī (362/973-*ca.* 442/1051)—perhaps the two most important scientists of the eleventh century anywhere in the world—gives us an insight into the inner dynamics of the Islamic scientific tradition as well as its modus operandi and mechanism of propagation.[29] In this correspondence, al-Bīrūnī raises ten questions regarding Aristotle's *De Caelo* (*al-Samā' wa'l-'Ālam*) along with eight additional questions of his own. Ibn Sīnā answered all questions one by one. But al-Bīrūnī was not satisfied. He responded by commenting on eight of the first ten responses and the seven of the last eight. Ibn Sīnā did not write back but asked Abū Sa'īd Aḥmad ibn 'Alī al-Ma'ṣūmī, one of his brilliant students, to respond on his behalf. This correspondence deals with some of the fundamental philosophical and scientific issues of the time and marks an exchange of ideas between a fiercely independent scientist, al-Bīrūnī, and the finest representative of Islamic Peripatetic tradition, Ibn Sīnā. Islamic Peripatetic tradition, it must be noted here, was the main school of natural philosophy in the Islamic civilization. It came into existence through a creative synthesis which combined Aristotelian tradition with certain elements of later Neoplatonism and Alexandrian commentaries of Aristotle's works. Al-Bīrūnī's criticism of this dominant

28. Dold-Samplonius, Yvonne, "al-Māhānī" in *DSB*, vol. 9, pp.21-2.
29. The Arabic text of this correspondence between Abū Rayḥān al-Bīrūnī and Ibn Sīnā was first published in 1914 in a collection entitled *Jāmi' al-Badāyi'*, without any reference to the manuscript used. In 1953, the Faculty of Letters of Istanbul University published the text of this correspondence in volume two of its *Rasā'il* of Ibn Sīnā (edited by Helmy Zia Ülkenon) on the basis of Ms. No. 3447 of the Ahmad Thalith Library. It was again published in a limited edition on the occasion of the al-Bīrūnī International Congress held in Tehran in 1973. Its most recent and complete edition was published in 1995. See Nasr, Seyyed Hossein and Mohaghegh, Mehdi, (eds.) (1995), *Al-As'ilah wa'l-Ajwibah,* International Institute of Islamic Thought and Civilization (ISTAC), Kuala Lumpur. The ISTAC edition, based on several well-known manuscripts, also contains response of al-Bīrūnī in the form of further questions and al-Ma'ṣūmī's defense of Ibn Sīnā's position.

school of philosophy is a sharp and powerful attack on Aristotelian physics. Though al-Bīrūnī does not reject Aristotle's view of circular motion of the heavenly bodies, he severely criticizes his thesis that circular motion is innate to heavenly bodies; he asserts that there is nothing innate about this motion; it could easily have been straight. He also rejects Aristotle's reasons for the spherical nature of the heavenly bodies. He shows that if an ellipse moves around the major axis and a lentil-shaped figure around the minor axis, they will revolve like a sphere without creating a void, as Aristotle had asserted.

The questions posed by al-Bīrūnī are equally poignant. "If things expand through heating and contract through cooling," he asks, "then why does a flask full of water break when its content freezes?" In other words, why is the density of water higher than that of ice—a question which was only answered in the twentieth century on the basis of hydrogen bonding. This correspondence, which was initiated by al-Bīrūnī, clearly shows that he was grappling with certain fundamental issues related to the properties of matter. He was interested in Ibn Sīnā's responses on a wide range of topics. Ibn Sīnā's responses are drawn from his well-known works—especially the *Shifā'*, *Najāt* and *Dānishnāma-yi 'alā'ī*—and others.[30] This correspondence is, by no means, a singular event in the history of Islamic thought. There are several other well-known cases.[31]

The contours of the Islamic scientific tradition will remain incomplete without the mention of representative examples from various branches of science. However, such details will take us away from the framework of the present study; they belong to the history of the tradition or rather to various topical histories. Here we will restrict our discussion to a small aspect of the tradition. But in general, it can be safely said that the Islamic scientific tradition encompassed a whole range of disciplines and dealt with both the applied as well as theoretical research. We have already

30. For a summary of Ibn Sīnā's views, see Nasr, Seyyed Hossein (1993), *An Introduction to Islamic Cosmological Doctrines*, State University of New York, Albany.

31. See the examples mentioned by Nasr in his "Prolegomena" to the aforementioned work, especially, the correspondence between Fakhr al-Dīn al-Rāzī and Ibn 'Arabī: Valsān M. (1961), tr. "Epître addresseé à l'Imām Fakhrud Dīn ar-Rāzī" in *Etudes Traditionnelles*, vol. 62, Juillet-Octobre, pp. 246-253; the discourse between Nāṣīr al-Dīn al-Ṭūsī and Ṣadr al-Dīn al-Qūnawī *cf.* Chittick, W. (1979) "Mysticism versus Philosophy in Early Islamic History: the al-Ṭūsī, al-Qūnawī Correspondence", *Religious Studies*, vol. 10, pp. 87-104.

mentioned some aspects of the alchemical tradition which was one of the first to develop (chapter 1). Soon after alchemy, there arose a monumental astronomical tradition supported by equally formidable mathematical and geometrical traditions. Mention must also be made of the outstanding tradition of medical sciences and studies in zoology and botany. We can safely assert that toward the end of its existence, the Islamic scientific tradition, once again, focused on astronomy and mathematics. This can be established by a cursory glace at the interests of major Muslim scientists of the fifteenth and the sixteenth century as well as from the scientific activities of the major centers of research in this period: the Maragha Observatory in northwest Iran which was directed, for some time, by Naṣīr al-Dīn al-Ṭūsī (598-671/1201-1272); the madrasa and observatory of Samarqand built by Ulugh Beg (796-853/1394-1449);[32] the works of such astronomers and mathematicians as Jamshīd Ghiyāth al-Dīn al-Kāshī (d. 833/429); the "universal scholar" Bahā' al-Dīn al-ʿĀmilī (954-1031/1547-1621) and his students, most notably Muḥammad Bāqir ibn Zayn al-ʿĀbidīn Yazdī.[33]

Although our current understanding of the making of the Islamic scientific tradition has emerged in small but definite steps during the last three centuries, there are still thousands of manuscripts waiting to be edited. But even though it has become evident that no final verdict could be passed on the tradition until a substantial amount of all available material has been thoroughly examined, hasty judgments remain the vogue. An interesting example of this phenomenon is the case of the Islamic astronomical tradition. This formidable tradition, which has religious significance for finding the direction and distance to Makkah as well as for various religious rites, was considered to have died sometime in the eleventh century. But then, new texts started to trickle into the mainstream research. During the 1960s, following E. S. Kennedy's discovery of the works of Ibn al-Shāṭir (*fl. ca.*751/1350), historians of

32. Ulugh Beg and his contributions are discussed in Sayili Aydin (1960), *The Observatory in Islam,* Publications of the Turkish Historical Society, Series VII, No. 38, Türk Tarih Kurumu Basimevi, Ankara, repr. (1981), Arno Press, New York, pp. 259-89; Kari-Niazov, T. N., "Ulugh Beg" in *DSB*, vol. 13, pp. 535-37.
33. On al-Ṭūsī, see the article by S. H. Nasr in *DSB*, vol. 13, pp. 508-14; al-Ṭūsī's major work, *Tadhkira* is now available in a critical edition: Ragep, *al-Ṭūsī's Memoir on Astronomy,* this work also contains an overview of his life, work and influence; Sayili (1960), *The Observatory in Islam,* pp. 189-223.

science came to realize that the solar, lunar and planetary models of Ibn al-Shāṭir were not an isolated example of an outstanding astronomer working alone; rather, they were part of an Islamic tradition that spanned eight centuries—from the ninth to the early seventeenth. The discovery of a series of Islamic astronomical treatises on planetary theories has also shown that, contrary to the earlier opinion which held that these theories were merely "based on philosophical speculations and physical reasoning (and a *malaise* with Ptolemy's equant)", it has been established now that the new theories were actually based on the new observational data as well as philosophical reasoning.[34] We also know now that Copernicus (1473-1543) developed his models on the basis of Ibn al-Shāṭir's planetary models.[35] Likewise, the so-called "problem of Alhazen" which was carried over to Europe, was not an isolated example of a Muslim scientist grappling with basic problems of Greek science and proposing a major departure from that tradition. This problem—which is related to the point of reflection on the surface of a spherical mirror, concave or convex, given the two points related to one another as eye and the visible object—was part of a long series of investigations of specular images discussed in Book V of Ibn al-Haytham's (*ca.* 354-433/965-1041) masterpiece, *Kitāb al-Manāẓir*.[36] The solution provided by Ibn al-Haytham was described by Christian Huygens in the seventeenth century as being *longa admodum ac tediosa* ("too long and

---

34. King, David, A. (1999), *World-Maps for Finding the Direction and Distance to Mecca,* Al-Furqān-Brill, Leiden, p. 43-4, n. 90. This book is a mine of information with hundreds of cross-references to other works on Islamic astronomy, many short biographical notes on major Muslim astronomers and references to various observatories and research institutions; it is undoubtedly the single most important reference work on Islamic astronomy.
35. See more details in the next section.
36. This reconstruction of the "Alhazen Problem" is based on Sabra, A. I. (1982), "Ibn al-Haytham's Lemmas for solving 'Alhazen Problem'" in *Archive for History of Exact Sciences,* vol. 26, Springer-Verlag, Heidelberg, pp. 299-324. The phrase "Alhazen's problem" or *"problema Alhaseni (or Alhazeni)"* was coined by the seventeenth century mathematicians to describe the solution provided by Ibn al-Haytham to this problem in his *Kitāb al-Manāẓir* (*Optics*), which was translated in the late twelfth or early thirteenth century into Latin by a yet unknown translator. Out of the twenty odd manuscripts now known to exist in Europe, one is dated 1269 but the earliest mention of the Latin version of the *Optics* goes back to Jordanus de Nemore (*fl. ca.* 1220-30). See Sabra (1982), nn. 1 and 2. Of particular interest are various references in Sabra's paper, which provide a useful bibliography.

wearisome"), though his own brief and elegant solution was based on the same idea as that of Ibn al-Haytham—the intersection of a circle and a hyperbola.[37] Ibn al-Haytham's solution was, in fact, one of the high achievements of the Islamic geometric tradition.

Assessing the Tradition

It would be instructive to conclude this section with a general statement on the progress of the tradition we are exploring. This is important because the western reappraisal of the Islamic scientific tradition in the seventeenth century has left a deep mark on all subsequent assessments and, in spite of a more balanced assessment that is now emerging through the work of a small group of historians of science, there remains a steady trickle of works tainted with that seventeenth century stain which saw hardly anything worthwhile in the Islamic scientific tradition. We will explore various social, religious and scientific currents that went into the making of that stain during the seventeenth century in more details in chapter six, but let us note here that contrary to the judgment passed by the seventeenth century Europe—a judgment that has been carried over to the twentieth century by a continuous flow of unfounded theories—there exists uncontroversial evidence that the Islamic scientific tradition was not merely a passive vehicle for the transfer of Greek science to Europe.

But in spite of new evidence, a certain strand of historically inaccurate scholarship continues to appear. For example, in his *The History of Science: From Augustine to Galileo*,[38] Crombie makes several contradictory statements, often within a single page, about the worth and contributions of "Arab science" to the Western Christendom. Examples abound: "Of the actual knowledge from the stores of Greek learning which was transmitted to Western Christendom by the Arabs, *together with some additional observations and comments of their own*, some of the most important was the new Ptolemaic astronomy...".[39] One can find such examples on almost every page of the chapters dealing with the "Arab science". Crombie is a

---

37. Ibid. p. 300.
38. Crombie, A. C. (1959, repr. 1970, 1979 and 1995), *The History of Science: From Augustine to Galileo*, 2 vols. in one, Dover Publications, Inc. New York, vol. 2, p. 121. A more recent example is the work of sociologist Huff, Toby E. (1993), *The Rise of Early Modern Science: Islam, China and the West*, University of Cambridge, Cambridge. See more on this in chapter 7.
39. Crombie (1995), vol. 1, p. 64, emphasis added.

forerunner of a peculiar breed of twentieth century historians of science who advance the thesis that all that Muslim scientists did during the so-called golden age of their science and civilization was to "add a few observations and comments of their own" to the received Greek science. These works should be counted as those of a special branch of Orientalist literature and though Orientalism has disappeared in its overt forms from the mainstream discourse on Islam, this breed continues to thrive.

Assessed in the most general terms, the Islamic scientific tradition can be seen as having passed through the following major phases:

(i) a formative period under the shade of Islamic religious sciences;
(ii) a quick maturation through the massive infusion of data, information and theories from the Greek, Indian and Persian traditions;
(iii) a phase of careful assessment, recasting and Islamization of the received material;
(iv) a gradual realization that there was something fundamentally wrong with some of the major concepts that had been received from other traditions;
(v) appearance of "doubt literature" which pinpointed major scientific and philosophical problems with the received material and suggested fundamental changes; and
(vi) a slow process of withering.

These six phases do not lend themselves to clearly differentiated periods and they should not; after all we are dealing with a tradition that covered a vast geographical region and all branches of science. What may appear to have matured in one place and time may only have begun to take roots in another region and, in many cases, the phases merged into each other, slowly and, often, imperceptibly. Their individual hues and colors only became distinct after enough time had passed from the previous phase. We have already seen various aspects of the first three phases; let us briefly mention the fourth and the fifth; the sixth phase, withering of the tradition is explored in chapter five.

The fourth and the fifth phases are characterized by the appearance of a new *genre* in the Islamic scientific literature: the *shukūk literature*.[40] Most of this "literature of doubt" is still inaccessible to the historians of science but

40. *Shukūk,* sing. *shakk,* lit. it means doubt.

what has been studied shows that this *genre* had made its presence felt as early as the ninth century and was in full vogue by the eleventh. In case of astronomy, the initial "doubts" may have appeared as a result of new observational techniques that showed the shortcomings of Ptolemaic data. So, the first task of the Muslim astronomers was to correct Ptolemaic values. Having done so, they moved on to the next step: that of examining the very methods used by Ptolemy to reach his values; this resulted in the invention of new methods. In the case of solar apogee, for instance, Muslims abandoned the old method of determining the length of the season by observing the times of equinoxes and the solstices—which had proved to be immensely difficult—and adopted the alternate *fuṣūl* method based on the observation of the declination of the sun during the middle of the seasons, when that declination could be determined with far more accuracy. A further refinement to this method, introduced a few years later, required only three observations, two of which were taken at opposition from one another.[41] These methodological developments led to the emergence of new commentaries and translations that reexamined the *Almagest.* By the eleventh century, this activity had definitely emerged as a major movement. The doubts raised by al-Bīrūnī in his aforementioned correspondence with Ibn Sīnā constitute a major link in the evolution of this literature. and the publication of Ibn al-Haytham's seminal treatise, *al-Shukūk ʿalā Baṭlīmūs,* certainly marks a high point in the evolution of this *genre.*[42]

This mature "doubt literature", which went beyond the basic questions about methodologies and procedures, was concerned with substantial theoretical issues. In the case of astronomy, this new and mature "doubt literature" should also be seen in the context of the *hayʾa* tradition that was purely Islamic in its origin. This *hayʾa* tradition is still an obscure area of history of science but its emergence has been related to *anwāʾ*, the pre-Islamic Arabic astronomy that investigated seasonal variations through the study of fixed stars. This *anwāʾ* tradition went through a fundamental

41. Saliba, George (1994), *A History of Arabic Astronomy,* New York University Press, New York, p. 15, *et passim.* My discussion of this section heavily relies on this ground-breaking work of Saliba. The book contains fifteen articles written over a period of two decades, all dealing with Islamic astronomy.

42. This important work is now available in a critical edition: Sabra, A. and Shehaby, N. (1971), *Ibn al-Haytham's al-Shukūk ʿalā Baṭlamyūs (Dubitationes in Ptolemaeum),* National Library Press, Cairo.

transformation under the influence of the Qur'ānic cosmology. But the *hay'a* was a mathematical astronomical tradition, dealing with the theoretical foundations of astronomy. However, there is still not enough clarity on how this tradition differed from the one that studied the structure of the celestial spheres. Many later sources refer to two kinds of texts that existed as early as the eighth century. We are told, for example, about the *zīj*-type texts and *Tarkīb al-aflāk* type texts of Yaʿqūb b. Ṭāriq who was active during the reign of al-Manṣūr—the same Yaʿqūb who cooperated with Ibrāhīm al-Fazārī (*fl.* second half of the 8th century) in the translation of the *sidhhantas* from Sanskrit into Arabic before the time of the translation movement which produced Arabic versions of the *Almagest* and the *Elements*.[43] Ibn al-Nadīm also mentions a *hay'a* text by Jābir b. Ḥayyān. We also know of a work by Abū'l-ʿAbbās Aḥmad ibn Muḥammad ibn Kathīr al-Farghānī (d. after 861) which was known by several titles including *Jawāmiʿ al-falak* and *Kitāb al-hay'a*.[44] Other works of this kind include *Kitāb al-hay'a wa-ʿilm al-ḥisāb* of Sahl b. Bishr (*ca.* 236/850), *Kitāb tarkīb al-aflāk* of ʿUṭārid b. Muḥammad (*fl.* 9th century), *Kitāb hay'at al-falak* of Abū Maʿshar (d. 273/886) and *Kitāb hay'at al-ʿālam* of Abū Bakr Muḥammad b. Zakariyyā al-Rāzī (*ca.* 250-313 /854-925). We also know of a tenth century Andalusian traditionalist and Qur'ānic exegete, Qāsim b. Muṭraf, who wrote *Kitāb al-hay'a*. None of these texts have been found so far but we do have at least one *hay'a* text from the ninth century which proves the existence of the *hay'a* tradition in that century; this work has been attributed to Qusṭā b. Lūqā (*ca.* 246/860) in one manuscript and to the sons of Mūsā in another.[45]

In any case, the emergence of a new observational methodology—the *fuṣūl* method—developed to determine the position of the solar apogee[46] and the value of the solar equation may have been the final cause which brought the whole range of Ptolemaic procedures and methodologies into question. It was because of this questioning that the need for continuous updating of data became clear; this also inspired the development of new

43. See Pingree, David (1970), "The Fragments of the Works of al-Fazārī," in *Journal of Near Eastern Studies*, vol. 29, pp. 103-23.
44. Copy of this work exists at Bibliotheque Nationale, Paris, Arabe 2504, 3, *cf. GAS*, vol. 6, p. 150, quoted in Saliba (1994), p. 42, n. 20.
45. Ibid. p. 17.
46. Apogee is the point in the orbit of a heavenly body, or of a man-made satellite, at which it is farthest from the earth. Solar apogee thus refers to the point when the sun is farthest from the earth; *cf.* perigee: the point in the orbit of a heavenly body or of an artificial satellite at which it is nearest to the earth.

and improved precision instruments. Thus the two traditions—instrument-making and compilation of new *zījes* tables—became a permanent feature of the Islamic astronomical activity. But the most significant aspect of this questioning was the merger of the *hay'a* tradition, which emphasized the theoretical side, with that of observational and mathematical astronomy during the second half of the tenth century. Hence, while the updated *zījes* tables had only produced new and more precise values for precession,[47] solar apogee,[48] solar equation and the inclinations of the ecliptic,[49] the merger of the two traditions produced texts which generally carried phrases like *tarkīb al-aflāk* and *hay'a* in their titles and which were based on these new values which were sometimes called *mumtaḥan zījes*, that is, the *zījes* produced as a result of fresh observations.

This merger of the two traditions served as the immediate cause for the emergence of the *shukūk* literature that questioned the very foundation of the Greek astronomy. Seen in this historical perspective, Ibn al-Haytham's aforementioned treatise is an important contribution to the growing literature that had begun to appear in the ninth century. Thābit b. Qurra is also known to have employed rigorous mathematical methods to explain observational phenomena and he later questioned Ptolemaic texts from a mathematical perspective.[50]

Thus from the ninth century onward, there appeared a continuous stream of texts—written in places as far apart as Aleppo and al-Andalus—that questioned various aspects of Greek astronomy.[51] By the middle of the

---

47. The precession of the equinoxes refers to the earlier occurrence of the equinoxes in each successive sidereal year because of the slow retrograde motion of the equinoctial points along the ecliptic, caused by the precession of the earth's axis of rotation; a complete precession of the equinoxes requires about 25,800 years.
48. The point in the orbit of sun at which it is farthest from the earth.
49. Inclination refers to the angle between the orbital plane of a planet and another given plane, usually the ecliptic; it also refers to the angle between the equatorial and orbital planes of a planet. Ecliptic refers to the great circle formed by the intersection of the plane of the earth's orbit with the celestial sphere; the apparent annual path of the sun in the heavens or an analogous great circle on a terrestrial globe.
50. *GAS*, vol. 6, p. 42, n. 25, which refers to the work of Régis Morelon, who has demonstrated the mathematical rigor of Thābit's methods.
51. For example, al-Qabīṣi (*fl. ca.*349/960), the famous astrologer of the Hamdānid ruler Sayf al-Dawla (d. 366/976), mentions in his treatise *fī imtiḥān al-munajjimīn* (*The Test of Astrologers*) that he has written another treatise, *al-Shukūk fī al-majisṭī* (*Doubts on the Almagest*) where he has given "several questions with which the members of this class of perfect

eleventh century, the *shukūk* literature had come in the full daylight and in the next century, there appeared two different groups of model builders. The first consisted of philosophers,[52] who tried to recapture the Aristotelian purity of the astronomical system. They objected to Ptolemaic eccentrics and epicycles on the basis of Aristotle's arguments (in *De Caelo*), which regarded the heavens to be spherical by necessity. They argued that the center of the universe was, therefore, at rest, just like the center of any moving sphere. This center, moreover, coincided with earth—the element of heaviness. Eccentrics violated this principle because they would require the presence of a fixed point (a center of a revolving sphere), other than the earth. This would create a new center of heaviness, a new earth, and that was impossible.

They also objected to the presence of Ptolemaic epicycles—the small circle the center of which moves around the circumference of a larger circle—that accounted for the observed periodic irregularities in planetary motions. Their objection was that epicycles would require a sphere, other than the one that surrounds the earth, to revolve around a center of heaviness placed in the realm of the celestial spheres; this was also an impossibility in Aristotle's system because, according to Aristotle, the celestial realm was made of the fifth element, ether, for which terms like heaviness and lightness could not be used. Thus this group of model builders objected to the Ptolemaic models because of their affiliation with Aristotle's philosophy.

The second group of new model builders consisted of working scientists and they objected to the Ptolemaic model on the basis of physical impossibilities. Their objection was that a sphere cannot move uniformly around an axis that did not pass through its center. Ptolemaic equant had done exactly that. A sphere moving uniformly would require that it describes equal arcs in equal times around its own center and any violation of that principle would mean that we are not consistent with the physical and mathematical properties of the sphere. Except for Ibn al-Shāṭir, this group had no problem with the violation of Aristotle's philosophical constructs; they could live with eccentrics and epicycles as long as there was no violation of the mathematical properties of spheres. In other words, as

---

astrologers can be tested". *GAS*, vol. 6, pp. 204, 293, *et passim,* reported in Saliba (1994), pp. 40-41, n. 9.

52. This included Ibn Bāja (d.534/1139), Ibn Ṭufayl (d.581/1185), Ibn Rushd (d.595/1198) and al-Biṭrūjī (d.597/1200).

long as these epicycles and eccentrics behaved like spheres—by revolving at uniform speeds around their own centers and not around some other center which is called an equant—this group of scientists had no problem with this model, except for Ibn al-Shāṭir who wanted to preserve the harmony of the whole system. But even he could not avoid epicycles that were an observational necessity. Thus, in his model, he allowed epicycles, accusing Aristotle of being inconsistent.

Links with the European Tradition

In its final phase, the Islamic astronomical tradition developed mathematical techniques as well as new models in search of a major alternative to the Ptolemaic system. Our present knowledge of this phase began in 1957 with the discovery of a remarkable treatise by Ibn al-Shāṭir of Damascus: *Nihāyat al-Sūl fī Taṣḥīḥ al Uṣūl (The Ultimate Quest regarding the Rectification of [Astronomical] Principles)*.[53] The legend has it that Edward Kennedy stumbled upon this work while he was at the Bodleian Library waiting for Ibn al-Shāṭir's *Zīj*.[54] But legends apart, there were already indications that our knowledge of this phase of Islamic scientific tradition was incomplete.

Prior to this accidental discovery, O. Neugebauer had already mentioned in Appendix I of the second edition of his seminal work, *The Exact Sciences in Antiquity*, that the method used by Copernicus for his lunar model was the same which was used for "the correction of Ptolemy's lunar model...about 200 years before Copernicus by Ibn al-Shātir (*sic*). Whether Copernicus knew about his predecessor or not is impossible to decide at the present moment."[55] Neugebauer had referred to a forthcoming article by Victor Roberts, which appeared in *Isis* shortly after Neugebauer's work.[56]

---

53. Saliba has mentioned that he has prepared a critical edition of this text which is based upon all the extant manuscripts. See his note 1, p. 258 in Saliba (1994), *op. cit.* He also says in the same note that about twenty years ago, Victor Roberts had completed an English translation based on one manuscript which was never completed and that he himself is preparing a new English translation and commentary; to the best of my knowledge, all three works remain unpublished to date.
54. Saliba (1994), p. 259.
55. Neugebauer, O. (1957), *The Exact Sciences in Antiquity*, Brown University Press, Providence; all references are to the 1969 reprint, Dover Publications Inc. New York.
56. Roberts, Victor (1957), "Pre-Copernican Copernican Model" in *Isis*, vol. 48, pp. 428-32.

This article was devoted to the solar and the lunar models of Ibn al-Shāṭir. In addition to Ibn al-Shāṭir, Neugebauer had already noticed "in order to account for this observation, Mercury is made to move on a straight line segment such that its distance from the center of its orbit varies with the proper period. A movement on a straight line seems not quite in conformity with the postulate of circular motions of the celestial bodies but fortunately Copernicus had at his disposal a device of aṭ-Ṭūṣī, who had shown that a point of the circumference of a circle of radius 's/2' moves along the diameter of a circle of radius "s" inside of which the first circle rolls."[57] This "aṭ-Ṭūṣī device" was later called "Ṭūsī Couple" by Edward Kennedy. It is interesting to note that while historians of science only "stumbled" upon this important phase of the Islamic scientific tradition in the second half of the twentieth century, the actual text of al-Ṭūsī in which he proposed his lunar model had been published in a French translation by Carra De Vaux in 1893![58]

This rediscovery prompted several new studies[59] and the results of this research brought to light a whole new phase of the Islamic astronomy which is often misleadingly associated with the work of the "astronomers of the Maragha School".[60] Most of the astronomers of this group were

57. Neugebauer (1957), p. 203.
58. See Appendix VI by Barron Carra de Vaux, in Tannery, P. (1893), *Recherche sur l'histoire de l'astronomie ancienne*, Paris.
59. Kennedy, Edward S. and Ghanem, Imad (1976), *The Life and Works of Ibn Al-Shāṭir*, Aleppo University, Aleppo; Kennedy, E. S. *et al.* (1983), *Studies in the Islamic Exact Sciences*, American University, Beirut; Hartner, Willy (1969), "Naṣīr al-Dīn al-Ṭūsī's Lunar Theory" in *Physics*, vol. 11, pp. 287-304; Saliba (1979), "The Original Source of Quṭb al-Dīn al-Shīrāzi's Planetary Model" in *Journal for the History of Arabic Science*, vol. 3, pp. 3-18; Saliba (1979), "The First Non-Ptolemaic Astronomy at the Maragha School" in *Isis*, vol. 70, pp. 571-576; Saliba (1980), "Ibn Sīnā and Abū 'Ubayd al-Jūzjānī: The Problem of the Ptolemaic Equant" in *Journal for the History of Arabic Science*, vol. 4, pp. 376-404. Also see other references cited in Swerdlow, N. M. and Neugebauer (1984), *Mathematical Astronomy in Copernicus's De Revolutionibus*, Springer-Verlag, New York.
60. There exists certain confusion about the first use of this term. Saliba makes two contradictory statements in the last section of his *History of Arabic Astronomy* (1994). He first attributes it to Roberts (p. 50, n. 10) but on page 260 of the same work, he says, "In 1966, while summarizing the results achieved up to that date, Kennedy coined the term 'Maragha School'". Perhaps both Victor Roberts and Edward S. Kennedy independently coined the term in 1966 and used it in their *Isis* articles: Roberts, Victor (1966), "The Planetary Theory of Ibn al-

working between the middle of the thirteenth to the middle of the fourteenth century, a period rightfully described as the "Golden Age of Islamic Astronomy".[61] The group includes such celebrated names as Mu'ayyad al-Dīn al-ʿUrḍī (d. 665/1266), Naṣīr al-Dīn al-Ṭusī (d. 673/1274), Quṭb al-Dīn al-Shīrāzī (d. 711/1311) and Ibn al-Shāṭir (d. 777/1375). They built upon the work of the astronomers of the previous two centuries who had written the *Shakūk* literature; Ibn al-Haytham and Abū ʿUbayd al-Jūzjānī (d. *ca.* 463/1070) being the two most outstanding astronomers in that previous group. Let us also note in passing that the discovery of this manuscript was followed by other discoveries, which have pushed the date of the so-called decline of Islamic science well into the fifteenth century.[62]

Since the initial reports of Roberts, Neugebauer and Kennedy, our knowledge of these developments in the Islamic scientific tradition has been enriched by studies published by Fuad Abbud, George Saliba, Jamil Ragep and others. They have brought to light many other models in the same tradition. The most important of these new models are those of Quṭb al-Dīn al-Shīrāzī and Mu'ayyad al-Dīn al-ʿUrdī.[63] Another text which

---

Shāṭir" in *Isis*, vol. 57, p. 210 as well as Kennedy, E. S. (1966), "Late Medieval Planetary Theory" in *Isis*, vol. 57, pp. 365-378. Let us note that no matter who invented the term, it is a rather misleading appellation as Saliba has rightly argued: "As our research is beginning to show, that name was not quite felicitous," he wrote in his *A History of Arabic Astronomy*, "since the type of activities conducted at the Maragha Observatory, namely the criticism of Greek astronomical models and the development of new models to replace them, was not restricted to Maragha nor to that time period. The name 'Maragha School' can therefore be sometimes misleading, especially when it is used in the sense of direct relationships among astronomers who lived centuries apart, or when it designates Maragha as a point of origin for such activities when we know that these activities began before the building of the Maragha Observatory." See Saliba (1994), p. 41, n. 11.

61. Saliba (1994), p. 252.

62. See more on this in Chapter 5.

63. Kennedy wrongly ascribed the model for the upper planets built by al-ʿUrḍī to Shirāzī. See Saliba (1979), "The Original Source of Quṭb al-Dīn al-Shīrāzī's Planetary Model" in *Journal for the History of Arabic Science*, vol. 3, pp. 3-18. Urḍī's text, *Kitāb al-Hay'a* was first used by Noel Swerdlow in his unpublished Ph.D. thesis, "Ptolemy's Theory of the Distances and Sizes of the Planets: A Study of the Scientific Foundation of Medieval Cosmology", Yale in 1968 and was identified as the "Anonymous Astronomical Treatise in Bodleian Arabic Ms March 621". The same manuscript was later used by B. Goldstein and N. Swerdlow (1970-71) in "Planetary Distances and Sizes in an Anonymous Arabic Treatise Preserved in Bodleian Ms March 621" in

criticized Ptolemaic astronomy came from al-Andalus testifying to yet another aspect of this tradition of criticism.[64] Written at the beginning of the thirteenth century (probably in 597/1200), Ibn Biṭrūjī's *The Principles of Astronomy* differs from the criticism of the later astronomers of the Marāgha school in a basic manner; Ibn Biṭrūjī was not interested in fixing the Ptolemaic model; he wanted to get rid of two of Ptolemy's basic principles: the eccentrics and the epicycles. He showed in his book how the apparent motions of the planets could be produced by means of concentric spheres without the use of eccentrics and epicycles.[65] Ibn Biṭrūjī's model was an unsuccessful attempt and left out many essential questions but it is the philosophical leap made by him that is important. Let us now return to the Marāgha school.

Further studies on the Marāgha school have established connections between the work of Muslim astronomers and Copernicus. Possible channels of transmission of these models to the Latin West have also been investigated. At least five works of Willy Hartner and Noel Swerdlow were specifically devoted to the exploration of these relations.[66] Hartner

---

Centaurus, vol.15, pp.135-70. George Saliba restored this anonymous Bodleian Ms to its rightful author, al-Urḍī; see Saliba (1979), "The First non-Ptolemaic Astronomy at the Maragha School" in *Isis*, vol. 70, pp. 571-6. Also see Saliba (1989), "A Medieval Arabic Reform of the Ptolemaic Lunar Model" in *Journal for the History of Astronomy*, vol. 20, pp. 157-64.

64. Goldstein, B. (1971), *Al-Biṭrūjī: On the Principles of Astronomy*, Yale University Press, New Haven.
65. Sabra, A. I. (1984), "The Andalusian revolt against Ptolemaic astronomy: Averroes and al-Biṭrūjī" in Mendelsohn Everett (ed.), *Transformation and Tradition in the Sciences: Essays in Honor of I. Bernard Cohen*, Cambridge University Press, Cambridge, pp. 133-153; reprinted in Sabra (1994), *Optics, Astronomy and Logic.*
66. My reconstruction of this historical account is based on Saliba's aforementioned book, *A History of Arabic Astronomy* (1994), p. 268, n. 18; also see further references cited by Saliba: Hartner, W. (1969), "Naṣīr al-Dīn al-Ṭūsī's Lunar Theory" in *Physis*, vol. 11, pp. 287-304; Hartner, W. (1970), "La science dans le monde de l'Islam après la chute du califat" in *Studia Islamica*, vol. 31, pp. 135-51; Hartner, W. (1973), "Copernicus, the Man, the Work and its History" in *Proceedings of the American Philosophical Society*, vol. 117, pp. 413-22; Hartner, W. (1975), "The Islamic Astronomical Background to Nicholas Copernicus", *Ossolineum, Colloquia Copernica* III, Nadbitka, pp. 7-16 [all now reprinted in Hartner, W. (1984), *Oriens-Occidens*, II]; Swerdlow, N. (1973), "The Derivation and First Draft of Copernicus's Planetary Theory: A Translation of the Commentariolus with Commentary", *Proceedings of the American Philosophical Society*, vol.117, pp. 423-512.

successfully established the history of textual transmission of the mathematical theorem which has been previously referred to as the "Ṭūsī Couple". In his 1973 article, Hartner reproduced the representational diagrams of the "Couple" and stated that both al-Ṭūsī and Copernicus had used the same alphabetical references to "refer to identical geometric points on their respective diagrams". But it was Swerdlow who made the most daring conclusion in his 1973 paper by stating that the "extent of indebtedness between Copernicus and the earlier Marāgha astronomers could not be attributed to coincidence".[67] Abbud had already compared the numerical parameters of Ibn al-Shāṭir's *Zīj* and Copernicus's *De Revolutionibus* and concluded that "although the tables of Ibn al-Shāṭir were similar to those of Copernicus, the latter's were not a direct copy of the first, despite the fact that they both deviate in the same direction from Ptolemy's tables."[68] But it was Neugebauer who, in 1975, published the photographs of a page from a Byzantine Greek manuscript—which had become part of the Vatican Collection sometime after the fall of Constantinople in 1453—wherein he noted the clear representation of Ṭūsī Couple.[69] Ten years later, Neugebauer and Swerdlow published another study in which they reproduced another page of the same Greek manuscript that contained the lunar model of al-Ṭūsī as well as a diagram demonstrating the transformation of the Ṭūsī Couple to a configuration of solid bodies.[70]

All of these studies have conclusively linked the final phase of the Islamic astronomy to the European tradition. But apart from their historic importance, which is significant in more than one respect, they have also

Saliba also states that "Hartner continued to explore this connection between Copernicus and the Maragha astronomers till the last years of his life. Just before he died, he published, for example, 'Ptolemaische Astronomie im Islam und zur Zeit des Regiomontanus,' *Regiomontanus-Studien, Österreichische Akademie der Wissenschaften,* Philosophische-Historische Klasse, Sitzungberichte, 364, Band (1980), Heraugegeben von Günther Hamann, 109 124." *op. cit.* p. 269, n. 20.

67. See note 18 of Swerdlow's previously mentioned article in the *Proceedings of the American Philosophical Society*.

68. Quoted in Saliba (1994), p. 260.

69. For a graphic representation, see Neugebauer, O. (1975), *A History of Ancient Mathematical Astronomy,* Springer-Verlag, New York, p. 1456; also see plate ix of *Vat. Graœc.* fol. 116r.

70. Swerdlow, N. and Neugebauer, O. (1984), *Mathematical Astronomy in Copernicus's De Revolutionibus,* Springer-Verlag, New York, p. 295, fig. 5 and 6.

drawn attention to a fundamental question: the originality of the Islamic scientific tradition. To be sure, these studies in the history of astronomy merely cover one small branch of what was the main concern of the Islamic scientific tradition. Similarly studies in mathematics, geometry, chemistry, botany, zoology and other branches of natural sciences are slowly producing a better understanding of the nature of Islamic scientific tradition and its connections with European science.[71]

These new areas of research are slowly changing the Orientalist accounts and as new texts are studied, we are beginning to understand both the range and depth of the Islamic scientific tradition. But since the main interest of this book is not the history of the Islamic scientific tradition, but the relationship between Islam and science, we cannot go into further details of this area. Rather, the next chapter will explore the connections that the Islamic scientific tradition had established with the fundamental doctrines of Islam. These connections form the core of what was Islamic in this tradition.

It is important to note that these connections often remain buried under the pure scientific data with which most scientists dealt in their research but they are never absent. This subtle guiding of the scientific enterprise, as it were, had profound impact on the direction of scientific research in the Islamic civilization as well as upon the fascinating process of transformation of the philosophical and metaphysical underpinnings of the Greek, Indian and Pahlavī scientific traditions—a transformation that made them Islamic.

71. Mention may be made of various studies on Ibn al-Haytham by A. I. Sabra, now conveniently combined in his aforementioned *Optics* (1994), where he has shown fundamental methodological and conceptual leaps in the theories and methods of Ibn al-Haytham. Also of interest is the tradition of criticism and reform of Euclid's works which spans several centuries—from the works of Thābit ibn Qurra in the 3rd/9th century to those of ʿUmar Khayyām (*ca.* 439-517/1048-1123).

CHAPTER FOUR

Islam and Science Nexus

Before the rise of modern science, the Islam and science discourse existed within the larger intellectual tradition of Islam and although there were many foreign currents that ran through the warp and weft of the tradition, it remained integrally linked to the Islamic worldview. This situation was to drastically change with the withering of the Islamic scientific tradition and its eventual replacement with the modern western science. These fundamental changes have altered the parameters of the Islam and science discourse and demand a different kind of exploration. We will explore these new and emerging facets of Islam and science discourse in chapter ten. In the present chapter, the exploration is restricted to the relationship between Islam and science before the rise of modern science—a restraint borne out of the very nature of the subject matter.

Let us begin by formulating questions about the Islam and science nexus: What was Islamic in the Islamic scientific tradition? How did it differ from the Greek, Persian and Indian scientific traditions from which it had received a large amount of scientific data as well as theories? What were the major issues in the Islam and science discourse? Who participated in this discourse? Within the scope of a single book, we can only draw an outline of the fundamental nexus that existed between Islam and the science it inspired. But even this is no small task. Any meaningful discussion of the basic questions involved will, by necessity, need to take into consideration the entire span of the Islamic scientific tradition during which this relationship saw a considerable change in many respects. Likewise, one would have to consider the whole geographical range—from Spain to Afghanistan—covered by the Islamic scientific tradition. And because this was not a static relationship, even a summary account will have to explore the dynamics of the relationship between Islam and science at various historical junctures. In addition, one needs to situate this discussion within the broader social, cultural and historical milieu in which science—as a social activity—found expression.

The Internal Links

The first important point to note in this exploration is the very absence of Islam and science as a differentiated discipline in the Islamic intellectual tradition. No one thought of "Islam" and "science" as two separate entities that had to be related to each other through an external mechanism. This fundamental aspect of the tradition is neither accidental nor does it point to any gap in the intellectual make-up of the Islamic tradition. Rather, it points to a profound understanding of the nature of science and its relationship to Islam. This relationship emerged naturally and because the scientific tradition was thoroughly rooted in the worldview created by Islam, no one ever thought it necessary to create an external apparatus to relate the two. This also explains why, contrary to the contemporary practice, we find no decorative uses of the Qur'ānic verses in the pre-seventeenth century Islamic scientific works. As already mentioned, al-Khwārazmi's famous *Algebra* starts with the customary invocation, *In the Name of Allah, the Most Beneficent, the Most Merciful,* followed by a paragraph in which he expresses thanks to God for his bounties and for God's mercy upon human race in guiding it by sending prophets and ultimately for sending Prophet Muḥammad. After this paragraph, he describes the purpose of composing his book[1] as being "[a book] on Calculating by [the rules of] completion and Reduction, confining it to what is easiest and most useful in arithmetic, such as men constantly require in cases of inheritance, legacies, partition, law-suits and trade and in all their dealings with one another, or where the measuring of lands, digging of canals, geometrical computation and other objects of various sorts and kinds are concerned…"; after this short introduction, he then goes directly to the subject matter.

The same pattern is followed in all other major scientific texts. Although they are all firmly rooted in the Islamic worldview, no overt effort is made to lace them with the Qur'ānic verses. Perhaps another reason for this is the fact that science in the Islamic civilization was part of a larger tradition of learning that arranged different disciplines in a hierarchical structure like the branches of a tree. The trunk of the tree in this case was none other than the central concept of Islam: the Oneness of God (*Tawḥīd*). Because of this central unifying concept, all branches of knowledge, including the natural sciences, were linked through an inalienable nexus with the metaphysical concepts of Islam. Each branch of knowledge was a contributing tributary to the main stream.

1. Al-Khwārazmi, Abū Ja'far Muḥammad bin Mūsā, *Kitāb al-Mukhtaṣar fi'l Ḥisāb wa'l-Jabr wa'l Muqābala,* tr. by Frederic Rosen (1989), Pakistan Hijrah Council, Islamabad, p. 66. It is interesting to note that this more recent reprint published in Pakistan contains the Qur'ānic verse (Q. 72:28): *God sets all things in numbers* at the beginning of the book whereas the manuscript of al-Khwārazmi does not.

The very structure of learning from which natural sciences emerged, as differentiated fields in a restricted sense, had a built-in mechanism for wedding these sciences to the heart of Islamic thought; this internal mechanism made it superfluous to sprinkle individual scientific works with the Qur'ānic verses. Furthermore, natural sciences were connected with the larger body of Islamic learning through internal links, thus needing no artificially construed pedagogical tools for such connections. This does not mean that there was no clear-cut division of various disciplines; quite the contrary. A considerable intellectual energy was devoted to enumerate, classify and explain the subject matter of each and every branch of knowledge. The science of nature (*al-ʿilm al-ṭabīʿī*) was clearly distinguished from the other subjects; this distinction was embedded in the broader classification that divided all inquiries into theoretical (*naẓarī*) and practical (*ʿamalī*).[2] There are obvious affinities to Aristotle in some of these classification schemes but there are also distinctions. For example, al-Fārābī (*ca.* 257-339/890-950) called physics "the science of nature" and distinguished it from that which comes after (*mā baʿd*) nature, that is, metaphysics. In his celebrated work on the subject of classification of sciences, *Iḥṣāʾ al-ʿulūm,* he states that metaphysics—the highest philosophical science—investigates (i) the nature and characteristics of bodily existence, (ii) the principles of demonstrations in particular sciences or meta-sciences, and (iii) the nature of non-bodily existents.[3] According to

---

2. It should be mentioned here that all leading Muslim philosophers have written on the subject of classification of sciences (*ʿulūm*) and that various classification schemes differ from each other in details or sometimes even in broader divisions. But they are all hierarchically arranged and in all such schemes, the metaphysical nexus is clearly established. For the division of sciences into theoretical and practical, see Ibn Sīnā's *Dānish Nāmaʾi ʿAlāʾī, Ilāhiyyāt,* ed. Moin, M. (1952), Tehran, ch. 1; *al-Shifāʾ, al-Ilāhiyyāt,* ed. Anawati, G.C., Mousa, Mohammad Yousef, Dunya, Solayman and Zayed, Saʿid (1960), Dār al-Fikr al-ʿArabī, Cairo, and *passim; ʿUyūn al-Ḥikma,* ed. Badawi, A. (1952), Dār al-Fikr al-ʿArabī, Cairo, p.16. Suhrawardī divides sciences into practical (*ʿamalī*) and theoretical (*naẓarī*), subdividing the latter into metaphysics (*ilāhī*), mathematics (*rīyāḍī*) and physics (*ṭabīʿī*); see *Shihābaddīn Yaḥyā As-Suhrawardī, Opera Metaphysica,* ed. Henry Corbin (1945), Istanbul, vol. 1, p. 196—these references are quoted from Parviz Morewedge, "The Analysis of 'Substance' in Ṭūsī's Logic" in Hourani, George F. (1975), *Essays in Islamic Philosophy and Science,* State University of New York Press, Albany, pp. 158-188, the above references are found in n.23, p. 183.
3. al-Fārābī, *Iḥṣāʾ al-ʿulūm,* ʿUthmān Amīn (ed., 1947), Dār al-Fikr al-ʿArabī,

al-Fārābī's scheme, natural science is the lowest in rank in the philosophical sciences because its subject matter consists of terrestrial bodies which are further divided into two categories: those that come into existence by nature and those that are brought into existence by human will. The natural bodies of different grades, such as rational animals, non-rational animals, plants, mineral and the four elements (fire, air, water, earth), belong to the world of generation and corruption in contrast to the incorruptible and eternal nature of the celestial world. Each natural body is made up of form (*ṣūra*) and matter (*mādda*); and bodies can be in potential existence or in actual existence. A body is said to be in potential existence as long as its matter continues to exist without its form and it becomes actual only when its form is present. None of the natural bodies is actual "from the outset"; in the beginning all natural bodies exist only potentially in their "common prime matter" (*al-māddat al-ūlā al-mushtarika*) and incorporeal existence that is the eternal outcome of celestial matter. Such a scheme, which may apparently look like a repetition of the Aristotelian scheme, attains a totally different character when we consider a more penetrating work of al-Fārābī, in which he distinguishes between "substance" (*jawhar*) and "being" (*mawjūd*).[4] In his discussion of "being", al-Fārābī points out the lack of an equivalent Arabic term corresponding to the Greek, Persian and Sogdian,[5] and then goes on to state that Arabic eventually resorted to using *wujūd* as a substitute.

This linguistic constraint provides an interesting example of the complexity of the relationship between the Islamic thought and the philosophical concepts of other thought systems. It was one of those situations in which "the translator [could] easily find himself helpless".[6] This problem of expressing the Greek concept of being in Arabic drew a lot of attention from many Muslim philosophers and it constitutes a case study for the influence of grammar on the formation of philosophical concepts. A

no term for 'being' in Arabic

Cairo, pp. 111-23.

4. This work is *Kitāb al-Ḥurūf, The Book of Letters: Commentary on Aristotle's Metaphysics,* ed. with introduction and notes, Mahdi, M. (1969), Dar el-Mashreq Publishers, Beirut. For the discussion of *jawhar* and its main usage in Arabic, see pp. 97-105; for a discussion of *mawjūd* as a term constructed to convey the concept expressed in Greek, Persian and Sogdian, see pp. 110-28.
5. Sogdian is the extinct Iranian language of Sogdiana, a province of the ancient Persian Empire between the Oxus and Jaxartes rivers.
6. Afnan, Soheil (1964), *Philosophical Terminology in Arabic and Persian,* E. J. Brill, Leiden, p. 29.

more recent work draws attention to this peculiarity as the problem arising from "the complete absence of the copula" in Arabic.[7] Another related aspect of the linguistic features is the sharp separation of the existential and the predicative functions in Arabic that is notably absent in classical Greek.

In addition to these built-in affinities, those who actually practiced science were themselves the product of an educational system that provided a firm foundation for the development of the Islamic worldview as a natural process. The first thing a Muslim scientist or scholar learned as a child was the Qur'ān. This repository of knowledge acquired so early in life not only provided the moral code for their lives; it also gave them an inexhaustible reservoir of technical terms, ideas and concepts. But above and beyond the intellectual tools, it acted as a magnetic field that oriented all subsequent learning in a particular direction. Depending on the individual, this magnetic field varied in intensity but in all cases where scholarship advanced beyond the primary level, it was inevitably present. This is not to say that this mechanism created a monolithic and fixed vision, quite the contrary. It was a tradition of learning that produced scholars as different from each other as Ibn Sīnā and al-Ghazālī. But what is central for any understanding of this tradition is the fact that these scholars, who differed from each other in many ways, did so on the horizontal axis while remaining firmly entrenched in the central vertical reality of Islam that establishes certain fundamentals about the Creator, His role in the cosmos and life.

Ibn Khaldūn (733-809/1332-1406) provides an insight into the central position of the Qur'ān in traditional Islamic learning. In the well-known prolegomena (*Muqaddima*) to his universal *History* (*Kitāb al-ʿIbar*), he has allocated a whole chapter (6) on "The Various Kinds of Sciences; The Methods of Instructions; [and] The Conditions that Obtain in these Connections". In a section of this chapter, "The Instructions of Children and the Different Methods Employed in the Muslim Cities", Ibn Khaldūn states:

> Instructing children in the Qur'ān is a symbol of Islam. Muslims have, and continue to practice, such instruction in all their cities because it imbues the heart with a firm belief in Islam and its articles of faith which are derived from the verses of the Qur'ān and Sunna

7. Ibid.

> (the Prophetic tradition). Thus, the Qur'ān is the basis of instruction, the foundation of all that is acquired later [in life]. The reason for this is that the things one is taught in one's early age take deeper roots; they become the basis for all later knowledge. The first impressions received by the heart, are the foundation of all later habits; the character of the foundation determines the condition of the building...[8]

"Islamic" versus "Foreign" Sciences

Another aspect of the Islam and science nexus is related to the questions of reception, cultivation and integration of the so-called "foreign sciences". This is particularly important because, following the 1916 article of Ignaz Goldziher, translated into English in 1981 with a misleading title, "The Attitude of Orthodox Islam Toward the Ancient Sciences",[9] it has become axiomatic pedagogical practice to divide Islamic tradition of learning into "Islamic" and "Foreign" and then draw certain conclusions which are permeated with nothing but "Goldziherism". This is particularly unfortunate because Goldziher's attitude toward Islam was formulated in the background of the colonization of the Muslim world by European powers which had, in turn, presented Islam as a spent force which could only be derided and vilified, not respected. This bias against Islam, which had penetrated all spheres of thought and imagination,[10] runs through many works dealing with the history of Islamic science. Goldziher's 1916 article ought to be seen in the light of his cultural background. But because of his position in the academic world, his attitude was not limited to his own work; it has affected succeeding generations as well. Numerous works take his "Islamic" versus "foreign" sciences hypothesis as if it were an axiomatic state which represented the only attitude of the normative

8. Ibn Khaldūn, *The Muqaddima,* tr. Franz Rosenthal (1967), Princeton University Press, abridged edition, pp. 421-2, translation emended.
9. Goldziher, Ignaz (1916) "Stellung der alten islamischen Orthodoxie zu den antiken Wissenschaften," *Abhandlungen der Königlich Preussischen Akademie der Wissenchaften,* Jahrgang 1915, Philosophisch-historische Klasse, no. 8, Berlin, Verlag der Akademie, 1916, pp. 3-46; translated by M. L. Swartz in his (ed., 1981), *Studies on Islam,* Oxford University Press, New York, pp. 185-215; [hereafter Goldziher (1916)].
10. Even in fiction; for example, Doestoyevsky's rage against the Prophet of Islam in *Brothers Karamozov*; a notable exception to this general trend in fiction is Herman Melville, who in his masterpiece, *Moby Dick,* called the Prophet of Islam "a man with a big soul".

Islamic tradition. What is worse, this attitude toward a particular strand of appropriated sciences is, then, made into a generalized attitude about *all knowledge* to draw conclusions which cannot be but erroneous. Although more recent and careful scholarship has pointed out fundamental flaws in Goldziher's approach,[11] this attitude still remains entrenched in many circles[12] and, as Berggren has so pointedly stated, "Goldziher must share some of the responsibility for this sort of reading of his data.... Indeed A. Heinen has even challenged the applicability of this division of knowledge to the intellectual situation in the first centuries of Islamic civilization."[13]

The fatal division on which Goldziher construed his thesis divides knowledge into sciences of the ancients (*ʿulūm al-awāʾil* or *ʿulūm al-qudamāʾ*), meaning all works "taken over from Hellenistic literature" and the sciences of the Arabs or the new sciences". By ancient sciences, he means "the entire range of propaedeutical, physical and metaphysical sciences of the Greek encyclopedia, as well as the branches of mathematics, philosophy, natural science, medicine, astronomy, the theory of music and others."[14] Although he acknowledges the extensive interest "that these sciences aroused from the second century AH on[ward] in religious circles loyal to Islam (and encouraged also by the ʿAbbāsid caliphs)", he states that "strict orthodoxy always looked with some mistrust on those who would abandon the science of Shāfiʿī and Mālik, and elevate the opinion of Empedocles to the level of law in Islam."[15] Thus pitted against each other, the Greek, Persian, Hindu and other pre-Islamic works on the one hand and purely Islamic sciences on the other find themselves in Goldziher's study as mortal rivals, clamoring for attention of the scholars.

But when one examines the data used by Goldziher to construct his

11. The most penetrating critique of Goldziher's hypothesis is to be found in Gutas, Dimitri (1998), *Greek Thought, Arabic Culture*, Routledge, London and New York, pp. 166-75 and Berggren, J. L. (1996), "Acquisition of the Foreign Sciences: A Cultural Approach" in Ragep, Jamil F. and Ragep, Sally P. (eds., 1996), *Tradition, Transmission, Transformation*, E. J. Brill, Leiden, pp. 270-83.
12. See, for example, the 1993 book by sociologist Toby E. Huff, *The Rise of Early Modern Science*, Cambridge University Press, Cambridge which is permeated with "Goldziherism". Huff is, by no means, the only contemporary scholar who relies on this approach to "prove" that the Islamic scientific tradition existed and survived not because of Islam but in spite of it.
13. Berggren (1996), pp. 269-70.
14. Goldziher (1916), p. 185.
15. Goldziher (1916), pp. 185-6.

battle lines, one realizes that these battle lines are boundaries drawn on sand with a clear and pre-conceived purpose which is none other than a specific interpretation of the whole intellectual tradition of Islam. In order to support his various claims, Goldziher had to rely on exceptions, rather than norms and on fatal distortions of the data by situating the quoted passages in *his* context, rather than in their proper historical context. For example, he states, as proof for his assertion, that "the pious Muslim was expected to avoid these sciences with great care because they were dangerous to his faith", because the Prophet had prayed to God for protection against a "useless science". Goldziher states that this Ḥadīth of the Prophet "was quoted frequently".[16] In the footnote to this statement, where one would expect to find references to the "frequent quotation", one finds only a note stating that the Ḥadīth is to be found in Muslim (V, 307) and not in Bukhārī, but that "it appears with *special force* in the *Musnad* of Aḥmad, VI, p. 318".[17] What does it mean for a tradition of the Prophet to appear in the *Musnad* of Aḥmad with *special force*? *Musnad* of Aḥmad, like all other *Masānīd*, is a collection of sayings and description of various acts of the Prophet of Islam, arranged according to the narrator (*rāwī*), systematically and in a uniform manner without any special treatment reserved for one Ḥadīth and withheld from another. But even if we ignore this special effect, we are left with no authority but Goldziher himself to assess the "frequency" with which this Ḥadīth was cited in support of the claim made by him. Furthermore, in the text of the Ḥadīth, the word used is *ʿilm,* which does not mean sciences of the type Goldziher is referring to; *ʿilm* means knowledge and taken within the context of Prophetic supplications, it is extremely unlikely that he would be referring to the "foreign sciences".

In any case, one needs to consider the attitude of Islam and its Prophet toward knowledge before passing any verdict. The importance of acquisition of knowledge in Islam can be judged from the fact that the very first revelation to the Prophet of Islam was a command: *Read*.[18] The Islamic testimony of faith (*shahāda*) is, in itself, a statement of knowledge. It can also be gleaned from the honor that the Qurʾān bestows on the learned: *Indeed, of His servants, it is the scholars* (ʿulāmāʾ) *who are in awe of Allah.*[19] The

16. Goldziher (1916), p. 186.
17. Goldziher (1916), p. 210, n. 18, emphasis added.
18. Q. 96:1.
19. Q. 35:28.

Arabic word for knowledge, *ʿilm*, appears over and over in the Qur'ān, which implores the believers to seek knowledge. It states in no unambiguous terms: *Only the learned understand these parables*,[20] and elsewhere, it says: *Say [O Prophet]: Are they equal: those who know and those who don't?*[21] God has called himself, *al-ʿAlīm* (The All-Knowing).

It is important to note that every Ḥadīth collection contains a permanent category: *Kitāb al-ʿilm* (*Book of Knowledge*). "Whoso walks in the path of Allah," the Prophet of Islam once said,

> seeking knowledge thereby, Allah will make him walk in the paths of paradise; and verily, the angels spread out their wings out of pleasure for the seeker after knowledge; and verily those who are in the heavens and the earth and fish also in the midst of water, all ask pardon for him; and, verily, the excellence of a learned man over a mere worshipper is as the excellence of full moon over the stars. And, verily, the learned men are the inheritors of the prophets; for verily, the prophets' heritage is not *dinār*, or *dirahim*, but the heritage of knowledge; Whoso then receives this, he has received ample good fortune.[22]

He also said: "When a man dies, his work also stops, except for three [things]: acts of charity, which continue, knowledge by which [all] profit, and a righteous child who prays for him."[23]

The Qur'ānic verse, *O my Lord, increase my knowledge* was one of the constant prayers of the Prophet of Islam who also asked God to "show him things as they really are". This prayer of the Prophet has echoed throughout the history of Islam in many forms but perhaps its most eloquent expression is by the Persian Sufi poet and scholar, ʿAbd al-Raḥmān Jāmī (d. 898/1492) who thus prayed to God:

> O God, deliver us from the preoccupation with worldly vanities, and show us the nature of things as they really are. Remove from our eyes the veil of ignorance, and show us things as they really are. Show us not non-existence as existent, nor cast the veil of non-existence

20. Q. 29:43: *And these are the parables we set forth for the mankind; but only those understand them who have knowledge.*
21. Q. 39:9.
22. Abū Dawūd/Book of Knowledge/44 and Tirmidhī/Book of Knowledge/55.
23. This famous saying of the Prophet of Islam is found in all major Ḥadīth collections, including Bukhārī, Muslim, and Tirmidhī.

> over the beauty of existence. Make this phenomenal world the mirror to reflect the manifestation of Thy beauty, not a veil to separate and repel us from Thee. Cause these unreal phenomena of the Universe to be for us the source of knowledge and insight, not the causes of ignorance and blindness. Our alienation and severance from Thy beauty all proceed from ourselves. Deliver us from ourselves, and accord to us intimate knowledge of Thee.[24]

From the very moment of birth to the last breath, a Muslim is required to seek knowledge. This extraordinary emphasis on acquisition of knowledge is not surprising for a religion based on a Book. This quest for knowledge does have a natural and integral relationship with the main thrust of Islam that imparts a definite orientation to all human endeavors. "The highest form of knowledge is the knowledge of God (may He be exalted!)," declared al-Ghazālī, "because all other forms of knowledge are sought for the sake of it and it is not sought for anything else."[25]

Thus, Goldziher's thesis cannot be validated and a careful reading of the extant material *within* the context of Islam's normative tradition shows that his backward reading of isolated texts to validate pre-conceived ideas neither sheds light on history to enhance our understanding of the subject matter nor yields solid scholarship; it merely clouds the intellect. Fortunately, many scholars have realized the need for corrective measures at the most fundamental level of the study of Islam and its intellectual tradition. This has given birth to a growing number of new texts that study various aspects of Islam from *within.* In relation to Goldziher's approach, in addition to the previously mentioned 1978 paper of A. Heinen in which he has seriously challenged the applicability of Goldziher's division of knowledge to the intellectual situation in the first centuries of Islam,[26] one can also say that the whole question of the division of knowledge into "foreign" and "religious" sciences needs to be examined within the context of the political, social and theological currents in which this division precipitated. One cannot just take such a division as an absolute

24. Jāmī, *Lawa'ih,* tr. by Whinfield, E. H. and Kazvini, M. M. (1914) as *Flashes of Light: A Treatise on Sufism,* Royal Asiatic Society, London, p. 2.
25. al-Ghazālī, Abū Ḥāmid, *Kitāb Jawāhir al-Qur'ān,* [henceforth *Jawāhir*], tr. by Quasem, Muhammad Abul (1983) as *The Jewels of the Qur'ān,* Kegan Paul International, London, p. 43.
26. Heinen, A. (1978), "Mutakallimūn and Mathematicians: Traces of a Controversy with Lasting Consequences" in *Der Islam,* vol. 55, pp. 57-73.

classification of knowledge in the Islamic tradition with total disregard to the hierarchical structure within which classification of knowledge in Islam made its appearance under a metaphysical principle that guided the process of classification. Nor can one divorce certain strict and harsh criticisms of one or the other trend from the immediate climate in which such verdicts were passed. In the final analysis, it is a question of emphasis, rather than exclusion, and that too, *within* a given historical situation. If we find al-Ghazālī overtly concerned about the rise of certain intellectual trends in his time, we cannot assume his criticism of such excessive tendencies to be a prima facie proof of a total repudiation of those disciplines. The foremost concern of a man like al-Ghazālī being none other than an inner certitude rooted in faith and knowledge with the ultimate aim of attaining what the Qur'ān calls the greatest success (*al-fawz al-kabīr*)—an aspiration held by all Muslims in utmost esteem—one cannot help to invoke the need to take into consideration a much wider perspective than mere isolated statements when pronouncing a judgment on an issue as vital as Islam's attitude toward natural sciences. In any case, the Goldziher thesis is based on premises that have been shown to be motivated by concerns other than unbiased understanding of the data.[27]

The Naturalization Thesis

It is true that a large body of religious and philosophical assertions also accompanied the flow of information and ideas from the Indian, Persian and Greek sources that brought scientific data and theories into Islamic thought over a period of three centuries. Ptolemy, Galen, Euclid, Plato and Aristotle did not only supply scientific data and theories; they also brought their philosophical and cosmological doctrines about the origin and destination of cosmos and life. Aristotelian physics was predicated on the distinction between what is divine (and hence eternal) and what is perishable. His heavens were composed of a single eternal element, the divine æther. He believed in the eternity of the world. Celestial bodies were divine for Ptolemy. Plato advocated religious piety and an ethics based in part on the divinity of the celestial bodies. He mentioned in the *Timaeus*

27. See, for example, Azmi, Mohammad Mustafa (1978), *Studies in Early Ḥadīth Literature,* Indianapolis, American Trust Publications; also (1985), *On Schacht's Origins of Muhammadan Jurisprudence,* King Saud University, Riyad and John Wiley, Chichester; Zaman, Iftikhar (1991), *The Evolution of a Hadith: Transmission, Growth and the Science of Rijal in a Hadith of Saʿd b. Abi Waqqas* (Ph.D. thesis) University of Chicago.

(39e-41a) that the heavenly bodies are gods who, together with the traditional gods of mythology, created all living things, including man.

These and related metaphysical and cosmological doctrines came into the intellectual currents that were flowing through the Islamic civilization during the period of translation and they did so with a clearly felt need to sift through this material because they were the product of other civilizations with their own characteristic worldviews, not necessarily shared by Islam. Thus there arose an inner tension between the received material and the faith tradition in which it was received. This tension expressed itself in various ways and provided the kinetic force for a vast and creative process during which the received material was "naturalized".[28] To be sure, it was a long and slow process that involved some of the best minds of the Islamic intellectual tradition. It was also not a homogeneous appropriation that would produce a monolithic Islamization of the received material. Rather, it was a process that took place in stages and through distinct modes that would later be associated with various representatives of the tradition such as the philosophers, the scientists, the mystics, and the mutakallimūn, though such a classification generally overlooks the fact that it is not always possible to delineate lines of demarcation in certain cases: al-Ghazālī was a philosopher, as well as a mutakallim and a mystic; even Ibn Sīnā, *al-Shaykh al-Raʾīs* (the Grand Shaykh) of Islamic philosophical tradition wrote mystical treatises toward the end of his life. Thus, these divisions are not watertight compartments; often, a single individual would combine various modes in his lifetime or even within a single work.

It is also problematic to consider this process of naturalization as some kind of algebraic operation which, having been once performed, produced a final solution. Rather, it was an organic process that examined and re-examined the material from various angles. It was also a long and slow process that naturally occurs in any living civilization and that continues to inspire fresh perspectives and angles of approach. This explains the tradition of commentary that accompanied this examination, even though some of this material became repetitious. In addition, there was the constant re-evaluation of the material that inevitably affected the nature of questions posed by the sciences in relation to the faith tradition within

28. This apt term is used here following A. I. Sabra's 1987 paper, "The Appropriation and Subsequent Naturalization of Greek Science in Medieval Islam: A Preliminary Statement", reprinted in Ragep and Ragep (1996), pp. 3-30.

which the practice of science was being carried out.

Thus, to do justice to the subject, perhaps it is best to explore affinities between natural sciences and other branches of knowledge within the intellectual climate created by Islam rather than static connections which are fixed in space and time. Through such an approach, we can employ a broader social and intellectual canvas to draw a picture of the integrated relationship that existed between natural sciences and other branches of knowledge through natural affinities instead of first construing "Islam" and "science" as two separate entities and then reading back our contemporary concerns into the body of literature that had come into existence without such a division.

Linguistic Affinities and Transformations

The mode of expression of the Islamic scientific tradition, Arabic, is the most obvious and the outer most layer of these internal and natural affinities. Being the language of the revealed book of Islam, Arabic enjoys a religious prestige that elevates it from being a mere cultural medium of a given society to being the mode of expression of the divine message, which is the nucleus around which the Islamic community and its social life grew. Thus the scientific tradition shared a nexus between the individual human creative acts and the divine expression of creativity through the letters of the language used to express this creativity. *He [God] created insān and taught him speech,* asserts the Qur'ān.[29] This sharing enabled the Islamic scientific tradition to draw from a large reservoir of Qur'ānic terms, concepts and ideas for its use. These terms played an important role in the emergence and developments of those sciences that had direct bearing on the question of origin of life and cosmos.[30] Certain branches of science, such as the *anwā'* tradition, were intimately connected with the Qur'ānic cosmology.

In addition, Arabic had a social dimension: it served as the language of discourse for Muslim scientists and enabled them to share the fruits of their

---

29. Q. 55:3-4. The Qur'ān uses the word *insān* to denote human beings, both male and female. The appropriation of this Arabic word into English can conveniently resolve the problem of inclusive language that involves various arbitrary techniques, such as alternate use of gender, use of he/she pair or variations thereof.
30. Some examples of these terms are: *'ilm, 'aql, idrāk, wahm, fikr, fiqh, naẓar, tadabbur, ithbāt, kalām, ẓann, ḥaqq, baṭil, ṣidq, kidhb, yaqīn, waḥy, ālam, wujūd, 'adam, dahr, zamān, ṣamad, ṭawḥīd, shirk, khayr, sharr, fiṭra, insān, bashar, irāda, 'amd, tawba, da'wa, qiyām, af'āl, 'amāl, tajallī, ma'rifa, nakira, majāz, ḥaqīqa, mufaṣṣal, mujammal, qidam, ḥadath.*

scientific research with colleagues over the entire geographical range of the Muslim world. The Arabic language also had a cultural role in the Islamic civilization; it allowed diverse regional cultures to find a common medium of expression, it provided shared symbols, metaphors and idioms and it served as the most important vehicle for the dissemination of ideas in an area that covered a vast region and climes. It was due to this shared language of discourse that the Islamic scientific tradition progressed over such a large geographical area, building upon the achievements of successive generations. Thus, it was essentially because of this shared language that a scientist from Bukhāra could understand the theories of his Egyptian colleague and a geographer from Spain could participate in the discussion of particular concepts first conceived by a geographer hailing from the small town of Ṭūs in western Iran.

The large amount of scientific data and theories that came into the Islamic scientific tradition from other civilizations came into it through a built-in process of linguistic transformation which "Arabicized" it in the very process of its arrival. This linguistic transformation had an enormous impact on the eventual naturalization of the received material. It created the necessity to coin technical terms in Arabic, which were further refined by the successive generations of translators and linguistics. It allowed metaphysicians to investigate the nexus between certain key scientific terms and the metaphysical doctrines that emanate from the concepts defined by these terms. This linguistic transformation removed the "foreignness" of the translated material to such an extent that the Arabic Aristotle translated back into Greek could not be the same that had been translated into Arabic. This was a monumental achievement of the translators who were faced with a formidable task—an achievement that would make it possible for the Islam and science nexus to develop in a seamless fashion.[31]

In addition, linguistic affinities were also playing their role in areas where one would expect them to be absent. Al-Fārābī's *Kitāb Taḥṣīl al-Sʿāda* (*On Attainment of Happiness*), for instance, does not start with a description of what happiness is or with an exposition of the way to happiness, as one would expect, instead, it begins by enumerating theoretical virtues, deliberative virtues, moral virtues and practical arts—four things whose

31. As an example, one may consider the works of al-Fārābī who wrote more than forty books on Logic and produced a large number of exact Arabic terms that became a rich repository for the successive generations.

presence in political communities leads to happiness in this world and to a supreme or ultimate happiness in the life to come. What is important for our discussion is the fact that al-Fārābī's vocabulary in this political work is full of Qur'ānic terms. Though al-Fārābī is generally characterized as a philosopher who is immersed in Greek thought, it is remarkable that he uses a characteristically Islamic vocabulary and, though he employs Greek logic and philosophy in all his philosophical writings, he does so for a purely Islamic synthesis that is rooted in the Qur'ānic worldview. His *Refutation of al-Rāzī's metaphysics*,[32] for instance, deals with al-Rāzī's anti-Aristotelian views on matter, time, space and atoms but in the course of his refutation, al-Fārābī also produces a metaphysical defense of prophecy, which was attacked by al-Rāzī.

There were several levels of linguistic transformations that affected the translated texts in a "scientific manner". In certain cases, this linguistic transformation was so fundamental that it produced a conceptual transformation that was to have a powerful impact on the whole field. Euclid's *Optika* (*ca.* 300 BC), for example, when translated into Arabic went through a peculiar transformation that laid the course of subsequent developments in visual theory. In contrast to Aristotle's philosophical and Galen's physiological approaches, Euclidean tradition was geometrical in both content and method. The *Optika* as well as other texts in the same tradition, such as those of Ptolemy (second century AD) and Theon of Alexandria (fourth century AD), formulate the discussion of vision around geometrical entities such as lines, angles, cones and circles. When appropriated into the Islamic scientific tradition, *Optika* went through an instantaneous linguistic transformation solely based on the phraseology of the Arabic versions of the fundamental assumptions of Euclid's visual model.[33] Euclid states that straight lines—or visual rays, as he called them later—extend from the eye to a distance of great magnitude. This first definition of Euclid's visual model is followed by the second definition that states that this extension is in the form of a cone with its apex in the eye and its base in the object. This single-cone model of Euclidean optics is

32. *Kitāb al-Radd ʿalā al-Rāzī fī'l-ʿilm al-Ilāhī.* It only survives in quotations embedded in other works; a complete manuscript of this important work is yet to be found.
33. This has been shown by a number of studies. See, for example, Elaheh Kheirandish (1996), "The Arabic 'Version' of Euclidean Optics: Transformations as Linguistic Problems in Transmission" in Ragep, and Ragep (1996), pp. 227-45.

transformed into a multiple radiation model based on an important optical principle—which has been called the principle of punctiform analysis of light radiation by David Lindberg.[34] The conceptual transformation of Euclid's first assumption—a single-vision cone issuing from inside the eye—to its Arabic version—cones of radiation issuing from every point on the eye's surface—was accomplished through a linguistic transformation: the Arabic word in all variants of this central assumption of Euclidean visual theory is *kathra*, a word that is in no way equivalent to the original Greek. The Arabic term *kathra* is ordinarily used in the sense of *multitude* as well as *magnitude*. Thus this part of the Arabic definition means: "Straight lines or paths constituting the visual cone *multiply* indefinitely."[35] The second conceptual transformation, likewise, follows from the Arabic terminology employed for the "inside of the eye" in the second definition of Euclid. Here the Arabic phrase used is *ʿalā al-ʿayn* or *yalī al-ʿayn* depending on the manuscript one uses. This means "outer extremities" rather than "inside of the eye". A third transformation occurs in the third Euclidean definition where the Arabic verb stating the visual requirement of the "falling of the rays on objects" is no longer plural, as in the Greek original, but the singular *waqʿa*. This, together with the use of the singular noun *al-shuʿāʿ* for "visual rays" completes the transformation, giving us the statement of the third definition as "that upon which *a* ray (or *a* conic collection of rays) falls is seen."[36]

But the Euclidean mathematical extramission theory of vision, as modified by al-Kindī, was not the only school of thought in the Islamic scientific tradition; there were at least two other: the Galenic and the Aristotelian. The former was represented by Ḥunain ibn Isḥāq[37] and ʿAlī ibn ʿĪsā, and the latter by Ibn Sīnā and Ibn Rushd. In addition, there is the towering figure of Ibn al-Haytham who obliterated the battle lines between the Euclidean, Galenist and Aristotelian schools by producing a synthesis of these theories in a single comprehensive theory which was a purely Islamic recasting and which was to become the source of fundamental conceptions

34. Lindberg, David, C. (1976), *Theories of Vision: From Al-Kindi to Kepler,* The University of Chicago Press, Chicago, p. 30.
35. Kheirandish (1996), p. 231.
36. Kheirandish (1996), p. 232.
37. Ḥunain was a Christian but since he was working within the framework of the Islamic scientific tradition, his works are considered to be part of the Islamic scientific tradition, just as the scientific works of thousands of Muslim scientists who are working in the contemporary West are part of the Western scientific tradition.

on which Kepler based his theory of retinal image.[38]

Ibn al-Haytham's conscious use of certain words which are different from the Aristotelian tradition are yet another example of linguistic transformation that shows a fundamental affinity with the conceptual framework which guided his scientific endeavors.[39] For instance, the word for induction used by Ibn al-Haytham is the regular term *istiqrāʾ* which was used in the Arabic translations of Aristotle but when he wants to say "experiment", he does not use the word *tajriba* which had been used in translations of Greek texts; instead he uses the nomen verbis *iʿtibār*, together with the verba *iʿtabara* and the nomen agentis *muʿtabir*. All of these are derived from the trilateral root *ʿBR*. The verb *ʿabara* means "to go through", "to traverse" and the eighth form, *iʿtabara* means "to draw an inference about one thing from another". What is interesting and important in the use of this term is the conscious attempt by Ibn al-Haytham to systematically operate with a concept of experiment which he associates with cognates of one and the same root. This explicit use of experimentation as a paradigmatic type of proof, to be distinguished from other types of proofs, is a unique situation of affinity of a scientific concept with the Arabic language.

Likewise, the appearance of experimentation in *Kitāb al-Manāẓir,* as an articulated methodological concept, is a distinct departure from the Aristotelian framework of science and this was accompanied by a linguistic transformation which was not a product of Ibn al-Haytham's fancy. By the time Ibn al-Haytham employed it in the eleventh century, it had already been established as a normative practice in astronomy with precisely the same emphasis as that of Ibn al-Haytham. In the second half of the ninth century, al-Battānī (*ca.* 244-317/858-929) had urged fresh testing, *miḥna* and *iʿtibār*, for the astronomical data. This, he said, was truly in the tradition of Ptolemy who had urged that observations and experiments be performed to correct his tables which might need correction after a long time had passed, just as he had to correct Hipparchus and others of his rank. Thus the idea of observation was already a part of the Islamic

38. Lindberg (1976), p. 86.

39. A. I. Sabra has drawn attention to this interesting case found in *Kitāb al-Manāẓir* (*Optics*) of Ibn al-Haytham in his article, "The Astronomical Origin of Ibn al-Haytham's Concept of Experiment" in *Actes du XIIe Congrès International d'Histoire des Sciences, T.III A, Paris 1968: Albert Blanchard, 1971,* pp. 133-36, reprinted in Sabra (1994); in my discussion of this example, I have drawn heavily from this source.

astronomical research and it was for this research that the astronomers of al-Maʾmūn's court had prepared *Zīj al-Mumtaḥan, The Tested Tables*. Furthermore, this tradition of preparing tested tables was not an isolated occurrence. The famous twelfth century *Zīj* prepared by ʿAbd al-Raḥmān al-Khāzinī also bears the title *al-Zīj al-muʿtabar, The Tested Tables*. And there are numerous other examples to show that this was, in fact, a tradition that lasted for centuries. The same concern for experimentation, with the same usage of Arabic words, *iʿtibār* and *imtiḥān*, can be found in al-Bīrūnī's *Ifrād al-Maqāl* and Ibn al-Haytham had himself used this term in astronomical reference in his *al-Shukūk ʿalā Baṭlīmūs:* "The movements of the planets asserted by [Ptolemy in the *Planetary Hypotheses*] are the same as those which he asserted in the *Almagest,* for he had proven them by observation and *iʿtibār.*"[40]

The shared vocabulary of science with the religious tradition is one level of affinities that related natural science with Islam. In the case of cosmological and life sciences—which have direct connections with the faith systems—the impact of Islam's revelatory data had a more apparent and decisive role in the formation and development of these sciences. Thus sciences which studied questions related to the origin of cosmos and life, divine role in the cosmos, nature of consciousness, dreams and eschatology were more discernibly linked to Islamic thought and even when they received ideas and theories from non-Islamic sources, they received them through a transforming process which Islamized them. Likewise, those sciences that were intimately connected with Islamic legal matters, such as the determination of the times for the canonical prayers and the beginning and the end of the month of fasting, received strong directing influences from the Qurʾān and the Prophetic tradition. Thus it is fruitful to examine more closely the relationship between Islam and cosmological sciences—a discipline that remains at the frontier of contemporary science-religion discourse.

Links with the Qurʾānic Cosmological Sciences

Was the cosmos created in time or is it eternal? If it was created, when did this act of creation take place and how? Who created it? Is there any teleology discernable in life and cosmos? These and similar contemporary issues also form the core of the Islam and science discourse during the pre-seventeenth

40. Bodleian Library Ms Arch. Seld. A.32, fol. 181v, quoted in Sabra (1994), p. 136, n. 7.

century era. Some of these questions had arisen in the Islamic tradition as a result of reflection on the cosmological data found in the Qur'ān; others arrived from non-Islamic sources, such as the Greek and the Hindu cosmologies which were either part of the philosophical texts translated into Arabic or were present as underpinnings of the scientific texts that were appropriated by the Islamic scientific tradition. The responses to these fundamental questions form the warp and weft of the Islam and science nexus. But before we examine this relationship, let us briefly summarize the Qur'ānic cosmological data; this will provide us the backdrop against which all cosmological schemes were analyzed and examined in the Islamic scientific tradition during the pre-seventeenth century era.

The Qur'ān contains a significant number of verses that describe the origin of cosmos and life. Thus it was natural for the Islamic scientific tradition to pay attention to these verses which had already been the subject of an intense reflection by the early commentators of the Qur'ān. Likewise, the eschatological verses, that recur throughout the Qur'ān with tremendous force and intensity, also received due attention. Thus philosophers, scientists, mystics, interpreters of the Qur'ān, and just about everyone related to the Islamic tradition of learning, has left behind significant amount of work on the subject.

Let us also note that there are profound differences between the Islamic cosmological sciences and contemporary cosmology. When we think of contemporary cosmology, we think of a branch of science that deals with the origin of the universe and with the laws that govern it. We think of theories that try to formulate initial conditions in physical terms. In contrast, the Islamic cosmological sciences, though dealing with the same fundamental questions, approached the subject matter from a distinctively different angle. These sciences were more concerned with the metaphysical principles related to the origin of cosmos *in* relation to the knower who was not a disembodied observer of the initial conditions and subsequent "evolution" of the universe; rather, the observer and the observed were wedded together in an inalienable relationship that cast light on the self of the observer as much as it did on the observed. Of course, the powerful quantitative tools at the service of modern science were also absent and so was the physical data such as the observed present cosmic abundances of helium and hydrogen gases.[41]

The Qur'ān describes the creation of the heavens and the earth in six

---

41. Considered to be 20-30 and 70-80 percent.

days with the express mention of the indeterminable nature of the Qur'ānic "day" in human terms.[42] It further specifies the stages of creation of earth in two days (Q. 41:9); and of the seven heavens in two days (Q. 41:12). It also mentions a cosmic smoke, engulfing the heavens (Q. 41:11) and the heavens and the earth being first together before they were rent asunder (21:30) and the creation of all things in pairs (Q. 42:11; 51:49)—all of this not for sport and play (Q. 44:38) but for a purpose and for an appointed term (Q. 6:2; 30:8). It speaks of the oceans being on fire and the mountains being pegs inserted into the earth's crust.

These essential features of the Qur'ānic cosmology had become the subject of theological reflection much before the beginning of the Islamic scientific tradition and they had given rise to various Kalām cosmological schemes which sought to establish proof for the existence of God from various aspects of the physical cosmos. The central issue of this debate was whether the temporal series of past events could be actually infinite. The proponents of the Kalām argument held that it could not be and sought to prove that the universe therefore had an absolute beginning and that beginning demanded the existence of a Creator. Though the arguments for and against temporal beginnings go back to the pre-Islamic era, they became the focus of intense debates within Islamic thought and were bequeathed to the West where they were bitterly contested. This is also a debate that is common to all three monotheistic religions—an area that has attracted some of the best minds in these traditions, often pitting one against another. Thus we have al-Ghazālī versus Ibn Rushd (623-698/1226-1298), Saadia (269-331/882-942) versus Maimonides (1335-1204) and Bonaventure (1221-74) against Aquinas (1225?-74). This debate is by no means over yet. In the contemporary science-religion discourse, this debate has expanded to include mathematics, physics, biology, cosmology, philosophy and theology and questions such as the nature of infinity, the beginning of time, the origin and destiny of the universe and the nature of God's role in the cosmos.

Science-Philosophy Nexus

In contrast to the Kalām cosmology, the Islamic philosophical tradition did not take the Qur'ān as its point of departure. The dominant school of Islamic

42. The creation theme recurs throughout the Qur'ān; see, for example: 2:164; 7:54; 10:3; 11:7; 25:59; 32:4; 50:22, 38; 57:4. For the indeterminable nature of the Qur'ānic "day", see: 32:5; 70:4.

philosophy spelled out the distinction between necessary and possible being on the basis of essence/existence distinction. These philosophers subscribed to Aristotelian theory of the four causes and ten categories, followed the main doctrines of his *Organon*, and adopted the Neoplatonic doctrine of emanation. But they did this in a manner that made their theories amenable to the revealed data. Ibn Sīnā, the most celebrated representative of this tradition and perhaps the most Hellenized of all Muslim philosophers, differs from Aristotle on the nature of the Primal Cause, which he redefined as the Necessary Being (*wājib al-wujūd*). But perhaps more important for his internally cohesive system is the way in which he derived the universe from the Necessary Being.

The first important characteristic of Ibn Sīnā's philosophy is the ontological distinction he makes between quiddity (essence, *māhiyya*) and existence (*wujūd*). If one knows the essence of something, one knows all its attributes, whereas existence is not a constitutive attribute of essence but a necessary one added accidentally to the essence. The existence of something, therefore, does not have its principle in the essence of that thing but derives its principle from the Being whose essence is the same as its existence, that is, the Necessary Being.[43] The second characteristic of Ibn Sīnā's philosophy is the tripartite division between the Necessary (*wājib*), contingent (*mumkin*) and impossible (*mumtaniᶜ*) beings. Only in the Necessary Being (*wājib al-wujūd*) are essence and existence inseparably united. Everything other than the Necessary Being is ultimately caused by the Necessary Being through a process of emanation; the emanation of the first intelligence from the thought of the Necessary Being forms the link between the Necessary Being and the contingent realm. This contingent realm is divided into two kinds: (i) the *essentially* contingent entities—those that receive from the First Cause the quality of necessity and hence are necessary in a contingent sense. These were the simple substances (*mujarradāt*), that is, the Intellects and angelic substances; and (ii) those entities that are *only* contingent, such as the non-simple (composed) bodies of the sublunary world which come into being and pass away.

The first category of possible beings is the result of an eternal effect of the Necessary Being and must therefore always be, while the second category contains in itself the principle of non-eternity, and hence has a beginning and an end. There are three simple substances (*jawāhar,* sing. *jawhar*) in the first category of contingent beings; they are all irreducible to

43. Nasr, Seyyed Hossein (1993), *An Introduction to Islamic Cosmological Doctrines*, State University of New York Press, Albany, p. 198, n. 6.

one another: (a) the substance whose being is one, which possesses contingency (*mumkin*) and is completely separate (*mujarrad*) from all matter and potentiality, this is Intellect (*ʿaql, noūs*); (b) the substance whose being is one but which accepts the form of other beings, is indivisible, and needs body for its action—this is Soul (*nafs, psychê*); and (c) the substance which is one but which is divisible and accepts the form of other beings, has the three dimensions of length, width, and depth—this is Body (*jism, hulê*).

These three substances—Intellect, Soul and Body—are separate entities though they all partake of the light of Being and have a "right to exist" and are hierarchically arranged in the following order: separated substances> form> body> matter. Contrary to Aristotle's scheme, the separate substances or angels stand highest in this scale and matter is the lowest in the hierarchy. Everything that exists in the universe derives its existence from this hierarchy through a process of emanation. Note that this ontological scheme establishes a single order of reality in which the Necessary Being, whose essence and existence are one and who is pure Truth and pure Goodness, is the source and origin of all existence. The Necessary Being is said to have no genus (*jins*), differentia (*faṣl*), definition (*ḥadd*), place (*maḥall*), subject (*mawḍūʿ*), opposite (*ḍidd*), species (*nauʿ*), companion (*yār wa nidd*), receptivity to motion (*taghayyur padhīr*), or receptivity to partition (*bahra padhīr*). It is the ultimate cause (*ʿillat al-ʿillat*) of all contingent entities. It is eternal (*qadīm*) in contrast to everything else, which is ephemeral (*muḥdath*), because being transient is related to being caused by something external that realizes the ephemeral entity in question. The Necessary Being is eternal because it cannot be realized by any other entity at any particular time.[44]

All of these descriptions remind us of the Qur'ānic attributes of God. But Ibn Sīnā's concept of "Necessary Being" is used here as an ontological principle, in the context of a cosmology where modalities of necessity and contingency play a crucial role. However, it is the close affinity of Ibn Sīnā's Necessary Being to the Qur'ānic God and of his single order of reality to the general thrust of the Qur'ānic teachings that makes this Hellenized scheme a compelling and powerful case of a fundamental recasting of the Greek legacy—an endeavor that was not always successful according to later Muslim scholars such as al-Ghazālī who severely criticized Ibn Sīnā, but an

44. For the Persian terms used in this description, see Ibn Sīnā's *Dānish Nāma-i ʿAlāʾī*, tr. by Parviz Morewedge (1973) as *The Metaphysica of Avicenna*, Routledge & Kegan Paul, London, pp. 293-325.

endeavor, which nevertheless earned him the honorific title of *al-Shaykh al-Ra'īs*, the Grand Shaykh. It is also important to note that Ibn Sīnā's cosmogony is likewise veiled in an Islamic cast because the universe that comes into being from his ontological order derives its existence from the pure Being in the following manner.[45] Ibn Sīnā says that from Unity only unity can come into being. The First Intellect (*al-ʿaql al-awwal*) is contingent in essence and necessary by virtue of the "Cause of Causes" (*ʿillat al-ʿilal*) or the Necessary Being Itself. Because of its contingency, the First Intellect generates multiplicity within itself; by intellection of the Divine Essence, it gives rise to the Second Intellect, and by intellection of its own essence to two beings, which are the Soul of the first heaven and its body. The Second Intellect through intellection generates in a similar manner the Third Intellect, the Soul of the second heaven and its body. This process continues until the ninth heaven and the Tenth Intellect, which governs the sublunary region, are generated.

In comparison to the Aristotelian doctrine that the generation of all substances is caused by their having the same form (*Metaphysica* 1070 a), Ibn Sīnā asserts that a body emanates from an intelligent substance and that matter is therefore generated out of intelligence. This difference accentuates an important distinction between the cosmologies of Aristotle and Ibn Sīnā. Ibn Sīnā depicts the world as an effusion from the Necessary Being and he asserts that entities belonging to different categories are generated out of one another and that the intelligence ascends toward the One. In contrast, Aristotle's doctrine is based on co-eternity of matter and the prime mover with fixed species. In this fundamental sense, then, the two philosophers stand far apart. In sum, Ibn Sīnā's cosmology rests on two fundamental premises: (i) that a material entity can emanate from an intelligence, and (ii) that there is in some sense a unity in the entire universe which is dependent upon the fact that the Necessary Being is the ultimate cause of every entity.

The relationship between Islam and science, as explored in the Islamic philosophical tradition, is a vast and enormously complex subject and we cannot hope to cover the whole field here. But our account cannot be left

---

45. For a discussion of the affinities between Ibn Sīnā's doctrine and the Islamic theory of creation, see Nasr (1993), pp. 212-13; for a refutation of this position, see Parviz Morewedge's critique of Nasr's position in Morewedge (1973), pp. 271-72. Nasr's position as well as Morewedge's critique revolves around the interpretation of Ibn Sīnā's terms *iḥdāth, ibdāʿ*, *khalq* and *takwīn*.

without the mention of some representatives of the latter philosophers such as Sayyid Bāqir Muḥammad Asṭarābadī, known as Mīr Damād (d. 1040/1631) whose *al-Qabasāt Ḥaqq al-Yaqīn fī Ḥudūth al-ʿālam* (or in its more popular short form, *Qabasāt*) is a *tour de force* philosophical work which combines the principles of Ibn Sīnā's philosophy with the doctrines of the School of Illumination. Mīr Damād is one of the most influential figures of the Ṣafavid period. His work is unique in the Islamic Wisdom tradition because the organization of his work did not follow the traditional pattern of Muslim philosophy that usually started with logic and then proceeded to natural philosophy (*ṭabīʿyyāt*), mathematics (*riyāḍiyyāt*) and theology (*ilāhiyyāt*). The ten chapters of his *Qabasāt* deal with various meanings of creation and the division of being, kinds of anteriority, multiplicity, sciences of the Qur'ān and the Ḥadīth, nature, time and motion, criticism of logic, divine omnipotence, intellectual substances, chain of Being and finally predestination.[46] Mīr Damād sought a solution to the old dispute between the notions of the world being created (*ḥādith*) or eternal (*qadīm*) by dividing reality into three ontological categories: *zamān* (time), *dahr* and *sarmad*; the latter two referring to two different kinds of eternities. But this scheme is within the Neoplatonic tradition of Great Chain of Being (*dā'irat al-wujūd*) rather the western secular scientific tradition.

After the death of Mīr Damād, Persia continued to enjoy a high degree of intellectual activity, mostly in its philosophical tradition. For example, Ḥājī Mullā Hadī Sabziwārī (1212-1298/1797-1881), the most famous *ḥakīm* of the Qajār period, produced, among other works, a complete and systematic summary of *ḥikma*, *Sharḥ-i Manzuma* (composed in 1239/1823) which forms the basic text of this Wisdom school along with *Shifa'* of Ibn Sīnā, *al-Isharāt* of Naṣīr al-Dīn Ṭūsī and *Asfār* of Ṣadr al-Dīn Shīrāzī (979-1050/1571-1640), the most important philosopher of the post-Ibn Sīnan era who is commonly known as Mullā Ṣadrā.[47] Ṣadrā's importance is enhanced because he brings together various strands of four major intellectual perspectives in Islam: the Kalām tradition, the Peripatetic school (*mashshā'ī*) of Ibn Sīnā and Naṣīr al-Dīn Ṭusī, the Illumination school (*ishrāq*) of Shihāb al-Dīn Suhrawardī (549-587/1154-1191) and the gnostic (*'irfan*) school of Ibn ʿArabī (560-638/1165-1240). Ṣadrā is also important because he brings to his subject a vast corpus of ideas of his teachers, peers

46. Nasr, Seyyed Hossein (1996), *The Islamic Intellectual Tradition in Persia*, edited by Mehdi Amin Razavi, Curzon Press, Richmond, pp. 248-49.
47. Nasr (1996), p. 306.

and contemporaries. Among his teachers were some of the best minds of the Ṣafavid period such as Bahā' al-Dīn Muḥammad al-Āmilī (d. 1031/1622) who is also known as Shaykh-i Bahā'ī. Ṣadrā's works range from cosmology and psychology to metaphysics and Qur'anic commentaries. His major work is, however, the monumental *al-Ḥikmat al-Muta'āliyya fi'l-Asfār al-'aqliyya al-Arba'a* (*The Transcendent Wisdom in the Four Intellectual Journeys*), known simply as *Asfār*.[48]

In *Asfār*, Ṣadrā has left behind a synthesis of various branches of Islamic philosophical tradition. In this work, four spiritual journeys form the external structure for an inquiry of almost all aspects of Islamic thought. The first journey, from the world of creation to the Truth and/or Creator (*min al-khalq ila'l-ḥaqq*), deals with metaphysics and ontology with precise descriptions of the meaning of philosophy, being (*wujūd*), quiddity (*māhiyya*), gradation of being (*tashkīk al-wujūd*), Platonic Forms (*al-muthūl al-aflaṭūniyya*), mental existence (*al-wujūd al-dhihnī*) along with a host of other ideas such as causality, substantial movement, time, temporal origination of the world, the intellect, and the unification of the intellect with the intelligible.

The second journey, "from the Truth to the Truth by the Truth" (*min al-ḥaqq ila'l-ḥaqq bi'l-ḥaqq*), provides a critique of the ten Aristotelian categories, substance (*jawhar*) and accidents (*'arḍ*), modes of existence of

---

48. Ṣadrā's *Asfār* (*Four Intellectual Journeys*) does not exist in English. There are three editions of the original Arabic: a lithographed edition by M. Ṭabāṭabā'ī, which is the oldest one; the nine volume Beirut edition by Raḍā al-Muzaffar, with extensive glosses of Sabzwārī, 'Abbās al-Qumī, Zunuzi, Ṭabāṭaba'ī *et al.*, was published by Dār Iḥyā' al-Turāth al-'Arabī, Beirut in 1981 and there is a currently under-print edition, being edited by S. Amulī; so far only three volumes of this new edition have been published. The Institute of Sadra Studies (SIPRIN) in Tehran is planning to translate the entire *Asfār* into English but it is still far from completion. Among Ṣadrā's other works are *al-Shawāhid al-rububiyya*, which deals with some of the most difficult questions of traditional philosophy; *Kitāb al-Mashā'ir*, which he wrote toward the end of his life and which is his own summary of his philosophical system which he calls "transcendent wisdom" (*al-ḥikmat al-muta'āliyya*). P. Morewedge's translation of *Kitāb al-Mashā'ir* has many problems. Nasr and Ibrahim Kalin have recently finished a new translation of this book into English with notes and commentaries. Ṣadrā's major works on eschatology are *al-Ḥikmat al-'arshiyya*, (translated by James Winston Morris (1981) as *The Wisdom of the Throne: An Introduction to the Philosophy of Mulla Sadra*, Princeton University Press, New Jersey) and *Risalāt al-Ḥashr*; his commentaries on the Qur'ān have been edited and published by Muḥammad Khwājawī in seven volumes.

physical entities (*hylé*), matter and form (hylomorphism), and the roots of the hierarchy of the physical order. In the third journey, "from the Truth to the world of creation with the Truth" (*min al-ḥaqq ila'l-khalq bi'l-ḥaqq*), Mullā Ṣadrā discusses metaphysics or "divine science in its particular sense" (*al-ʿilm al-ilāhī bi'l-maʿna'l-akhaṣṣ*). This section deals with all of the major issues which had formed the core of Kalām discourse: the unity of philosophy ('wisdom', *ḥikma*), the Divine law (*sharīʿa*), the notions of unity and existence of God, Necessary Being, the Names and Qualities of God, God's knowledge of the world, His power, Divine providence, speech (*Kalām*) as a Divine quality, good and evil (theodicy) and the emanation of the world of multiplicity from the One. The last journey, "from the world of creation to the world of creation with the Truth" (*min al-khalq ila'l-khalq bi'l-ḥaqq*) is devoted to the discussion of the Great Chain of Being, psychology, resurrection, and eschatology.

What makes Ṣadrā a major figure in the Islamic philosophical tradition is his remarkable achievement in synthesizing various strands of Islamic thought in a structured and organized system which combines all branches of Islamic learning, including the transmitted sciences (*al-ʿulūm al-naqliyya*) as well as the intellectual sciences (*al-ʿulūm al-ʿaqliyya*). The same synthetic distinction holds for his commentaries on the Qur'ān as well as his hermeneutics of Qur'ānic exegesis in which the Qur'ānic terminology is combined with the philosophical vocabulary. Like all other major philosophers of Islam, Ṣadrā's ontology plays a major role in the formulation of his natural philosophy, which introduces the notion of substantial motion (*al-ḥarakat al-jawhariyya*) as a major premise. Ṣadrā maintains that everything in the order of nature—including the celestial spheres—undergoes substantial change and transformation as a result of the self-flow (*fayḍ*) and penetration of being (*sarayan al-wujūd*) which gives every concrete individual entity its share of being. Unlike Aristotle and Ibn Sīnā, who accept change only in four categories,[49] Ṣadrā defines change as an all-pervasive reality running through the entire cosmos including the category of substance (*jawhar*). And he supports his premises through a carefully built system of thought which postulates that change in the accidental qualities of physical bodies has to come from their substance and not the accidents because accidents can not have existence independent of the substance to which they belong. In fact, every accidental change is the result of a deeper change or motion (*ḥaraka*) that takes place in the very

49. Quantity (*kamm*), quality (*kayf*), position (*waḍʿ*) and place (*ʿayn*).

substance and constitution of things. In both the accidental and essential processes of change, physical bodies undergo a substantial change. This holds true even for cases where we do not observe essential transformation in the physical constitution of things such as in the case of positional movement, such as when an object A moves from point B to point C. Ṣadrā calls this kind of motion accidental and describes it as a "movement-in-movement" (*ḥaraka fi'l ḥaraka*). Thus, every accidental change, which is immediately available to our five senses, can be traced back to substantial motion. Hence, Ṣadrā transforms substantial motion or change into an intrinsic quality of things. And because every positional movement, which we take to be the measure of time, is ultimately a modulation of substantial movement, time should be redefined in tandem with the existential transformation of physical substances. Once we accept this, we come to the conclusion that time is a dimension of physical bodies. From here, it is only a step away to the notion that the celestial spheres—whose circular motion had been taken by the Peripatetics to be the ultimate measure of time—are *themselves* subject to substantial motion, hence we can no longer turn to them for the measure of linear time.

Applied to the question of origin of the world, Ṣadrā's notion of substantial motion explains everything in the cosmos to be under constant change and hence always different from what it was before and from what it will be the next instant of its existence. In other words, we come to conclude that every physical being is preceded by non-existence (*masbūq bi'l-ʿadam*), and such an order of being, taken as a whole, can neither subsist by itself nor, in contrast to the Peripatetics, could be eternal (*qadīm*). Thus the world of physical existence is temporally originated and renewed at every successive phase of its existential transformation. Furthermore, according to Ṣadrā, this existential transformation is only possible because of nature (*ṭabīʿa*), used here in a particularly Ṣadrean sense, and not because of an external agent that acts upon the world of nature antecedently. Nature, as defined by Ṣadrā, signifies the *immediate cause* of movement and transformation in physical bodies. Thus, in this sense, nature is the principle of change as an *essential quality* of things. But it should also be noted that in Ṣadrean philosophy, nature is the principle of continuity and permanence because the preservation of natural forms, in spite of their ceaseless change, is a constant phenomenon in nature. Thus, we come to a rather complex notion of nature which possesses both change and permanence. Because of the absence of an external agent acting on nature accidentally, we perceive, rather easily, the central notion of Ṣadrā's schema: nature is teleological because chance or accidental coincidences (*ittifāqiyyāt*) are not the properties of nature.

Thus, Ṣadrā affirms that everything in nature moves toward a "universal purpose" (*aghrad kulliya*), which is nothing but the existential actualization and perfection of the cosmos. The ever-continuous 'intensification' (*tashaddud*) of the order of nature comes about as a result of the self-effusion (*fayḍ*) of Being. Nature is wholly dependent upon the Command of God (*kun*) but it has been created in such a fashion that it possesses a remarkable regularity and constancy. These two apparently paradoxical aspects of nature overcome the problem faced by the Islamic occasionalists, especially the Ashʿarites, who had come to the radical conclusion that they had to accept vertical causality at the expense of horizontal causality in order to make space for miracles. Ṣadrā, being acutely aware of occasionalism's intrinsic difficulties and inconsistencies, defines the two lines of causality as in a perfect accord, in that God sustains the world of creation in such a way that it is bound to be causal and rule-governed in the most concrete sense of the term. The Great Chain of Being, in its Ṣadrean expositions, is construed as a unified structure that allows for a self-regulating dynamism on the one hand, and the perpetual presence of the creative act of God, on the other.[50] This is one of the major achievements of Ṣadrā's philosophy.

Ghazālian Synthesis

Let us conclude this section with the views of another major figure of the Islamic tradition whose honorific title, the "proof of Islam" (*Ḥujjat al-Islām*), indicates the esteem with which he is held in the tradition: Abū Ḥāmid al-Ghazālī, who remains one of the most celebrated scholars of Islamic thought

50. Useful references for various aspects of Mulla Ṣadrā's doctrines include Nasr, Seyyed Hossein (1994), "Mullā Sadrā: His Teachings" in S. H. Nasr and O. Leaman (eds., 1996), *A History of Islamic Philosophy*, Routledge, London, vol. I, pp. 643-62; Açıkgenç, Alparslan (1993), *Being and Existence in Sadra and Heidegger*, ISTAC, Kuala Lumpur; Dhanani, Alnoor (1994), *The Physical Theory of Kalam: Atoms, Space, and Void in Basrian Muʿtazili Cosmology*, E. J. Brill, Leiden; Nasr, Seyyed Hossein (1967), "Mulla Sadra" in *The Encyclopedia of Philosophy*, Paul Edwards (Editor in chief), Macmillan Company and The Free Press, New York, vol. 5, pp. 411-13; Rahman, Fazlur (1987), "Mulla Sadra" in *Encyclopedia of Religion*, vol. 10, pp. 149-53, New York and Nasr, Seyyed Hossein (1975), *The Philosophy of Mulla Sadra*, Albany: State University of New York Press, Albany.

and who lived in that turbulent period of Islamic history which, according to the historian Abū'l-Fidā', was marked by a state of abasement and decline. Faced with internal strife and external threats,[51] the Muslim world lived with a marked presentiment of a coming calamity. Trained in Islamic jurisprudence (*fiqh*), a practitioner of Kalām in the Ashʿarite tradition, philosopher and, eventually, a mystic who would write one of the most celebrated works of Islamic thought, *Iḥyā' Ūlūm al-Dīn* (*The Revival of the Religious Sciences*),[52] al-Ghazālī's various works contain direct references to his ideas on the relationship between Islam and science. He is also often accused of having given a *coup de grace* to philosophy as well as being the cause of decline of the scientific tradition in Islamic polity, a charge that will be explored in the next chapter.

What made al-Ghazālī's corpus of varied works—ranging from intricate branches of jurisprudence to philosophy and mysticism—so important for the subsequent generations was a transparent growth of an inner clarity and certitude he acquired through a painful period of "spiritual crisis" which has been vividly recorded in his autobiography, *al-Munqidh min al-Ḍalāl* (*Deliverance from Error*).[53] For an understanding of al-Ghazālī's views on the relationship between natural sciences and Islam, it is imperative to view his works on the subject within the framework of his other works, otherwise one risks the reading of texts in isolation and out of context, leading to erroneous conclusions—something that has been repeatedly done in the case of al-Ghazālī. Working within the framework of Ghazālian

---

51. Al-Andalus was in revolt, the ʿAbbassīd caliphate was at its lowest state of power, Peter the Hermit was summoning men for Crusades which would result in the founding of a princedom in Rahā in the Euphrates valley in 490/1097, in Antioch in 491/1098; Jerusalem was conquered by the Crusaders in 492/1099, Tripoli (of Lebanon) fell in 495/1102. Internally, Shīʿites and Sunnīs were fighting each other, Ashaʿrites and Muʿtazilites were pitched against each other and the Bāṭinite threat was gaining force.
52. Numerous editions exist of this major work of Islamic scholarship. I have used the five volume edition published by al-Maktaba al-ʿaṣriyya, Beirut in 1996; the English translation of this seminal work is currently being published by the Islamic Text Society, Cambridge, England; some books of *Iḥyā'* have also been published by Fons Vitae, Louisville, USA.
53. Many editions of the Arabic text exist; for references, see the edition published by Mu'assat-ul-Kitāb al-Thaqāfiyya, Beirut in 1991 and the excellent English translation by R. J. McCarthy, Fons Vitae, Louisville in 1980. This annotated edition also contains five other key texts by al-Ghazālī.

thought, we understand that when he uses the word *ʿilm*—often translated as "science" with obvious reduction of the meaning of the Arabic term—he uses it in the sense in which it has been understood as a comprehensive term, covering all subjects. Given to an almost obsessive habit of carefully defining his terms, al-Ghazālī devoted a whole chapter, "On the nature of sciences" (*al-Kalām fi Ḥaqāʾiq al-ʿulūm*), in his book on the principles of jurisprudence, *Uṣūl al-Fiqh*. "Knowledge (*al-ʿilm*)," he said, "cannot be defined".[54] Explaining his statement, he said that our inability to define knowledge does not indicate our ignorance about it and that we can merely define it by its branches and what they are. But what is more important for our discussion is neither the two major divisions of knowledge that he enumerates as being Eternal and Accidental, nor his clear exposition of the Eternal Knowledge as being solely the property of the Creator but the fact that he states that when one has attained knowledge of the second category, which he divides into immediate and theoretical, there remains no difference between the various branches of knowledge because knowledge itself obliterates all such divisions. This profound insight into the Islamic epistemology is often overlooked in Ghazālian studies and stress is placed on al-Ghazālī's classification of knowledge and the seekers of knowledge; the latter into four types: the Mutakallimūn, the esoterics (*al-Bāṭiniyya*), the philosophers, and the Sufīs. In *Maqāsid al-Falasifa* (*The Aims of the Philosophers*), al-Ghazālī divided sciences of the philosophers into four major categories: mathematical (*al-riyādiyyāt*), logical (*al-manṭaqiyyāt*), natural (*al-ṭabīʿyyāt*) and metaphysical (*al-ilāhiyyat*) with politics, economics and ethics being subdivisions of metaphysics. In the second section of *Ihyāʾ*, knowledge is divided into *ʿulūm al-sharīʿyya* (sciences of the *Sharīʿa*) and *ghayr-sharīʿyya* (non-*Sharīʿa* sciences). To the latter belong mathematics and medicine, which al-Ghazālī described as praiseworthy sciences and *farḍ kifāya,* meaning that there should be enough Muslims who are experts in these fields to the degree that they can fulfill the needs of the Islamic society. This last point brings us to the major thrust of Ghazālian thought and concerns.

Al-Ghazālī's whole life seems to have been devoted to the revival of the Islamic polity in all aspects and most of all to the revival of the same pristine spirit of Islam that had once given birth to a civilization deeply conscious of its relationship with the Eternal and the Everlasting. This

---

54. See *al-Mankhūl min taʿliqāt al-uṣūl,* ed. Muḥammad Hasan Hitu (1970), Dār al-Fikr, Damascus, p. 42.

pronounced and oft-articulated concern in Ghazālian thought was in direct response to his times, rife as they were with powerful political, social and intellectual conflicts that threatened to annihilate the Islamic community as a cohesive community of believers.

Deeply concerned as he was with the overall well-being of the Islamic society, al-Ghazālī felt compelled to classify and set limits of each science in as precise a manner as possible and with a clear aim of regulating the life of the community which, in his view, was at the brink of a major catastrophe. Thus when he defines sciences such as mathematics and medicine as *farḍ kifāya*, he is actually placing the practice of these sciences within the larger framework of the goals and aims of the Islamic society as he sees them. This means that the society at large would be committing a sin if it neglected these sciences. Likewise, when he criticizes excessiveness and indulgence, he has the same goal in mind. But his critique is often taken as his opposition to the cultivation of natural sciences *a la* Goldziher; this totally ignores the fact that al-Ghazālī uniformly applies the same criteria against over-indulgence to the "religious sciences", even to jurisprudence, the queen of Islamic sciences. Thus when he blames students of jurisprudence for their indulgence in minute details of the *Sharīʿa*, he does so with the clear understanding of the goals of acquisition of knowledge within the lifespan granted to individuals—a human condition to which he was excessively sensitive.

Ghazālian thought is deeply rooted in the Qur'ān. Moreover, having passed through his "spiritual crisis", he attained a gnosis of the external reality that is characteristically mystical. Thus when he declares in his *Kitāb Jawāhir al-Qur'ān* (*The Jewels of the Qur'ān*), "Rather, I should say that through clear insight free from doubt, it has become apparent to us that in possibility and potentiality, there are sciences which have not yet come into existence, although they are within human reach and there are sciences which once existed but which have now been effaced so that there is not a man on the surface of the earth who knows [them]",[55] he is making an epistemological claim and when he states that "there are still other sciences the understanding and acquisition of which are by no means in the power of human beings but which are possessed by some of the angels drawn near [to God] because possibility is limited in the case of human beings while in the case of the angels it is limited to the relatively highest perfection", he is

55. *Jawāhir*, p. 46 of the English translation, slightly emended.

making explicit reference to a hierarchy.[56] And when he makes the claim that "the principles of those sciences which we have enumerated and of those which we have not, are not outside the Qur'ān, for all of these sciences are drawn out of one of the seas of knowledge of God (may He be exalted), that is, the sea of [knowledge of His] works," he is making an ontological statement that all things, including human knowledge, depend for their existence on the Divine.

Al-Ghazālī considered knowledge of many branches of natural science as an essential prerequisite for understanding the Qur'ān. Narrating the words of Abraham from the Qur'ān, *When I fall ill, it is He Who restores me to health,*[57] he says that this can only be understood by "him who knows the science of medicine completely, for this science means nothing but all aspects of diseases together with their symptoms and the knowledge of their cure and its means."[58] Again, quoting the verses, *The sun and the moon move according to a fixed reckoning,*[59] and *He ordained stages for the moon so that you might learn the method of calculating years and determine time...,*[60] he says that "the real meaning of the movements of the sun and the moon according to a fixed reckoning and of the eclipse of both, and of the merging of the night into the day and the day into the night, can only be known by the one who knows the knowledge of the composition of the heavens and the earth, the science of astronomy."[61]

But perhaps more telling of Ghazālī's attitude toward natural sciences and his understanding of the integration of all knowledge is a short passage in the same work which ought to be quoted in full:

> Likewise, the complete meaning of God's words, O insān, what has deceived you concerning your Gracious Lord, Who created you, then perfected you, then proportioned you aright? He fashioned you in whatever form He pleased, can only be known to him who knows the science of anatomy of human limbs and internal organs, their number, their kinds, their

---

56. Already mentioned in *Iḥyā'*, where he states: "Among the creatures of God, only the angels, human beings and jinn are endowed with intelligence. Man's position is below that of the angels, whose qualities he should try to acquire." *Iḥyā'*, vol. i, p. 236.
57. Q. 26:80.
58. *Jawāhir*, p. 46.
59. Q. 55:5.
60. Q. 10:5.
61. *Jawāhir*, p. 47.

> underlying wisdom and their uses. God indicated these in many places in the Qur'ān, and [knowledge of] these belongs to the sciences of the ancients and the moderns (*'ulūm al-awwalīn wa 'ulūm al-ākharīn*); [in fact] in the Qur'ān lies the confluence of the sciences of the ancients and the moderns. In the same way, the complete meaning of God's words, I perfected his [i.e. Adam's] shape and breathed My spirit into him, cannot be understood so long as [the knowledge about the] perfection of shape, breath and spirit are not known. There are such obscure sciences behind these that most people are heedless to them; sometimes they even fail to understand these sciences when they hear from the one who knows them.[62]

For our discussion of Islam and science nexus, the most important work of al-Ghazālī is his *Incoherence of the Philosophers* (*Tahāfut al-Falāsifa*), which "marks a turning point in the intellectual history of medieval Islam."[63] In this work of enduring interest, al-Ghazālī refuted twenty philosophical doctrines which were considered to be essential features of the Islamic neo-Platonism so painstakingly and thoroughly perfected by al-Fārābī and Ibn Sīnā who became the main targets of al-Ghazālī's attack. In particular, three propositions were singled out by al-Ghazālī as particularly running against the faith tradition to which both he and the philosophers he condemned belonged. Note that the question here was not the faith of individual philosophers. In fact, it was generally accepted that their entire philosophical system was directed toward an affirmation of the existence of God, as opposed to some Hellenistic philosophers and furthermore, they tried to establish their system of thought in a manner as to affirm the uniqueness of one and only one God. The problem, as al-Ghazālī saw it, was that their doctrines *forced* God to produce the world by necessity through a process of emanation, in more or less the same manner in which an inanimate object like the sun was said to produce its light by its very nature, by its essence, necessarily. Thus he found the three propositions—the eternity of the world, God's knowledge of universals only, and the

62. *Jawāhir,* pp. 47-8. The Qur'ānic verses, italicized in the quotation, are in order of citation: Q. 82:6-8 and Q. 32:9.

63. See the parallel English-Arabic edition of *Tahāfut al-falāsifa* [hereafter *Tahāfut*], translated, introduced and annotated by Michael E. Marmura (2000), Brigham Young University Press, Provo, Utah, p. xv. Another translation, now out of print, was published by Sabih Ahamd Kamal (1963), Pakistan Philosophical Congress.

denial of the resurrection of the body—particularly offensive because they reduced God's omnipotence and denied the divine attributes of Will, Power, and Knowledge. *Tahāfut* achieved its high rank in the history of Islamic tradition because it was the first sustained, well-argued and thorough critique of the emanative metaphysics, causal theory and psychology of Ibn Sīnā which was built on a cohesive internal structure and which, in spite of its professed religious and theological aims, was ultimately philosophical.

Written between 484-9/1091-5, when al-Ghazālī was at the prestigious Niẓẓāmiyya Madrasa in Baghdad, along with three other closely related works,[64] *Tahāfut* is divided into two parts. The first part, consisting of sixteen metaphysical questions, covers natural sciences. Two out of three most condemned propositions—the pre-eternity of the world and the theory that God knows only the universals—are covered in this part; the third doctrine in this category (Ibn Sīnā's denial of a bodily resurrection) is refuted in the second part, in the eighteenth through twentieth discussion, the most focused and thorough refutation being in the twentieth discussion.

The refutation of the first proposition, "the eternity of the world" takes up the bulk of the *Tahāfut*. Central to the debate is the question of divine causality in the sense of God's operative principle: Does God act by the necessity of His nature or voluntarily? For al-Ghazālī, the doctrine of an eternal world means the denial of the divine attribute of will, putting an arbitrary limitation on God's absolute power. It is interesting to note that before refuting their claims, al-Ghazālī had to expound the doctrines of the philosophers and he did it in his own crystal clear manner of exposition that made it accessible even to non-philosophers. In the introduction, after the "Preface", al-Ghazālī clearly states that he is not going to plunge into narrating the differences between the philosophers because that would involve too long a tale, but he would restrict his discussion to showing the contradictions of their leader, "who is the philosopher par excellence and 'the first teacher'...namely Aristotle and [his] most reliable transmitters and

64. The first of these three is *Maqāṣid al-falāsifa* (*The Aims of the Philosophers*), written, according to al-Ghazālī, as a prelude to his refutation of these aims in *Tahāfut*, though in the latter work, there is no reference to it; the second work, *Miʿyār al-ʿilm* (*The Standard for Knowledge*), which is a critique of Ibn Sīnā's *Logic*, which for him was a philosophically neutral tool; this work was to serve as an appendix to *Tahāfut*; the third work was *Al-iqtiṣād fi'l-iʿtiqād* (*Moderation in belief*), a kind of sequel to *Tahāfut*.

verifier among the philosophers in Islam, Abū Naṣr al-Fārābī and Ibn Sīnā."[65]

Having explained the boundaries of his work, al-Ghazālī states that in spite of many disagreements among the philosophers on the question of the past eternity (*qidam al-ʿālam*) of the world, a great majority of them uphold its past eternity, "that is [to say], it [the world] has never ceased to exist with God, exalted be He, to be an effect of His, to exist along with Him, not being posterior to Him in time, in the way the effect coexists along with the cause and light along with the sun; that the Creator's priority to [the world] is like the priority of the cause to the effect, which is a priority in essence and rank, not in time."[66] He then goes on to explain the Platonic view, which held that the world was created in time,[67] and finally the view of Galen who suspended judgment on this issue.

In his rebuttal of the eternality thesis, al-Ghazālī first cites the claims of the philosophers and refutes them one by one: "They say, 'it is absolutely impossible for a temporal to proceed from an eternal.'" His exposition of this position is thorough: If we suppose the Eternal at a stage when the world had not yet originated from Him, then the reason why it had not originated must have been that there was no determinant for its existence, and that the existence of the world was only a possibility. So, when later the world comes into existence, we must choose one of the two alternatives to explain it: (i) either that the determinant has emerged or (ii) that it has not. If the determinant did not emerge, the world should still remain in the state of mere possibility, in which it was before. But if it has emerged, who is the originator of the determinant itself? And why does it come into being now, and did not do so before? Thus, the question regarding the origin of the determinant remains unanswered. But since all the states of the Eternal are alike, either nothing shall originate from Him, or whatever originates shall continue to originate forever.

Why did He not originate the world before its origination? It is not possible to answer this by saying that this is because of His inability to bring the world into existence, nor could one say that this is because of the impossibility of the world's coming into being. For this would mean that He

65. *Tahāfut*, p. 4.
66. *Tahāfut*, p. 12.
67. "It is related that Plato said: 'The world is generated and originated in time.' But, then, some among [the philosophers] have interpreted his language as metaphor, refusing [to maintain] that the world's temporal origination is a belief of his." *Tahāfut*, p. 12.

changed from inability to power, or that the world changed from impossibility to possibility. And both senses are absurd. Nor can it be said that, before the time of the origination of the world, there was no purpose and that a purpose emerged later. Nor is it possible to ascribe (the non-origination of the world before it actually originated) to the lack of means at one stage, and to its existence at another. The nearest thing to imagine is to say that He had not *willed* the world's existence before. But from this it follows that one must also say that the world is the result of His having become willing to will its existence, after having not willed so. This would mean that the will should have had a beginning in time. But the origination of the will in the Divine Being is impossible; for He is not subject to temporal events, and its creation—not through or by Him—would not make Him a Willer.

But even if we leave the question concerning the substratum in which the will originated, al-Ghazālī argued, the difficulty regarding the very act of origination still stands. Whence does the will originate? And why does it originate now and not before? Does it now originate from a source other than God? If there can be a temporal existent which has not been brought into existence by anyone, then the world itself should be such an existent, so as to be independent of the Creator. For what is the difference between one temporal existent and another?

So, if the origin of the world is ascribed to God's action, the question remains: Why now, and why not before? Was it due to the absence of means, or power, or purpose, or nature? If so, the transition from this stage to that of existence will revive the difficulty we had to face at the outset. And if it is said to have been due to the absence of will, then one act of will will stand in need of another, and so on ad infinitum. From this it is absolutely clear that the procession of the temporal from the eternal is impossible, unless there were a change in the eternal in respect of power, or means, or time, or nature. And it is impossible to suppose a change in the state of the eternal. For as a temporal event, that change would be like any other change (in non-eternal beings). Therefore (in case of the eternal), change of any kind whatsoever is impossible. And now that the world has been proved (always) to have existed, and the impossibility of its beginning in time has been shown, it follows that the world is eternal.

Before refuting their doctrine, al-Ghazālī acknowledges, "this, then, is the most imaginative of their proofs. In general, their discussion in the rest of the metaphysical questions is weaker than their discussion in this, since here they are able to [indulge in] various types of imaginings they are unable to pursue in other [questions]. For this reason we have given priority to this question, presenting first the strongest of their proofs." He then presents two objections to their proof: "How will you disprove the one who says that the world came into being because of the eternal will which demanded its existence at the time at which it actually came into existence, and which demanded the non-existence (of the world) to last as long as it lasted, and (demanded) the existence to begin where it actually began? So, on this view, existence of the world was not an object of the eternal will, before the world actually existed; hence its non-actualization. And it was an object of the will at the time when it actualized. What can prevent us from believing such a thing, and what is the contradiction involved in it?"[68]

Al-Ghazālī then advances a mathematical argument against the Neo-Platonic assertion of the eternity of the world.[69] He states that the past eternity of the world logically entails that an infinite number of revolutions of the heavens has already elapsed which is impossible because there exists a finite ratio between the revolutions of the sun and the other spheres. This is based on the fact that the sphere of the sun rotates in one year, whereas Saturn's rotates in thirty so that the rotations of Saturn are a third of a tenth of those of the sun. The rotations of Jupiter are a half of a sixth of the rotations of the sun for it rotates once in every twelve years. Now, according to their assertion, if the number of the rotations of Saturn is infinite, the number of the solar rotations, although a third of a tenth [of the latter], will [also] be infinite. Indeed, the rotations of the sphere of the fixed stars, which rotates [once in] every thirty-six thousand years, will also be infinite, just as the sun's movement from east to west, taking place in a day and a

68. *Tahāfut*, pp. 14-15.

69. The impossibility of an infinite number of revolutions of the different planets is not found in Philoponus in this connection, as asserted by Fakhry (1983) in his *A History of Islamic Philosophy*, 2nd ed. Columbia University Press, New York, p. 224, n. 40, cf. Averroes' *Tahāfut al-Tahāfut*, II, 7 where the note on page 7 merely states that it *derives* from him [that is, from Philoponus] but is not found in his works in this connection; even in his lost refutation of Aristotle's doctrine of the eternity of the world, where "it is given as a quotation from him by Simplicius in his commentary on the *Physica* (Diels, 1179, pp. 15-27). Philoponus says in his first argument that if the world were eternal, there would be not an infinite number of men, but also of horses and dogs; infinity therefore would be triplicated, which is absurd, because nothing can be greater than infinity." *Averroes's Tahafut al-Tahafut (The Incoherence of the Incoherence)*, tr. by Simon Van Den Bergh (1954), Luzac & Co., Oxford, vol. ii, p. 7.

night, will be [likewise] infinite and this is a clear impossibility. Moreover, these revolutions are either even or odd and hence must be finite. For the infinite is neither odd nor even, since it can be increased indefinitely. To top it all, the Neo-Platonists assert the possibility of an infinite number of Souls, existing in a disembodied condition, as Ibn Sīnā held, despite the logical contradiction that the concept of an actual infinite involves.

Al-Ghazālī also refuted Ibn Sīnā's assertion that God is prior to the world in essence, rather than in time, by showing the creation of time. The statement that God is prior to the world, he said, merely means that God existed while the world was not, and continued to exist together with the world after its creation. Likewise, al-Ghazālī showed that the proposition of post-eternity was merely a logical offshoot of the proposition of pre-eternity.

He then moves on to the question of God's attributes (questions iii-xi). According to the Neo-Platonists, the world emanates from God—whom they liked to call the First—*necessarily* just as the effect emanates from the cause or the light from the sun. Al-Ghazālī returns to the philosophers' assertion that the world is eternal and asks how could it be said that it is created by God for creation or making means the act of bringing forth an entity out of nothing, and the eternal is forever in being. Moreover, the Neo-Platonists claim that out of one only one can come, but since God is one and the world multiple, there can be no sense in saying that He is its Maker. In his treatment of question four, al-Ghazālī shows that according to Neo-Platonists' own logic, they cannot even prove the existence of God because all their arguments rest on the impossibility of an infinite regress and necessity of ultimately positing an Uncaused Cause. However, bodies are eternal, according to them, and hence require no cause and an infinite series is not impossible since it follows from their thesis of the eternity of the world that an infinite series of effects has already come and gone.

At the end of his critique of the four proofs of the philosophers, al-Ghazālī states that the *Tahāfut* is intended only to refute their claims and "as regards the true doctrine, we will write a book concerning it after completing this one—if success, God willing, comes to our aid—and will name it *Qawāʿid al-ʿaqāʾid* (*The Principles of Beliefs*). We will engage in it in affirmation, just as we have devoted ourselves in this book to destruction."[70] There is, in fact, a book by that title in the *Iḥyāʾ*. But, as noted by Michael Marmura, the work that best qualifies as a sequel to *Tahāfut* is

70. *Tahāfut,* p. 46.

al-Iqtiṣād fī'l-I'tiqād.

This brings us to al-Ghazālī's refutation of causality, most coherently formulated in Part Two of the *Tahāfut*, where it starts with a preamble that states, "Regarding what are called 'natural sciences', these consist of many sciences, whose divisions we will [now] mention so that it would be known that the religious law does not require disputing them nor denying them, except in places we will mention".[71] Then he goes on to give details of his eight-fold division of the roots of natural sciences. Having done so, he states "the connection (*al-iqtirān*) between what is habitually (*fī'l-'āda*) believed to be a cause (*sabbab*) and what is habitually believed to be an effect (*musabbab*) is not necessary (*laysa ḍarūriyyan*)." He, then, provides a list of pairs that are usually thought to be cause and effect by the philosophers (quenching of thirst and drinking, satiety and eating, burning and contact with fire…). And then states that "their connection is due to the prior decree of God, who creates them side by side (*'alā'l-tasāwuq*),[72] not to its being necessary in itself, incapable of separation. On the contrary, it is within [divine] power to create satiety without eating, to create death without decapitation, to continue life after decapitation, and so on to all connected things. The philosophers denied the possibility of [this] and claimed it to be impossible."[73]

This criticism of the philosophers' position is on the basis that their proof of causality was dependent on observation (*mushāhada*), which depends on the senses—a source of knowledge that he could not accept on its own merit. Thus his position regarding causality is consistent with his theory of knowledge. Using the example of fire and burning, he said that observation could only prove that burning took place when there was fire, and not *by* the fire or the fact that there was no other cause [for burning]. Thus he establishes that something's existence *with* a thing does not prove that it exists *by* that thing. He then shows that the inert and lifeless objects such as fire are incapable of action and thus cannot be the agent (*al-fā'il*) that causes burning. To prove his point, al-Ghazālī used several examples and employed a neo-platonic device of the philosophers some of whom

---

71. *Tahāfut*, p. 161.
72. "Side by side" or "one alongside the other" but not "one following the other" and not "in a successive order." What al-Ghazālī means is concomitance, where the priority is not temporal. His critique is of Ibn Sīnā's concept of essential cause, where cause and effect are simultaneous. *Tahāfut*, p. 240, n. 3.
73. *Tahāfut*, p. 166.

held that accidents (*a'rāḍ*, sing. *'arḍ*) and incidents (*ḥawādith*) emanate at the time of contact between "bodies", from the provider of forms (*wāhib al-ṣūwār*), whom they thought to be an angel. Accordingly, one cannot claim that fire is the agent of burning:

> Indeed, we will show this by an example. If a person, blind from birth, who has a film on his eyes and who has never heard from people the difference between night and day, were to have the film cleared from his eyes in daytime, [then] open his eyelids and see colors, [such a person] would believe that the agents [causing] the apprehension of the forms of the colors in his eyes is the opening of his sight and that, as long as his sight is sound, [his eyes] opened, the film removed, and the individual in front of him having color, it follows necessarily that he would see, it being incomprehensible that he would not see. When, however, the sun sets and the atmosphere becomes dark, he would then know that it is sunlight that is the cause for the imprinting of the colors in his sight.[74]

Al-Ghazālī reduced the problem of causality to that of "will" which makes it rationally possible for the agent, whom he held to be the Creator Himself, not to create burning even though there is contact. This makes room for the existence of miracles (*mu'jizāt*) that were associated with the prophets, without resorting to allegorical interpretations of the Qur'ānic verses as the philosophers did. He gives the example of the Qur'ānic account of Abraham's ordeal when he was thrown in the fire but no burning took place. The Qur'ān (21:69) states clearly that it was Allah's Will that the fire did not harm Abraham and al-Ghazālī maintained that Allah is the agent (*fā'il*) of every action, either directly or indirectly (that is through the angels).

His short work, *al-Maqṣad al-Asnā fi Sharaḥ Asmā' Allah al-Ḥusnā* (*The Highest Aim in the Commentary on the Beautiful Names of God*),[75] written approximately at the same time as *Iḥyā'*, is one of the best representative works in the traditional Islamic reflection on metaphysical and cosmological meanings of God's beautiful names (*al-asmā' al-Ḥusna'*). In a

---

74. *Tahāfut*, p. 168.
75. This work has been translated into many languages. A more recent English translation is by David B. Burrell and Nazih Daher, The Islamic Texts Society, Cambridge, 1992, reprint 1999; all references are to this edition; [henceforth *Maqṣad*].

passage describing the three names of God—al-Khāliq, al-Bāri, al-Muṣawwir—al-Ghazālī states that "everything which comes forth from non-existence to existence needs first of all to be planned; secondly, to be originated according to the plan; and thirdly, to be formed after being originated."[76] These operative functions are signified by the aforementioned three names.

Al-Ghazālī remains enormously important for the contemporary science-religion discourse but his continuous relevance does not rest on his position on a particular issue; rather it rests on his general approach to some of the fundamental questions now being debated in regard to the cosmos, the human condition and God's role in the world. His personal journey, his formal training in many branches of learning and, most of all, his clear insight into the nature of the human condition together with an accessible prose contribute to the contemporary interest in his works. Furthermore, in the vivid account of his personal experience of a spiritual transformation that made him what he was, one discovers many strands of a universal nature. By making his intellectual and spiritual journey accessible to subsequent generations through an inspiring and lucid account, he has not only drawn numerous seekers into the folds of his intensely personal experience, but has also provided a matrix for sharing such experiences within the larger body of literature dealing with spiritual transformations. This, together with his works written after the transforming experience, gives a significantly unique dimension to his contribution on such contemporary issues as the nature of God's action in the universe, the reality of miracles, the question of good and evil, suffering, hope and salvation. In addition, his ideas on many fundamental questions which are being debated in disciplines such as cosmology and eschatology deserve to be seriously studied because, although he remains thoroughly rooted in the Islamic tradition, the treatment he imparts to his subject matter raises it to a level that is accessible from all faith traditions.

Teleology: God, Cosmos and Science

Teleological arguments pursue two distinct lines: the evidence of design on a minor scale and on a cosmic scale. The evidence of design in both cases is either the functionality of nature or an aesthetic quality in nature, that is, its orderliness and beauty. Socrates, for example, is known to have pointed out the diversity of man's physiological and psychological endowments and

76. *Maqṣad,* p. 68.

the phenomena surrounding him that contributes to his well-being. He postulated that what "clearly is for a purpose" must be the result of "forethought", not "chance". And he concluded that man must have been made by a "wise demiurge...[for]gods take care to furnish men with the things they need... nature discloses divine 'providence' and 'love of man'."[77] Cicero goes further. The spokesman for Stoicism in his *De Natura Deorum* offers botanical, zoological, meteorological and geological data to heap a wealth of evidence that discloses functionality and hence design. "The world is governed by the providence of the gods," he declares, "everything in the world is governed, for the welfare and preservation of all, by divine intelligence and deliberation and not by chance."[78] Galen was to follow a similar line of reasoning, adding details from human and animal physiology.[79]

The second line of teleological arguments spans the whole cosmos. "There are sympathetic, harmonious, all-pervading affinities between things," so goes the general argument of this type, that is sufficient for one to recognize "a single divine, all-pervading spirit,"[80] as Cicero's stoic spokesman says in *De Natura Deorum*. These arguments refer to the immense beauty and the regularity of the celestial bodies as a self-evident proof for a "mind" that governs the universe. Several cosmic schemes and plans are extant in literature from ancient times that employ this type of elaborate reasoning to show that the cosmos is designed.

Both of these lines of teleological arguments lend themselves to a demonstration of unity in the universe; this was particularly true for the second line that took the whole cosmos as its point of departure. If there was beauty, compelling harmony, functionality, and interdependency, it was argued, then there must be a single overall design and by extension, a single designer.

---

77. Xenophon, *Memorabilia*, I, iv; Iv, iii. Quoted by Davidson, Herbert A., (1987), *Proofs for Eternity, Creation and the Existence of God in Medieval Islamic and Jewish Philosophy*, [hereafter *Proofs*], Oxford University Press, New York, p. 217.
78. Ibid.
79. Galen, *De Usu Partium*, X, 9; XVII. Ibid., p. 217. Davidson notes that the theme had already appeared in Aristotle's *De Partibus Animalium*, but there design in nature is clearly regarded as immanent and nonconscious. See *De Partibus, Animalium*, I, 641b, 12; III, 1, 661b, 23-24; IV, x, 687b.
80. *Proofs*, p. 218.

These ancient arguments had arrived in the Islamic intellectual tradition after the transmitted sciences had been thoroughly established during the two centuries of intense reflection on the Qur'ān. Among the most astonishing aspects of the Qur'ān was an emphatic invitation to all humankind to reflect on the grand design in nature that exhibits itself in such a compelling manner that no one with heart and soul and mind can fail to recognize an underlying unity in the cosmos and hence a single Designer, Allah. Though compelling in its own way, these are, however, not the arguments that were used to establish a nexus between faith and science in the Islamic scientific tradition because it was recognized that these arguments originate in a text that skeptics did not accept. Hence they would easily render these powerful arguments irrelevant by stating that had they accepted the Grand Designer, they would not be arguing against the Design. However, let us note that the Qur'ān does not use its ontological premise while inviting humankind to reflect on the signs that are spread throughout the universe—signs that speak to the innate human intelligence in the most extraordinary manner. These include the water cycle; the regeneration of earth after it has been dead; the periodic and orderly movement of the heavenly bodies; the alternation of night and day *so that ye may rest during the night and seek sustenance during the day*; the six stages of development of fetus in mother's womb; and a host of other natural phenomena.[81] Indeed, an oft-repeated refrain in the Qur'ān is *in this* (sometimes *in these*) *are signs for those who reflect.*

Let us trace the arrival of one analogy in the Islamic tradition. One of the metaphors employed by Cicero goes back to the Cleanthes and Chrysippus of the old Stoa. They argued that the design in the universe can be compared to the design apparent in a house. This argument is based on aesthetics. Cleanthes contended that when someone comes into a well arranged and regulated house, he cannot suppose that the order in the house came about without a cause, hence with far more reason, the motion and order of the world, which over an infinite past time have never played false, must convince every observer that nature is directed by a mind.[82] This analogy was also used by Chrysippus who compared the beauty of the heavenly bodies and the great magnitude of the oceans and lands to a giant and beautiful house, thereby inferring that the world must have been constructed by the immortal gods as a "domicile for

81. For example, Q. 2:164; 3:190; 30:20-25; 45:3-5.
82. *De Natura Deorum,* II, v, 15, quoted in *Proofs,* p. 200, n. 44.

themselves".[83] Philo, too, mentions the analogy, crediting it to "those whose philosophy is reputed to be the best", the Stoics, who maintained: "Should a man see a carefully built house...he will get a notion of the craftsman... just so, anyone entering, as it were, the great house of the world...and beholding the heavens...planets, stars...which move rhythmically, harmoniously, and for the benefit of the whole,...beholding as well the [arrangement and variety of] earth, water, air, and fruits, will surely conclude that these [things]" are the works of "a creator, God."[84]

This analogy was to reappear in the Islamic intellectual tradition, perhaps through the route of translation. The earliest example is in an Arabic work, attributed to al-Jāḥiẓ which has been referred to by various titles all of which contain the term Reflection. An extant version is entitled, *The Book of Proofs and Reflections regarding Creation and Divine Governance.*[85] In its Arabic construction, the argument attempts to show that the universe not only has an intelligent cause on the grounds that it shows a remarkably unified design but also that a single creator must be behind this design who made it and who provides for it. The argument further states that the planning (*taqdīr*), governance (*tadbīr*) and order apparent in the universe must come from one single creator who fitted the parts together and arranged them. Note, the terms here have been transformed from the Greek philosophical tradition to the Qur'anic usage; *Taqdīr* and *Tadbīr* are oft-repeated terms used in the Qur'ān in reference to the creation of the universe and its maintenance by one single God.

Another example that can be traced from Socrates to al-Jāḥiẓ is, interestingly, the argument which is also used in the Qur'ān. Socrates had insisted that the alternation of night and day has been made for man's proper function: "...gods provided [man] with a most beauteous time for resting."[86] The Spokesman for the Stoics in Cicero's *De Natura Deorum* counts "the alternation of day and night which afford a time for acting and another time for resting among the gifts of divine providence." *Kitāb al-dalā'il* repeats this theme: "The rising of the sun permits men to busy themselves in their affairs" and its setting furnishes them with the

---

83. *Proofs*, p. 220, n. 15.
84. *Proofs*, p. 220, n. 46.
85. *Kitāb al-Dalā'īl wa'l-I'tibar 'alā'l-Khalq wa'l-Tadbīr* (1928), al-Jāḥiẓ, Aleppo; also found in Aya Sofia, MS. 4836/2, described by Gibb (1948), "The Argument from Design," in *Ignace Goldziher Memorial Volume*, vol. 1, Budapest.
86. Xenophon, *Memorabilia*, IV, 3.

opportunity of "repose for the recovery of their bodies," and indeed in forcing them, when necessary, to rest; for human greed is so great that "many would never rest except for...the darkness of...night." Note, once again, the resemblance with the Qur'ānic theme of the alternation of night and day which the Qur'ān presents as one of the proofs of Divine Design: *Behold! in the creation of the heavens and the earth, in the alternation of night and day, in the sailing of the ships through the ocean for the profit of mankind; in the rain which God sends down from the skies, and the life which He gives therewith to an earth that was dead; in the beasts of all kinds that He scatters through the earth; in the change of the winds and the clouds which they trail like their slaves between the sky and the earth; indeed [in all of these] are signs for people who are wise.*[87] Muslim scientists were not innocent of these facts. Just one source, our *Kitāb al-Dalā'il,* accumulates hundreds of details from plant biology, zoology, human physiology and psychology in support of its argument from Design. Some examples are: the human eye, providentially protected by eyelids, lashes and eyebrows; the digestive and excretory functions; man's erect posture; the willingness of animals such as the ox, the horse, the dog, the ass, the camel and the elephant to submit to man, although they are stronger than he—all of these are mentioned in detail in this early source and they become much more refined in later sources such as *The Wisdom in God's Creation (al-Ḥikmah fi Makhlūqāt Allah),* a book attributed to al-Ghazālī.

One can continue to quote examples of teleological arguments from this tradition ad infinitum. Suffice it to say that the Islamic intellectual tradition was not only aware of the need for formulating the argument for Design independent of the ontological premises which were at the heart of Islamic faith, but it also carried it out to its ultimate limits with increasing refinement. One can trace this thread from Muḥāsbī (d. 243/857), who has a teleological argument for the unity of the cause of the universe, to Qāsim b. Ibrāhīm (160-246/785-860) for whom the "imprints" of perfect wisdom and the "signs" of good governance manifest in the universe prove that a wise and good deity must be responsible. In addition, there are the arguments that range from the "wondrous wisdom exhibited in the universe", which al-Māturīdī (d. 333/944) was to use in his *Kitāb al-Tawḥīd,*[88]

87. Q. 2:164.

88. Al-Māturīdī's *Kitab al-Tawḥīd* has been reprinted from Beirut (1970), cited in *Proofs,* p. 260.

to the arguments of Ikhwān al-Ṣafā', the Brethren of Purity,[89] who offer a teleological argument for the existence of God in which the very structure of planets and stars supplies the evidence of Design. In this scheme of things, the universe is considered as a single unit, "as a city is one, or as an animal is one, or as man is one," the Ikhwān noted in their *Rasā'il.*[90] For Ikhwān, the creation of the universe proceeds in the following manner:

1. Creator—who is one, simple, eternal, permanent.
2. Intellect (*'aql*)—which is of two kinds: innate and acquired.
3. Soul (*nafs*)—which is of three kinds: vegetative, animal and reasonable.
4. Matter (*hayūlā'*)—which is of four kinds: matter of artifacts, physical matter, universal matter, and original matter.
5. Nature (*ṭabī'a*)—which is of five kinds: celestial nature and the four elemental natures.
6. Body (*jism*)—which has six directions: above, below, front, back, left and right.
7. The sphere—which has its seven planets.
8. The elements—which have eight qualities, these being in reality the four quantities combined two by two: Earth—cold and dry; Water—cold and wet; Air—warm and wet; Fire—warm and dry.
9. Beings of this world—which are the mineral, plant, and animal kingdoms, each having three parts.[91]

89. For the identity of the group of scholars from Baṣra who are commonly known as *Ikhwān al-Ṣafā'*, the Brethern of Purity, see Nasr, Seyyed Hossein (1992), *An Introduction to Islamic Cosmological Doctrines*, State University of New York Press, Albany, pp. 25-74; this work first appeared in 1964, published by the Belknap Press of the Harvard University Press, Cambridge.
90. Cited from *Proofs*, p. 226.
91. Nasr (1992), p. 52. Nasr notes the elegance inherent in this table of generation: "The first four numbers are simple, universal beings—the numbers 1 to 4 already containing in themselves all numbers, since 1 + 2 + 3 + 4 = 10—while the other beings are compound." He points out that it is from this point of view that the Ikhwān divided the

Nasr also notes that the "chain of being described by the Ikhwān possesses a temporal aspect which has led certain scholars to the view that the authors of the *Rasā'il* believed in the modern theory of evolution."[92] In a footnote, Nasr mentions Dieterici as one such proponent of evolution who saw the Brethren as Darwin's precursor and states that in 1933, De Boer had already correctly refuted this thesis of Dieterici.[93] Nasr has also clarified that according to the *Rasā'il,* all changes on earth occur as acts of the Universal Soul and not by an independent agent acting within bodies here on earth. Secondly, Ikhwān construe this world as a shadow of another world that is more real than it, and the "idea" of everything in this world actually exists in the other, so that there is no question of the species changing into another, because the "idea" of each species is a form which is beyond change and decay.[94] The Ikwān had said:

> The species and genus are definite and preserved. Their forms are in matter. But the individuals are in perpetual flow; they are neither definite nor preserved. *The reason for the conservation of forms, genus and species in matter is fixity of their celestial cause* because their efficient cause is the Universal Soul of the spheres instead of the change and continuous flux of individuals which is due to the variability of their cause.[95]

Nasr mentions that there exist certain similarities between the doctrines held by the Ikhwān and modern theories of evolution. For example, both believe that the time of existence of terrestrial plants precedes that of animals, minerals precede the plants, and organisms adapt to their environment but he asserts that the conception of Ikhwān was teleological: Everything existed for a purpose, the final purpose of the cosmos being the return of multiplicity to Unity. He also makes the distinction between modern ideas and those of Ikhwān by stating: "In the deepest sense, what separates all these ideas of the Ikhwān from their modern counterparts is

---

hierarchy of Being into the four-fold division of God, Universal Intellect, Universal Soul and *hylé*.

92. Nasr (1992), p. 71: *Der Darwinismusèim X und XI Jahrhundert* (Leipzig, 1878).
93. Tj. de Boer (1933), *History of Philosophy in Islam*, London, p. 91, cited from Nasr (1992), p. 71, n. 97.
94. Nasr (1992), p. 71 and *passim*.
95. See Nasr (1992), p. 72, wherein the text has been quoted from Carra de Vaux, *Les Penseurs de l'Islam* IV, 107, emphasis added by Nasr.

that for the Ikhwān the hands of God were not cut off from creation after the beginning of the world—as is the case with the deists."[96]

But let us note that the position of the Ikhwān is rather marginal in Islamic thought. Most modern scholars tend to agree that they were Ismāʿilīs. Al-Ghazālī, who himself was to put together a simple teleological argument along with the argument from creation, refuted their ideas. A similar case was made by T. I. Raïnow concerning al-Bīrūnī. He stated that in "Alberuni's fine and substantial work entitled *India*, which is devoted to the history of all fields of Hindu thought, one may find the whole theory of Darwinism already expounded more than eight hundred years before the publication of the theory of natural selection."[97] Professor Jan Z. Wilczynski, of the Lebanese State University refuted this claim in his "On the Presumed Darwinism of Alberuni Eight Hundred Years before Darwin".[98]

Al-Bīrūnī also used this medieval scheme in which human beings are perceived in relation to their position within the universe. The "migration" mentioned by al-Bīrūnī, however, once again signifies the gradation of being in the Universe which according to him and most of his contemporaries, is a hierarchy in which each creature occupies a position in the ontological scale in conformity with its own nature. The mineral kingdom forms the base of support for the plants and animals. Al-Bīrūnī also accepts the analogy of microcosm and macrocosm, which is closely related to the concept of Chain of Being.

Ibn Ḥazm (384-456/994-1064) was to add biological and botanical data to the astronomical data of the Ikhwān along with an argument from aesthetics that would build on the functionality of the argument. Thus he admires the skill by which the limbs of the human body fit together and the texture of the palm tree fiber, which is woven so skillfully that it seems to be worked on a loom. But the important point to note is that Ibn Ḥazm's final appeal is to the intellect: it is in the human intellect that it must be undoubtedly known that the celestial and terrestrial regions must have come about by the "deliberation of a maker" who "exercises choice and invention" and the evidence from both the macrocosmic and microcosmic

96. Nasr (1992), p. 74.
97. T. I. Raïnow (1943), *Wielikije Uczenyje Usbecistana (IX-XIIbb)* [The Great Scholars of Uzbekistan (IXth to XIth centuries)], Edition Ousphan, Tashkent, p. 62.
98. *Isis*, vol. 50 (1959), pp. 459-66.

planes is "sufficient to conclude not only that the universe has a maker, but that it has a single maker."[99]

This appeal to the inborn faculty and intellect of human beings is central to the Islamic intellectual tradition. Al-Ghazālī employs it in his characteristic lucid style: he begins by quoting the teleological verses from the Qur'ān (2:164), and then declares that no one "possessing the least intelligence who reflects upon these verses, who gazes upon the wonders of God's creation on earth and in the heavens, who gazes upon the marvelous formation of animals and plants," can doubt that "the well adapted arrangement" must depend on a "maker who governs...and adapts it."[100] Al-Ghazālī also wrote a separate book, *al-Ḥikmah fī Makhlūqāt Allah (Wisdom in the Creation of Allah)*, in which he points out to the wisdom and design inherent in the sky, earth, sun, moon, oceans, water, air, fire, man as well as birds, bees, fish and minerals. He mentions mosquitoes, flies and pearls. In his *Kitāb Jawāhir al-Qur'ān (The Jewels of the Qur'ān)*, in the chapter "Secrets of the Sūra of the Opening, and how it comprises eighth of the ten valuables of the Qur'ān", he had already pointed out a remarkable fact about the spiders:

> Look at the spider, how God has created its limbs and has taught it the device of weaving, and how He has taught it the tricks of hunting without two wings, for He has created for it sticky saliva by which it attaches itself to a corner, lying in wait for the passing of a mosquito. [When the mosquito passes close by], it throws itself onto the mosquito, catches it, shackles it with its threads, made from its saliva, and thus disables it from escaping until it eats it or puts it in store. Look at the spider's method of weaving its abode, how God has guided it in its weaving according to the geometrical proportions in the order of its warp and woof.[101]

One of the most interesting examples cited by al-Ghazālī is that of the bees. "Look at the bee and the innumerable wonders of its gathering honey," he wrote,

---

99. Ibid.

100. *Al-Risāla al-Qudssiya*, tr. A. Tibawi (1965), as *Al-Ghazali's Tract on Dogmatic Theology*, Curzon, London.

101. Al-Ghazālī, *Kitāb Jawāhir al-Qur'ān*, ed. and tr. by Muhammad Abul Quasem (1983), as *The Jewels of the Qur'ān*, [henceforth *Jawāhir*], Kegan Paul International, London, p. 68; translation emended.

> and [at its producing] beeswax. We should like to make you aware of the geometry of its hive. It is built on the figure of a hexagon so that the space [in the hive] may not be insufficient for all the bees who crowd in one place in great numbers. If hives were circular, there would remain outside the hives an empty space since circles do not pack contiguously. Likewise are all other shapes. As to squares, though they do pack contiguously, but the shape of the bee is inclined to roundness and so inside the hive there would remain empty corners as in a circular shape there would be empty corners outside. Thus none of the figures other than a hexagon approaches the circular figure [of the bee] in contiguity, and this is known by geometrical proof. Consider, then, how God has guided the bee to the characteristic of this figure.[102]

Let us note that all varieties of bees all over the world have been constructing hexagonal beehives whose apex angle is always 70.529^0.[103]

Ibn Rushd also derives two simplified arguments from the Qur'ān: a cosmological argument concluding that some entity must be responsible for the occurrence of events in the world and a teleological argument in the following manner: The functionality exhibited throughout the universe cannot conceivably be due to "chance"; it must "perforce" be the doing of an "agent" who intends and wills it.[104]

Science, Technology and Society

Let us conclude this chapter with a brief mention of yet another aspect of the Islam and science nexus that can still be "experienced", at least to some extent. Walking through the winding streets of Fez, one sees old houses which provide the outer "clothing" of a nourishing and nurturing inner

---

102. *Jawāhir,* p. 68-9, translation emended.

103. Note that the hexagonal structure is the most optimal structure for it is capable of holding the maximum amount of honey, using the minimum amount of beeswax. By solving the optimality problem for a hexagonal pyramid, we find out that in order to achieve the maximum capacity for the minimum surface area (and hence the minimum amount of beeswax), the apex angle of the individual cells would have to be exactly 70.529^0. For further details of this interesting example, see ANALYS, "Chance or Intelligent Design" in *Islamic Thought and Scientific Creativity,* vol. 2, 1991, pp. 73-7.

104. M. Mueller (ed., 1859), *Kitāb al-Kashf,* Munich, pp. 27-8, quoted from *Proofs,* p. 229.

space for families; these winding streets were planned hundreds of years ago in a manner that was typically Islamic. They were planned to exclude the external world from the privacy of the home. Closed and windowless to the outer world, the walls of these houses protect an open courtyard from where the dwelling places inside receive their light and air. The streets are circular because these concentric circles are etched around a center, which is not only the center of the material world thus constructed, but also the spiritual center of the community: the *Jāmiʿ* mosque. These streets and the side streets that come out from the center, like the spokes on a wheel, provide maximum access to the mosque as well as to the commercial activity yet do not allow the outside world to impose into the privacy of the homes. And when the call to prayer is chanted from the high minaret of the mosque, all have easy access to the mosque where the space transforms from its silence into a chanting remembrance, that renews the nexus between God and those who respond to his urgent invitation.

The traditional Islamic cities such as Fez, Iṣfahān and Damascus fully utilized technologies but these technologies were based on the same principles that had guided the Islamic tradition; hence there was no incongruity in their development. Now they are coming under increasing dangers of various kinds due to the intrusion of modern technological advances that have no regard for the sacred dimension of these cities or for the living space that they enclose. But in spite of these rude intrusions, these cities still present a living testimony to the integral nexus that existed between all things in the traditional Islamic society. The sciences, the arts and the crafts that utilized Islamic science and technology, the open spaces in the cities and in the mosques, the covered bazaars and the guilds—all of these varied aspects of the Islamic civilization functioned in relation to each other as well as in relation to a center. In the microcosm, this centrality is the human heart; in the outer world, it is the sacred city of Makkah, or more precisely the Kaʿba in Makkah, toward which all Muslims turn while praying. "This act of orientation has a profound significance. It represents an awareness that there is a right direction—the 'Straight Path' mentioned in every unit of the ritual prayer—and that every other direction leads away from the goal of human life. At the same time, this act of turning towards the Center, both within and without, is an act of integration in accordance with the basic Islamic principle of unity."[105]

105. Eaton, Charles Le Gai (2000), *Remembering God: Reflections on Islam*, ABC International Group, Inc, Chicago, pp. 55-6.

This concentric pattern, together with the urban planning which was involved in the construction and maintenance of these cities, is inextricably linked to an aesthetic sensibility that visualizes space as a sacred dimension of existence, stretching out to the heavens. The circular streets—which appear like cul-de-sacs but lead to an intricate pattern of life—are living reminders of the importance of privacy that Islam cherished in all matters of individual life. The market place in these old cities is not merely an impersonal space where faceless traders and equally anonymous customers exchange money and goods; rather these are warm places where relationships are established, news and pleasantries are exchanged, goods are bought and sold and when, in the middle of a bargain, the call to prayer is heard, both the seller and the buyer go together to the mosque, where they stand shoulder to shoulder, facing the same direction. Likewise, goods sold and bought are also the product of craftsmen who work nearby and whose art is not merely for decoration—though it serves that purpose as well—but for daily use. Whether it is carpets, utensils or clothing with intricate designs and motifs, they were all living expressions of a tradition that are part of daily life. These ancient cities still support artisans as well as guilds. Islamic arts and crafts, which employ a number of traditional scientific and technological tools, provide yet another dimension of the nexus that existed between the scientific tradition and the aesthetic and spiritual dimensions of Islam. A feature still existent in these cities is the presence of various bazārs (*aswāq*) known by the artistic or the commercial activity associated with a particular trade, such as the weavers, dyers, metal workers or glass blowers. These *aswāq*, where masters train their apprentices and pass on their arts to successive generations, still stand in remembrance of the close links that existed between Islamic spirituality and the sciences and the crafts it inspired.

The sense of transcendent implies the consciousness of an inner human desire to transcend the limitations of the earthly state. Whether it is in the sciences or the arts and crafts, this yearning expresses itself in countless ways which involve the search for the true principles of the natural world as much as it involves the expression of beauty and harmony, may that be in sciences or the arts. Within the traditional civilization of Islam, these expressions are fused together through certain principles that provide internal avenues and links to a tapestry of various branches of science, arts and crafts. Even a glance at an astrolabe—the most versatile instrument of the Islamic astronomical tradition—is enough to realize these inner connections, which express themselves in the instrument's engravings and its fine metal work.

The striking characteristics of mathematical patterns in Islamic art and architecture are an obvious example of the nexus between qualitative mathematics and Islamic spirituality. This "mathematical nature of Islamic art and architecture does not derive from external historical influences, Greek or otherwise. It derives from the Qur'ān whose own mathematical structure is bewildering and reveals an amazing rapport between Islamic intellectual and spiritual concerns and mathematics."[106] A building such as the Great Mosque of Córdoba, one of the finest expressions of Islamic architecture, still provides a glimpse of these inner connections. Though this mosque now stands in isolation from its historical environ that once housed almost eighty thousand shops and artisan workshops, and although there is no sign of the public baths and inns or of the multitudes of citizens, merchants and mules passing over the bridge on the Guadalquiver (the Great River, *al-wad al-Kabīr*) into the center of the city, one can still see numerous connections between Islamic spirituality, sciences and practical arts in this structure. However, one has to use one's imagination because even the interior of this monumental mosque is not what it used to be; the presence of a "dark church structure that was built between the Renaissance and Baroque periods, and arbitrarily placed at the center of the light forest of pillars like a giant black spider"[107] makes it extremely difficult to clearly distinguish the features of the mosque which looked like a broad grove of palm trees. The mosque also stands today without the fabulous royal city, *Madīnat al-ẓahra*, which once provided the backdrop to the city or the famous library of al-Ḥakam II, with its 400,000 volumes, many of them containing annotations about their authors in his own hand. It is also devoid of the traditional courtyard with fountains for washing the face, hands and feet for the ritual purification before prayers. But some things still remain and among them are the prayer niche and the marvelous array of columns and arches with their hypnotic symmetry. "The pillars are linked by horseshoe-shaped arches immediately above the abaci...the upper arches are heavier than the lower ones and the abutments of both increase in size with the height of the pillars. This feature, too, is

106. Nasr, Seyyed Hossein (1987), *Islamic Art and Spirituality*, State University Press of New York, Albany, p. 47.
107. Burchardt, Titus (1999), *Moorish Culture in Spain*, tr. by Alisa Jaffa and William Stoddart, Fons Vitae, Louisville, pp. 9-10.

reminiscent of palm branches—and the whole, contrary to the classical European conception of architecture, rests on comparatively slender columns. Yet the effect of the vaulting is in no way oppressive; the arches appear to be suspended like so many rainbows in the sky."[108]

Harmoniously embedded in the seven-sided prayer niche of the Córdoba Mosque are many features of various Islamic sciences, arts, architectural motifs and a peculiar Islamic usage of colors and forms. This blend creates a unique space inside the niche—where the word of God was once recited—a space that evokes the feeling of awe and reminds one of the mysterious "niche of light" passage in the celebrated "Light Verse" of the Qur'ān (24:35). The fluted shell-like vault, designed to create extraordinary acoustics for the transmission of the recitation of the Qur'ān to the far corners of the mosque, and the horseshoe shaped arch that seems to breathe "as if expanding with a surfeit of inner beatitude, while the rectangular frame enclosing it acts as a counterbalance. The radiating energy and the perfect stillness from an unsurpassable equilibrium."[109]

It is no wonder that this extraordinary mosque has remained, up to our own times, one of the enduring sources of inspiration and reflection on that period of Islamic civilization that had nurtured a scientific tradition which seamlessly blended its various connections with the metaphysical sources of Islam. Seen in its totality, Islamic scientific tradition is not only rooted in the metaphysical truths of Islam, it is also integrally linked to Islamic art, Arabic language and literature and all other expressions of human creativity that emerged within Islamic civilization. It is this integral aspect of the nexus between Islam and the science it inspired that was to be lost through the implantation of modern Western science in the Muslim world. But before modern science could come into existence, a large body of Islamic tradition had to be transmitted to Europe. This process of transmission, and the subsequent transformation of this material forms another link in the emergence of a new Islam and science discourse and is explored in chapter 6. The next chapter is, however, devoted to an examination of a question that has vexed several generations of historians: the withering of Islamic scientific tradition.

---

108. Burchardt (1999), p. 11.
109. Ibid.

CHAPTER FIVE

Withering of the Tradition

The withering of the Islamic scientific tradition presents many unresolved and enigmatic challenges to historians of science. Why did the Islamic scientific tradition suffer such a fatal collapse after centuries of sustained flowering? Why did it die? How and when? In a narrow sense, these questions belong to the discipline of history of science and not to the present work but because the relationship between Islam and science was fundamentally altered by the decline of the Islamic scientific tradition, we cannot ignore this phase of history without seriously compromising the integrity of our inquiry, especially its historical dynamics. Hence, it is imperative that we explore this question, at least to the extent necessary for understanding its impact on the relationship between Islam and science.

But even that small subset of the bigger question cannot be adequately answered without first understanding the nature of the question itself. To be sure, this question has been asked numerous times by historians of science and it is one question that is bound to arise in every discussion dealing with the Islamic scientific tradition. But there are many different perspectives in which this question can be and has been asked. One particularly telling formulation of the question of decline runs like this: Why did Muslim scientists not produce "the scientific revolution"? This is revealing because in the very formulation of the question, a benchmark has been used against which a prior tradition is being judged. But even in formulations where this benchmark is not so obvious, it always remains just below the surface. Perhaps it is not avoidable. Perhaps it is even natural. But it is also important to direct the inquiry without this ubiquitous criteria and formulate the question *within* its own parameters. Furthermore, this peculiar formulation (the "why-not question") has also been applied to other scientific traditions, such as the Chinese, and it would be beneficial to draw upon those resources to the extent possible and useful.[1] Asked in this

1. See Needham, Joseph (1954—), *Science and Civilization in China,* 7 vols. Cambridge University Press, Cambridge and its critique by Sivin, Nathan (1982), "Why the Scientific Revolution did not take place in China—or didn't it?", text of Edward H. Hume Lecture, presented at Yale University in 1982 and first published in *Chinese Science* (1982), vol. 5, pp. 45-66; reprinted in Mendelsohn, Everett (1984),

broader sense, the "why-not question" may provide certain common denominators which may be helpful to understand a related question: Why did the Scientific Revolution occur where it occurred and why did it take place at the time when it did? Such inquiries would, by necessity, judge all other scientific traditions in reference to the European Scientific Revolution; nevertheless, there are some gains to be made from these explorations.

In the case of the Islamic scientific tradition, such an inquiry seems unavoidable because the origins of modern science are integrally bound with the Islamic scientific tradition temporally as well as through the scientific data and theories which came from the Islamic scientific tradition to the European scientific enterprise during its formative period. However, for the purpose of this chapter, we will have to restrict the parameters of our inquiry in deference to the main subject of this work. A useful point of departure is the formulation of question.

Formulating the Question

There can be no two opinions about the fact that the Islamic scientific tradition withered and eventually died, at least in a practical sense, even though some remnants can still be found, especially of the Islamic medical tradition which is still a living tradition in some parts of the Muslim world, notably in the Indian subcontinent. Therefore, the first task that can establish our inquiry within a framework is to assign a date to the occurrence of the decline of the Islamic scientific tradition. But as soon as we attempt to do this, we run into difficulties that arise both from the conceptual framework of the question as well as from the paucity of resources.[2]

Transformation and Tradition in the Sciences, Cambridge University Press, Cambridge, pp. 531-54. All references are to this latter reprint.

2. In order to understand the magnitude of the untapped resources on Islam, one has only to look at the bio-bibliographies of Carl Brockelmann, *Geschichte der Arabischen Litteratur,* and Fuat Sezgin, *Geschichte des Arabischen Schrifttums* (see full citation in the bibliography), which, however, only give a partial listing of the library holdings. There exist numerous other libraries whose manuscript holdings have not even been catalogued. Then there are private libraries and the possibility of still finding those works which have been listed in classical catalogues such as the *Fihrist* of Ibn al-Nadīm and the *Kashf al-Ẓunūn* of Ḥājjī Khalīfa (*Kashf al-Ẓunūn 'an Asāmī'l-Kutub wa'l-Funūn* (1945-47), Istanbul). In addition, there is a need to study the works of individual scholars in their totality—a task that has been

Conceptually, what do we mean by the withering, decline or death of a tradition? Obviously, it could not have been a sudden event that happened on the fourth day of the fifth month of a particular year. Hence, we should be searching for a period of time, rather than a particular date. But even in this case, we must ask: Will this period of time, which we hope to find, be universally applicable to all branches of the Islamic scientific tradition *at once* and in *all* regions of the Muslim world? After all, we are dealing with a tradition that lasted longer than the Greek or the Latin medieval or, even the modern science, as George Sarton once remarked,[3] and that was spread over a very large geographical region. A third related question is: Did the tradition come to a cul-de-sac where it died a slow and agonizing death over a "period of time" or were there attempts to cure the malady? If yes, where were these attempts made, by whom, and did they produce any results?

In addition, we must also ask a few other related questions: Was the withering of the Islamic scientific tradition an isolated phenomenon or was it part of a general decline of the intellectual tradition to which it belonged? If it was part of a larger process of decline, then how did this larger process start and at what stage of its decay did it affect the scientific tradition? Where and when did it begin? Why? What were the social, political and economic circumstances that were responsible for this general intellectual decline, which must have spread to a large geographical region with tremendous force? Were there any early signs and corrective measures?

We cannot do justice to these questions without the discovery, annotation and publication of a large number of manuscripts pertaining to the social, economic and political situation of the period of decline. Nor

---

made somewhat easier by the appearance of specialized catalogues dealing with the works of a single scholar. For example, the bibliography of Ibn ʿArabī by O. Yaḥyā (1964), *Historie et classification de l'oeuvre d'Ibn ʿArabī*, Publications de l'Institute Français de Damas, Damascus; of al-Ashaʿrī by R. J. McCarthy (1953), "The Theology of al-Ashʿarī" in *Bibliographical Notes*, Beirut, pp. xvii-xxii; of al-Jāḥiẓ by Ch. Pellat (1953), *Le Milieu Baṣrien et la formation de Ǧaḥiẓ*, Paris; of Ibn Qutaiba by G. Lecomte (1965), *Ibn Qutaiba, l'homme, son oeuvres et ides*, Publications de l'Institute Français de Damas, and of Ibn ʿAqīl by George Makdisi (1963), "Essai bibliographique sur l'oeuvre d'Ibn Aqīl" in *Ibn ʿAqīl et la resurgence de l'Islam traditionaliste au XI siècle*, Publications de l'Institute Français de Damas, Damascus, pp. 509-21.

3. Sarton, George (1931-48), *Introduction to the History of Science*, 3 vols., published for the Carnegie Institute of Washington by The Williams & Wilking Company, Baltimore, vol. ii, part 1, p. 1.

can we begin to formulate any theory of decline in the absence of a rigorously documented history of the Islamic scientific tradition. But such studies have to wait for the cataloguing, documentation and eventual publication of source material upon which they must be based. In order to get a glimpse of the enormity of the task, let us mention just one work, *Kitāb al-Funūn* of Ibn ʿAqīl, which is preserved in the Bibliothèque Nationale in a manuscript (*Fonds arabe,* no. 787) of 267 folios, about 800 printed pages.[4] This work was written in approximately four months and according to a conservative estimate,[5] Ibn ʿAqīl is said to have written two hundred other works of the same type, amounting to one hundred and eighty thousand pages in which he gives lists of works of other scholars as well as details of scholarly discussions which took place in Baghdad in his own presence and in which he himself took part.[6] And yet, this is only *one* example of a single author from so many who remain unknown. Considering all of this, the following formulations have to remain tentative. With this caveat in place, let us first attempt to explore the question of dating the phenomenon of decline.

The When Question

The existing literature on dating the phenomenon is of little help. Various scholars mention different centuries—not years or decades—as the period of decline. At least one view even suggests that there was, in fact, no such thing as the decline of the Islamic scientific tradition because no such tradition ever existed. The proponents of this view argue that it was merely a question of "hosting" the Greek tradition in the Muslim world for three centuries during which it failed to take roots in the Islamic polity because of a fierce opposition from the religious scholars and then it was finally transferred to Europe—its rightful heir—where it prospered and bloomed into what we now know as the modern science. A slight variant of this extreme view is the "marginality thesis" which limits the practice of natural sciences in the Islamic civilization to a small group of scientists who had no emotional, spiritual and cultural ties with the main body of Islam and who

4. This example has been cited by George Makdisi (1981), "Hanbalite Islam" in *Studies on Islam,* translated and edited by Merlin L. Swartz, Oxford University Press, New York, p. 218.
5. Ibid.
6. Ibn ʿAqīl's *Kitāb al-Funūn* has been published as *The Notebooks of Ibn ʿAqīl: Kitāb al-Funūn,* Arabic text, edited with Introduction and Critical Notes by Makidisi, G. (1970-71), Recherches, *ILOB,* vols. 44-45, Beirut.

practiced their science in isolation from the rest of cultural and religious currents.[7] While Sabra has attempted to show "the falsity of the marginality thesis...by offering a description of an alternative picture—one which shows the connections with cultural factors and forces, thereby explaining (or proposing to explain) not only the external career of science and philosophy in Islam, but at least some of their inherent characteristics, possibilities and limitations",[8] his refutation remains limited to a "few general remarks". But a more serious problem with this refutation is its acceptance of the "two-track thesis" which is the cornerstone of the marginality thesis which he tries to refute. This "two-track thesis" views the Islamic scientific tradition in opposition to—or at least in competition with—what it calls the Islamic religious sciences. In the previous chapter, we have shown numerous internal links between all branches of knowledge in Islam as well as the process through which an integrated and holistic theory of knowledge had emerged from the twin sources of revelation and the tradition of the Prophet of Islam. True, formulations such as the "sciences of the ancients" (*ʿulūm al-awāʾl*) do occur in the body of Islamic texts and there are documented cases of a fierce and sustained attack against certain subjects such as astrology, but this diverse material has to be seen in its proper context and from within the matrix of the tradition that gave birth to these debates. Seen from within the perspective of the monocentric tradition of Islam, based as it is on the concept of Unity of God (*tawḥīd*), that body of literature which came into the Islamic intellectual tradition from non-Islamic sources could not have been received without critical appraisal and sorting. All living traditions do this. There is nothing special about the Islamic tradition in this respect. The problem arises when one construes the arrival of the new sciences into the framework of the existing tradition as if it was *en masse* arrival, like some kind of gatecrashing which met severe opposition from the upholders of traditional Islam. The historical facts tell a different story.

The translation movement was not a minor or isolated activity; rather, it was a massive process that stretched over three centuries and that was actively pursued by the most influential and wealthy members of the

7. This has been cogently formulated by A. I. Sabra in his previously cited paper, "The Appropriation and Subsequent Naturalization of Greek Science in Medieval Islam: A Preliminary Statement" first published in 1987 and reprinted in his previously cited collection of articles *Optics, Astronomy and Logic: Studies in Arabic Science and Philosophy* in 1994.

8. Sabra (1994), p. 230.

society. It was a movement that attracted a large number of people of diverse temperaments and racial and intellectual composition. It was also a process that brought material into the Islamic intellectual tradition from at least three major traditions. And, finally, it was a process that met with several levels of transformations—from instant linguistic to more fundamental and substantial transformation of the content and metaphysical underpinnings; this latter process was also not a one-act play but a long and constant process that was often repeated several times in the course of history by various scientists and scholars, as we have shown in the previous chapter. Hence to construe the Islam and science relationship as a case of Islamic orthodoxy versus a small group of scholars and scientists enamored by Greek science, as Goldziher did in his previously mentioned 1916 paper,[9] is to distort the historical data. Furthermore, as George Makdisi has shown, the phrase "Islamic orthodoxy" is a highly problematic term:

> The use of the term "orthodoxy" implies the possibility of distinguishing between what is true and what is false. This term implies the existence of an absolute norm as well as an authority which has the power to excommunicate those whose doctrines are found to be false or heretical. Such an authority exists in Christianity, in its councils and synods. It does not exist in Islam.[10]

Returning to the question of dating, it seems logical to ask the question in a much broader conceptual framework and in terms of setting the timeframe for decline in individual branches of science and in various regions of the Muslim world. This approach promises richer rewards because of the very nature of the Islamic scientific tradition and its relationship with the general intellectual makeup of the Islamic civilization. By applying a general conceptual framework to the question, we can reformulate the question of decline of the scientific tradition as a subset of a much broader decline and by careful investigations into each branch of natural science we can arrive at a more comprehensive understanding of the growth and decay within that branch. Furthermore, it is important to refrain from hasty conclusions. Such familiar categorizations as the "Golden Age of Islamic Science" are devoid of real content and have no

---

9. Goldziher (1916), *op. cit.*
10. Makdisi (1981), p. 251.

correspondence to the actual historical reality. These catch phrases merely reflect an inexactness that distorts historical situations and cultivates stereotypes. For instance, up until the first half of the twentieth century, the Western historians of Islamic intellectual tradition had "established" that the golden age of Islamic scientific tradition lies in the ninth-tenth centuries after which it was said to have declined. In his monumental work, *An Introduction to the History of Science,* George Sarton sets the eleventh century as the end of the vigor of the Islamic scientific tradition, with the twelfth century, and to a lesser extent the thirteenth century, as being the centuries of transition of the vigor to Europe.[11] But the discovery of new texts pushed this boundary further and eventually the very idea of a Golden Age was seriously challenged.[12]

Similarly, the oft-repeated notion of the "end of the thirteenth century" being the beginning of the decline of the Islamic science has also been shown to contradict historical data. In fact, it has been plausibly argued by many historians of science that the "Golden Age of Islamic Astronomy" lies between the middle of the thirteenth and the middle of the fourteenth centuries and not in the ninth-tenth centuries, as was previously assumed. For instance, in his 1994 work, *A History of Arabic Astronomy: Planetary Theories during the Golden Age of Islam,* Saliba has expressly stated that

> the subtitle of the book intentionally designates this period [of so-called decline] as the Golden Age of Islam. This may be disturbing to students of Islamic intellectual history who are used to dismissing the works produced during this period as insignificant. What the evidence presented here now suggests is that if we can find such original work in astronomical planetary theories, and such mathematical sophistication and maturity in the presentations of these results, shouldn't we consider other disciplines as well, and try to find out if such vigorous scientific activity can be substantiated in other fields? In fact, at various points in these articles [of the book] I suggest

---

11. Sarton (1931-48), *op. cit.*, vol. 2, part 1, pp. 1-2.
12. There exist many schemes connected with this idea of a Golden Age with different periods of Islamic history being mentioned. See, for example, such classifications in Hodgson, Marshall G. S. (1974), *The Venture of Islam,* 3 vols. University of Chicago Press, Chicago; Lapidus, Ira M. (1988), *A History of Islamic Societies,* Cambridge University Press, Cambridge; Lewis, Bernard (ed.,1976), *Islam and the Arab World,* Knopf, New York.

> that such research would promise to be extremely rewarding.[13]

Surely the most original works of the thirteenth and the fourteenth century astronomers and mathematicians such as Athīr al-Dīn al-Abharī (d. *ca.* 638/1240), Mu'ayyad al-Dīn al-ʿUrḍī (d. 665/1266), Naṣīr al-Dīn al-Ṭūsī (d. 673/1274), Quṭb al-Dīn al-Shirāzī (d. 711/1311) and Ibn al-Shāṭir (d. 777/1375), cannot be discounted as isolated incidents, especially when they are part of a well-established tradition and when they are related to each other in more than one way. Likewise, the work of scientists such as al-Jazārī (d. *ca.* 602/1205) in mechanics and Ibn al-Nafīs (607-687/1210-88) in medicine cannot be ignored. We even have a first hand account of a very telling nature that sheds light on the nature of sophistication of the Islamic astronomical tradition in the fifteenth century. This extraordinarily lucid account is preserved in a private letter written by Jamshīd Ghiyāth al-Dīn al-Kāshī (d. 833/1429),[14] the celebrated author of *Sullam al-Samā'*, to his father, shortly after his arrival in Samarqand around 1420. This letter, which has been collated, annotated from two manuscripts and published in the original Persian,[15] starts with a quotation from the Qur'ān,

> indicative of filial piety, and [with the] statement that the writer [that is Ghiyāth al-Dīn al-Kāshī] has been too busy with the observatory to do anything else. He then writes that the Sultan [meaning Ulugh Beg] is an extremely well-educated man, in the Qur'ān, in Arabic grammar, in logic, and in mathematical sciences. As an illustration of the latter he tells how the king [that is Ulugh Beg], while on horseback, once computed in his head a solar position correct to minutes of arc. Kāshī then goes on to describe how, upon his arrival at Samarqand, he was put through his paces by the sixty or seventy other mathematicians and astronomers in

13. Saliba (1994), p. 8.
14. He was one of the most important scientists working at the Samarqand Observatory. Two of his works, written towards the end of his stay in Samarqand, deal with the computation of 2π and the sine of 1^0, both fundamental qualities in mathematics, to nine significant sexagesimal fractional digits (equivalent to 16 decimal places). His *Khāqānī Zīj* was a revision of al-Ṭūsī's *Īlkhānī Zīj* and it contained geographical and trigonometric tables independent of those found in the Ulugh Beg's *Zīj*. On al-Kāshī, see sources cited by King (1999), p. 44, n. 92.
15. Ṭabāṭabā'ī, M. (1319 Hijrī Shamsī), *Nāmeh-i Pesar beh Pedar, Āmūzesh va Parvaresh*, vol. 10, no. 3, pp. 9-16, 57.

> attendance there. He gives as examples, four of the problems propounded to him. The first involved a method of determining the projections of 1022 fixed stars on the rete of an astrolabe one cubit in diameter. The second required the laying out of the hour lines on an oblique wall for the shadow cast by a certain gnomon. The third problem demanded the construction of a hole in a wall, of such a nature that it would admit the sun's light at, and only at, the time of evening prayer, the time to be that determined by the rule of Abū Ḥanīfa. Lastly, he was asked to find the radius, in degrees of arc on the earth's surface, of the true horizon of a man whose height is three and a half cubits. All these and others, says Kāshī, which had baffled the best minds of the entourage, he solved with ease, thus quickly gaining intellectual paramountcy among them.[16]

This letter written in the fifteenth century indicates the presence of "sixty or seventy" astronomers and mathematicians in Samarqand at the madrasa and observatory of Ulugh Beg (797-853/1394-1449), both still standing with their impressive tile designs, though both are now only sites to visit. Other accounts of this center are also extent: "At the time Ulugh Beg's observatory flourished it was carrying out the most advanced observations and analysis being done anywhere. In the 1420s and 1430s Samarqand was the astronomical and mathematical 'capital of the world'."[17]

Also relevant to the question of dating is the discovery of two scientific instruments of a kind previously unknown to the historians of science. These instruments, which were made available to David King in 1989 and 1995, have prompted him to make an interesting statement pertinent to our discussion:

> If one finds a microchip in a tomb in a pyramid then

16. This is a treatise on the sizes and distances of the heavenly bodies, finished on Ramaḍān 21, 809/March 1, 1407 in Kāshān, and preserved in many extant copies, including the one at the Shrine Library in Mashhed, Iran, also called *al-Risālat al-Kālīyya,* in a Tehran lithograph edition of 1306 AH; see the extensive references in al-Kāshī, Jamshīd Ghiyāth al-Dīn, *The Planetary Equatorium,* tr. and commentary by Kennedy, E.S. (1960), Princeton University Press, Princeton, pp. 251-55.
17. Krisciunas, Kevin (1993) quoted in Kennedy, E.S. "Ulugh Beg" in *Cambridge History of Iran,* Cambridge University Press, Cambridge, p. 11.

> either some modern put it there or we should revise our opinions of the technological achievements of the ancient Egyptians. If the chip is essentially made of stone and bears inscriptions in hieroglyphics, then either the person who put it there was an Egyptologist with a somewhat perverse sense of humour, or we historians really do have a problem.[18]

The two metal instruments are engraved with world-maps of a kind previously unknown to the history of cartography. The instruments are not dated but, according to King, their provenance is clearly Iran. Both are copies of earlier world-maps of the same kind. Both instruments have highly ingenious mathematical markings which allow one to simply read the direction and distance to Makkah. To situate these two instruments in their historical settings, King had to completely revise his previous estimation of medieval Islamic cartography.[19]

In December 1995, when King inspected the first of the two instruments with Assadullah Souren Melikian-Chirvani, "one of the world's leading authorities on Iranian metalwork, [the latter] was much taken by the elegance and precision of the engraving and suggested a dating of 1700±20 years".[20] The discovery of these world-maps is not simply a matter of two isolated instruments which have surfaced; rather, as King has observed, their study takes us into many other fields including the history of cartography, mathematical geography, applied mathematics, especially trigonometry as well as the technologies associated with Islamic crafts and metalwork.

This discovery and the extensive treatment it has received also points out another dimension of the dating question:

> For the reader unfamiliar with Islamic science in general it may be well to point out that Western historians have been pre-occupied with the scientific heritage that was transmitted to the West. We are dealing here with materials that were not transmitted to the West, indeed—at least for the time when the two world-maps were made—we are dealing with the time when European science and technology had surpassed Islamic science and technology. This actually happened

18. King, David (1999), *World-Maps for Finding the Direction and Distance to Mecca,* E. J. Brill and Al-Furqān, Leiden and London, p. xiii.
19. Ibid.
20. King (1999), p. xxi.

> no earlier than the 16th century, and we shall be dealing mainly with what are ostensibly two late-17th century objects. These could not have been devised by Muslims in the 17th century, and it still surprises me that the Ṣafavid instrument-makers were in a position to make them, and to make them so well as they did.[21]

These examples are enough to show that there is ample evidence to suggest that the question of dating the decline has not been resolved. Moreover, as the various dimensions of the question mentioned in the foregoing abundantly show, it is not a question of finding a year, decade or even a century; rather, it is a complex issue which requires careful studies in the history of various branches of natural sciences in various regions of the Muslim world and of the establishment of the definitive dates of substantial and significant discoveries *within* each discipline. Only after these developments have taken place in our existing reservoir of knowledge, will we be able to state with confidence that such and such branch of science came to a state of decline in such and such region of the Muslim world at such and such time.

Likewise, to understand both the "When" and the "Why" questions related to "the decline of Islamic science (a subject on which very little reliable material is available) it is also important to take into consideration the regional schools which dominated the scene from the eleventh or twelfth century onwards."[22] Moreover, we cannot establish any reliable date for the decline of the Islamic scientific tradition without knowing much more than we know at present about the scientific enterprise in the later Iranian, Indian and Ottoman empires.[23] Until we have the source material available, no definite verdict can be passed. So far, we only know of about 1,000 Muslim scientists who worked between the eighth and the eighteenth centuries; there are thousands more about whom we have no information or we merely know their names and titles of their works. There are over 200,000 manuscripts in Iran alone, of which about three-quarters are as yet uncatalogued.[24]

---

21. King (1999), p. xxiii.
22. King (1999), p. 7. In a related footnote (1:15), King gives some of the more important studies of regional schools of astronomy in the later period.
23. Some studies on the regional schools of astronomy in the later period are listed by King (1999), p. 9, n. 15.
24. For the estimate of the number of known scientists as well as for the manuscripts in Iran, see King (1999), p. 4, n. 4 and p. 5. "In 1994,

The Why Question

The decline of the Islamic scientific tradition has been variously ascribed to the opposition to the scientific enterprise by the "Islamic orthodoxy"; to a book that al-Ghazālī wrote against the philosophers; to the Mongol invasion of Baghdad in 1258; to the lack of institutional support for science; to the disappearance of patrons and even to some inherent flaw in Islam itself which allegedly makes it inimical to science. This bewildering array of "causes"—and the list is by no means complete—has been cited in respectable academic publications in authoritative manner with citations and references in support of various claims being made. Yet, our understanding of this complex question remains fragmented, incomplete and inconclusive. Once again we have a question where paucity of available material has permitted personal preferences, inclinations, even biases, to play a leading role in providing the answer.

Most of the existing material also examines this question with the overt or covert inclusion of a related question: Why did the Scientific Revolution not occur in Islam? This inclusion is more than the addition of a related issue; it transforms the very perspective from which the question of decline of the Islamic scientific tradition is studied because, it reads back into the history of the Islamic tradition, a vast corpus of western notions, such as progress, scientific development, and the nature of relationship between science and society. Added to the complexity of the situation are the contemporary realities of the Muslim societies, especially the status of their science. While there is no doubt that a conclusive or at least satisfying answer has to wait until we have enough source material—manuscripts, social, political and economic surveys, detailed information about the state of educational institutions and the like—to answer this complex question, the following section is devoted to a critical analysis of the prevailing answers and to providing a few pointers toward the directions from where real answers may come. The former is an essential task for clearing the

---

during my research on the first world-map," writes King, "the index to a 21 volume catalogue of over 8,000 manuscripts in the public library of Āyatallāh al-ʿUẓmā Marʿashī Najafī in Qum landed on my desk. There are over 400 titles relating to mathematics and astronomy, including some of the works hitherto thought to be lost." p. 4, n. 4. King's book is a mine of information about various aspects of the Islamic scientific tradition, especially of Islamic astronomical tradition and instruments. It cites 9,002 instruments, over 80 manuscripts and 38 pages of bibliography.

foreground that has been clouded by these oft-repeated variants of a few basic ideas; the latter may suggest new avenues of research.

Perspective from the History of Science

Devoting less than two pages to the question of the decline of Islamic science and basing his arguments on the utilitarianism, David Lindberg states that "during the thirteenth and fourteenth centuries, Islamic science went into decline; by the fifteenth century, little was left. How did this come about?" He repeats the obvious that "not enough research has been done to permit us to trace these developments with confidence" and then goes on to identify several "causal factors."[25] The first of these causal factors is none other than what Goldziher had "identified" in 1916: "conservative religious forces".[26] The second is the "debilitating warfare, economic failure, and the resulting loss of patronage" without which "the sciences were unable to sustain themselves" and the third is, once again, a rehashing of Goldziher's hypothesis:

> In assessing this collapse, we must remember that at an advanced level the foreign sciences had never found a stable institutional home in Islam, that they continued to be viewed with suspicion in conservative religious quarters, and that their utility (especially as advanced disciplines) may not have seemed overpowering. Fortunately, before the products of Islamic science could be lost, contact was made with Christendom, and the process of cultural transmission began anew.[27]

At least one aspect of this approach has been adequately discredited by J. L. Berggren in his study of mathematical sciences in Islam from a cultural perspective.[28] What Berggren has said about the transmission and transformation of mathematics can be justifiably expanded and applied to the growth of science in general: When we look at cultural factors in the growth of a scientific tradition, a problem arises because "there are cultural

---

25. Lindberg, David C. (1992), *The Beginnings of Western Science,* The University of Chicago Press, Chicago and London, p. 180.
26. Goldziher (1916), pp. 192-3.
27. Lindberg (1992), pp. 181-82.
28. Berggren, J. L. (1996), "Islamic Acquisition of the Foreign Sciences: A Cultural Perspective" in Ragep, Jamil and Ragep, Sally, *Tradition, Transmission, Transformation,* pp. 263-83. This paper is a revised version of an earlier version which appeared in *The American Journal of Islamic Social Sciences (AJISS),* vol. 9, 1992, no. 3, pp. 310-24.

factors that condition *our* thought, not the least of which is the fact that we do so as members of a civilization whose mathematical development depended importantly on the contributions of the medieval Islamic civilization."[29] In such studies, judgments passed on the scientific achievements of a previous civilization are invariably based on the developments in modern science, this creates many historiographic problems and entails the danger of unconsciously slipping from the historical fact into the Whiggish view of history, as if the final purpose of the cultivation of science in the other civilization was merely to create modern science. "This approach has had two quite opposite, but equally regrettable, results," says Berggren:

> The first is a treatment of medieval Islam as a civilization deserving of attention only for its role as a channel through which the great works of the Greeks were carried safely to the eager minds of the European Renaissance. The emphasis falls on the two great periods of translations, that into Arabic in the ninth century and that into Latin in the twelfth and thirteenth centuries, and the developments of the intervening centuries provide little more than a series of anecdotes about one curious result or another that was proved by an occasional great figure.
>
> The second result of this Whiggish attitude is a selective and tendentious reading of medieval Arabic texts to show how Islamic science prefigured that of modern times...it would be invidious to cite contemporary examples of either of these approaches—and of little interest to cite earlier examples—and I shall only observe that both of these results, which on the surface seem to place such different values on Islamic civilization, should concur in valuing it only insofar as it served ends not its own; this is hardly surprising, since both are motivated by a fundamental interest not in the past but in the present.[30]

One can cite text after text to show the truth of Berggren's statement. The track etched by Goldziher was so deep that most subsequent works have fallen in his steps.[31] His "Islamic Orthodoxy versus Foreign Sciences"

29. Berggren (1996), p. 266.
30. Berggren (1996), pp. 266-7.
31. If one were to compile a list of this repetitive literature, it would become abundantly clear that all of this literature is reducible to the attitudes

hypothesis, first published in German in 1916, was to remain paradigmatic for almost all subsequent studies until the close of the twentieth century. But, as recent scholarship has clearly established, this hypothesis is untenable for several reasons, not the least of which is the very foundation of the work which rests on undefined notions of Islamic "orthodoxy" and "old orthodoxy".[32]

In his perceptive critique of Goldziher's position, Dimitri Gutas states:

> "Old Orthodoxy" is obviously to be contrasted to some 'new' orthodoxy, and this is identified as Islam in Goldziher's day, which he mentions in his very last sentence: "Contemporary Islamic orthodoxy in its modern development offers no opposition to the ancient sciences, nor does it see an antithesis between itself and them." This statement points to the source of Goldziher's rationalist and even political bias. His intention clearly appears to be to portray as anti-rationalists those Muslims who opposed the ancient sciences, the representatives, that is, of what he calls "old orthodoxy".[33]

The "bias" that Gutas has mentioned is

> the anti-Ḥanbalī bias of Goldziher, which has misled not a few scholars writing after him...and [which] has been discussed, notably by George Makdisi. In the political realities of Goldziher's day, as Makdisi has

---

summarized in the foregoing paragraphs. For specific examples, one can see the treatment of the question of decline in such works as Grant, Edward (1966), *The Foundations of Modern Science in the Middle Ages*, Cambridge University Press, Cambridge, pp. 176-86 and Crombie, A. C. (1995), *The History of Science: From Augustine to Galileo*, Dover Publications, Mineola.

32. As mentioned in chapter 4, the most penetrating critique of Goldziher's thesis is to be found in Gutas, Dimitri (1998), *Greek Thought, Arabic Culture*. For a more charitably phrased criticism of Goldziher's essay, see Sabra, A. I. "The appropriation and subsequent naturalization of Greek science in medieval Islam," in Sabra (1994), *op. cit.*, especially pp. 230-2.
33. Gutas (1998), p. 167; Gutas cites the original German in a footnote (n. 24) and states: "I have adapted Swartz's translation: he reads 'Orthodox Islam' for 'Contemporary Islamic orthodoxy' and adds 'study of' before 'ancient sciences' (p. 209). The pleonastic 'neuzeitliche' in the first phrase is significant for the concern it shows on the part of Goldziher to differentiate the contemporary and modern orthodoxy from the 'old'".

> shown, the Wahhābīs of Sa'ūdī Arabia were the (neo-) Ḥanbalīs while their enemies, the Ottoman Turks, were the Ḥanafīs. Given this tendentiousness, the import of his study is the light it throws on Goldziher's ideology and the political climate of Europe in his time rather than on the attitude of a presumed "old Islamic orthodoxy" to the ancient sciences.[34]

The second, and more grave, weakness of Goldziher's position is his failure to explain and identify what he has called Islamic "orthodoxy"—a doctrinal pillar upon which rests his whole edifice.

> To begin with, as Goldziher himself doubtless knew, "orthodoxy" is not something in Sunnī Islam that is legislated by a centralized religious authority (as in the Orthodox and Catholic Christian Churches)—there are no such authorities; at most what one could claim is the prevalence of a certain religious approach at a specific time and in a specific locality. But even this has to be qualified by stating to *whom*, among the different strata of society, this approach belonged, because an assumption of "prevalence" as meaning "majority view" is not necessarily always true.[35]

Let us now move to the more general domain of sociological treatment of the "Why" question.

Perspectives from the Sociology of Science

A more recent and comprehensive study of the "Why" question from the perspective of the sociology of science identifies four strands in the sociology of science: the idea of the role of the scientist; the social norms of science; the common elements of the scientific communities and the comparative, historical and civilizational study of science.[36] These are then

---

34. Gutas (1998), p. 167; the work of George Makdisi to which the quoted statement refers is: "The Hanbali School and Sufism" in *Boletin de la Asociacion Española de Orientalistas*, Madrid, 1979, vol. 15, pp. 115-26, reprinted in Makdisi, George (1991), *Religion, Law and Learning in Classical Islam*, Variorum, no. v, both cited from Gutas.
35. Gutas (1998), pp. 168.
36. Huff, Toby E. (1993), *The Rise of Early Modern Science: Islam, China and the West*, University of Cambridge, Cambridge, especially chapters 2-6. See p. 15 where he identifies the first idea with the work of Joseph Ben-David (1971), *The Scientist's Role in Society*, Prentice-Hall, Englewood Cliffs, N.J.; the second with the extension of Max Weber's 1949 work,

applied to the phenomenon of the emergence of modern science as well as to the failure of the emergence of the Scientific Revolution in Islam and China. Though this approach inherently suffers from the above-mentioned Whiggish attitude—it examines all other traditions from the perspective of modern science and is primarily concerned with the non-emergence of the Scientific Revolution in Islam and China—there are some gains to be made by examining these arguments.

The inherent flaw of this approach, even within the narrow set of conditions that it imposes on the inquiry, is its backward reading of the conditions which produced the Scientific Revolution in Europe from which it draws the logical conclusion: only the presence of these conditions could have given birth to the Scientific Revolution and these conditions were not present in China or in the Muslim world, hence the Scientific Revolution did not take place in those civilizations. A corollary of this hypothesis is that the Scientific Revolution of the European type was the *only* possibility left to all other scientific traditions for their further development. Although the question "Why did the Scientific Revolution not take place in Islam" is not linked to our "Why" question, an examination of this question, even within the four parameters mentioned above, is not without some merit. The least one can gain from it is a clear understanding of the reasons for the inapplicability of these parameters to the question of decline. The following section will, therefore, examine these parameters within the context of Huff's study.

In a section called "Role-sets, institutions, and science", Huff has brought together a vast array of miscellaneous ideas and data, ranging from the examples of multiple roles of certain Muslim scientists, such as Ibn al-Shāṭir and Ibn Rushd, to the connections between institutions and ideas and the concept of law. "I must stress the fact that, from a sociological point of view, institutions are ideas," he states, "that is, social institutions are ideas that have been given paradigmatic expression so they are ready

---

The Methodology of the Social Sciences, Free Press, New York, by Robert K. Merton especially in his "classic dissertation" published in 1970 as *Science, Technology and Society in Seventeenth-Century England,* Harper and Row, New York; the third with the work of Thomas Kuhn (1962) resulting in the idea of *paradigms, cf.* his *The Structure of Scientific Revolutions,* University of Chicago Press, Chicago; and the fourth with a comprehensive approach which calls for going beyond Max Weber and takes into consideration such works as Joseph Needham's "monumental study" *Science and Civilization in China.*

and available to Everyman in a particular society and civilization."[37] Sifting through this narrative, one finds that ultimately, Huff's position can be summarized in the following manner:

> Modern scientific worldview rests on certain assumptions about the regularities and lawfulness of the natural world and the presumption that man is capable of grasping this underlying structure...modern science is [also] a metaphysical system which asserts that man, *unaided by spiritual agencies or divine guidance*, is single-handedly capable of understanding and grasping the laws that govern man and the universe...Accordingly, it is imperative that we view the problem that modern science arose in the West and not elsewhere as a set of intellectual struggles over these very issues. Above all they are intellectual struggles in the domain of moral decision. As the history of Western culture reminds us, people like Galileo had to join battle with established church authorities in order to warrant the claims they made for their scientific knowledge as well as their human capacity to achieve it. The rise of modern science was not just the triumph of technical reasoning but an intellectual struggle over the constitution of the legitimating directive structures of the West...In order to decipher the fate of Arabic-Islamic science, we must attend to precisely these dimensions of the philosophical, religious, and legal reconstructions of social roles in the medieval period.[38]

Having established these parameters, this study reverts to the same old pattern of positing various groups of a fully stratified society against other groups. Thus we have our familiar case of philosophers against the religious orthodoxy *a la* Goldziher who is expressly cited. But what is more, we have such diverse individual thinkers as al-Kindī, al-Fārābī, al-Rāzī, Ibn Sīnā, al-Baghdādī, al-Bīrūnī and Ibn Rushd, all lumped together in this

---

37. Huff (1993), p. 64.
38. Huff (1993), p. 65; emphasis added. The use of such terms as "Arabic science" or "Arabic-Islamic science" poses serious problems. To categorize the Islamic scientific tradition in terms of its linguistic features is to completely misconstrue the whole enterprise that arose within the mutually connected domains of Islamic intellectual tradition. This also acts as a limiting factor, depriving a substantial amount of literature written in Persian, Turkish, Urdu and other Islamic languages their inalienable right to be an integral part of the Islamic scientific tradition.

category of philosophers who are then equated with "free thinking" and classified as those who "suggested that revealed religion was little more than superstition."[39] Next, we have a case of mutakallimūn against the fuqahā' and the conclusion: "In general, the structure of thought and sentiment in medieval Islam was such that the pursuit of the rational or ancient sciences was widely considered to be a tainted enterprise. This has been shown most systematically in the work of Ignaz Goldziher."[40]

We have cited this work in detail because it is full of references to the extant literature on the subject and because it expresses, more forcefully than many other works, the embedded biases in the methodology applied to the question. But, like all other works of this type, it suffers from the same defects, the most glaring of which is an imposition of modern western concepts on a civilization whose goals and aims, aspirations and models vastly differed from the modern West. Needless to say that it also suffers from gross generalizations; no two men can be as different as al-Rāzī and al-Bīrūnī in their attitudes toward philosophical thought and religion, yet they are all lumped together. Then there is the ample use of selective citations of the primary sources with total disregard to their context. Even the normative practices of Islam in regard to its sacred texts are ridiculed: "Even today many Muslims claim that the Qur'an is a perfect, unchanged, and uncorrupted text because Muslims from the beginning committed every word to memory, and thus no forgery of this living text was possible because many Muslims had memorized it. No account was thus taken of the possibility of faulty memories."[41] Historically established facts are denied. Even well-established traditions and practices, such as the existence of guilds, which are still extant in the Muslim world, are denied on the authority of certain scholars whose work has been often cited totally out of

39. Huff (1993), p. 67.
40. Huff (1993), p. 68.
41. Huff (1993), p. 72. Let us note here that Muslims believe the Qur'ān to be a perfect, unchanged and uncorrupted text, *not* because there exists an uninterrupted tradition of its memorization in the Islamic polity and not because of the presence of thousands of men, women and children who have committed it to memory and who have existed in all societies all over the Muslim world throughout the Islamic history but *because* of their belief in the incorruptibility of the Qur'ān attested to by the Qur'ān on behalf of none other than the One who sent it; see Q. 15:9: *Indeed, We have sent down this Reminder and verily, We are its Guardian.*

context and without any regard to the main intent of their work.[42] The fundamental precepts of Islam, its integral unity and inner framework—all are distorted through a "scholarly apparatus" that takes the western norms as the universal criteria. For example, we are told that

> the separation of the ecclesiastical jurisdiction from the secular jurisdiction of emperors and kings was a necessary precondition for the development of the modern European conception of corporate autonomy and, quite possibly, for the development of science as an autonomous enterprise as well...Some students of the Islamic legal profession argue that even lawyers (qadis) [*sic*][43] were not an autonomous group until the introduction of the Western civil codes in the nineteenth and twentieth centuries...What was unique about the European guilds, including cities and universities, was the fact that they were able to make their own laws—that is, internally valid rules and ordinances—which the church and political authorities recognized as valid. The phrase 'city air makes one free' is the classic illustration of this level of social autonomy. Clearly this is not something that occurred in Islam.[44]

This is in total disregard of the fact that in Islam there is no ecclesiastic authority, no such thing as "give unto Caesar what belongs to Caesar and unto God what belongs to God", not even a lawgiver in any human terms; the legislative authority being the sole right of the Creator.[45]

---

42. See, for instance, the citation of Gabriel Baer's work as proof of the non-existence of guilds in the Middle East. The cited work is Baer, G., "Guilds in Middle Eastern History" in Cook, M.A. (ed.,1970), *Studies in the Economic History of the Middle East,* Oxford University Press, London. In spite of such "scholarly works" one only needs to walk in the bazārs of contemporary Fez, Damascus or Iṣfahān to find out that guilds continue to thrive even now.
43. A *qāḍī* is not a lawyer, but a judge.
44. Huff (1993), p. 81
45. It is important to point out that even before this faulty theoretical frame of inquiry is applied, the author has already concluded the results and passed the judgment. He opens the sixth chapter of the book, "Cultural climates and the ethos of science" with the following statement: "We turn now to a consideration of the larger context of Arabic-Islamic civilization and to the *structural impediments* that prevented the break-through to modern science there." (p. 202; emphasis added.) This chapter is perhaps the best example of the

A sociological perspective on the question of decline can render a more definitive summary of the causes, provided it is rooted in the Islamic tradition. However, the framework for Huff's inquiry is based on the synthetic model of Robert Merton who had made no use of any Islamic sources or concepts dealing with the theory of knowledge or social organization.[46] In any case, let us look at the answers provided by Huff's inquiry in some detail. He attributes the decline of the Islamic scientific tradition to the following "internal factors": The failure to develop universalism; the failure to develop autonomous corporate bodies; the persistence of particularism in institutions of higher learning; elitism versus communalism; disinterestedness and organized skepticism.[47] Let us briefly examine these five "internal factors", which are said to have been the reasons for the "failure of Arabic (*sic*) science to give birth to modern science".

The first thing to note is that these causes are premised on the idea that the *only* way of further development left for all non-European scientific traditions was to give birth to a scientific revolution of the kind that occurred in Europe in the seventeenth century. Secondly, they have been formulated as a result of a backward interpretation of the causes for the emergence of the scientific revolution in Europe. Even so, further examination of these causes is not entirely a futile exercise, because it will bring into sharp relief the inherent limitations of the models of some contemporary sociologists and prepare ground for examining the question from within the Islamic tradition.

> The norm of universalism, in Merton's sense, consists in the standardizing of "pre-established impersonal criteria" for judging individual achievements. I would suggest that this impersonalism is parasitic on the

---

author's biases against Islam and though he cannot completely overlook history ("As one surveys the domains of knowledge in which Islamic civilization left its imprint, above all in the natural sciences (astronomy, mathematics, medicine, pharmacology, optics, and so forth), the achievements of this civilization assume singular proportions."), his judgments are vindictively harsh: "If Spain had persisted as an Islamic land into the later centuries—say, until the time of Napoleon—it would have retained all the ideological, legal, and institutional defects of Islamic civilization." (p. 205).

46. Merton, Robert, K. (1973), "The Normative Structure of Science" in Storer, Norman (ed.) *The Sociology of Science: Theoretical and Empirical Investigations,* University of Chicago Press, Chicago.

47. Huff (1993), pp. 213-26.

> larger cultural norms that establish universalism (and personal standards of conduct) for classes of social actors. This is paradigmatically the domain of legal norms, and it is here that we see most dramatically the contrasting images of idealized conduct in the two civilizations. It is here that we see the greatest resistance to the creation of a rationally ordered, hierarchical set of universal legal norms, and therewith the failure to produce universal scientific norms for a scientific community...In the case of Arabic-Islamic culture, it proved virtually impossible to achieve this level of moral and ethical neutrality in the realm of thought. And this is so, above all, because of the particularistic nature of Islamic law itself. Consequently, all developments in Islamic law served to reinforce a great variety of particularisms, instead of creating a universal level of discourse.
>
> In addition to being a sacred law, Islamic law is a composite of four major schools of law: the Hanafi, Maliki, Shafa'i, and Hanbali, each named after its personal founder...In short, Islamic law in its spirit and its application institutionalized a thoroughgoing particularistic and personalistic approach to all human encounters. For that reason it proved impossible to establish a neutral zone of scientific inquiry in which a singular set of universal standards—free from the incursions of religious law—could apply without interference.[48]

Let us begin by noting that all of the "internal factors" summarized in the foregoing section suffer from a general problem: these "internal factors" were *already present* when the Islamic civilization gave birth to and nourished its scientific tradition. It is unreasonable think that the Islamic legal system, which came into existence in the seventh century before the emergence of the scientific tradition, would first allow a scientific tradition to flourish for six centuries and then become an impediment to the emergence of a "neutral zone of scientific inquiry in which a singular set of universal standards" could be applied.

Second, this construction, founded as it is on the basis of the now thoroughly discredited work of Joseph Schacht,[49] totally ignores centuries

48. Huff (1993), p. 213-4.
49. Schact, Joseph (1950), *The Origins of Muhammadan Jurisprudence*, Oxford University Press, Oxford; also (1964), *An Introduction to Islamic Law*, Oxford University Press, Oxford, both of which have been shown to

of Islamic reflection on what is undoubtedly the most important area of Islamic scholarship, the *fiqh*. It also ignores the normative practice which allows the right to define fundamental terms of a particular tradition to that tradition and its representatives. In any case, in the Islamic tradition, Islamic law (*ḥukm sharʿī*), is, by definition, a "communication from God, related to the acts of the subjects through a demand or option or declaration".[50] The word *sharīʿa* occurs in the Qurʾān (*We have set you on a Sharīʿa of command, so follow it.*),[51] where it clearly denotes the divine prerogative which has always been understood in the Islamic tradition as a universal principal of Islamic law. It should also be remembered that the first and the most important source of Islamic law is the Qurʾān which Muslims believe not to be a human construction.[52] They also interpret all other material sources in the light of the Qurʾān.[53] Therefore, to classify the Islamic law as being "composed of four major schools, each named after its personal founder", is to totally distort one of the fundamental tenants of Islam. The four *madhāhib*, named after the aforementioned four individuals, are not "schools of law" in the sense in which the above quoted passage construes them; rather the systematic expressions of legal nature which eventually found a more cohesive and organized form in the interpretive works of Abū Ḥanīfa (d. 150/767), Mālik b. Anas (d.179/795),

---

exhibit fundamental misinterpretations, lack of competence in reading Arabic texts and outright distortions by a number of Muslim scholars, notably by Azmi (1978), *Studies in Early Hadith Literature,op.cit.* The article under the entry "Sharīʿa" in *EI,* vol. ix, pp. 321-8, is also of little help because it is based on similar non-Islamic and Orientalist sources; it even states that "the word *Shāriʿ* (law-giver) refers characteristically to Muḥammad in his function as model and exemplar to the law." (p. 322) No Islamic source ever describes Muḥammad as law-giver; a right exclusively reserved for God.

50. Ṣadr al-Shaiʿa, ʿUbayd Allāh ibn Masʿūd, *al-Tawḍīḥ fī Ḥall Jawāmid al-Tanqīḥ,* vol. 1, p. 28, quoted in Nyazee, Imran Ahsan Khan (2000), *Islamic Jurisprudence,* Islamic Research Institute, Islamabad.
51. Q. 45:18.
52. In Islamic law, the term used for "source" is *dalīl* (pl. *adilla*), which means guide; the person leading a caravan is called *dalīl*.
53. In Islamic jurisprudence, the sources of Islamic law are the following: the Qurʾān, Sunna, *ijmāʿ* (consensus of legal opinion), *qiyās* (analogy), *istiḥsān* (juristic preference), *qawl al-ṣaḥābī* (the opinion of a Companion), *maṣlaḥa mursalah* (jurisprudential interest), *sadd al-dharīʿa* (blocking lawful means to an unlawful end), *istiṣḥāb al-ḥāl* (presumption of continuity of a rule), *ʿurf* (custom) and earlier scriptural laws. The Qurʾān and the Sunna are the two sources upon which there is a universal agreement among all the jurists.

al-Shāfiʿī (d. 204/820), and Aḥmad b. Ḥanbal (d. 241/855) preserved the fruit of reflection of numerous scholars of Islam. This literature, collectively called Islamic law, ultimately traces its origins to the universally applied twin sources of Islamic law—the Qur'ān and the Sunna of the Prophet of Islam. These schools emerged, in the general sweep of Islamic history, to fulfill the needs of the Muslim community in an era of rapid expansion when it faced new situations, both at practical as well as at the intellectual levels. None of the four "founders" named their "schools" on their own names; these are convenient interpretative categories that emerged in the body of Islamic literature after the death of the four towering personalities who held no ecclesiastic position whatsoever. Moreover—and this is important—these data of legal opinions are *not* different versions of a prototype which has been personalized by these individuals.

The second internal cause, "the failure of legally autonomous corporate bodies to emerge in Arabic-Islamic civilization (prior to the borrowing of Western civil codes in the nineteenth century)," we are told, "is likewise a product of the unique character of Islamic law".[54] Once again, we have a category based on ubiquitous Schacht, replete with Orientalists' biases toward Islam and its foundations. This total disregard to one of Islam's central tenets, which led Schacht to conclude that in Islam "the whole concept of an institution is missing",[55] also leads the sociological discourse to conclude that "any form of corporate autonomy—guild, city, university, scientific society, business, or professional corporation—was ruled out by the Islamic conception of sacred law",[56] defies all historical data which provides examples of thousands of texts granting specific rights to guilds, traders, specific groups of people, and cities. In fact, one of the first acts of the Prophet of Islam after his arrival in Madinah was the writing of a legal deed, which recognized the legal identity and rights and obligations of three distinct corporate communities then residing within the city of Madinah: the Jews, the Aws and the Khazraj. This document, known as *Ṣaḥīfat al-Madīnah*, which is extant,[57] and which has been commented upon

54. Huff (1993), p. 218.
55. Schacht (1964), p. 398.
56. Huff (1993), p. 220.
57. For English translation of the text of *Ṣaḥīfat al-Madīnah*, see Hamidullah, Muhammad (1408/1988), *The Prophet's Establishing a State and His Succession*, Pakistan Hijra Council, pp. 65-78. Also see Ibn Isḥāq's *Sīrat Rasūl Allāh*, tr. Guillame, A. (1995) as *The Life of Muhammad*, Oxford University Press, Oxford, pp. 231-5.

and cited in almost all classical sources of Islamic history, not only established the legal framework of interaction between Muslims and non-Muslims but also recognized the right of the people of Book to continue to administer their own affairs according to their own religious code—a right that was to be granted to all subsequent groups, including the Christians, in all parts of the Muslim world. Then we have the "Treaty of Jerusalem", signed by the second Caliph ʿUmar ibn al-Khaṭṭāb, and finally, we have the legal description of thousands of *waqf* institutions that came into existence in the Muslim world as distinct and autonomous bodies with well-established and well-recognized legal provisions. These *waqf* institutions continue to exist in the Muslim world.

The third internal cause, "the persistence of particularism in institutions of higher learning", makes mockery of the whole tradition of the Islamic education system—a tradition that continuously provided the intellectual base for the Islamic scientific tradition. This distinctly Islamic tradition of learning, which seeks to transform the learner in the process of learning, is, no doubt, built upon the system of receiving *ijāza*, permission, from a qualified individual who acts as a teacher as well as a companion on the Way. But even in the modern impersonalized educational system based on institutions, where knowledge is dispensed in classrooms in which the teacher is supposed to serve as a disembodied repository of knowledge, could not completely dispense with the fundamental importance of the teacher, even though it has seriously damaged the crucial emotional and spiritual aspects of the process of learning. However, the Islamic system, based on a direct teacher-learner relationship, which acted as one of the most important built-in mechanisms for the dissemination of scholarship in the vast regions of the Muslim world and which gave birth to the tradition of journeying for the sake of knowledge (*ṭalab al-ʿilm*), can in no way be said to have "run against the scientific ethos"; the two are totally unconnected. Likewise, the contention that the normative Islamic tradition was secretive and that "Arabic-Islamic culture was highly ambivalent about the question of disseminating knowledge",[58] are totally devoid of any solid proof. Such assertions are not only contrary to the well-established norms of the Muslim society; they also go against the injunctions found in the legal sources of Islamic tradition. The Islamic theory of knowledge is clearly established on the solid principle of making known to all whatever one knows; a principle enshrined in the Qurʾān as well as the traditions of the Prophet of Islam.

---

58. Huff (1993), p. 224.

One can hardly do more than to point to such sayings of the Prophet as "the one who hides knowledge, Allāh will seal his mouth with a leash of fire on the day of qiyāma."[59]

Finally, the last "internal cause" mentioned by Huff are the two elements of scientific ethos, "disinterestedness and organized skepticism" which

> seem to represent preeminently modern values and, for that reason, one might suppose that it would be futile as well as anachronistic to look for them in this early period. On the other hand, it would be equally unhistorical to imagine that any form of skeptical and disinterested inquiry had to wait for the age of reason of the seventeenth century to makes (*sic*) its appearance...In the West, however, this new metaphysics created an intellectual space within which men could entertain all sorts of questions about the constitution of the world. And this the medievals [i.e., medieval Europeans] did. They asked whether the world had a beginning or whether it had always been in existence; whether there were other worlds and, if so, would the same physical laws obtain in such worlds. In that domain concerning speculation about time, space, and motion, they asked questions about the existence of a vacuum and its properties. Could God cause the earth to be instantaneously accelerated in a straight line, and if he could, would this produce a vacuum?..these and dozens of more such questions were asked. It is difficult to imagine a more crowded agenda of disinterested inquiry, and organized skepticism among natural thinkers in any other period of time, or any other civilization.[60]

This is the most confusing of all the "internal causes" and the one that is supported by glaring historical inaccuracies. The questions cited above had remained the focus of uninterrupted attention in the Islamic scientific tradition for hundreds of years; we have summarized some aspects of these debates in the previous chapter. Yet, we are told that this was distinctly a European phenomenon!

But perhaps nothing reveals the inaptness of such sociological inquiries than their complete disregard for the distinctive realms of knowledge

59. "*Man katama ʿilman lijamhullāhu bi lijāmi min al-nār yawm al-qiyāma.*" Bukhārī/book 35/67.
60. Huff (1993), pp. 226-32.

maintained in the Islamic tradition of learning in which each realm was studied through a method proper to it with due care taken for the use of source material appropriate to that realm. Thus, while no one in the Islamic tradition would ever think of applying the Prophetic tradition regarding innovation in religion ("worst things are those that are novelties, every novelty is an innovation, every innovation is an error and every error leads to Hell-fire"), to the domain of scientific inquiry, Huff and others of his kind build their whole edifice on such improper applications of source material to draw conclusions which defy the most obvious historical data: "The role of scientist, above all as the innovator, was neither institutionally permissible nor culturally tolerated in Arabic-Islamic civilization during this period."[61] Such conclusions not only defy all rational and logical discourse, they totally ignore the established grounds for research that have been painstakingly enacted by successive generations. Above all, they seem to be naïve and totally innocent of a considerable body of literature within the field of history of science. To cite just one example, on this very question (of innovation), let us note what Sabra has to say:

> In Medieval Islam the concept of innovation in intellectual endeavor found expression in terms like *istikhrāj* or *istinbāṭ* (*discovery*), which denoted accomplishments that went beyond merely elucidating, emending, or completing an earlier contribution to knowledge; and a critical attitude clearly revealed itself in the not infrequent composition of *shukūk* (*aporia, dubitationes*), a form of argument in which difficulties or objections were raised against ancient authorities. Indeed, it would be impossible to explain the high quality of much of Islamic scientific writings without noting the intellectual ambition and independence of mind their authors often possessed to a remarkable degree.[62]

---

61. See Huff (1993), p. 234, where this Prophetic tradition is quoted in support of the lack of innovation in the Islamic scientific tradition and the conclusion is drawn about the status of scientists.
62. Sabra (1984), "The Andalusian Revolt against Ptolemaic Astronomy: Averroes and al-Biṭrūjī" first published in Mendelsohn, Everett, (ed., 1984), *Transformation and Tradition in the Sciences: Essays in Honor of I. Bernard Cohen,* Cambridge University Press, Cambridge and reprinted in his (1994), *Optics, Astronomy and Logic, op. cit.* p. 133. Although Huff quotes this paper elsewhere in his book, he makes no mention of it in his erroneous notion of innovation.

Indeed, the Islamic tradition has preserved for us concrete proof of the existence of considerable reflection on the very idea of innovation. For example, Ibn Ḥazm of Córdoba lists seven orders of innovation, headed by "that in which an author puts forward something that has not been previously discovered";[63] the same idea already occurs in the opening sentences of al-Khwārazmī's *Kitāb al-Jabr wa'l Muqābala*, which uses the same term, *istikhrāj*, for unprecedented discovery.[64]

In conclusion, these "internal factors" are merely a backward reading of the conditions which supposedly gave birth to the Scientific Revolution in Europe and their application to non-European scientific traditions. As we have seen, they suffer from certain internal defects such as the use of selective, and often irrelevant, material sources, and are flawed because of their basic premise that the European scientific revolution was the *only* valid path for progress in science—a Eurocentric premise that is not necessarily valid for other traditions.

Perspectives from Within

The perspective from within seeks to explore the causes of the decline of the Islamic scientific tradition by first defining what is meant by decline, then de-linking the "Why" question from the extraneous parameters—such as the assumption that the only possible way for the survival of the Islamic tradition was for it to have a scientific revolution of the kind that occurred in Europe in the seventeenth century—and, finally, by situating the question *within* the framework of Islamic civilization. These fundamental requisites stem from the simple fact that the Islamic scientific tradition was not an isolated phenomenon that evolved in the Muslim world as an alien entity; rather, it was integrally linked to the Islamic tradition of learning and therefore whatever befell it, could not have been an isolated event; the whole tradition must have been affected by it.

Defining the Question

In general, the Islamic scientific tradition can be shown to have remained committed to the basic premises of a hybrid of the Artistotelian-Ptolemaic tradition. This meant a reliance on the four causes and ten categories to explain generation, corruption and change of substances which were

---

63. See his *al-Taqrīb li-ḥadd al-mantiq...*, Iḥsān 'Abbās (ed., 1959), Dār al-Ḥayāh, Beirut, quoted by Sabra (1994), p. 145, n. 1.

64. Ibid.

perceived as composites of matter and form. These premises were, however, informed by the Neoplatonic doctrine of hypostases and emanation. But let us note that these premises were not simply taken over from the Greek tradition in a passive manner, as we have shown in the previous chapters; they were incorporated into the Islamic scientific tradition through a radical recasting that made them amenable to Islam's revealed data. This is also not to say that there existed, in the Islamic tradition, a monolithic process of recasting that was arbitrarily applied to the received material. In fact, there exists not one, but a wide range of dynamic processes of assimilation which emerged in the tradition in an organic manner, in a vast region and over many centuries. Thus, we have the Hellenized philosophers who dominated the scene for centuries but we also have individuals like Abū Bakr Zakariyyā al-Rāzī who stand like towering giants, both in the history of medicine and of natural philosophy and who defy all classification, even though al-Rāzī himself claims to be a follower of Plato. However, his atomistic natural philosophy clearly shows Indian and Harranian elements integrated into a framework of a non-Aristotelian, non-Neoplatonic kind. Al-Rāzī, who has been dubbed as a "freethinker" who dismissed prophecy,[65] and the one who "destroyed the ordered cosmos of Aristotle" is also the one who "reintroduced God in a reconstructed metaphysical system based on his five eternal principles—God being the eternal principle of creation, *al-Bāri'* (*Demiurgus*). Thus, despite his rebellious independence and freethinking, Rāzī transformed Aristotle's cosmology into a thoroughgoing *theistic* system".[66]

In the case of cosmology and related sciences, this meant a conception based on the notion of the spherical shape of the universe and of all bodies in its celestial part as well as the circular and uniform motion of all such bodies, the impossibility of a void, the incorruptibility of the heavens, and the impossibility for any celestial body to combine contrary motions or tendencies toward such motions. This was true in a general sense yet there exist, in the Islamic astronomical tradition, radical departures from this model as well as its consistent and sustained criticism such as the previously discussed works of Ibn al-Shāṭir and others whose modifications were based

65. For a recent study on this see Stroumsa, Sarah (1999), *Freethinkers of Medieval Islam*, E. J. Brill, Leiden.
66. See Haq, Nomanul S. (2002), "Moments in the Islamic Recasting of the Greek Legacy: Exploring the Question of Science and Theism" in Peters, Ted; Iqbal, Muzaffar; and Haq, Nomanul S. (eds., 2002), *God, Life and the Cosmos: Christian and Islamic Perspectives*, Ashgate, Aldershot.

on a genuine concern for the observational data.[67]

Seen from within, the question of decline cannot be associated with the failure of the Islamic tradition to completely break away from the Aristotelian-Ptolemaic models for two reasons: these models did work, rather successfully, for centuries, and there appears to have been a gradual and sustained effort to re-examine and reform these models. We also know from the evidence now fully documented that the mathematical techniques needed for a total break with the heliocentric system already existed in the Islamic astronomical tradition before the same was used by Copernicus.[68] However, from a purely sociological point of view, the question of decline neither rests on a radical break with the past models, nor on any methodological breakthroughs, nor on the development of particular instruments because all of these are aspects of a tradition that emerge as need arises. Rather, the question of decline is related to the disappearance of a vigorously pursued scientific research that could respond to a changed sociological order of the society in the post-fifteenth century Muslim world. In purely scientific terms, the question of decline cannot be merely a question of breaking away from a previous authority, for such breaks did occur, as has been shown in the case of Ibn al-Haytham's experimental theory, in the successive refinements of the theory of vision, and most conclusively, in al-Biṭrūjī's refutation of the Ptolemaic system.[69] In other words, the question of decline is not related to the absence of *a* specific paradigmatic shift that failed to occur, but to the failure to produce *series of successive* paradigmatic shifts which are, in turn, responsible for the appearance of "scientific revolutions".[70]

Let us cite one example. We now understand the nature of light on a basis of the quantum mechanical model in which light is treated as photons. This model—first developed by Planck, Einstein, and others during the first half of the twentieth century—produced a paradigmatic shift from the notion of light as being a transverse wave motion as defined by Young and Fresnel in the early nineteenth century, which in turn, had

---

67. In addition to numerous references cited in chapter 4, see the following important article on this aspect, Saliba, George (1994), "Theory and Observation in Islamic Astronomy: The Work of Ibn al-Shāṭir of Damascus" in his *A History of Arabic Astronomy, op. cit.*, pp. 233-41.
68. See chapter 4.
69. The case of Ibn al-Haytham has been discussed in Chapter 4; for the model of al-Bitrūjī, see Sabra (1984), *idem.*
70. Kuhn, Thomas S. (1962), *The Structure of Scientific Revolutions,* University of Chicago Press, Chicago, 3rd revised ed. p. 12.

replaced the Newtonian notion of light as being material corpuscles. But the Newtonian model had worked for some time, in some limited ways and cannot be regarded as primitive. Similarly, various models produced by the Islamic scientific tradition had worked for some time, in their own way. The problem is not the *nature* of these models, but the absence of new, more refined models. In purely practical and utilitarian terms, the fact that the Islamic medical tradition was able to generate a vast corpus of literature related to various diseases and their cures and was adequate to provide the scientific knowledge needed for the emergence of a sophisticated health-care system that reached the far corners of a vast empire and that provided for the needs of the community even in the distant villages, is in itself a proof of its sufficiency from a social point of view. Likewise, and from the same perspective, the sciences such as chemistry, mechanics, geology, zoology, mineralogy and others, did provide sufficient foundation for the needs of the society up to a certain point as is evident from the presence of a large infra-structure which regulated both the urban and rural life and which used sophisticated technologies to construct bridges, clocks, irrigation systems, and other structures.

Delimiting the Question

Just as the question of decline needs a "disengagement" with the European scientific revolution, likewise, it needs a "de-linking" with the nature and role of the madrasa in the Islamic polity. As mentioned in the previous section, the sociological treatment of the question of decline makes its case primarily on the argument that there was no institutional support for the scientific endeavor, an institutional support that it seeks to find in the madrasa system which is said to be the institution of higher education in the Islamic civilization and hence the natural home for sciences on the pattern of western universities. Because natural sciences were not taught in the madāris, so goes the reasoning, science, therefore, was never institutionalized in the Muslim world and hence it disappeared.[71]

This line of reasoning needs careful attention because it is related to some of the most fundamental aspects of Islamic institutions in general as well as to its peculiar mechanisms of transmission of knowledge. As such, this is not a peripheral matter that can be treated lightly. The first thing to note is that the madrasa made its earliest appearance in Islam *within* another institution of enduring strength—the mosque. The Prophet's

71. Huff (1993), especially chapter 6.

Mosque in Madinah was the first such mosque where the earliest organized teaching activity was initiated by the Prophet himself. Then there is the familiar case of the prisoners of war captured during the Battle of Badr,[72] the ransom for some of whom was to teach reading and writing skills to the children of Madinah.[73] In addition, we have the well-documented history of the *Aṣḥāb al-Ṣuffa,* the People of the Bench, whose dwelling place—a raised bench in the Mosque of the Prophet—was considered to be an extension of the Prophetic household.[74] These people had devoted themselves to living continuously in the Mosque and to a perpetual life of piety, devotion and learning; they are among some of the most important transmitters of the traditions of the Prophet. With the establishment of other mosques in Madinah and later in other parts of the Muslim world, these early teaching institutions spread, developed and changed. But in all cases, the mosque in Islam perpetually remained a place of worship as well as that of learning. And because the Qur'ān imparted such high station to the mosque as being a place exclusively reserved for God,[75] and because it lavished praise on those who make the mosque their place for remembrance of God,[76] any activity that was carried out within this consecrated enclosure achieved religious significance far exceeding that which could be granted to activities in any other edifice.

Thus even though various words, such as *majlis* (meeting) and *ḥalaqa* (study circles), have been used for these teaching institutions which existed within mosques, the applicability of such words as technical terms, denoting distinct types of institutions of learning in the early centuries of Islam remains unsubstantiated, a fact that has been acknowledged by George Makdisi: "The terminology used for the designation of institutions of learning is not always easy to pin down. This is especially true of the early centuries of Islam, when the terminology was fluid, during a stage of development when institutions were still in flux."[77] And yet, the irony of this debate is that Makdisi himself applies these terms to various institutions in order to differentiate them. The normative practice in Islam

---

72. This battle took place in the month of Ramaḍān in the second year of Hirah (624 CE).
73. See Ibn Sallām, *Amwāl,* p. 116, also Ibn Sa'd, *Ṭabāqāt,* vol. 2, p. 14, quoted by Azmi (1978), *op. cit.*, p. 4, n. 3.
74. See Watt, Montgomery, "Ahl al-Ṣuffa" in *EI*, vol. 1, p. 266.
75. Q. 72:18.
76. Q.7:29.
77. Makdisi (1981), p. 12.

allowed any pious individual or a group of individuals to establish a mosque by dedicating a piece of land and/or a building for that purpose. As opposed to what Makdisi states, we must assert that there is no such thing as a caliphal authorization required for this purpose; at least not in the normative practice and certainly not in the legal system of Islam. The example cited by him, without providing any historical or textual context, merely tells us about one specific case of a specific mosque and cannot be taken as a general rule. In any case, even from such examples, one cannot draw the conclusion that there existed two types of mosques in Islam: "the Congregational Mosque, jāmiʿ, and the ordinary, everyday, mosque, masjid", as Makdisi has done.[78] Likewise, the example following this case, where Ibn al-Jawzī is quoting al-Khatīb al-Baghdādī, who mentions that he loved to attend Friday prayers in six mosques of Baghdad, cannot be taken as a proof that there were only these six *jāmiʿs* in Baghdad in the fifth/eleven century out of three thousand mosques which existed in Baghdad at that time. It is absurd to assume that a population of more than a million could be accommodated in only six mosques for Friday prayers while the other 2,994 mosques remained "non-congregational type". Even in the fourth/tenth century, Baghdad's population had reached 1,120,000 inhabitants who lived in approximately 160,000 houses.[79]

This is a case of the application of a scholar's own pre-conceived ideas on the historical material. Makdisi's description and definition of two kinds of mosques in Islam is a gross misrepresentation of historical data of early Islam. He states: "The term *jamiʿ*(*sic*) is elliptical, being originally the adjective in the phrase *al-masjid al-jāmiʿ*". But then goes on to say that "the elliptical term, jamiʿ (*sic*), came to be used for the Friday Congregational Mosque in contradistinction to the term masjid, for the non-congregational mosque; the former being the mosque which had the chair of the preacher, designated as the khatib (*sic*), who delivered the Friday khutba (*sic.*)". In Islam, there is no such thing as an ordinary mosque and an extra-ordinary mosque. The term *al-jāmiʿ* simply means "the collector", and a mosque was generally given this epithet because people gather in it at a certain time. Traditionally, cities in Islam were always founded around the central

78. Makdisi (1981), pp. 13-14. Even in this example, the case was referred to the jurisconsults for their legal opinion.
79. Massignon (1982), *The Passion of al-Hallāj*, *op. cit.* vol. 1, pp. 238-9, based on the number of *hammāms*; this chapter in Massignon's work contains a fascinating discussion on Baghdad, its population, mosques, madāris, professions, social life and numerous other facets.

mosque and they spread in concentric circles so as to provide maximum access to the maximum number of people. However, this does not mean that other mosques in the city did not hold Friday congregational prayers. The case is self-evident. A city of half a million people would not rely on one mosque for its Friday congregational prayer. Furthermore, there are specific religious requirements for a mosque to be designated as a place for the Friday congregational prayer. One of these being that the Friday congregational prayer can only be held in the mosque where all five congregational prayers are held on a regular basis. Hence, technically, all such mosques where the five prescribed prayers are held on a regular basis, can hold Friday congregational prayer and the actual practice of not holding such prayers in mosques within close proximity to each other was purely for social reasons: a central mosque in a given locality where people could gather provided a convenient meeting place for social purposes; such gatherings also facilitated the task of those who sold fruits, vegetables and other goods by providing them a place where people from various nearby localities came at a specific time. Thus these Friday markets became a regular feature of the Muslim social life.

The madrasa, like the mosque, is simply a *waqf* (endowed) institution, which could be established by any Muslim and which operated under the Law of Waqf. While it is true that a great many madāris did not teach natural sciences, it is also true that many did. Ulugh Beg's madrasa in Samarqand was one such example where some of the most distinguished astronomers of Islam had gathered in the fifteenth century. But even the fact that a large number of madāris did not have natural sciences in their curriculum, does not automatically lead us to the conclusion that this is the reason for the decline of the Islamic scientific tradition. The more organized chain of madāris that came into existence in the fifth/eleventh century Baghdad came into existence in response to a very specific intellectual crisis in the Muslim world and they served the purpose for which they were established. There is no reason to assume that they should have been the institutions for the Islamic scientific tradition. This assumption is based on another assumption: that these madāris were the institutions of higher learning in Islam therefore; it is natural to assume that they should have been the institutions of scientific research as well. This is based on our familiar western institutions of higher learning, the universities. But why the same should be applied to the Islamic institutions of the fifth/eleventh century is not clear.

Another fact that needs to be stressed is that the Islamic scientific tradition came into existence and flourished for centuries in the presence of these madāris that did not teach natural sciences, so how can they be the cause of its demise? Does this not indicate that we should not be looking for the causes of decline in the direction of madāris?

Thus, we must define our question within its own boundaries and dissociate it from all extraneous considerations. Formulated in this way, the question of decline will become independent of comparisons of two different traditions, which are products of two different civilizations, and which existed in two different eras as well as it will be de-linked from the supposed internal constraints which were *always* present and which *did not* stop the Islamic scientific tradition to flourish for centuries. This formulation will then lead us to the causes for the decline of the Islamic scientific tradition. This delimited inquiry has more likelihood of directing us toward certain social, political and economic circumstances that contributed to the decline; rather than to some "inherent" flaws in Islam itself, which would, ironically, first allow the birth and nourishment of sciences for centuries and then strangle their further pursuit.

Having isolated the question itself, we must also re-examine its temporal and geographical domains. As already mentioned in the previous chapters, the Islamic scientific tradition was not a localized phenomenon that took place in Baghdad in a certain year. We are concerned here with a tradition that existed at two levels *simultaneously*. It existed *locally*, in various distinct regions of the traditional Muslim lands and it existed *globally* in the entire region that had come into the fold of Islam. These two aspects of the tradition were not mutually exclusive but they did exist as distinctly as any two entities can be said to exist. This is not easy to grasp because of the extensive movement of scholars and scientists from one region to another and also because of the common language of discourse. But at the same time, there exists at least one distinguishing aspect of the tradition that provides considerable and substantial evidence for the existence of local scientific traditions in various regions. This has been preserved for us in the distinct manner of Muslim names[80], which not only indicate the patrimony of the person but also give the place name, indicating the place of residence or birth, sometimes both. It is natural to assume that most scientists of Islam must have received a substantial portion of their science education in their early years. It is, therefore, safe to assume that there must have been a local system for providing such education. For instance,

80. See Fleisch, H., "Ism" in *EI*, vol. vi, pp. 181-2.

we are told by none other than Ibn Sīnā himself that he learned arithmetic from a vegetable seller until the famous mathematician Abū ʿAbd Allāh al-Nātilī came to Bukhāra, who was then invited to stay with his family in order for him to teach Ibn Sīnā *Almagest*, the *Elements* and logic.[81] Likewise, we know of thousands of other student-teacher relationships which existed in various regions of the Muslim world. Next, it is a self-evident premise that the Muslim scientists whose names and works we know today are only a fraction of the total number of scientists who existed in the Islamic civilization; not every researcher in medicine was an Ibn Sīnā and not every chemist was a Rāzī. Even with the contemporary electronic means of documentation, out of thousands of scientists who are currently working in various laboratories around the world, it is likely that a thousand years from now, we will only be able to trace the work of a small percentage.

Next, we know of very few Muslim scholars and scientists who did not travel from their place of birth to other cities. These itinerants were not only traveling in search of patrons, although that was one reason, they were also traveling to perfect their own learning and their character. Traveling for the sake of knowledge had an unusually high merit as the previously quoted tradition of the Prophet indicates. Thus there came into existence a pattern of advancement of knowledge, scientific or otherwise, that did not rest on stationary structures for its propagation but in the moving and living entities who traveled in search of knowledge and who disseminated knowledge from region to region. Given the nature and level of instrumentation in the scientific tradition, this movement was not problematic. The ubiquitous astrolabe could be taken anywhere as conveniently as one takes a palm-held computer these days and the same was true for surgical instruments of medical research. In the case of theoretical sciences, the movement was even easier. In addition, there existed a vast network of public libraries that could be consulted anywhere in the Muslim world. We are told of such marvelous libraries as the one in Shīrāz in the fourth/tenth century, which is said to contain 360 vaulted rooms with cabinets especially built for books, a library that was surrounded

81. The most authentic account of the life of Ibn Sīnā is the one written by himself and completed by his student ʿAbd al-Wāḥid Abū ʿUbayd al-Jūzjānī, who joined him in 403/1012 and remained with him until his death. It has been translated into English. See Gohlman, W. E. (1974), *The Life of Ibn Sina*, State University of New York Press, Albany.

by lakes and gardens.[82] And the historian Yāqūt tells us about the existence of ten libraries in the city of Merv in eastern Persia in the fourth/thirteenth century.[83] Madāris had attached libraries; in addition, there were thousands of private libraries. We have a first hand account of one such library:

> One day I asked him [that is, the Sulṭān of Bukhāra, Nūḥ ibn Manṣūr] to permit me to go into his library, to get to know it and to read its books. He gave me permission and I was admitted to a building which had many rooms; in each room there were chests of books piled one on top of the other. In one of the rooms were books on the Arabic language and poetry, in another, on jurisprudence and likewise in each room [were books on] a single science. So I looked through the catalogue of books by the ancients (*faṭāla't fihrist kutub al-awā'il*) and asked for whichever one I needed".[84]

Note that all of this was there *before* the advent of the printing press; this is indicative of the enormous amount of energy and resources that had gone into the making of the Islamic tradition of learning in which books played a major role; no wonder the arts related to the publication of books, such as book binding, glues used for the purpose, inks of various colors, the decorative arts related to the book covers—all have received tremendous attention in the Islamic tradition. Even the wonderful little ribbon that used to be inserted in the binding as a handy bookmark, was not neglected.[85]

---

82. Pedersen, Johannes (1984), *The Arabic Book,* tr. by Geoffrey French and ed. with an introduction by Robert Hillenbrand, Princeton University Press, Princeton, p. 31.
83. Yāqūt bin 'Abd Allāh, Shihāb al-Dīn, *Mu'ajam al-buldān,* (reprn. 1995), Dār Ṣādar, Beirut, vol. 5, p. 114.
84. Gohlman (1974), pp. 35-6.
85. Most Western scholars find fault with Muslims on their late acceptance of printing presses completely overlooking the fact that at least some of this reluctance was connected with aesthetics as well as economic considerations. A tradition that had flourished for centuries and that had been responsible for the emergence of several related trades and crafts, such as calligraphy, book binding, ink production and that was supporting longstanding family traditions devoted to the art of book publishing, could not be replaced overnight. No one ever mentions these reasons; only the reasons which have been given by *some* religious leaders are mentioned and in that case too, only partially, with emphasis placed on one statement: the Book of God could not be printed on a machine!

There exists enough historical data to construct the contours of the "local traditions" in al-Andalus and in some other regions of the Muslim world.[86] The Islamic scientific tradition was an aggregate of these local traditions but it was also a case of the sum being more than its constituting parts because what has survived is the distilled and the enduring aspect of a tradition that operated in miniscule scale, in the lives of thousands of men and women, in the silent corridors of observatories, libraries and laboratories. Thus, in order to understand the question of decline, we need to look at the fate of these local traditions, which worked through an observatory in one place and through a library attached to a madrasa in another place and through a living vegetable seller in yet another. There is, indeed, a case to be made for the existence of modern science being solidly rooted and grounded in its institutions: research laboratories and universities which share a certain kind of instruments and one language of discourse. But a much more interesting and fascinating case can be made for a tradition that was based on a combination of "mobile" and "grounded" institutions and that worked through the interaction of living human beings who could teach mathematics as well as sell vegetables. There is something fundamentally different between the two traditions—a difference that expresses itself in many realms but perhaps most eloquently in the epic traditions of the two civilizations. The one, "built upon Homer by Virgil, Dante, Milton and Goethe, is a sequential architectural structure," as Herbert Mason has stated in a penetrating analysis,

> [which] recalls and projects; [which] builds a world view on world views; [which] assumes the authority of survival...; while the other, which is sequential in an older, more primitive, unVirgilian way...is a religious epic [in which] civilization collapses...one immortalizes the structures of this world, the other knows immortality exists only in the world to come...".[87]

Naturally, it would be futile to look for a scientific research program sponsored and funded by the defense department of the state or by the multinational pharmaceutical companies; we are not only dealing with an entirely different era, but also with an entirely different milieu and

---

86. A useful resource on al-Andalus is Jayyusi, Salma Khadra (ed., 1994), *The Legacy of Muslim Spain*, 2 vols.; for natural sciences, see the section on "Science, Technology and Agriculture", vol. 2, pp. 937-1058.
87. Mason, Herbert (1986), *A Legend of Alexander and the Merchant and the Parrot,* University of Notre Dame Press, Notre Dame, pp. 1-2.

civilization. In the era under consideration, the state did not act as the most potent and tangible instrument that ordered the affairs of large sections of humanity. The science had also not yet become the instrument of the state in the sense in which it would, following Francis Bacon's prescription. What we are dealing with in our inquiry is, therefore, something far less structured than solidly grounded institutions with external funding and vast research programs geared toward certain definite goals, linked to economic, political or military needs.

For understanding the reasons for decline, we must make an attempt to look at the state of the Muslim world in minute details at the dawn of the fifteenth century—a time when Ibn al-Shāṭir was actively employed in the Jāmiʿ Mosque of Damascus and Ulugh Beg was conducting the most advanced astronomical observations and theoretical research. The following section is a small beginning toward this important task. It excludes al-Andalus for two reasons: Whatever happened to the tradition in al-Andalus did not have a far-reaching impact on the scientific tradition; although important for its own sake as well as for the sake of its relationship with the rest of the Islamic tradition, al-Andalus presents a special case of the Islamic tradition of learning because of its multi-faith, multi-racial composition. Thus, delimiting the question allows us to focus on the period of three hundred years, between the fifteenth and the seventeenth century. This is the most crucial period for understanding the causes of decline of the Islamic scientific tradition.

To begin with, let us note that, unlike the popular perception that constructs a tale based on supposed lack of material resources, geopolitical developments related to internal conflicts, and political instability, the actual historical data of this period does not support any of these "causes". On the contrary, this data shows that this period was actually a time of great prosperity and of three stable and internally cohesive empires: the Ottoman (689-1343/1290-1924), the Indian Timūrī Empire (933-1274/1526-1857),[88] and the Ṣafavī (907-1135/1501-1722). During the reign

88. Commonly known as the Mughal Empire, a term which is awkward and imprecise, if not altogether incorrect, as Marshall Hodgson has noted: 'The term is awkward when the history of India is considered in a wider Islamicate context. The Chaghatay Turks, under rulers of Timur's line, were not Mongols; in the Syr-Oxus basin they were sharply distinguished from the Mongols or Mughals of 'Mughalistân'... [thus] to use the term 'Mughal' rather than 'Timurî' is unsuitable...", Hodgson, Marshall G.S. (1974), *Venture of Islam,* 3 vols., The University of Chicago Press, Chicago and London, vol. 3, p. 62ff.

of Shāh 'Abbās, the splendor of Iṣfahān was literally raised to its true proverbial proportions, *Isfahān nisf jahān,* (Iṣfahān is half the world). The magnificent public parks, palaces, great open squares, impressive mosques, hospitals, schools, great irrigation works, and caravanserais sprang up everywhere in the empire, especially in Iṣfahān, which was like a huge garden and showpiece of the artistic flowering of the age. The colored tiles that decorated public buildings, great noble domes that still stand, the resplendent blue that recalls the splendor and majesty of Samarqand of the Timūrī era, and the gem-like style of miniature painting—all testify to a concentration of wealth that had been seldom achieved before. In addition to the royal wealth, there were great merchant families who maintained representatives in many European cities as well as in China who oversaw their far-flung trade. The Ottoman and the Timūrī Indians were not far behind in wealth and splendor.

The one and a half centuries between the sacking of Baghdad in 1258 and the dawn of the fifteenth was a period which not only continued to produce first-rate astronomical texts,[89] but it was also a period that made these empires possible. It was during this century and a half that the traditional Muslim lands recovered from the large-scale destruction that followed in the wake of the Mongol conquest. During this period, the three major Mongol realms, which had emerged with distinct spheres of influence, were all absorbed in the religious and cultural milieu of the lands they had conquered. The descendants of Hülegü, called the Īl-khāns, who ruled over much of the Iranian mountains and plateaus and in the Tigris-Euphrates valley, with their capital at Marāgha, gradually accepted Islam, just like their cousins, the Chughtā'ī Mongols, who controlled the Syr and the Oxus basins, the Yedisu steppes and the region surrounding Kabul and eventually the whole of Punjab in the Indian subcontinent. The third Mongol realm of influence, the Golden Horde, which was centered in the Volga basin but extended its sway much further westward, was the first to accept Islam because the population of this region was already Muslim with strong commercial ties with Khwārazm by the Aral Sea. This Muslim population, mostly Turkic Bulghārs, was able to have a Muslim ruler as early as 1290. But even in the Īl-Khanate, as early as during Hülegü's own

---

89. This astronomical tradition was based in the land of the later Timūrī rulers of Transoxania and Iran, such as Timūr (772-808/1370-1405), Khalīl (r. 808-812/1405-09), Shāh Rūkh (808-851/1405-47), and Ulugh Beg (796-853/1394-1449).

life, the old administrative structure had been restored. This was administered by experienced Persian administrators.[90] Thus, first the Golden Horde and then the Īl-Khānī state turned to Islam and when Ghazan took the throne in 1295 and became Muslim, most of the other Mongol nobles followed his example. Their new capital, Tabrīz, became the intellectual centre for the whole empire and when Ghazan's wise vizier, the physician and scholar, Rashīd al-Dīn Faḍl Allāh (d. 718/1318), built a town for scholars near the capital Tabrīz, it quickly became the most desired destination for scholars and scientists from as far away as Egypt, India and China. The eventual disintegration of the Mongol power resulted in the emergence of smaller independent dynasties.

During the time of the Mamlūks of Egypt, who had defeated the Mongols at ʿAyn Jālūt, south of Damascus in 1260, Cairo had become the heart of the Islamic intellectual tradition in that part of the world and it retained its supremacy until the Mamlūks were over-whelmed by the Ottomans in 923/1517. The Delhi Sultanate, the counterpart of the Mamlūks in the Indian subcontinent, also attracted many Muslim scholars fleeing Mongol invasion. Established in the Punjab in the Ganges valley at the start of the thirteenth century, the Delhi Sultanate had continuously expanded under a series of brilliant rulers, such as ʿAlā al-Dīn Khiljī (r. 696-716/1296-1316) and Muḥammad Tughlaq (727-753/1325-51), until Timūr sacked Delhi in 801/1398. These Sultanates were absorbed in the Indian Timūrī empire in the following century. Thus, by the dawn of the fifteenth century, the Ottoman, the Indian Timūrī, and the Ṣafavī empires had emerged through a historical realignment of the Muslim world following the sacking of Baghdad.

General Features of the New Empires

Built on the ruins of the ʿAbbāsid Empire, through a century and a half of conflicts, confrontations, and realignments, these three empires inherited the Islamic scientific tradition in a broken form in the sense that major centers of learning, libraries, and patrons had been uprooted. The large-scale devastation that accompanied the Mongol invasion and the subsequent strife had a deep impact on the social fabric of the society. It

90. In 659/1259, Hülegü had appointed a Muslim scholar, ʿAṭāʾ Malik Juvaynī, from the old administrative family of Khurāsān, as the head of fiscal divān; ʿAṭāʾ Malik's brother rose to become the chief minister of the whole Īl-Khānate in 1262.

created new ruling elites, new centers of power, and new interests. Baghdad was no longer the social, intellectual and economic capital of the Muslim world; instead, there arose other cities to claim the honor: Tabrīz, Delhi, Iṣfahān (after 1599), and Istanbul (after 1453).[91] For the purpose of our study, the following new factors are important.

1. After the Mongol invasion, when the dust finally settled and the new empires emerged as stable entities, the Islamic scientific tradition did not find a new home (or homes) where it could re-establish itself in a manner that would not create a break with what had gone before. This is because most of the old centers of scientific research had been destroyed, patterns of social life were disrupted and numerous libraries had been plundered.
2. A new political situation arose: For the first time in Islamic history, there appeared three powerful empires with adjacent borders, two of which fought one another for supremacy and control of the areas that were previously held under one empire. This was not the same as the small-scale disputes at the borders of the ʿAbbāsid Empire or even claims to authority within the empire. The Ottomans, often together with Ozbegs, opposed the Ṣafavids on religious, economic, political and territorial grounds, and though the Indian Timūrīs remained out of this long-term conflict, they were often courted by the other two for help.
3. The Ṣafavids not only chose the Shīʿī interpretation of Islam as their official creed, they also established their institutions, legal system, and social organization on this basis. This created parallel, and often conflicting, claims to loyalty and patronage. This division had a deep impact on the pace of scientific research.
4. In all three empires, there arose 'model emperors', who ruled for long periods, greatly expanded their empires, laid the foundation of stable bureaucracies and administrative structures and vastly

91. Known to the Slavs as Tsargrad, the Emperor's city, to the Greeks and Romans as Byzantium and Constantinopolis, the city of Constantine, who founded his new imperial capital there in 330 CE, and to the Muslims as Qustantinniyya (from Constantinople), Istanbul, the modern name, was not legalized as such until 1930.

increased the revenues of the state through efficient use of resources, but placed little priority in science.[92]

5. Out of the three empires, the Indian Timūrī empire had a uniquely new historical situation: a large non-Muslim population, which outnumbered the Muslims. This gave birth to a tension in the social fabric of the society and often rulers were pre-occupied with wars, rebellions and conflicts.
6. When new centers of intellectual activity emerged in any stable form, the interest of rulers and patrons had changed from patronizing science to building impressive monuments of architectural splendor and to supporting other forms of artistic expression; all civilizations take this route when large amounts of wealth are accumulated in the hands of few institutions or individuals. Thus in all three empires, the greatest amount of energy and resources were devoted to architectural and artistic expressions, rather than natural sciences. Hence we see the emergence of monumental buildings, great poetry and paintings in all three empires.[93]
7. In the Ṣafavī Empire, the Islamic philosophical tradition re-established itself through a new synthesis that combined elements of falsafa and Ishrāqī mysticism that recast the vision of Philosophia in Ṣūfī terms.[94] But this renewed interest in philosophy was not accompanied by an interest in natural sciences to any significant degree.
8. Although both the Indian Timūrī and the Ottoman empires were Sunnī, none could claim the universalistic nature of the caliphal authority that was held by the ʿAbbāsids.
9. Because there existed, more or less, permanent borders between the three empires, the free flow of people, goods and ideas was not like it used to be. Of the three empires, the Ṣafavī held the greatest share of the traditional centers of Islamic scholarship, followed by the Ottomans in their Arab domains. But these old centers of intellectual

---

92. Suleymān (1520-66), Ṭahmasp I (1524-76) of the Ottoman empire; Akbar (1556-1605), Jahāngīr (1605-27), Shāh Jahān (1627-58), and Aurangzeb (1658-1707) in India; and Shāh ʿAbbās I (1587-1629) and Ḥusayn (1694-1722) in Iran.
93. Painters such as Bihzād (*ca.* 834-942/1450-1536), buildings such as the Tāj Mahal and the great squares of Iṣfahān with their monumental buildings displaying intricate tile work.
94. Mīr Damād (d.1065/1631) and Mulla Ṣadrā (979 or 980-1050/1571-1640) are the two most important representatives of this school.

scholarship were not revitalized in the new empires, which had their own intellectual centers.

10. The position of Arabic, as the universal language of discourse, did not remain the same in the new realignment. Although it was still accepted as the language of scholarship in large areas, Persian emerged as an important second language; Turkish and various Indo-Muslim languages also drew attention. This produced a restrictive impact of its own. Great scholars came to India from the other empires but the Indian scholars rarely left India, except when they went to settle in Ḥijāz, which became the conduit for the spread of their works and ideas. Consequently, books written in India reached the Ottomans via Ḥijāz but the books written by the Ottomans were practically unknown in India.

What does all of this suggest? Certainly not a case of a civilization having come to its lowest ebb. The least one can gather from this data is that there existed, during these three centuries, a set of unique circumstances common to all three empires. The most striking facets of this set is neither the paucity of wealth, nor weakening of intellectual vigor, but an unusual interest in artistic expression: great mosques decorated with wonderful calligraphic designs and artwork, lavish palaces, vast public squares suitable for polo and troop movement, miniature paintings which show rich details and poetry. All of these features are common in all three empires and many great architectural works still stand to testify to an age rich in expression of beauty, splendor and wealth.

Writing toward the end of the fourteenth century, Ibn Khaldūn (733-809/1332-1406) was conscious that a new level of civilization might be on the horizon in the Muslim world—a level of civilization which only comes when sedentary culture has reached a certain degree of stability and prosperity. The new political and social circumstances of the three empires show exactly that kind of flowering. "It is true," wrote Ibn Khaldūn, "that the old cities, such as Baghdad, al-Baṣrah, and al-Kūfah, which were the [original] centers of scholarship, are in ruin. However, Allāh has replaced them with even greater cities. Science has been transplanted in the non-Arab ʿIrāq of Khurāsān, to Transoxania in the East, in Cairo and the adjacent regions in the West."[95]

95. Ibn Khaldūn, *Muqadamah*, tr. by Rosenthal, Franz (1967), Princeton University Press, Princeton, p. 341.

Compared to the austerity of the Prophetic times, these empires seem to be driven by an internal desire to express and display the accumulated cultural riches of a civilization that had turned its focus and attention to a this worldliness with a concentration never before seen in the Islamic civilization, not even in the fabulous times of Hārūn al-Rashīd. The high culture of the Ottomans, Ṣafavids, and the Timūrī Indians displays such a florescence of arts that no other time in the Muslim history is comparable to it. The cultivation of Turkish language by the Ottomans, that of Persian by the Ṣafavids and the Timūrī Indians produced rich poetry and imaginative prose works which speak of this worldly splendor in an exalting language that is almost alien to the Islamic emphasis on moderation. And though individuals like Kātib Çelebī (called Ḥājjī Khalīfah, 1015-1068/1606-57), an encyclopaedist who was at home with a broad range of Arabic, Persian and Ottoman texts as well as aware of new developments in geography and astronomy in the West, did make their appearance, they were rare in a culture of pleasure, almost bordering on decadence.

It is in this pleasure-seeking high culture of this age, that the real causes of decline are to be found. The courts at Delhi, Istanbul and Iṣfahān, now captive of their extravagant routines and almost alienated from the realities of the vast empires they controlled, the courtiers and the elite families who contributed so much to the decadence and absolutism of the courts and the concentration of wealth in fewer and fewer hands are the indicators of a civilization at the brink of disastrous ruin. The Islamic scientific tradition became a caricature of its past glory in these three centuries and those who had cultivated it, were replaced by those who preferred to seek pleasure in the finite realm of the senses, rather than the splendors of the spirit.

When this interlude of three centuries came to its close, and the high culture and the decadent practices felt threatened by the approach of foreign armies at their doorsteps, it was already too late. The West had achieved a decisive edge over the Muslim world through remarkable advancements in science which were quickly translated into technologies which produced superior weapons, enhanced industrial production and, most of all, a vast reservoir of energy which sought to expand their frontiers, both physically as well as intellectually. The future historians of Islam must divert their attention to these three centuries in order to understand the causes of decline and the withering of the Islamic scientific tradition. Those who have sought "internal causes" in the very foundations of Islam have misled these efforts for too long and with disastrous results. It is time for a total new orientation and a new search.

One should also not forget the impact of the timing of certain inventions in Europe. One of the most important and fateful aspects of the new developments was a rapid shrinking of the globe. Science produced skills, tools and techniques. Technology produced weapons and means of transportation; all synchronized with a time when wars could still be fought in distant lands and victories could still be held for long time without endangering global repercussions. It was a time when victories and defeats were still isolated and localized affairs. It was also a time when the Muslim world was so divided that one part of it could not come to rescue the other part. This global dimension of the impact of modern science, this rapid shrinking of the planet, passed through that phase and then came to a new phase in the post World War II era. The timing of events was a major factor in deciding the fate of the Islamic scientific tradition and thus of the relationship between Islam and science.

It is also important to mention that before it faded from the Muslim lands, a large part of the Islamic scientific tradition had been transmitted to Europe. This transmission and the subsequent transformation of the Islamic scientific tradition in Europe is an integral episode in the emergence of a new Islam and science discourse and is the focus of the next chapter.

CHAPTER SIX

Transmission and Transformation

The relationship between the Islamic scientific tradition and modern western science forms a crucial link in the exploration of the contemporary Islam and science discourse. Fortunately, the transmission of the Islamic scientific tradition to the West is not as obscure a subject as the transmission of the pre-Islamic traditions to the Islamic tradition. Likewise, the paths leading to the appropriation and transformation of the material received by the West are also more amenable to scrutiny, though many texts have not been studied yet and many questions remain unresolved. However, inquiry into the process of transmission and transformation of the Islamic scientific tradition in Europe can only yield fruitful results if it is studied within the larger historical context in which it took place. In order to understand this larger context, we will start with a brief description of the European scientific tradition in the Middle Ages and then examine the process of transmission of the Islamic scientific tradition and finally explore the ultimate fate of the received material.[1]

The European scientific tradition of the Middle Ages was primarily situated in the network of Christian monasteries, spread throughout Europe. These monasteries had started as early as the fourth century. By the time St. Benedict (d. *ca.* 550) established his monastery at Monte Cassino, south of Rome, this way of life had matured to the extent that rules were formulated to govern the lives of those who chose to live in these monasteries. The Benedictine Rules were widely adopted within Western monasticism. The monastic life was primarily devoted to contemplation and worship but there are enough examples to dispel the generally held view that natural philosophy (as science was then called) was totally absent from the monastic tradition. The well-known examples of Isidore of Seville (*ca.* 560-636) and the Venerable Bede (d. 735) testify to the presence of a tradition that was not wholly devoid of interest in nature and its study.[2] His

1. This section is partially based on my paper "Islam and Science: Formulating the Questions", *Islamic Studies,* vol. 39 (2000), no. 4, pp. 517-70.
2. For further details on Isidore, see Stahl, William H. (1962), *Roman Science: Origins, Development and Influence to the Later Middle Ages*, University of Madison Press, Madison, pp. 213-23.

works range from biblical studies to theology, literature and history. Two of his works, *Nature of Things* and *Etymologies,* are monumental treatises of the Middle Ages that offer encyclopedic accounts of the whole range of classical learning. Bede, who entered the monastery of Wearmouth in Northumbria in northeastern England near modern Newcastle at the age of seven to spend the remainder of his life there, has also left his mark on a whole range of subjects taught in the eighth century. Among his works are *Ecclesiastical History of the English People* and *On the Nature of Things* as well as two textbooks on timekeeping and the calendar.[3]

The focus of monastic tradition was ecclesiastical but this does not mean that medicine, logic and other Greek and Roman sciences were altogether absent from the communal life. We know for sure that Boethius (480-524) translated parts of Aristotle's logic and composed handbooks on the liberal arts. Gregory (*ca.* 550-604), who became Pope in 590, left behind a respectable body of sermons, lectures, dialogues and biblical commentaries. Toward the end of the eighth century, there was another burst of energy that revived the tradition of learning, this time under the patronage of Charlemagne who inherited a Frankish kingdom in 768 that contained parts of modern Germany and most of France, Belgium and Holland. By the time of his death in 814, he had enlarged his kingdom to include more German territory, Switzerland, part of Austria and more than half of Italy. His empire, known as the Carolingian Empire, was the first centralized empire to appear in Europe since the Roman Empire. Charlemagne instituted a state-wise educational enterprise under Alcuin (*ca.* 730-804), headmaster of the cathedral school at York in northern England, who was especially brought to the court of Charlemagne to direct the new educational enterprise.[4]

It was this educational system established by Alcuin that was to initiate the transmission of Greek learning (through the Arabic route) into Western Europe. An imperial edict mandated the establishment of cathedral and monastery schools. This laid a foundation on which was built the grand edifice of learning in the later centuries.[5] Alcuin attracted a group of scholars who were interested in serious theological reflections and it was this system of schools that produced men like John Scotus Eriugena (*fl.*

3. Stahl (1962), pp. 223-32.
4. For these details, see Lindberg, David (1992), *The Beginnings of Western Science,* University of Chicago Press, Chicago, p. 185.
5. Ibid., and *passim.*

850-75)—an Irishman attached to the court of Charlemagne's grandson, Charles the Bald. Scotus was the most influential and ablest scholar of the ninth century Latin West with an excellent command of Greek, learned in the monastic schools. He was to translate a number of important Greek works into Latin, in addition he wrote several original works in Latin.

A century later, another beneficiary of Carolingian educational system, Gerbert (*ca.* 945-1003), was to become one of the first intellectual links between Islam and Latin Christendom. Gerbert arose from his humble beginnings to the high office of Pope through a series of dramatic events that exhibit his sharp intelligence as well as scholarship. His election as Pope Sylvester II in 999 provided him an institutional structure for the pursuit of his scholarly ambitions. But already in 967 when Gerbert crossed the Pyrenees into the northeastern corner of Spain to study mathematical sciences with Atto, the bishop of Vich, he had forged a link with the Muslim Spain which was to serve as a decisive point of contact between the Islamic scientific tradition and the Latin West.

Gerbert's letters are our source for ascertaining the extent of his interest in Islamic sciences at this early stage of intellectual interaction between Muslim Spain and Europe. *The Letters of Gerbert with His Papal Privileges as Sylvester II*,[6] provide ample testimony to Gerbert's wide-ranging interests as well as influence. In these letters, one finds Gerbert asking for specific manuscripts and books. In one letter, he asks for a book on numbers by the Arabic speaking Christian Joseph the Spaniard, in another, he asks for a book on astronomy which had been translated from Arabic by Luptins. He instructs friends on mathematical and geometrical problems and imparts instructions on the construction of astronomical models as well as on the use of the abacus for multiplication and division, using Arabic numerals.

Transmission

After the Viking and Magyar invasions of the ninth and tenth centuries which devastated much of Europe, there came a period of strong monarchies, political stability and economic growth. The reasons for these developments are complex and beyond the scope of the present study. Suffice it to say that after being a receiver of foreign armies for centuries, Western Europe reversed the pattern and became an aggressor, first in Spain and then in the Holy Land where it dispatched armies of crusaders.

6. Lattin, Harriet Pratt (ed. and tr., 1961), *The Letters of Gilbert with His Papal Privileges as Sylvester II,* Columbia University Press, New York.

Amidst rapid urbanization, a new educational system emerged. Stable, prosperous monarchies, continuous economic growth and increased agricultural production between 1000 and 1200 contributed to a population explosion during which the population of Europe may have quadrupled.[7]

During the eleventh and the twelfth centuries, along with the population explosion, there arose a chain of new schools throughout Western Europe with far broader aims than those of monastery schools. What is important for our purposes is the fact that these schools were centered on the interests of the "master" who directed them, just like the schools in the Islamic civilization that attracted students to a particular teacher whose name was synonymous with that of the school. And just like their counterpart in the Muslim world, these European schools were not fixed geographically; they went where their master-teacher went.[8] These new schools multiplied. The number of students and teachers increased and some of them became large enough to need organization and administration; this was the beginning of universities that would subsequently become home to an intense scientific activity.

These universities arose in Western Europe as spontaneously as the schools had. At that early stage, universities were not educational institutions with buildings and charters; rather, the early universities were merely voluntary associations or guilds where teachers and students pursued their common interests. The word "university" (from the Latin *universitas*) merely meant a guild, corporation or association where people pursued common (universal) ends; it had no structural and organizational connotations. Nonetheless, the customary date for the masters of Bologna to have achieved university status is 1150, for those of Paris, about 1200 and those of Oxford by 1220.[9]

---

7. Herlihy, David (1982), "Demography" in Joseph R. Straye (ed.), *Dictionary of Middle Ages* [henceforth *DMA*], 13 vols. Scribner, New York, vol. 4, pp. 136-48.
8. On the medieval schools, see Orme, Nicholas (1973), *English Schools in the Middle Ages*, Methuen, London and Contreni, John J., "Schools, Cathedral" in *DMA*, vol. 11, pp. 59-63.
9. None of these dates can be taken as fixed. They represent a development in the history of Western Europe that spanned two centuries. For an introduction to the history of universities, see Astrik L. Gabriel, "University" in *DMA*, vol.12, pp. 282-300. Also see Makdisi, George (1981), *The Rise of Colleges: Institutions of Learning in Islam and the West*, Edinburgh University Press, Edinburgh.

The presence of stable monarchies created opportunities for employment of learned scholars at courts as well as the need for administrators for growing state institutions. This meant expansion of universities and their curricula. Education in these early universities followed the centuries-old tradition of guilds that had been established all over the world. A student entered university at about age fourteen and studied with a teacher for three to four years, attending lectures and discussing various books and authors. At the end of that period, the student would present himself to be examined for young man's degree. Having passed this examination, the student now became a sort of journeyman who could impart instructions to new students under the direction of a master, while he continued studies. After another period of three to five years, the student could present himself for a higher examination that would confer full rights on him and give him full membership in the faculty of arts. These universities were bigger than schools; numbers varied from 200 to 800 students. Oxford probably had 1,000 to 1,500 students in the fourteenth century, Bologna was of similar size but Paris may have had up to 2,500 students.[10]

For our study, more than the number of students, we need to know the curriculum of these universities. What was taught changed over time but an interesting feature of these early universities was their uniformity in curriculum. There were minor differences in emphasis but almost all universities taught the same subjects from the same texts. This may have been the result of paucity of texts at this stage but this common curriculum produced a phenomenal result: medieval Europe acquired a universal set of Greek and Arabic texts as well as a common set of problems which facilitated a high degree of student and teacher mobility across countries. Thus teachers earned their *ius ubique docendi* (right of teaching anywhere) and moved between different universities, all of which used Latin as their language of instruction. This, again, demonstrates an important parallel between medieval Europe and the Muslim world where Arabic was the universal language of scholarship and where students and teachers easily moved across a vast geographical expanse.

Perhaps the most important characteristic of the Aristotelian tradition in the medieval European university curriculum is the fact that from its modest beginnings in the twelfth century, it grew to hold center stage by the second half of the thirteenth century. This was, partly, due to the

10. Ibid.

intense transmission activity that had brought the whole Aristotelian corpus from its Arab home to Europe. This was done through the links between the Muslim world and Europe that had always remained active because of travelers, traders and bordering cities with their multi-lingual populace. As early as 950 CE, there was an official exchange of ambassadors between the courts of ʿAbd al-Raḥmān (277-350/890-961) at Córdoba and Otto (912-973) in Frankfurt. As already mentioned, Gerbert had gone to northern Spain in the 960's to learn Arabic mathematical sciences. A century later, Constantine (*fl.* 1065-85 CE), a North African who had become a Benedictine monk, went to the monastery of Monte Cassino in southern Italy where he translated medical treatises from Arabic into Latin. These included the works of Galen (d. 129) and Hippocrates (*ca.* 460 - *ca.* 377 BC), which were to become the foundations of medical literature in the West.[11]

These were, however, "harmless translations"; they did not impinge upon faith nor pose any problems for the new class of educated Europeans who found a most attractive intellectual reservoir in Spain. The presence of Mozarabs,[12] a cosmopolitan culture, ample supply of Arabic texts and generous patronage combined to produce a translation movement which was to transform European learning over the course of a century and a half. While this translation activity was beginning, the reconquest of Spain further helped the process. The fall of Toledo in 1085 into Christian hands provided an excellent library that was exploited to the maximum extent during the next hundred years.

In an atmosphere ripe with enthusiasm, adventure, conquest, patronage and texts, there was no dearth of translators. Many Spaniards were fluent in Arabic. John of Seville (*fl.* 1133-42) translated a large number of astrological works; Hugh of Santalla (*fl.* 1145) also translated works on astrology and divination and Mark of Toledo (*fl.* 1191-1216) translated Galenic texts. Those who came from abroad included Robert of Chester (*fl.* 1141-50) from Wales, Hermann the Dalmatian (*fl.* 1138-43?), a Slav and the Italian, Plato of Tivoli (*fl.* 1132-46).

The first translations were done without a scheme and merely for the sake of transmission of knowledge. But soon there arose need for translation of specific works whose references had been found in earlier translations and these were done by able translators who searched for these texts. Among the greatest of these translators was Gerard of Cremona (*ca.*

11. McVaugh, Michael, "Constantine the African" in *DSB*, vol. 3, pp. 393-5.
12. Spanish and often Arabic-speaking Christians.

1114-87) who came to Spain in the late 1130s or early 1140s from northern Italy in search of Ptolemy's *Almagest.* He found a copy in Toledo, where he remained until he could master Arabic to translate it. But once in Toledo, Gerard also found a host of other texts that were simply astounding in character. Over the next thirty to forty years, he was to produce an enormous number of translations, no doubt with the help of a team of assistants. Thus, in addition to *Almagest,* he is credited with the translation of al-Khwārazmī's *Algebra,* Euclid's *Elements* and fifteen other works on mathematics and optics; fourteen works on logic and natural philosophy, including Artistotle's *Physics, On the Heavens, Meterology,* and *On Generation and Corruption;* he translated twenty-four medical works, nine of these were Galenic treatises and one was *Canon of Medicine,* Ibn Sīnā's monumental work which was to remain as the mainstay of medical curriculum all over Europe for at least four hundred years. The total number of books translated by Gerard of Cremona is between seventy and eighty; all of these were of high quality because of his excellent command of languages as well as subject matter.[13]

The Greco-Latin translation movement continued well into the thirteenth century. Just like the Greco-Arabic translation movement, it became more refined over time and as the technical terms and ability of

13. Gerard is comparable to Ḥunayn ibn Isḥāq, the Nestorian Christian who is credited with a large number of translations, ranging from medicine, philosophy, astronomy, mathematics to magic and oneiromancy (divination through dreams) from Greek and Syriac into Arabic. Out of the 129 titles enumerated by him in his *Risāla,* he himself translated about 100 into Syriac or Arabic or into both. The list is not exhaustive. To my knowledge no study exists which compares the impact of the life and work of these two men, separated by three centuries but so comparable in their roles as transmitters of knowledge from one civilization to another. Ḥunayn's life is a fascinating story, both of one man's commitment to a life devoted to scholarship as well as of the vibrant currents that were flowing into the Islamic scientific tradition during his life. Biographical material on Ḥunayn has been collected by G. Gabrieli (1924), "Ḥunayn ibn Isḥāq" in *Isis,* vol. 4, pp. 282-92; by Lutfī Sa'dī (1934), "A Bio-bibliographical Study of Ḥunayn ibn Isḥāq al-'Ibādī" in *Bulletin of the History of Medicine,* vol. 2, pp. 409-46, and in Meyerhof's notes to al-Bayhaqī (1948), *Tatimmāt, Osiris,* vol. 8, pp. 122-217. For a short biographical note see entry by G. Strohmaier, "Ḥunayn b. Isḥāq al-'Ibādī", *EI,* vol. 3, pp. 578-81. Likewise the medieval European translation movement can also be compared with the earlier Baghdad translation movement which brought a large number of Greek, Persian and Syriac texts into Arabic during a period extending from eighth to tenth century.

the translators improved, many works were retranslated. William of Moerbeke (*fl.* 1260-86) was one such translator who provided a complete Aristotelian corpus to Latin Christendom along with translation of major Aristotelian commentators. He also revised older translations and translated a number of Neo-Platonic works.

Reception of the Islamic Scientific Tradition

With this background in mind, let us now examine how this received Greek and Islamic tradition was to first become the dominant intellectual force in the medieval West and then give way to a new and opposing force out of which grew the worldview that was to produce modern science. The first thing to note is the texts that were translated. The medieval West seems to have been interested in medicine and astronomy at the beginning of the translation movement in the tenth and eleventh centuries. During the first half of the twelfth century, a large number of astrological works were translated along with enough mathematical works to allow a successful practice of astronomy and astrology. But medicine, astronomy and astrology in the Islamic tradition were grounded in a powerful metaphysical foundation and they could not have been understood without understanding the foundations on which they were constructed. Thus, a large number of philosophical works were also translated at the beginning of the second half of the twelfth century; this activity continued into the thirteenth century and eventually almost all metaphysical works dealing with the foundations of Islamic scientific tradition in general and medicine in particular were translated into Latin. This meant philosophers who had been interested in the Aristotelian corpus—from al-Kindī to Ibn Sīnā, as well as others, such as Abū Bakr al-Rāzī, whose works were needed to properly understand and grasp the philosophical foundations of the Islamic scientific tradition.

Let us also note that, contrary to the commonly held notion prevalent in the works of many Muslim scholars, it was not the Islamic scientific tradition that had arrived in Europe to take it out of its so-called Dark Ages—if anything like that ever existed. It was the *inner dynamics* of the European civilization that had created a particular need that was fulfilled by making use of the material from the Islamic scientific tradition. Even a cursory glance at what was translated makes this point abundantly clear. Fortunately, we can reconstruct, with reasonable accuracy, what was translated as well as when and by whom:[14] Ibn Sīnā was one of the first to be translated into Latin. The physical and philosophical parts of his *Kitāb al-Shifā'* were translated by Dominicus Gundissalinus and John of Seville in Toledo in the twelfth century; Alfred of Sareshel translated the chemical and the geographical parts in Spain at the beginning of the thirteenth century and *al-Qānūn fi'l-Ṭibb* was translated by Gerard of Cremono in Toledo in the twelfth century. Among other translations done between the eleventh and the thirteenth centuries are the works of Ibn Rushd by Micheal Scot in the early thirteenth century; of Ibn al-Haytham translated by more than one translator toward the end of the twelfth century; of al-Fārābī by Gerard of Cremona in Toledo in the twelfth century; and of Abū Bakr al-Rāzī by Gerard of Cremona and Moses Farachi in Toledo and Sicily in the twelfth and thirteenth centuries. Works by al-Kindī were translated by Gerard of Cremona in Toledo in the twelfth century; those of al-Khwārazmī by Adelard of Bath and Robert of Chester in the twelfth century and Jābir ibn Ḥayyān's numerous works were translated by various translators in the twelfth and thirteenth centuries.

This somewhat incomplete, but representative, list clearly shows that the European intellectual tradition was looking for a particular type of material; that it was not interested in the Islamic tradition *per se*; rather, in the course of its development, it needed to recover its own antiquity; it found it in Aristotle's Arab home and recovered it. In this process, it came across Ibn Sīnā, al-Kindī and Ibn Rushd and took them as well—not as representatives of the Islamic scientific tradition but as commentators of Aristotelian corpus. Notice that those whose works were translated were translated because of their importance for Aristotelian studies and *not* for their contributions to the Islamic scientific tradition. Had the Islamic scientific tradition been the need and focus of the European science, the list of translated material would not have been restricted to the above group of scholars and scientists, all of whom were profoundly interested in Aristotle. In that case, it would have been interested in the works of science as such and would not have omitted such important scientists as Abū Rayḥān al-Bīrūnī, Ibn Sīnā's able contemporary whose vast corpus of writing, which includes 180 works of varying length embracing all known fields of science. These omissions are more than accidental. In fact, the real appreciation of al-Bīrūnī had to wait until the twentieth century. And this is not an isolated example. Medieval Europe was equally uninterested in a

14. Crombie (1995), pp. 56-8.

host of other Muslim scientists whose contributions did not fit the requirements of the nascent science in Europe.

Intellectual Milieu

In order to understand the true meaning of this translation movement and its impact on the subsequent developments, we need to reconstruct the intellectual milieu in which these translations arrived, first as a trickle and then as a torrent. Until the twelfth century, European intellectual life was relishing a peaceful but fervent expansion of the educational system. During the early part of the twelfth century, recovery of the writings of the Latin church fathers, a few translations of Greek works (Plato's *Timaeus* and parts of Aristotle's *Logic*) and a few new translations both from Greek and Arabic quietly flowed into the main stream of the new educational activity.

But the large-scale translation activity of the thirteenth century that opened the floodgates of knowledge from a civilization that was considered to be hostile, pagan and dangerous, posed a serious threat to the intellectual life. The new material was simply irresistible in its utility, power and quality. And some of it was harmless, as far as the religious and philosophical beliefs were concerned. Thus treatises on mathematics, optics, meteorology and medicine were welcomed. Euclid's *Elements,* al-Khawārazmī's *Algebra,* Ibn al-Haytham's *Optics,* Ibn Sīnā's *Canon of Medicine* and even Ptolemy's *Almagest* posed no serious threat but when it came to works which had profound metaphysical implications, there was no easy solution. Once translated and circulated, these works could not be un-translated and removed from the intellectual horizon of Western Europe and their presence posed a serious threat to the religious beliefs, and demanded immediate response.

Aristotle and his Muslim commentators were the first to meet resistance. In 1210, a council of bishops issued a decree forbidding instruction on Aristotle's natural philosophy within the faculty of arts; this decree was renewed in 1215 by the papal legate Robert de Courçon.[15] Though this decree was only applicable to Paris, it marks the beginning of a long process that would eventually cast shadows over the later history of science and religion discourse in the West. Bans on Aristotle (1210, 1215 and 1231) had a short life and by 1240, Aristotle's works on natural philosophy

15. On reception of Aristotle in Paris, see Fernand Van Steenberghen (1955), *Aristotle in the West,* tr. by Leonard Johnston, Nauwelaerts, Louvian.

were being taught in Paris as they had been taught in Oxford and Bologna. By 1255, Aristotle had won a respectable place in the academia; in that year the faculty of arts at Paris passed new statutes that made it mandatory to include all known works of Aristotle in the curriculum. This change was accompanied by another change that is of interest for our topic. Aristotle did not barge upon the intellectual tradition of the West unaided; he was received in company of Ibn Sīnā whose Platonized versions of Aristotelian corpus posed serious threats of pantheism.

However, around 1230, the commentaries of Ibn Sīnā started to be replaced by those of Ibn Rushd, in whom the Latin West discovered a more authentic and less Platonized commentator. It was for this reason that Ibn Rushd, who became known as *the* Commentator, was to enjoy immense respect and popularity in the West. But in spite of his new companion, Aristotle was still as unacceptable to the Christian West as he had been to the Muslim East when he first arrived in his Arab home. Both the Islamic and the Christian traditions had to struggle with an Aristotelian cosmos that was made up of eternal elements and destined to last forever because the elements had not come into being at any moment and hence they will not cease to be.

This was obviously in direct contradiction to the opening chapters of Genesis. Likewise, both traditions were threatened by the Aristotelian notion of the Prime Mover as the deity that was eternally unchanging and hence incapable of intervening in the operation of the cosmos that ran on its own on the basis of cause and effect relationships. Obviously there was no room for miracles—a central element in both the Islamic as well as the Christian traditions. But this was not all. There were other troubling elements in Aristotelian system which had sparked intense debates in the Muslim world and which now arrived in the Latin West: the astrological theories which accompanied Aristotle's philosophy taught that human acts and will were influenced by celestial objects and hence they impinged upon Christian notions on sin and salvation; the nature of soul in Aristotle's philosophy which argued that the soul was the form and organizing principle of the body and had no independent existence. It needed a body to exist and hence at death, both the individual's form (i.e. body) and soul ceased to exist—a notion which was, once again, incompatible with Christian teachings on the immortality of the soul.

But these specific concepts which were incompatible with Christian teachings were merely the tip of the iceberg; at a more fundamental level, Aristotle posed the same threat to Christianity as he had posed to the

Islamic tradition: his system was taken to be a rational alternative to the revealed knowledge. This opened floodgates of another kind; now Aristotelian philosophy was standing at par with theology and as a rival to biblical studies. A chasm had opened; one could follow theological methods and arrive at one conclusion or follow philosophical methods to arrive at a totally opposite conclusion, with both claiming to be true. This was the beginning of the classical fight for authority: the rivalry between Athens and Jerusalem, a fight that would be won by Jerusalem for a short while and then lost forever.

As the century ran its course, Aristotle bloomed in the new universities. The most attractive feature of Aristotelian philosophy was its completeness. Aristotle had constructed a cosmos in which everything was in place; everything followed a simple basic set of logical assumptions. He offered a cosmology in which the universe and its constituents were convincingly mapped—from the outer heavens to the earth in the centre, everything had a function and all functions were explained. He provided details that the West had never heard before. From his account of motion to the rich and detailed descriptions of his biological corpus, everything fitted well in his orderly cosmos which was explained in terms such as form, matter, substances, actualities and potentialities, the four causes, the four elements, contraries, nature, change, purpose, quantity, quality, time and space. By the second half of the thirteenth century, new commentaries had started to appear and the Latin West had started to come to terms with Aristotle. Robert Grosseteste (*ca.* 1168-1253) was one of the first to produce a commentary on Aristotle's *Posterior Analytics,* which tried to harmonize Aristotelian notions with Christian beliefs through Platonic and Neoplatonic influences. Grosseteste's cosmology made use of Neoplatonic emanationism to reintroduce the biblical account of creation *ex nihilo* into Aristotle's cosmology.[16]

Roger Bacon (*ca.* 1220-*ca.* 1292) was to continue Grosseteste's work well into the thirteenth century. Bacon was a tireless champion of the new learning and he saw no conflict between Aristotelian philosophy and his own theology. But others were more cautious. In particular, the attitude of the Franciscan order around the middle of the thirteenth century was one of extreme caution. Bonaventure (*ca.* 1217-74), who had studied liberal arts

16. For details of Grosseteste's cosmology, see James McEvoy (1982), *The Philosophy of Robert Grosseteste*, Clarendon Press, Oxford, pp. 149-88 and pp. 369-441.

and theology at the University of Paris and then stayed on to teach theology from 1254 to 1257 before resigning to become a minister general of the Franciscan order, respected Aristotelian philosophy but he was much more cautious than Bacon about the utility of philosophy in matters of faith. Grosseteste, Bacon and Bonaventure made important contributions in finding a way out of the impasse that the Aristotelian corpus had produced but it was left to two Dominicans, Albert (*ca.* 1200-1280) and Thomas Aquinas, who were active in the middle and later years of the thirteenth century to forge a powerful synthesis between Aristotelian philosophy and Christian faith. Albert was born and raised in Germany, educated at Padua and the Dominican school in Cologne. He arrived in Paris in the early 1240s to study theology and became the master of theology in 1245. From 1245 to 1248, he was the Dominican professor at Paris; Thomas Aquinas studied under him and when Albert was called back to Cologne in 1248, Thomas accompanied him.

Albert wrote his voluminous commentaries on Aristotle after his departure from Paris. Before him, no one in the Western Christendom had paid so much serious and sustained attention to Aristotle. In many ways, he resembled Ibn Sīnā. Both men were profoundly impressed by Aristotle, both wanted to remain independent of Aristotle's influence and both tried to harmonize their faiths with Aristotelian philosophy. No wonder, Albert was heavily influenced by Ibn Sīnā's works. The twelve volume nineteenth-century edition of Albert's works, consisting of more than 8,000 pages, stands as a monumental testimony to Albert's contribution in forging a synthesis between Aristotelian philosophy and Christian faith. Albert was able to produce this synthesis because he not only knew his Aristotle, he was also at home with the works of masters of Islamic philosophy who had produced their own synthesis of Islam and Aristotelian philosophy before him. Thus one finds in Albert's works a heavy dependence and borrowing from a range of Muslim and Greek authors such as al-Kindī, Ibn Rushd, Plato, Euclid, Constantine the African and many others.

Albert's able student, Thomas Aquinas (*ca.* 1224-1274), was to add to the contributions made by his teacher. Both respected philosophy but not at the expense of theology, both understood the power of philosophy and both tried to use that power in service of faith. But in many ways Aquinas went further than his teacher in addressing thorny issues. In his book *On the Unicity of the Intellect, Against the Averroists,* he dealt with the issue of monopsychism and the nature of the soul. He agreed with the Aristotelian doctrine that the soul is the substantial form of the body, but he argued that this is a special kind of form; one capable of existing independent of body so that when body perishes, soul does not.

Along with these efforts to harmonize Aristotelian philosophy with Christian faith, there was a parallel current in the later half of the thirteenth century Europe that disregarded the dictates of theology and opted for pure philosophy. Siger of Brabant (*ca.* 1240-84), in his earlier years and Boethius of Dacia (*fl.* 1270) were two representatives of this current. Both felt that a compromise between philosophy and theology is not possible. As a philosopher, one has to remain true to its principles and, though in the end he remained attached to his faith as a Christian, Boethius felt that as a philosopher, he could not defend his belief in a created universe. Natural philosophy cannot admit the possibility of creation, he felt, because such an admission will introduce an element of supernatural to the natural causes. Although Boethius had professed his faith openly, he and other members of his group were considered radicals and in 1270 and 1277, two condemnations were issued by Etienne Tempier, the bishop of Paris. The former condemned thirteen philosophical propositions allegedly taught by Siger and his fellow radicals in the Faculty of Arts and the latter condemned 219 propositions. This was a strong official response to the radical Aristotelianism that spread in academic circles in Paris. Rather than serve a severe blow to Aristotelian philosophy, this condemnation merely added fuel to the fire. Aristotle had arrived in Europe from his Arab home to stay. And men like Thomas Aquinas had made a place for him in the main discourse. The force of condemnation wore off with time and in 1323, Pope John XXII elevated Aquinas to the rank of saint and in 1325, the bishop of Paris revoked all articles of the condemnation of 1277 applicable to Aquinas' teachings.

The problems were not resolved, however. With time, they became more sophisticated. It was realized that at the heart of the problem lie two epistemological claims: one by philosophy and the other by theology. Toward the end of the thirteenth century and early in the fourteenth, men like John Duns Scotus (*ca.* 1266-1308) and William of Ockham (*ca.* 1285-1347) tried to diminish the area of overlap between theology and philosophy by questioning the ability of philosophy to address articles of faith with demonstrative certainty. In this attempt to separate theology and philosophy, there was also an effort to achieve peace and cohabitation. The central doctrine of this peace plan was that the articles of faith could not be challenged by philosophy and natural philosophy could not encroach on religious grounds.

The influence of Islamic scientific tradition and the debates that it sparked in the theological circles ran their course, often echoing an earlier era when these issues were bitterly contested within the Islamic world. A good example is the emphasis on divine omnipotence in the theological debates of the fourteenth century—a theme which was central to Christianity. If God is absolutely free and omnipotent, this means that the physical world is contingent rather than necessary. This means that there is no necessity that it should be what it is; it is entirely dependent on God's Will in all respects: in its form, function, operation, in fact, in its very existence. The observed physical laws are not necessary; they are imposed by the divine will. The cause and effect relationships, too, are not necessary; they are contingent. Fire burns but not because fire and the act of burning are necessarily connected; rather it is so because God chose to connect them, empowering fire for the function of burning. God is free, and can choose to "disconnect" the relationship between fire and its power to burn, as He did in the case of Shadrach, Meshach and Abednego when they were cast into the burning furnace but were not harmed, as the Book of Daniel recounts (in chapter 3); this miracle represented a perfect example of God's omnipotence and His right to suspend natural causation when He chose. It is no accident that while reading these arguments, one feels as if one is reading al-Ghazālī: "In our opinion, the connection between what is habitually believed to be a cause and what is habitually believed to be an effect is not necessary," al-Ghazālī had written in his seminal work, *Tahāfut al-Falāsifah (The Incoherence of the Philosophers)*,

> But [with] any two things, where "this" is not "that" and "that" is not "this" and where neither the affirmation of the one entails the affirmation of the other nor the negation of the one entails negation of the other, it is not a necessity of the existence of the one that the other should exist, and it is not a necessity of the nonexistence of the one that the other should not exist. For example, the quenching of the thirst and drinking, satiety and eating, burning and contact with fire, light and the appearance of the sun, death and decapitation, healing and the drinking of medicine...so on, to include all observable among connected things in medicine, astronomy, arts and crafts. Their connection is due to prior decree of God, who creates them side by side, not to its being necessary in itself, incapable of separation. On the contrary, it is within [divine] power to create satiety without eating, to create death without decapitation, to continue life after decapitation, and so

> on to all connected things. The philosophers denied the possibility of [this] and claimed it to be impossible.[17]

This is not an isolated coincidence; the medieval European debates on natural laws and their relationship with religion bear a striking resemblance to similar debates in the Muslim world. This resemblance is the result of a similar process in two different contexts in the two civilizations. In the Muslim world, al-Ghazālī's reflections on causality were the mature product of discourse on Aristotelian philosophy which had gone through a full circle—from initial encounter through translation to acceptance and then appropriation and critical reflection. The debates in the fourteenth century Europe were likewise a product of refinement and critical reflection on fundamental questions that arose from the encounter between Christianity and the Aristotelian corpus. In both cases, this produced two divergent views. According to the first view, nature did not have its own permanently assigned laws; rather, it depended, wholly and without exception, on divine will for the continuous validity of its laws. According to this view, any other explanation of natural laws would amount to compromising God's omnipotence. According to the second view, it was held that God could have chosen to create any world He wished, but He chose to create *this* world with its laws; hence natural philosophy can only discover the laws which this world exhibits, laws which are universal and can be discovered by going out to look for them.

The former view provided an easy explanation of miracles. It also created room for God's absolute and ordained powers by arguing that God's omnipotence gave Him the power to create any kind of world out of an infinite number of possibilities but having created *this* world, God chose to manifest His power in a particular mode and since He is a consistent God, He does not tinker with His creation and having created *this* world, God's activity manifests within the existing order (i.e. His ordained power); of course there are exceptions to this general rule, but they are extremely rare. According to the latter view, unless the natural world was taken on its own absolute value, with its own well-established laws, there was no serious way of studying the order and laws that were inherent in the world. These latter arguments were a powerful motivation for going out and discovering these laws though that did not happen until three centuries later and by

17. Al-Ghazālī, *Tahāfut, op. cit.*, p. 166.

the time it happened, the medieval world had been shattered and pushed into the confines of history.

Transformation

The Islamic scientific tradition provided a large amount of data and theories to the European tradition but all of this was appropriated and eventually transformed. It was this transformed tradition that gave birth to modern science. No doubt this transformation is intimately linked to the internal dynamics of the European civilization, but the famous "continuity debate", which has received a lot of attention within the history of Western science, links this process to the transformation of the material received from the Islamic tradition. This debate revolves around the crucial issues of "continuity" and "discontinuity" of modern science with the medieval science. One group of historians of science claims that modern science is the natural outcome of an internal process of growth of science in which the medieval science was but one step in a continuity that goes back to antiquity. The opposite camp holds that modern science has nothing to do with its medieval precursor. In between these two extremes lie a host of intermediate positions. This is not a place to delve deeply into this debate but we do need to briefly outline the broad concerns of this discourse because an understanding of the relationship between the Islamic scientific tradition and modern science depends on how the central issues in the "continuity debate" are understood.

The central questions in the "continuity debate" have been well formulated by David Lindberg in his 1992 work, *The Beginnings of Western Science*:

> What difference did the ancient and medieval scientific tradition make in the long run? Did it have a permanent or continuing influence on the course or the shape of Western science, or was it an inconsequential cul-de-sac that ultimately led nowhere? Or to pose the question in its most common form, were medieval and early modern science continuous with each other, or discontinuous?[18]

In retrospect, the normative Western tradition was to pass a judgment on the Middle Ages as a period of darkness, stagnation and decay. This was already the verdict of the major voices in the seventeenth century. Francis

18. Lindberg (1992), *The Beginnings of Western Science*, p. 355.

Bacon (1561-1626), Voltaire (1694-1778), his younger contemporary Condorcet (1743-94) and the Swiss historian Jacob Burchhardt (1818-97), who is generally credited with the coinage of the ubiquitous term "Renaissance", all thought of the Middle Ages as the dark period. This judgment was to remain unchallenged until the early years of the twentieth century when theoretical physics opened a chasm in the certainty of scientific knowledge. But by then, the popular notion about the Middle Ages as the dark ages had attained a universal currency and anyone voicing an opposite view had to fight a difficult battle.

But slowly, a respectable body of literature did emerge which challenged the prevalent view.[19] Shortly after World War II, the revisionist history witnessed a dramatic expansion, both in quality as well as in quantity. There were many reasons for this. The worldview which had produced the condescending attitude toward the Middle Ages (and in fact toward the whole history) was badly shaken through the experience of the war; a significant number of new scientific and mathematical texts were carefully studied and the works of historians such as Marshall Clagett (b. 1916), Anneliese Maier (1905-1971) and especially those of the French historian of science, Alexandre Koyré (1892-1964), powerfully articulated an alternate view which was supported by impressive scholarship.[20]

19. One of the earliest to cast a stone was the French physicist and philosopher Pierre Duhem (1861-1916). While inquiring into the intellectual predecessors of Leonardo da Vinci, Duhem discovered a series of remarkable medieval texts and authors to whom he attributed many later discoveries. These included the works of Jean Buridan (d. *ca.* 1358) and Nicole Oresme (d. 1382). This led Duhem to formulate his influential, but flawed theories, about the anticipation of Copernicus' theory of the diurnal rotation of the earth, Descartes' analytic geometry and Galileo's law relating time and distance traveled in free fall by Oresme. See Pierre Duhem (1913-1959), *Le Système du Monde,* 10 vols., Hermann, Paris, vol. 7, p. 534. Somewhat later, historians like Charles Homer Haskins (1870-1937) and Lynn Thorndikc (1882-1965) were to add considerable weight to the counter arguments which tried to rehabilitate the Middle Ages. See Haskins, Charles Homer (1924), *Studies in the History of Mediaeval Science,* Harvard University Press, Cambridge and Thorndike, Lynn (1923-1958), *A History of Magic and Experimental Science,* 8 vols., Columbia University Press, New York and also his *Science and Thought in the Fifteenth Century* (1944), Columbia University Press, New York.
20. For examples, see Clagett, Marshall (1957), *Greek Science in Antiquity,* Abelard-Schuman, London; Clagett (1959), *The Science of Mechanics in the Middle Ages,* University of Wisconsin Press, Madison; Clagett (1979), *Studies in Medieval Physics and Mathematics,* Variorum, London; and

According to Koyré, what the founders of modern science did was neither refinement, nor improvement of what they had inherited; they had to actually "destroy one world and to replace it with another. They had to reshape the framework of our intellect itself, to restate and to reform its concepts, to evolve a new approach to Being, a new concept of knowledge, a new concept of science."[21]

One of the cornerstones of the continuity debate is the question of scientific methodology. The proponents of continuity thesis, especially the enormously influential Alistair Crombie (b. 1915), contend that the experimental methods of the early modern science had an integral continuity with the Middle Ages. Crombie claims that "there can be little doubt that it was the development of these experimental and mathematical methods of the 13th and the 14th centuries that at least initiated the historical movement of the Scientific Revolution culminating in the 17th Century".[22]

This claim has been seriously challenged by a number of subsequent works, including those by Koyré and A. Rupert Hall (b. 1920). But what is more important for our purpose is the fact that recent scholarship has made a powerful case for a fundamental shift in the very foundation of the medieval and modern science. For example, commenting on the continuity debate, David Lindberg wrote:

Maier, Anneliese (1982), *On the Threshold of Exact Science: Selected Writings of Anneliese Maier on Late Medieval Natural Philosophy*, selected and translated with an introduction by Steven D. Sargent, University of Pennsylvania Press, Philadelphia. Anneliese Maier is one of the most insightful historians of science who paid special attention to the philosophical underpinnings of the medieval science. Most of her work remains unavailable in English. Her other works on the subject include the nine volume series *Storia e Letteratura* (1966), Edizioni di Storia e Letteratura, Rome; five volumes of her *Studien zur Naturphilosophie der Spätscholstik* (*Studies on late scholastic natural philosophy*) all published by Edizioni di Storia e Letteratura, between 1949 and 1958; three volumes of *Ausgehendes Mittelalter*, collective essays on fourteenth-century intellectual history published in 1964, 1967 and 1977 by Edinioni di Storia e Letteratura. A memorial volume in her honor was published in 1981 as *Studi sul XIV secolo in Memoria di Anneliese Maier*, ed. A. Maierù and A. Paravicini Bagliani (1981), Edizioni di Storia e Letteratura, Rome, which includes an updated bibliography of her works.

21. Koyré, Alexandre (1968), *Metaphysics and Measurement: Essays in the Scientific Revolution*, Chapman and Hall, London, p. 21.
22. Crombie (1995), vol. 2, p. 121.

> An even stronger case for discontinuity can be made, I believe, if (following Alexandre Koyré's lead) we shift our focus from methodology to worldview or metaphysics. The specific metaphysical developments that I have in mind are the rejection, by the "new scientists", of the seventeenth century (Galileo, Descartes, Gassendi, Boyle, Newton, and others) of Aristotle's metaphysics of nature, form and matter, substance, actuality and potentiality, the four qualities, and the four causes; and the resuscitation and reformulation of the corpuscular philosophy of the ancient atomists. This produced a radical conceptual shift, which destroyed the foundations of natural philosophy as practiced for nearly two thousand years.[23]

This assessment is shared by many other historians of science, such as Anneliese Maier, whose insightful studies of the medieval science have enormously enriched the field and A. Rupert Hall, the author of the celebrated *The Revolution in Science 1500-1750.*[24] Maier's various works corrected the ideas forwarded by Duhem and along with Koyré, she demonstrated in rich details, the definite break between the medieval past and the discoveries of Bruno, Galileo and Descartes.

This is not to say that the seventeenth century scientists were consciously attempting to break away from the past; they were busy in the construction of large-scale systems and with the formulation of new worldviews. Nor was the break with the past an abrupt process; it was a gradual process in which the medieval worldview gave way to the triumphant modernity in various stages. A case in point, amply demonstrated by Maier, is the concept of motive force. For the medieval world, its metaphysical content, *vis motrix,* was the active quality that produces motion; only the Cartesians tried to eliminate completely the qualitative aspect of motive force.[25]

Ibn Rushd had formulated this problem in *Physica* in the following manner. He first postulated both possibilities and then chose one as being more correct. Here is how he conceived the problem: motion differs from "perfection" attained as a result of the motion only in degree and not in

23. Lindberg (1992), p. 361.
24. Hall, Rupert, A. (1983), *The Revolution in Science 1500-1750*, Longman, London.
25. Maier, Annelies (1982), "The Nature of Motion" in *On the Threshold of Exact Science*, pp. 21-39.

essence; thus from this standpoint, motion belongs to the same category as the goal to which it is directed, since motion is nothing but the gradual creation of the "perfection" in question. On the other hand, one can consider motion to be the process by which the "perfection" is attained; in this respect, motion is a genus unto itself, since the "way to the thing" (*via ad rem*) is different from the "thing" itself. Thus considered, motion actually represents a special category. Ibn Rushd then states that the second opinion is more popular but the first is more correct.[26] In contrast, the new metaphysics of the seventeenth century was to construct a mechanical "world of lifeless matter, incessant local motion, and random collision," to use David Lindberg's expression. The new metaphysic thus "...stripped away the sensible qualities so central to Aristotelian natural philosophy, offering them second-class citizenship, as secondary qualities, or even reducing them to the status of sensory illusions"; this was, indeed, a real transformation.[27] For the explanatory capabilities of form and matter, it offered the size, shape, and motion of invisible corpuscles—elevating local motion to a position of preeminence among the categories of change and reducing all causality to efficient and material causality. And for Aristotelian teleology, which discovered purpose *within* nature, it substituted the purposes of a creator God, imposed on nature from the outside.[28]

To be sure, the Islamic scientific tradition had a contribution in the process that led to the emergence of the Medieval European scientific tradition that viewed nature from a perspective that was not wholly alien to Islamic perspectives. The overlap was never complete, as is natural for any two distinct civilizations but, nevertheless, there was a broad sphere of commonality in the way the two traditions viewed nature. But this shared perspective was short-lived and as the Middle Ages gave way to Renaissance and medieval science to the seventeenth century Scientific Revolution, the common area between the Islamic scientific tradition and the new science emerging in Europe rapidly shrank and finally there remained nothing of that old commonality. The breach thus produced was only to widen with time. The inner dynamics of the post-Renaissance European civilization, the abandonment of the essential natures of qualities which were

26. *Averroes, Aristotelis stagiritae de hysico auditu libri octo cum Averrois cordubensis variis in eosdem commentaries*, vol. 4 of *Aristotelis stagiritae omnia quae extant opera*, Juntas Venice, 1550, cited by Maier (1992), p. 25.
27. Lindberg (1992), p. 362.
28. Ibid.

considered to be an integral part of matter in the Islamic as well as in the Greek scientific traditions, the emphasis on the geometric properties of corpuscles (shape, size, motion) and finally the mathematization of nature at an unprecedented scale was to produce a final cleavage with whatever was received from the Islamic scientific tradition.

Thus prior to the Scientific Revolution of the seventeenth century, there was a common universe and a common language of discourse between the sciences that were emerging in Europe and those that had developed in the Islamic civilization. But this common universe collapsed, once and for all, as Nasr has eloquently stated in his *Religion and the Order of Nature*:

> It was this common universe of discourse that was rent asunder by the rise of modern science as a result of which the religious view of the order of nature, which is always based on symbolism, was reduced either to irrelevance or to a matter of mere subjective concern, which made the cosmic teachings of religion to appear as unreal and irrelevant...From the idea of cosmic order and laws created by God through His Will and applicable to both men and nature to the idea of "laws of nature" discoverable completely by human reason and usually identified with mathematical laws, divorced from ethical and spiritual laws, there is a major transformation that played a central role in the rise of modern science.[29]

Let us also note with Nasr that this new idea of laws of nature was to play a significant role in the process that eclipsed earlier Christian understanding of nature. Such an event did not take place in the Chinese, Indian, and Islamic civilizations. "This is of great significance in the parting of ways between the modern West and other civilizations as far as the understanding of the order of nature and its religious significance are concerned."[30]

Reassessment of the Tradition

The transformation of the Islamic scientific tradition in Europe is also associated with the European reassessment of Islam and the civilization it produced. In the process of its re-awakening, European civilization not only reclaimed Greek and Roman intellectual tradition, it also received a vast

29. Nasr (1996), *Religion and the Order of Nature*, pp. 129-33.
30. Nasr (1996), p. 133.

reservoir of knowledge from the Islamic tradition. But as soon as it could become independent of the source material, it started a thorough revision of its earlier appreciation of the Islamic tradition. This can be gleaned from various developments within Europe. One interesting case is that of Chaucer (*ca.* 1340-1400). The intellectual make up of his "Doctor of Physic" could not be complete without a predominant Islamic presence:

> *Well knew he the olde Esculpius*
> *And Deyscorides, and eek Rufus,*
> *Olde Ypocras, Haly and Galyen,*
> *Serpion, Razis and Avicen,*
> *Averrois, Damascien and Constantyn,*
> *Bernard and Gatesden and Gilbertyn.*[31]

Out of the fifteen authorities quoted, there are five Greeks,[32] seven Muslims, one Frenchman and two Englishmen. Written in the 1390s by a man who was a public servant, a courtier and a diplomat trusted by three successive English kings—Edward III (1312-1377), Richard II (1367-1400) and Henry IV (1366-1413)—these tales, told by a group of about thirty pilgrims, reflect the general status of these men and an appraisal of their contributions to the Medieval Ages. The European civilization looked toward the Islamic civilization with respect, awe and expectation. This interest, which produced a phenomenal amount of translated literature was not limited to natural sciences, but covered all aspects of learning. By the end of the fifteenth century, the intensity of the translation activity had abated in reference to the scientific works but the diffusion of learning from the Islamic civilization to Europe was by no means over. In fact, it has been plausibly argued that the sixteenth and the seventeenth centuries were the "golden age of Arabic studies in Europe".[33] This intense activity rested on the appearance of a

> spirited community of scholars eager both to pursue the language and heritage of Islam and to provide contemporaries with learned editions in Arabic (and not merely translations as had been the case during the

31. Chaucer, Geoffrey (1979), *The Canterbury Tales*, University of Oklahoma Press, Norman, vol. ii, p. 429.
32. Including one mythical figure.
33. Feingold, M. (1996), "Decline and Fall: Arabic Science in Seventeenth Century England" in Ragep and Ragep (1996), *Tradition, Transmission, Transformation, op. cit,* pp. 441-69.

> Middle Ages). Several professorships of Arabic were funded in European universities, scores of scholars made their way East in search of instruction in the language or for Arabic manuscripts—thousands of which made their way to Europe—and various publishers as well as individual scholars acquired Arabic type in anticipation of a significant publication enterprise.[34]

Note the significant difference in this renewed interest—which lasted for almost a century, between 1580 and 1680—and the previous translation movement. This time around, the interest was focused on producing Arabic texts, with commentaries, annotations and translations. This marked interest in the primary sources, while indicative of a mental attitude formed by reformation and humanism, as noted by Feingold,[35] was also entangled in the intellectual atmosphere of the age as well as in the theological debates that proliferated during the sixteenth and the seventeenth centuries. In any case, through patronage, internal politics of the European academic community and necessity, the study of Arabic did become an indispensable component of the late Renaissance humanists who applied it to gain access to their cherished classical texts preserved, and enriched, by the Muslim scholars.

> The dignity conferred upon Arabic by the greatest scholars of the day further boosted its status. Joseph Scaliger, Isaac Casaubon, and G. J. Vossius helped transform Arabic into an integral and esteemed part of erudition, both through the work they carried out and their instrumentality in stimulating scholars like Peter Kirsten and Thomas Erpenius to apply themselves to its life-long pursuit. Indirectly, the stature of these scholars and the public support they garnered helped fire the spirits of a whole generation of scholars who made Arabic their domain of expertise, as well as galvanized patrons to endow professorships, support individual scholars, and amass important collections of manuscripts.[36]

Although this phase of the transmission of knowledge from the Islamic civilization to Europe remains least studied, and hence inconclusive, it is remarkable that what little we know is rich in detail and insights. Most

---

34. Feingold (1996), p. 441.
35. Ibid.
36. Feingold (1996), pp. 441-2.

importantly, it is based on many first hand accounts which show a great interest, zeal and eagerness in learning Arabic and in acquiring works of Islamic tradition, as late as the seventeenth century.[37] Arabic was wielded into the academic world through the establishment of chairs, research programs and ambitious projects. For instance, Sir Henry Savile, a highly respected mathematician and Greek scholar of the seventeenth century England, who wished to restore the purity and originality of the mathematical sciences through philology and the new tools of the textual analysis toward the recovery and better understanding of the classical texts, established geometry and astronomy chairs at Oxford in 1619 and considered the knowledge of the Islamic scientific tradition an indispensable tool for his chairs. In a public lecture, delivered at Oxford in 1620, he cited the examples of Jābir ibn Aflaḥ, al-Battānī, and Thābit ibn Qurra as instances of Arab mathematicians who had gone beyond their Greek teachers.[38] Edward Pococke (1604-1691), the first Laudian professor of Arabic mentions that John Bainbridge, the first Savilian professor of astronomy, had said "Brahe and Kepler had scarcely improved on the observations made by the Arabs centuries earlier."[39]

But this appraisal was going to change within the lifetime of these patrons and enthusiasts. Islam and Muslims were going to be cast out of the European memory as major players in the advancement of science and their role was to be delegated to the second class citizenship—a position that was to remain firmly entrenched in Western scholarship for almost five hundred years and only yield to a revised appraisal toward the end of the twentieth century. By the time William Laud, James Usher, John Selden, and Gerard Langbaine died, they had already lost their interest in the Islamic scientific tradition and their students showed nothing but scorn toward what their teachers had found. In sciences like geography, this was

---

37. Our knowledge of this neglected phase of transmission has been enriched by a recent study, Toomer, Gerald (1995), *The Study of Arabic in England during the Seventeenth Century*, Oxford University Press, Oxford. Also see, Feingold (1996), "Oriental Studies" in Tyacke, Nicholas (ed.), *The History of the University of Oxford*, Oxford University Press, Oxford.
38. Savile, Henry (1621), *Praelectiones tresdecim in principium elementorum Euclidis*, Oxford, p. 35, quoted in Feingold, Mordechai (1996), p. 446.
39. Smith, Thomas (1707), "Commentariolus de vita et studiis...Joannis Bainbridgii" in *Vitae quorundam eruditissimorum et illustrium virorum*, London, pp. 10-11; (1661), *The Works of Francis Bacon, Carmen Tograi*, Oxford, fol. *7, both quoted in Feingold (1996), p. 447, f. 9.

partly due to the more accurate information that the European sailors had gathered by then. "John Greaves, for example, griped to Pococke in 1646, that the drudgery he had put himself through the editing of Abulfeda's *Geography* was simply not worth it:

> To speak the truth, those maps, which shall be made out of Abulfeda, will not be so exact, as I did expect; as I have found by comparing some of them with our modern and best charts. In his description of the Red sea, which was not far from him, he is most grossely mistaken; what may we think of places remoter? However, there may be good use made of the book for Arabian writers.[40]

By 1700, there had appeared Latin editions of all the Islamic material that was needed by the scholars, including a translation of the Qur'ān.[41] Now, oriental publications could be produced solely on the basis of these Latin texts. Thus Humphrey Prideaux published his *The True Nature of the Imposture fully display'd in the Life of Mahmet*, based on the poor Latin translation of the Qur'ān by Bibliander, published in 1543, "while all his references to Muslim historians were derived from the footnotes to Pocock's *Specimen histoiae Arabum*."[42] This derived scholarship became the foundation of the Orientalism that reigned supreme until the middle of the twentieth century.

The European Renaissance had attempted to rebuild a civilization based on its antiquity, the triumph of early modern science, with its characteristic distaste for authority, books and scholastic learning and

40. Feingold (1996), p. 448. "Abulfeda", the text quoted by Feingold, is from Ward, John (1740), *The Lives of the Professors of Gresham Colledge*, London, repr. New York, p. 151.
41. The first Latin paraphrase of the Qur'ān, made by Robert of Ketton at the behest of Peter the Venerable, Abbot of Cluny, and completed in 1143, exists in the autograph of the translator in the Bibliothèque de l'Arsenal in Paris; an Italian version was published by Andrea Arrivabene in 1547 and "though its author claims that it is made directly from the Arabic, it is clearly a translation or paraphrase of Robert of Ketton's text as published by Bibliander. Arrivabene's version was used for the first German translation made by Solomon Schweigger...which in turn formed the basis of the first Dutch translation, made anonymously and issued in 1641." *EI*, vol. v, p. 431. Most of the subsequent translations of the Qur'ān in various European languages were derivative products of these works, which were not accurate in the first place.
42. Feingold (1996), p. 452.

elevation of experiment, saw little commendable in the Islamic tradition. Already in the fourteenth century, Dante Alighieri (1265-1321) had placed Ibn Sīnā and Ibn Rushd in Limbo—in the First Circle of Hell, with the greatest non-Christian thinkers, Electra, Aeneas, Caesar, Aristotle, Plato, Orpheus, Cicero where they must live without hope of seeing God, in perpetual desire, though not in torment.[43] The propagandists of the new science were quick to single out Arabs as harbingers of scholasticism whose learning was derivative and irrelevant in the light of their own accomplishments. This attitude was to solidify with the appearance of Francis Bacon. "The sciences which we possess come for the most part from the Greeks," he wrote in *Novum Organum,* "for what has been added by Roman, Arabic, or later writers is not much nor of much importance; and whatever it is, it is built on the foundations of Greek discoveries."[44] He goes on to say:

> For only three revolutions and periods of learning can properly be reckoned; one among the Greeks, the second among the Romans, and the last among us, that is to say, the nations of Western Europe, and to each of these hardly two centuries can be assigned. The intervening ages of the world, in respect of any rich or flourishing growth of sciences, were unprosperous. For neither the Arabians, nor the Schoolmen need be mentioned; who in the intermediate times rather crushed the sciences with a multitude of treatises, than increased their weight.[45]

This verdict was to be repeated in all fields of learning, until it was engraved on the European conscience. Almost every historian of science

---

43. See Alighieri Dante, *The Divine Comedy, Inferno,* tr. Mark Musa (1971), Penguin, New York, 101, Canto IV: 142-144. Note that Dante had placed Prophet Muḥammad (and 'Alī) among a group of "sowers of scandal and schism", whose mutilated and bloody shades, many of whom are ripped open, with entrails spilling out, bemoan their painful lot. See Ibid., 326, Canto XXVIII: 31-33: "See how Mohomet is deformed and torn!/In front of me, and weeping, Ali walks,/his face cleft from his chin up to the crown".

44. Robertson, John M. (ed., 1905), *The Philosophical Works of Francis Bacon,* George Routledge and Sons Ltd. London, p. 275; Bacon adds in a footnote: "M. Chasles appears to have shown this with respect to the principle of position in arithmetic. We derive it, according to him, not from the Hindoos or Arabs, but from the Greeks." n. 37.

45. Robertson (ed., 1905), p. 279.

and philosopher from this period has left a testimony of disrespect. Even men like Ibn Sīnā, whose *Qānūn* was considered to be the Summa of medical sciences in the European universities, were not spared: "George Starkey criticized all of the Arabic writers because of their reliance on Galen and opined that 'Avicenna was useless in the light of practical experience.'"[46]

The criticism spread from the scientific realm to the general learning, and from the examination of achievements and limitations in various sciences to the Arabs and Muslims as people. By the turn of the eighteenth century, these opinions could be articulated in broad terms. "It is certain that the Arabs were not a learned People when they over-spread Asia," wrote William Watton (1666-1727), "so that when afterwards they translated the *Grecian* Learning into their own Language, they had very little of their own, which was not taken from those Fountains."[47] The verdict was also passed in specific terms:

> Their *Astronomy* and *Astrology* was taken from *Ptolemee*, their *Philosophy* from *Aristotle*, their *Medicks* from *Galen*; and so on...there is little to be found amongst them, which any Body might not have understood as well as they, if he had carefully studied the Writings of their *Grecian* Masters...[48]

Watton goes on to complain:

> There have been so many thousands of *Arabick* and *Persick* manuscripts brought over into *Europe*, that our learned Men can make as good, nay, perhaps, a better Judgment of the Extent of their Learning, than can be made, at this distance, of the *Greek*...There are vast Quantities of their Astronomical Observations in the *Bodleian* Library, and yet Mr. *Greaves* and Dr. *Edward Bernard*, two very able judges, have given the World no Account of any Thing in them, which those *Arabian* Astronomers did not, or might have not learnt from *Ptolemee's Almagest*, if we set aside their Observations which their *Grecian* Masters taught them to make; which, to give them their due, Dr. Bernard commends,

46. Greaves, Richard, L. (1969), *The Puritan Revolution and Educational Thought*, Rutgers University Press, New Brunswick, p. 90.
47. Watton, William (1694), *Reflections upon Ancient and Modern Learning*, London, p. 140.
48. Watton (1694), pp. 140-43.

as much more valuable than is commonly believed...[49]

Interestingly, the invalidation of Islamic learning was not merely a result of the advancements in European science but it was based on a genealogy of learning from the remote antiquity to the present time in which the contribution of the Islamic tradition as a whole was seen as no more than a phase of history in which the Greek learning was "parked" in the Arab lands, where it was corrupted and mutilated. This tradition of censure first appeared among the humanists and was built upon by the historians of philosophy in the seventeenth century. Leonhart Fuchs demanded the liberation of medicine "from the Arabic dung dressed with the honey of Latinity"; then he went on to state his true intent: "I declare my implacable hatred for the Saracens and as long as I live shall never cease to fight them. For who can tolerate a past and its ravings among mankind any longer—except those who wish for the Christian world to perish altogether. Let us therefore return to the sources and draw from them the pure and unadulterated water of medical knowledge."[50]

With the waning of interest in Arabic, there appeared yet another kind of "scholar" who could fabricate his "translation" of the Arabic original on the basis of a limited knowledge of Arabic vocabulary or by having a contact with the few remaining Arabists whose own understanding of the intricacies of Arabic was rather shallow. Thus we have several recorded instances in which the Arabists were asked to provide translations of specific information from the works of Muslim scientists. John Wallis, for instance, used the services of Pococke in "solving" Euclid's fifth postulate by asking him to provide a translation of al-Ṭūsī's solution for the problem and many mathematicians who attempted to solve the celebrated "Alhazen problem" used the same device to obtain a limited and often imperfect understanding of Ibn al-Haytham's own work.[51]

---

49. Watton (1694), p. 143.
50. Pagel, Walter (1977), "Medical Humanism: A Historical Necessity in the Era of the Renaissance" in Maddison, Francis; Pelling, Margaret; and Webster, Charles (eds., 1977), *Linacre Studies: Essays on the Life and Works of Thomas Linacre c. 1460-1525*, Clarendon Press, Oxford, pp. 375-86 at 384.
51. Regarding the "Alhazen problem", see Sabra, A. I. (1982), "Ibn al-Haytham's Lemmas for Solving 'Alhazen's Problem'" in *Archives for History of Exact Sciences*, vol. 26 (1982) pp. 299-324. There are many other examples. For instance, Robert Boyle's request in 1663, that Pococke "give account of all the longitudes and latitudes in Abulfeda", of young Thomas Hyde eagerly providing Boyle various translations in

While this transformation was taking place in Europe, there was a growing realization in the Muslim world that something has gone wrong; that something was needed to restore the balance in the society; the sheer weight of decadence was making its presence felt. Muslims had realized that European science and technology had surpassed their own learning. Perhaps the Ottomans were the first to realize this but the rest of the Muslim world was not far behind because, equipped with superior arms, the European armies and missionaries were already knocking at their doors.

---

the hope of handsome remuneration and patronage, etc. See more examples in Feingold (1996), p. 462-4.

CHAPTER SEVEN

Winds of Change

In the Islam and science discourse, the eighteenth century stands as the great watershed. It was a century in which the winds of change acquired a ferocity that would leave nothing intact in the whole fabric of Islamic civilization, including its tradition of learning. It would inaugurate an era in which the Islam and science discourse would go through its first great transmutation. But this transmutation would only be a small part of a much greater calamity that this century before the deluge would bring to the entire Muslim world. From an Islamic perspective, this sterile century, so fatefully synchronized with the appearance of certain events on the world history that made it more than a passing lapse, became the beginning of the great collapse that would alter the geopolitical map, uproot established empires and bring about total collapse of the Islamic scientific tradition.

This fateful century, which saw the unleashing of unprecedented economic and political power in the West, was a century whose scientific course had been set by Isaac Newton (1642-1727). Newton had already shown, in the 1680s, that the orbits of the planets are the result of an attractive force between the sun and each planet, thus bringing into science a revolutionary concept, gravity, which worked in a universal manner, whether the bodies upon which it operated were heavenly or not. In Newton, two centuries of European science had found a synthesis that articulated the nature of the world in the form of equations through a novel mathematical technique, differential calculus. His *Principia,* first published in 1687 in Latin, firmly established the mechanical model in which bodies were endowed with mass and subjected to external forces, such as gravitational attraction. The century was rich in discoveries that would help transform the way humans lived and states expanded. For Europe, it was the unprecedented century which would not only bring to it the exhilarating music of such men as Johann Sebastian Bach (1685-1750) and Wolfgang Amadeus Mozart (156-1791) but also the inventive power of men like James Watt (1736-1819), the inventor of steam engine, and Joseph Bramah (1748-1814), who invented the hydraulic press in 1795. It was also a century of consolidation of previous learning[1] through the publication of encyclopaedias.[2] And of numerous new discoveries—such as that of chromium, chlorine, uranium and nitrogen[3]—that would have fateful consequences for the world. A century of triumph for humanism—a century in which Voltaire (pseudonym of François-Marie Arouet, 1694-1778), Jean-Jacques Rousseau (1712-1778), Immanuel Kant (1724-1804), Alexander Pope (1688-1744), David Hume (1722-1776) and Gottfried Wilhelm Leibniz (1646-1716) lived. The eighteenth century is also remembered for the emergence of modern chemistry to which Antoine Lavoisier contributed so much before his execution in 1794 during the French Revolution and the systematic classification of animals and plants by Carl von Linné (1707-1778), who is better known as Linnaeus. The French Revolution, that began in 1789 with the removal of the absolute monarchy of the Bourbons and the system of aristocratic privileges, and ended with Napoleon's overthrow of the Directory and seizure of power in 1799, was also not a localized event that happened in France; it had tremendous impact on the rest of the world. When Napoleon arrived in Egypt in 1798, he was accompanied by a number of scientists who would find, among other things, the Rosetta Stone[4] in the Nile Delta in 1799, which would prove to be the key to deciphering the Egyptian hieroglyphs. Napoleon's arrival in Egypt was symptomatic of a major transformation of the Islam and science discourse that had been taking shape during the course of that critical century and which would remain the reigning paradigm until the present time. His arrival in the Islamic heartland crystallized the "catching

1. For example, Lavoisier's *Méthode de nomenclature chimique* (1787) as well as his "Table of Thirty-One Chemical Elements" (1790).
2. The French *Encyclopédie* (1751-72) was edited by Diderot and Jean le Rond d'Alembert (1717-83), and the first edition of the *Encyclopaedia Britannica* was published in 1771.
3. Chromium was discovered by French Chemist L. N. Vauquelin (1763-1829) in 1797; uranium by German chemist M. H. Klaproth (1743-1817); and nitrogen independently by Scottish chemist Daniel Rutherford (1749-1819) and English chemist Joseph Priestley (1733-1804).
4. The stone bears a decree of the Egyptian priesthood in 199 BC. The script was written in three columns; the first was hieroglyphs; the second, demotic, a late form of ancient cursive Egyptian script, and the third Greek. Everyone, including Napoleon, understood the importance of the stone. Despite the state of war between France and England, Napoleon ordered plaster copies of the stone to be sent to scholars all over Europe but the defeat of his armies meant that the stone ended up in the British Museum, where it remains to this day.

up syndrome" that had already made its appearance all over the Muslim world. Briefly stated, this syndrome is a myopic statement that summarizes the cause of decline of Muslim power by ascribing the loss to falling behind Europe in science and technology. As a corollary, it suggests that as soon as Muslims catch up with the West in science and technology, all will be set aright.

Henceforth, Islam and science discourse was overshadowed by the "catching up syndrome". Those who held centre-stage would bring in the whole weight of the religious tradition, along with its primary sources—the Qur'ān and the Sunna—to support their program by emphasizing that these two sources support acquisition of science. Another aspect of this changed nature of discourse would manifest itself in the rise of mounds of apologetic literature that would attempt to prove that all modern scientific discoveries can, in fact, be traced back to the Qur'ān and Sunna. In the course of time, there would appear institutions sponsored by governments for just this purpose and international conferences would be held to promote a discourse focused on proving modern science through the Qur'ān and the divine nature of the Qur'ān through modern science. But these aspects will be the focus of the next chapter. In this, let us briefly trace the developments which led to the changes in the discourse during the two and a half centuries between 1700 and 1950—a period that would bring almost all the Muslim world under a colonial yoke.

Instruments of Change

A number of complex, interconnected and diverse forces operated on the Muslim world between 1700 and 1950 to produce changes that destroyed old institutions, disrupted centuries-old social patterns of life, and replaced old languages of discourse with new and alien languages which could be understood by only a small percentage of the population. All of this led to a total collapse of the Islamic scientific tradition and this, in turn, completely transformed the nature of discourse between Islam and science; from being a discourse *within* the tradition, it became a discourse between Islam and modern science—a tradition that was rooted in a different civilization.

These changes were the product of historical forces that were reshaping the map of the world during this era. From being major players in world history, the three powerful Muslim empires that had emerged in the traditional Muslim lands after the destruction of ʿAbbāsids were rapidly becoming a backwater. And this was happening not only due to the internal weakness of these empires, but also due to the fact that, precisely at this time, Europe was taking a dynamic lead in the events that would eventually transform the world. It was a dramatic and fateful reversal that took place through a highly complex interplay between diverse factors including international commerce, politics, military techniques, science, technology, social customs, fashions and arts.

The most dominating feature of this period is an inner vacuum that characterized the Islamic civilization at all levels. As if it had been hollowed from within, the civilization that had created a grand infrastructure of legal, administrative and social organizational systems appeared to be suspended in the air without any support. It was this great inner vacuum that made it possible for any maverick general with finesse to rise and conquer large regions merely on the basis of his personal abilities, without any institutional structure. Likewise, stray ideas, fashions, cultural symbols, and ad hoc power structures seem to float through this vacuous era. It was a civilization that had been hollowed from inside and left with no immune system to resist the onslaught of foreign aggression and infiltration.

During this period, all three empires suffered humiliating defeats and contractions. In the course of this period of two and a half centuries, vast regions of the traditional Muslim lands were colonized by foreign powers. The Ṣafavī and the Indian Tīmūrī empires totally disappeared, the Ottomans lost their past glory, their vast empire shrunk drastically, and was finally dissolved, giving birth to modern Turkey. In all three empires, it was a combination of internal and external causes that led to the collapse. But, for the first time in Muslim history, a new factor arose: all three empires were forced to measure their strength and weakness in reference to an outside force: the European military and economic power which was knocking at their doorsteps with increasing force. Out of the three, the Ottomans were the most conscious of the imminent danger to their empire and they made desperate attempts to arrest the decay.[5] These attempts were, however, only partially successful and eventually, they proved inadequate.

5. In the seventeenth century, Kochu Bey (d.1650) wrote his *Risale* (1631) in which he advised the Sultan to return to the direct management of the government, restore the authority of the Grand Vizier, reconstruct the *timars* and suppress factions. Kātib Çelebi (known as Ḥājjī Khalīfa, 1609-1657) analyzed the decline in terms of loss of production and revenue and abuse of peasants. Mustafa Naima (1665-1716), an official historian of the Ottoman court, advised the government to balance its income and expenditures, pay stipends to the military and rid the system of incompetent soldiers.

When the Ottomans signed the humiliating treaty of Karlowitz in 1699, they had come to realize that Europe had gained a decisive edge over them in military technology and economic organization. Despite some short-term gains against the Russians and the Venetians, in 1718 they had to sign another treaty with Austria (at Passarowitz), in which even Belgrade was lost. But most telling of a chronic internal weakness was the succeeding period under the Grand Vizier Ibrāhīm Pasha, which became famous as the "Tulip Age", so called because of craze for tulips. It was a period in which the high culture, which had by then become enamored of European civilization, openly displayed its preference. Thus, in a short burst of cultural flowering, traditional patterns of design, architecture, music, painting, poetry, and furniture lost their appeal, at least in the cities. Instead of the traditional geometric and Arabesque ornamentation, there appeared French-inspired rococo and floral naturalistic styles. Poets broke away from the old Persian patterns, and painters produced wall murals based on European models. This new sensibility was an early sign of what was to follow. And although Belgrade was regained from the Austrians in 1739, this was a short-lived victory. The center could no longer hold its parts and various regions of the empire became virtually independent. By 1774, the Ottomans had lost control of the Black Sea to Russians and in 1783, Russia annexed the large territory around the Sea of Azov. In 1792, Salīm III undertook far reaching military and political reforms, which he called *Niẓām-e Jadīd,* the New Order.

When Napoleon arrived in Egypt in 1798, the Egyptian Mamlūk troops proved helpless against him. The French started to establish modern hospitals, scientific laboratories, and a new administrative system in order to turn Egypt into a supporting economy for that of France. But in 1801, they had to vacate Egypt. Muḥammad ʿAlī,[6] who had been sent by the Ottomans against the French, then succeeded in restoring something of the former structure. However, he was not content to leave Egypt in the same state in which he had found it. Between 1803 and 1805, he successfully established himself as the major player in the local military and political setup. By 1807, he had broken the power of Mamlūks and by 1813, he had re-established peace (under Ottoman suzerainty) in Ḥijāz, where the

6. Known in the Ottoman histories as Meḥmed ʿAlī Pasha (d. 1849), he was born in the late 1760s in the small Macedonian port of Kavala, to an Ottoman soldier of Albanian origin who had arisen to command the local irregulars and who was married to the daughter of the local governor.

reformist Wahhābīs of Najd had overthrown Ottoman rule in 1803-4. He was recognized as the governor of Egypt by the Ottomans and between 1805 and 1811, he consolidated his power. He spent the next fifteen years (1812-27) in carving out a powerful state for himself out of the Ottoman sovereign's vast domains. He expanded his influence and empire by aggressive campaigns in the Sudan, Crete and the Morea. Above all, Muḥammad ʿAlī brought modern science and technology to Egypt. He set up new schools, factories and training colleges for modernizing his military.[7] However, in the 1830s, he turned all his military might against the Ottomans and brought Britain and France into the power struggle; this eventually led to the colonization of the entire region.

Similar power struggles marked the disintegration of the Indian Tīmūrī empire and resulted in the colonization of the Indian subcontinent by the British. The Ṣafavids were attacked by Afghans. Iṣfahān was occupied in 1722 but the Afghans failed to establish their power in Iran; they could only destroy the Ṣafavīd power and destroy their cherished city. Nādir Khān, a talented general, reorganized the Ṣafavī army and expelled the Afghans. But then he declared himself ruler as Nādir Shāh and set on a course of destroying the neighboring Muslim empires. He fought with the Ottoman armies of Aḥmed III in 1730, thus ending the "Tulip Age" and attacked India in 1739 and sacked Delhi, ruining the city of Tīmūrī king Muḥammad Shāh. To the north, he attacked the chief of Ozbeg capitals along Zarafshān and Oxus rivers. In the wake of this wave of destruction, nothing was built. Nādir Shāh, like Muḥammad ʿAlī, found a vacuous region and ascended to its kingship, merely on the basis of his personal power. When he was killed in 1160/1747, his family could only hold power for a few months. Karīm Khān Zand, the general of Shīrāz, tried to restore the Ṣafavīd empire but could not succeed. Finally he gave up his attempts in 1753 and ruled whatever region he could in his own name till 1779. After this, there arose another tribal power, the Qajār, which consolidated its hold over the entire region and founded an empire, carved out of the

7. Between 1825-1836, his government founded the following schools: military and naval institutions for training officers and soldiers in the various military professions, such as the infantry, cavalry, and artillery, a medical school; a school for veterinarians; a school for arts and crafts; a school of pharmacy; a school for applied chemistry; a school for midwifery; a school for agriculture; a school for civil engineering; a school for administration; a school for languages and translation. *EI*, vol. vii p. 427.

ruins of the Ṣafavīd empire. This lasted for almost one hundred and fifty years until a military *coup d'état* brought Riḍā Khān to power in 1921 who, in 1925, extracted constitutional kingship from the Assembly in his own name, thus establishing the Pahlavī dynasty that was overthrown in 1979 in a popular uprising.

The detailed story of these instruments of change that transformed the Muslim world and the vast cultural synthesis that had come into existence in the traditional Muslim lands between the seventh and the eighteenth centuries belongs to the domain of history proper. The short preceding description would suffice our purpose, which was to lay the background for the transformation of the Islam and science discourse during this period. However, let us conclude this chapter by pointing out those transforming forces that worked in the Muslim world during the period of colonization.

Routes of Transformation

Nothing is more significant for the understanding of the present phase of the relationship between Islam and science than the period of colonization of the Muslim world. It was during this period that the Muslims as well as their scientific tradition encountered modern western science in the traditional lands of Islam, *Dār al-Islām*. Moreover, it was an encounter in which Muslims were decidedly at the receiving end; their political strength had already been sapped and they were subjects of a vast ruling apparatus that treated them like second-class citizens. Just prior to their colonization, the vacuous remains of their own tradition had seen a large-scale effort of reform and revival that had emerged throughout the Muslim world during the eighteenth century.

At the time of colonization, there were a number of reform-renewal movements throughout the traditional Muslim lands: these included the movement led by Sidī al-Mukhtār al-Kuntī (*ca.* 1750-1811) in the Sahara along with two West African movements, ʿUthmān Dan Fodio and Shaykh Aḥmad of Massina who were influenced by Siddī al-Mukhtār. In the Indian subcontinent, the eighteenth century witnessed a major reform-renewal movement led by Shāh Walī Allāh al-Dihlawi (1702-1762). In Egypt, which in the eighteenth century was a province of the Ottoman Empire, the *ʿulamāʾ* emerged as a distinct social and political force. Al-Azhar University had, by that time, developed a great reputation throughout the Muslim world and was a focal point for interactions among Muslim scholars. Likewise, the spiritual centers of the Muslim world, Makkah and Madinah, were also important seats of learning in the eighteenth century. A cosmopolitan community of scholars lived in these cities and much emphasis was placed on *ijtihād*, or fresh thinking. Out of this environment, a spirit of social and moral reconstruction was evolving.[8]

This process of inner struggle and reform was, however, cut short by the invasion and colonization of these societies by the European powers. During the colonial rule, Muslim societies were transformed at the most fundamental level by the replacement of their basic institutions, models, ideology and in most cases, language of learning. Following the conquest, assimilation or annexation, the colonized societies were subjected to a reign of terror. Old and established families were uprooted. Leading figures were executed or exiled, ruling classes and people of wealth and fame were made targets of special retribution. The continuity of institutions was disrupted and in many cases, they were destroyed in both the physical and the functional sense. The following changes affected all regions.

The first and the most important was the political transformation. Throughout their history, Muslim societies had functioned as units of a larger community. This concept of community (*umma*) transcended national, tribal and regional barriers and worked as a basic operating entity, which provided the framework for a unique spiritual and ideological orientation. This is not to say that the individual states or empires did not function as independent political and administrative units at certain times or that these states had no rivalry with each other. What is important to note is the fact that the transnational notion of the Muslim community as a whole superseded these regional units. The institution of Caliphate was a symbol of this concept. Cities like Makkah and Madinah were held in great esteem by all Muslims in various parts of the world. There were certain centers of learning that were open to all Muslims and to which scholars came from all over the Muslim world. The tradition of traveling for the sake of knowledge, *raḥla fi'l ʿilm,* provided a most natural and stable means of dissemination of ideas throughout the vast region. These centers of learning also provided a forum for resolving issues that affected the whole community. In addition, the trade routes which ran through a geographical region that stretched from the Arab heartlands to the Central Asian steppes formed a lifeline of economic, intellectual and cultural growth as well as a means for regular links among communities of Muslims living in diverse environments.

---

8. See Levtzion, N. and Voll, John, O. (eds., 1987), *Eighteenth Century Renewal and Reform in Islam,* Syracuse University Press, Syracuse.

During the colonial era, this transnational concept of *umma* was replaced by another operating concept that was characteristically western in its origin. This new concept was that of nationalism which gave rise to the idea of state as a basic political unit, defined by concrete boundaries. This change was more than a mere theoretical formulation of two concepts; it had far-reaching implications for the Muslim world. The spirit of nationalism is based on cultural and linguistic grounds. In the West, this concept gave birth to distinct political units that were, by and large, defined on the basis of language, culture and geographical boundaries. These states demanded loyalty from their citizens in the name of patriotism. For instance, the foremost duty of a Russian was defined as loyalty to Russia, and for a German it was loyalty to Germany. Islam does not recognize any fragmentation of humanity on the basis of culture and language. The emergence of nationalism in the Muslim world during the colonial rule produced, for the first time in their history, an idea that divided the *umma* on national and regional grounds—a division from which they are still suffering. This division gave rise to numerous countries in the Muslim world and created nations and states, divided and at war with each other.

The second change which affected the Muslim world deeply was the position of the Arabic language. Being the language of the Qur'ān, Arabic had achieved the status of *lingua franca* in the Muslim world. In countries where it was not the usual spoken language, it was commonly taught at the elementary level and those who continued their studies beyond the basic level invariably learned it as the language of scholarship. This shared language was the single most important vehicle of communication in the Muslim world. Thus it was possible for an Indian Muslim, for instance, to communicate with his Egyptian trade partner or fellow student in a language that was not foreign to either of them but had centuries of shared terminology, metaphors and parables. The wisdom and teachings of the ancestors were preserved for all generations and for all regions in this language. The colonial rulers replaced this with their own languages and, within a short span of time, in countries where Arabic was not the usual language of people, it became a foreign language. This change produced two effects: it destroyed the vehicle of communication among various Muslim communities and, in those countries where Arabic was not used as a spoken language, it made the Qur'ān and the vast corpus of traditional knowledge inaccessible even to the educated class. Thus removed from the language of the divine revelation, Muslims in these countries were left defenseless against the onslaught of Western ideology.

The third significant change in the colonized societies was the replacement of the traditional system of education by the Western educational system. In the Muslim societies, the governing principle was Unicity (*tawḥīd*) of God and submission to His Will; education was one way to achieve knowledge of the divine attributes, of the Qur'ān and the Sunna, of sciences related to the cosmos and its organization and rhythms, to the physiological functioning of the body and of understanding numerous other marvels of creation. The set of beliefs forming the core of Islamic teachings was operative in the development of curricula. The universe was created by an omnipotent God, it was subject to His Will, it was created with a purpose, and there was an end for it and a Day of Reckoning. These beliefs formed the basis of all activity. Further, knowledge was acquired in a manner that required a period of apprenticeship, reverence and respect for teachers and it was not an end in itself, but a means. It was not linked with the gains of this world and least of all with jobs in the administrative system. One learned because it was an obligation (*farīḍa*) and for the sake of understanding the nature of this life and the universe. All of this was replaced, with far-reaching ramifications, by the Western educational system which had evolved out of a spirit of free thinking and inquiry, in which nothing was taken as a given. The universe may have been created by God or it may have evolved out of its own. Darwin and the Church Fathers were treated equally and the function of education was to prepare the student for an impartial inquiry, not necessarily based on Faith. This system was invariably linked with the jobs in the new administrative system. Most of those Muslims who received their "education" in the new schools found themselves struggling with two opposing worldviews. Their education created a secular, this-worldly ideal, their faith pulled them toward a profoundly different world. This inner struggle made it very difficult for them to build any social organization on the basis of their faith which became mere rituals, repeated on occasions of birth, marriage and death. This education had only one profane and utilitarian purpose: access to jobs. In time, this new system of education produced a generation of "educated" men and women who had little knowledge and far less faith in their own tradition. The Islam and science discourse, thus, lost its most essential fertile ground—the educational system—in the very process of the emergence of modern science in the Muslim world; the new scientists had no grounding in their own tradition.

The fourth important change was the introduction of the Western political system in the colonized societies. At the time of colonization,

Muslim societies were engaged in an intense inner struggle to develop a new system of governance. The period of large empires, ruled by single families, was coming to an end. The introduction of the Western political system made this evolution impossible.

These changes uprooted centuries-old traditions, social customs, and destroyed the organic growth and continuity of the institutions. As a result, when the struggle for independence started, its point of departure was based on the transformed societies that were already looking toward a new Western educated elite for guidance. The genuine representatives of the Islamic tradition had been removed from the role of leadership. Because the concept of state as the basic operating unit was already established and a strong nationalist lobby had emerged, all colonized lands fought for the independence of their countries, instead of re-establishment of some form of pan-Islamic unit. In many cases, artificial boundaries were drawn to create nation-states out of geographical regions that had existed as one unit for centuries. A nation-state was the only political entity that was recognized by the international organizations, such as the League of Nations and, later, the United Nations, hence the task of carving out non-viable states, which would perpetually remain dependent on the West, was made easier. Thus, the map of the world was redrawn by the departing colonial powers, leaving very little room for the transnational concept of *umma* to become an operative reality. Most leaders of the independence movements in the colonized lands were actually products of the Western institutions. Thus independence, in most cases, essentially meant a change of rulers rather than ideologies.

When the first phase of independence was over, the Muslim masses realized that their struggle had changed little in their lives. This led to a widespread resentment followed by a series of coups and changes of governments through mass uprisings. In the sixties, this instability gave rise to a series of "revolutions" across the whole central belt of the traditional Muslim lands. The most frequent label for these so-called revolutions was "socialism", though often with some qualitative adjective, such as Arab or even Islamic, attached to the label. These "revolutions" changed nothing.

The dawn of the fifteenth century of Hijra (November 1979) saw a great upsurge in the Muslim world. The Iranian Revolution, the newly found wealth through the export of oil and the Prophetic promise that God will revive his *Umma* at the head of each century—all combined to produce a new hope. A number of international conferences were held. Many new institutions were established and there was a renewed awareness to reclaim the intellectual tradition that had once flourished in the Muslim world. But this was a short-lived hope.

There was neither the material revival, nor the intellectual and spiritual resurgence. All that this short spring of hope could create was a small vanguard of Muslim scholars who were able to pinpoint the malaise of the *Umma* with ever more precision. But they were not allowed to exercise their legitimate role as the revivers of the intellectual tradition. Those who could not be subdued or silenced, were killed. Sayyed Quṭb, the celebrated Egyptian exegete whose commentary on the Qurʾān, *Fī Ẓilāl al-Qurʾān*, is now the most widely read commentaries in the Muslim world, was among such intellectuals who paid the price of their convictions with their life.

The new Islam and science discourse that emerged from this background is intimately linked to the social, political, economic and educational changes that affected the Muslim world during the eighteenth and the nineteenth centuries; in many ways, it is the product of these winds of change as we will see in the next two chapters.

CHAPTER EIGHT

The Colonial Cut

The Islam and science discourse entered a new phase in the nineteenth century. This new dimension of the discourse was the natural outcome of the arrival of the Western science in the Muslim world. Until then, the Islam and science discourse had been rooted within the larger Islamic intellectual tradition; now it acquired a new dimension because one of the two entities of the discourse, science, had a matrix situated outside the Islamic tradition. The arrival of this foreign entity, which was premised on its own philosophical and religious foundations, was not like the arrival of the material from the pre-Islamic civilizations into the Islamic scientific tradition because that material had come into a living tradition, through an active process of appropriation. The new science, on the other hand, came to a tradition that was neither actively seeking it, nor was able to appropriate it into its own matrix. As a result, there emerged a completely new phenomenon that produced novel effects previously unknown.

Numerous questions, which hold center stage in this new Islam and science discourse, had little to do with what was until then considered to be the essential features of the discourse. The new questions arose from a widely held view that the Muslim world had fallen behind Europe in science and technology. This is not an altogether false premise, though this was only *one* of the contributing causes. However, this has been generally taken to be *the* cause for the colonization of most of the Muslim world in the late eighteenth and the early nineteenth centuries. This reductionist approach then sought the remedy in the same reductionist manner; this is how the demand for the acquisition of Western science (and technology) became the roaring cry of the age. This had a significant effect on the Islam and science discourse, which became hostage to the question of acquisition of Western science and technology. This myopic attitude is still prevalent in many circles in the Muslim world. The sole purpose of Islam in this new attitude is to sanction, justify, and encourage the acquisition of modern science. Two other facets of this new discourse are attempts to prove the prefiguration of the findings of modern science in the two primary sources of Islam, the Qur'ān and the Sunna; and the large-scale attempts to establish what has become known as *al-'ijāz al-'ilmī fi'l-Qur'ān,* the scientific miracles of the Qur'ān. This chapter is devoted to an examination of the origins, motives and nature of these new factors which led to the emergence of a "colonized Islam and science discourse" which will be the focus of the next chapter. The brief summary of events and currents in the previous chapter provides a convenient backdrop for tracing these developments. It will be useful to examine the process of arrival of the Western science in the Muslim world along with the accompanying political, economic and social conditions prevalent at that time and then discuss the general transformation of the discourse on Islam and science. This will allow us to see the complex interdependence of various social, political, economic and scientific forces that gave birth to the new facets of Islam and science discourse.

Science in the Service of the Empire

The arrival of Western science in the Muslim world is intimately connected with a much larger transformation of the traditional Muslim lands. The connections between the implantation of the new science and the colonial designs for the people and the occupied land are deep, insidious, and often ignored in the larger framework of Islam and science discourse. But these connections form an integral part of the discourse and must be brought to light for any understanding of the transformation of the discourse during this period. Allegedly benevolent actions, such as the establishment of botanical gardens, would appear to have no connection with the destruction of the indigenous tradition, but when seen in the proper historical context, and through the well-documented records, the establishment of these institutions proves to be integrally linked to the economic and political designs of the colonizing powers and it becomes abundantly clear that the new science arrived in the colonized lands in service of the empire. The mechanisms adopted for the implantation of the new science slightly varied in the various Muslim regions but their overall impact was the same. We will explore the case of the Indian Timūrī empire as a model.

The arrival of western science in India is intimately connected with the transformation of a trading company to a colonial state. When the directors of the East India Company (EIC), appointed Thomas Roe as an official ambassador from James I to the Timūrī emperor Jahāngīr in 1615, it already had a factory on the west coast of Surat but, as compared to the Portuguese and the Dutch, the English presence was far from being secure. During the next one hundred years, the rivalry between the Dutch, the Portuguese and the English companies and the local political considerations played a major role in the eventual victory of the EIC which was able to obtain the royal decree (*farmān*) of 1717 in its favor. However, it was cotton, and not the Indian spices, that became the deciding factor in the large-scale operation of EIC in the Indian subcontinent. The "Calico Craze" in Britain that bestowed high esteem on Indian calico, muslin and chintz, together with the ban on French linen, had a significant impact on the British woolen and silk industry though perhaps not to the extent mentioned in a pamphlet of the time, *The Trade to India Critically and Calmly Considered* (1720): "Europe like a body in warm bath with its veins opened lies bleeding to death and her bullion, which is the life blood of trade, flows to India...to enrich the Great Moghul's subjects."[1] But it was the perception of the impact of import of Indian cotton on the British industry—rather than the actual amount of bullion involved—that triggered the Weavers' Riots in 1719. The riots forced the British Parliament to pass the "Calicoe Bill" which became an act in 1720. The Bill banned the use or wear of all "printed, painted, stained and dyed calicoes" of non-British and non-Irish origin from the Christmas Day of 1722. But the demand prompted John Kay to invent his flying shuttle for weaving and within the next thirty years, new inventions by men like James Hargreaves (d.1778), Richard Arkwright (1732-1792), and Samuel Crompton (1753-1827) turned Lancashire into a major producer of cotton textile produced from staple that was not grown in Britain. Within a short time, the revenue generated from the export of this cotton textile triggered the Industrial Revolution, which, in turn, enabled Britain to flood the markets of India with cheaper cotton textile produced in Britain and strangle the age-old art of producing hand-loomed cotton of the finest kind in Bengal. Thus, prohibitive duties imposed on textiles coming from India on the one hand, and the unrestrained export of woven cotton to India on the other, would turn India, which had been an exporting country, into an importing one, as Karl Marx observed: "The great workshop of cotton manufacture for the world since immemorial times, became now inundated with English twists and cotton stuffs."[2]

> However, to flood India with cotton produced by the power looms, the British first had to gain ascendancy

---

1. Cited in Baber, Zaheer (1996), *The Science of Empire*, State University of New York Press, Albany, p. 116. This section borrows heavily from this major study of the relationship between colonialism and science.
2. Quoted in Baber (1996), p. 118.

> over other rival powers like the Dutch and the French. The EIC also had to gain actual control over Indian territories. And this was anything but a smooth process. It was hardly a case of the British deciding on a clear-cut colonial policy and putting it into practice just as they pleased. It was a complex and, at times, convoluted process that involved a mix of the implementation of specific policies and their unintended consequences...The eventual establishment of English territorial power in India, starting with the Battle of Plassey in 1757, occurred against the background of relatively rapid social change within the erstwhile centralized Mughal empire.[3]

The fatal battles of Plassey (1757) and Buxar (1764), which consolidated the hold of the British EIC over Bengal, which, in turn, proved a stepping stone for the expansion of EIC control over Bihar and Orissa, were followed by the India Act of 1784, which led to the creation of the Board of Control and placed the activities of the EIC under the direct supervision of the British Parliament. Then came the 1793 Permanent Settlement Act of Cornwallis which removed all barriers to treating Indian land as a commodity to be bought and sold. Now the stage was set for a rapid expansion of the Indian holdings. When the army of EIC won the final encounter between the armies of the Company and those of Tīpū Sultān, the visionary ruler of Mysore, in the closing year of the eighteenth century, the fate of India was sealed. The defeat of Tipu's army represents the last real resistance to colonization of India. In 1813, the British government decided to increase its direct control over the Company and the new charter of 1813 ended all monopoly of the EIC in India and paved the way for full colonial structure. It was then that the modern science arrived in India—primarily in the service of the empire.

The first major activity of the newly arrived science was in the area of scientific geography. This was to build on the efforts of the EIC which had started as early as the 1760s and which were aimed at producing accurate surveys for revenue collection. No wonder, the first "great English geographer in India was the Surveyor-General James Rennell, who had arrived in India in 1760 and was employed by the navy to produce extensive surveys of the coastal areas of southern India and Ceylon. When

3. Baber (1996), pp. 119-20.

Robert Clive returned to India as governor of Calcutta in May 1765, he created the post of Surveyor-General of Bengal and appointed Rennell as the first holder of this post with funds from the Company along with a company of sepoys for his protection.

> By the mid-1770s, Rennell had compiled enough maps and charts to prepare the Bengal Atlas and the Map of Hindoostan. Assured of a pension of six hundred pounds by Warren Hastings, Clive's successor, the first surveyor-general of Bengal collected all his charts, drawings, and maps and set sail for England in March 1777...First published in 1779, the Bengal Atlas was followed by a second edition in 1781. From the point of view of the colonial administrators based in Bengal, the significance of the publication of the Bengal Atlas cannot be overemphasized. It was the first modern atlas of the province, drawn on a scale of three miles to an inch, prepared after years of detailed mapping and fixing of positions through the use of innovative measurement techniques...the atlas, running into fourteen folios, of a province that constituted "the British Bridgehead", was deemed by Clements Markham as a "work of the first importance both for strategical and administrative purposes." Keenly aware of the significant role of the various officers of the East India Company in patronizing his scientific interests, Rennell dedicated the Bengal Atlas to governors Robert Clive, Cartier, Warren Hastings, and other key administrators.[4]

This was followed by several other trigonometric, topographical, and statistical surveys of various regions of India. On January 15, 1784, William Jones, a judge at the Supreme Court of Calcutta, set up the Asiatic Society of Bengal on the model of Royal Society of London. Four years later, the Society's journal, *Asiatic Researches,* was launched. Whatever the overt purpose of the Society and the journal may have been, Jones was convinced, as early as 1785, that "on the sciences, properly so named in which it must be admitted that the Asiaticks, if compared with our western nations, are mere children", but by 1790, after the publication of Samuel Davis' paper "Astronomical Computations of the Hindus," and Reuben Burrow's "A Proof that the Hindus had the Bionomial Theorem" in the

4. Baber (1996), p. 142.

second volume of *Asiatic Researches,* Jones had changed his initial assessment as he wrote, "Give us time, we may say, for our investigations, and we will transfer to Europe all the sciences, arts, and literatures of Asia."[5] However, Jones, who would became known for his interest in and patronage of Indian languages, literature and philosophy, was also an amateur botanist who had worked closely with Johan Gerard Koenig, a student of Carl Linneaus. He realized the significant relationship that existed between the local medical traditions and the plants and herbs used in the extensive pharmacology that was practiced throughout India. In planning his "Treatise on the Plants of India", Jones wanted to reduce the various indigenous classification systems to a modern taxonomical scheme based on the Linnean natural order of genera and species. Here, we see clearly the connections between language and science. Various plants and vegetables that had been known to the inhabitants of the subcontinent by a certain name for centuries were to be reclassified for no reason other than to facilitate their passage into the European repository. Many of these local names had also existed in the rich mythical, literary and folklore traditions—all of which now were deemed to be primitive, outdated, and non-sensical.

William Jones was one typical example of the instruments of change. In establishing the Asiatic Society, his goals were to investigate the indigenous state of science and technology for devising "the best mode of ruling" Bengal; he wanted to separate "accurate and rational knowledge" from "mythology" and "clouds of fables". On the basis of having spent a few years in India and having an amateurish interest in botany, Jones had become an expert on all things Indian to the extent that he could mock traditions that were rooted in centuries of human experience. "Geography, astronomy, and chronology have, in this part of Asia, shared the fate of authentic history," he wrote, "and like that, have been so masked and bedecked in the fantastic robes of mythology and metaphor, that the real system of Indian philosophers and mathematicians can scarcely be distinguished..."[6]

This scientific tradition, which had been understood by its savants for centuries and which was an integral part of the larger tradition rooted in the fabric of a civilization that had emerged in the Indian subcontinent from various historical currents over centuries, was incomprehensible to a

5. Jones, W. (1799) [1790]: 345, quoted by Baber (1996), p. 156.
6. Baber (1996), p. 159.

representative of the European science, and hence it had to be changed! The instruments of change were the new institutions that were to be planted in rapid succession. First came the Asiatic Society, then its journal *Asiatic Researches,* then its successor, *Journal of the Asiatic Society,* and then a torrent of institutions—all styled on the European models, with complete disregard to the local traditions, customs and ways. The new institutions included the Royal Botanical Gardens, the Indian Museum, the Zoological Gardens, the Survey of India, His Majesty's Mint, the Meteorological Department of the Government of India, the Linguistic Survey, the Medical College of Bengal, the School of Tropical Medicine, the Geological Survey, and the Anthropological Survey of India.

This was, however, only the beginning of the new era. There was an immediate benefit to EIC in terms of extraction of revenues at extremely high rates of assessment despite crop failures. The Company also showed total disregard for the preexisting irrigation systems. Then there were the monopolies in grain trade which were dominated by the officers of the EIC and their chosen Indian traders, this led to hoarding and diversion of rice by the colonial administration to feed its armies in various regions of India. Eventually, this led to the devastating famine of 1770. Famines do not come suddenly and like all famines, the famine of 1770 gave ample forewarning. In the wake of early signs, many warnings were sent to the administration. In one such warning, a British district collector wrote to the government on November 23, 1769, "It is with great concern, Gentlemen, that we are to inform you that we have a most melancholy prospect before our eyes[,] of universal distress for want of grain...insomuch that the oldest inhabitants never remembered to have known anything like it, and as to threaten a famine."[7] And on January 4, 1770, Maharajah Shitab Roy wrote to the government "such is the scarcity of grain in this province that fifty poor wretches in a day perish with famine in the streets of Patna." But nothing was done. Not only that, the revenue collection continued with the same brutality and, in the following year, when the impact of the famine had become widely known, the Governor General Warren Hastings boasted, "the nett collections of the year 1771 exceeded even those of 1768."[8] More than one-third of the total population and more than half of the cultivators, "the source of revenue", perished in one year. Those who remained were faced with the persistent demands of the revenue collectors which they

7. Baber (1996), p. 161.
8. Hunter (1868) 405, quoted in Baber, p. 162.

could not meet. Hence, they started to abandon their lands and moved to big cities to find employment as laborers.

The situation worsened by the Permanent Settlement instituted by Lord Cornwallis on March 22, 1793. The Permanent Settlement transformed agra-rian relations by conferring private rights of land ownership to *zamindars*; this effectively created a new class of absentee landlords who lived in cities and extracted large incomes from the labor of another class, the peasants. But this did not increase the revenue. As a solution to the problem of decreasing revenues, science and technology were pressed into colonial service. This was initiated by a Lieutenant-Colonel by the name of Robert Kyd, who wrote a letter to the Board of Revenue in Calcutta, on April 15, 1786, proposing the introduction of the Malayan sago palm to India, a plant "affording a species of food, highly valued, and eagerly sought after by the natives of every denomination of our Government."[9] Kyd followed his letter with another, written on June 1, 1786, this time proposing the transfer of cinnamon trees from Assam to Calcutta, in order to offset the commercial advantage the Dutch had from their possession of cinnamon plantations in Ceylon.

These letters were received by the Company at a time when its revenues were continuously falling and the Directors were looking for new commodities, especially botanical products like drugs, dyes and spices. Kyd's proposals were eventually picked up by Henry Dundas, the president of the newly constituted Board of Control, overseeing the financial affairs of the Company, who referred his proposals to Sir Joseph Banks, the president of the Royal Society, who had considerable experience in the establishment of botanical gardens in St. Vincent in the West Indies for the introduction of breadfruit from Tahiti as "food for slaves".[10] Joseph Banks wrote back, enthusiastically supporting the proposal on the basis of availability of "Labour excessive cheap: raw materials of many sorts, dying, drugs, Medecines, Spices &c sure of a ready and advantageous market and of producing a most beneficial influence upon the Commerce of the mother Country."[11] Consequently, the Board of Control and the Court of Directors sent a letter to the Governor-General at Calcutta on July 31, 1787 in which they conveyed their "great pleasure from the perusal of

9. Baber (1996), p. 165.
10. Mackay, David (1985), *In the Wake of Cook: Exploration, Science and Empire, 1780-1801*, Croom Helm, London, p. 172, quoted in Baber (1996), p. 167.
11. Ibid.

Lieutenant-Colonel Kyd's letter...proposing the establishment of a Botanical Garden, and give our most hearty approbation to the institution."[12] Kyd's proposal to introduce sago palms was never implemented, but within four years, grants from the Company led to the establishment of botanical gardens at Calcutta, Madras, Bombay, and St. Helena. Robert Kyd was appointed as the first superintendent of Calcutta Botanical Garden. With the help of these gardens, the Company was able to transfer many commercial plants and crops across continents to raise revenues. The case of tea and cinchona[13]—two plants that significantly increased the fortunes of the British Empire—is instructive.

Various kinds of tea had been cultivated in the Indian Timūrī empire for centuries. It was used for medicinal purposes. But the kind of tea that was popular in Britain was imported from China and it was paid for in bullion. For example, in the year 1786, the Company had paid approximately eight hundred thousand pound sterling for purchase of tea from Canton. The Company now proceeded to transplant this particular kind of tea from China to India. The superintendent of the Company's Botanical Garden at Saharanpur had reported to the Company that India's Himalayan foothills would be ideal for the cultivation of tea. The area between Bengal and Bhutan was selected for the first experiments in tea transfer. Joseph Bank had suggested that the Company should import some Chinese tea cultivators along with the plants and place them under the "able and indefatigable superintendent" of the Calcutta Botanical Gardens.[14] But there were problems in obtaining both the plants and the Chinese cultivators from Canton. However, small consignments of plants arrived in Calcutta in 1789 and 1790 and grew well. But this situation changed dramatically after the Opium Wars.

In 1848, the Company commissioned Robert Fortune, a botanist with experience in China, to obtain suitable tea plants from China. He was successful. In 1851, he arrived in India with seventeen thousand tea seeds, together with Chinese farmers. By then, the Company's botanists working at the gardens in Calcutta and Sharanpur had "discovered" that the tea was indeed grown in the north-eastern regions of India. William Griffith, the superintendent of the Calcutta gardens (1842-44), had traveled to Assam in

12. Ibid.
13. Any of the several trees and shrubs of the genus *Cinchona,* of the madder family, esp. *C. Calisaya,* native to the Andes, cultivated for its bark, which yields quinine and other alkaloids.
14. Mackay, David (1985), p. 175, quoted in Baber (1996), p. 169.

search of tea, teak and mines and he reported in 1847 "the article [tea] is procurable here," including "bitter tea."[15] The Company acquired land around Darjeeling in northeastern India, and with the help of its botanists and the Chinese and Indian cultivators and laborers, began cultivating indigenous varieties of tea on large plantations.

By the latter half of the nineteenth century, tea became one of British India's principal exports and the Indian tea supplanted Chinese tea in the international market. The term "Darjeeling tea" became a household word, a symbol of finest quality tea all over the world. As for the imported Chinese cultivators, they were disposed as soon as their services were deemed to have become redundant. But most of them could not return to China and ended up as displaced and uprooted families who would later open Chinese restaurants in various cities of the Indian subcontinent; some of these restaurants still exist.

The story of the cinchona tree is no less instructive. In 1857, there arose an armed uprising aimed at liberating India from the overbearing rule of the Company. It was ruthlessly crushed but the shock was such that Britain took some drastic steps. The rule of the British East India Company was abolished and the Crown took direct charge of its Indian dominion. A new institution of the Secretary of State for India was established together with a Council for India. This led to a number of important social and political changes. During the rule of the Company, Englishmen had been discouraged from bringing their families to India and they had tended to establish alliances with Indian women. Now, such alliances were discouraged. The Indians could not be trusted anymore. The perceived disloyalty of the Indian sepoys led to the restriction of the artillery to British troops. All higher administrative posts were reserved for the Englishmen. The bureaucracy was expanded and a large number of English administrators arrived in India with their families. This led to increased concerns for their safety and health. These new social conditions drastically increased the consumption of cinchona in India, which was a sure cure for malaria to which the British were increasingly vulnerable in India, having little resistance to it because it had disappeared from England and France by the seventeenth century.

In 1855, the medical board in India sent an urgent letter to the

---

15. Griffith, William (1971) [1847], *Posthumous Paper Bequeathed to the Hounourable East India Company*, Ch'eng Publishing Company, Taipei, pp. 91-2, 96.

"President in Council" at Fort William, expressing their concern over the "danger of a failure of the cinchona supply in America, under the annually increasing demands for the medicinal bark from nearly all parts of the world."[16] This concern eventually led to the dispatch of Clements Markham to Peru. Markham, along with Richard Spruce, a Kew botanist already in Ecuador, and Robert Cross accomplished a daring mission. On the last day of 1860,

> knowingly violating stringent Peruvian and Bolivian laws against the export of cinchona, which was a government monopoly, Markham and his colleagues were eventually successful in shipping out nearly one hundred thousand dried seeds and 637 young plants for India via England. The plants were reared in the Calcutta botanical garden for a while, before being transplanted on plantations in the regions of the Nilgiri Hills by convict laborers. Later, new plantations were established in a number of other areas like Sikkim and Ceylon. The whole process of the transfer of cinchona from South America to India was a colossal undertaking in which the botanists, botanical expertise, and the network of botanical gardens both in India and England played crucial roles. A number of botanical and chemical experiments were carried out before the plantations and the production of quinine was successful...[17]

The far-reaching implications of this "scientific enterprise" can be judged from the fact that this transplantation contributed to the subsequent expansion of the British empire to Africa:

> The cinchona cultivation and the production of quinine were also indispensable for the British conquest of [the malaria-prone regions of] Africa. The connection between the botanical gardens of Calcutta, the application of the botanical knowledge for the transfer of cinchona from South America to India and the expansion and exercise of colonial power was best expressed by Surgeon Major G. Bidie of the British Army of Madras presidency: "To England, with her

16. Medical Board. Letter to the Hon. J. A. Dorin, President in Council. Fort William, 9 June 1855. Parliamentary Papers. House of Commons. 1863:13, quoted by Baber (1996), p. 171.
17. Baber (1996), pp. 172-3.

> numerous and extensive Colonial possessions, it is simply priceless; and it is not too much to say, that if portions of her tropical empire are upheld by the bayonet, the arm that wields the weapon would be nerveless but for Cinchona bark and its active principles." ...Overall it should be evident that although the scientific research initiated in the early phases of colonial rule contributed to the reproduction of colonialism, it also led to the production and development of new scientific knowledge. There emerged a symbiotic relationship between the production of scientific knowledge and exercise of colonial power. The connections among science, technology, and colonialism were further strengthened in the later phases of the colonial rule in India...[18]

After 1857, the British government established a number of new scientific institutions in India. However, throughout the British rule in India, these institutions remained a shadow of their parent institutions in England where modern science developed into a formidable enterprise. In India, it could only produce second-rate imitators of western science, assistants and technicians for the new scientific machinery of the colonial government.

Institutional Collapse

The Islam and science discourse could not have attained its new dimension without a significant change in the institutional structure that evolved. This new institutional structure drastically affected all spheres of life in all colonized lands.

In India, the educational institutions were part of a vast system that had functioned for centuries. As late as 1822, Thomas Munro, the governor of Madras, had stated that "every village had a school," and a senior official of the Bombay presidency, G. L. Pendergest, had observed "there is hardly a village, great or small throughout our territories in which there is not at least one school."[19] This indigenous network of schools had come into existence—just like the extensive medical system—over centuries, through endowments of land and property for education and it was organically linked to the civilization which had given birth to this system and which

18. Ibid.
19. Di Bona, Joseph (1989), *Critical Perspectives on Indian Education*, Bahri, New Delhi, pp. 42-5, 69, cited in Baber (1996), p. 187.

honored the village school master, just like it honored the local religious scholars who performed the rites of passage from birth to death. Attached to houses of worship, these local schools had provided education to countless generations before the arrival of the colonial masters—an education that was sufficient for their purposes. Likewise, the local *panchiat* system had provided an effective justice system and the sharing of information by farmers had been sufficient for raising crops that fed the whole subcontinent for centuries. All of these traditions were interwoven with a way of life, social customs, and with history, religion, beliefs, literature and myths that had sustained life in this part of the world for centuries.

The educational system in India primarily rested on the extensive endowments that supported madāris for Muslim students and *pathshalas* for Hindus. But the British East India Company considered these rent-free lands sheer loss and wastage because they could not collect any revenue from such lands. Consequently, various laws were passed in the late nineteenth and the early twentieth centuries for the "resumption of land", or the right to collect revenue on previously rent-free land grants. In Bengal, this resulted in the increase of five hundred thousand rupees as revenue and in the northwest provinces the amount of revenue reclaimed was over 2,321,953 rupees.[20] These laws choked the lifeline of a centuries-old tradition and within a few decades, whole regions were left without schools. This, combined with the belief that whatever these institutions were providing was insufficient, backward, inadequate, and absurd, completed the prescription for the collapse of this system. "The absurd systems of Hindoo geography and astronomy," wrote J. W. Massie, the author of *Continental India: Travelling Sketches and Historical Recollections*, "and their stupid fictions in natural science, rest upon one foundation, which demonstrations and experiment could easily overthrow; the extension of true science would, therefore, undermine the fortress of error and delusion..."[21]

But this was not all. There were a number of debates in the ruling circles about the state of the society they were ruling. There were those, like Charles Grant, one of the members of the Court of Directors of the

20. Di Bona (1989), p. 71, cited in Baber (1996), p. 188.
21. Massie, J. W. (1985) [1840], *Continental India: Travelling Sketches and Hitorical Recollections*, 2 vols. B. R. Publishing, Delhi, vol. 2, pp. 470-1, cited in Baber (1996), p. 184.

Company, as well as a member of Parliament, who considered educated natives better governable than the uneducated and there were those who invoked the designs of the "Supreme Disposer" who had put India "providentially into our hands...not merely to draw an annual profit from them, but that we might diffuse among their inhabitants, long sunk in darkness, vice and misery, the light and the benign influences of Truth, the blessings of well-regulated society, the improvements and the comforts of active industry."[22] Grant argued that these religious objectives could be pursued along with the extension of commerce and in fact, the two would go hand in hand. Grant's recipe for the achievement of these two goals was the introduction of scientific and technical education and establishment of industry. When the renewal of the charter of the Company was being considered in 1813, a "Committee of the Protestant Society" met in a New London Tavern and appealed to the Parliament, that

> as Men, as Britons, and as Christians, this committee continue to regard with anguish, the moral dispersion and religious ignorance of very many millions of immortal beings who people the plains of India, subject to British power...[C]onvinced by history, observation, and experience, that Christianity would affirm inestimable benefits, and that their diffusion is practicable, wise, and imperative, they cannot but persevere eminently to desire its speedy and universal promulgation throughout the regions of the East.[23]

However, the Company knew from its experience of past incidents that such efforts would incite "violent irritation...in the minds of the natives of India," and thus jeopardize the rule. Hence it refrained from direct imposition of Christianity on India but let the missionary activity spread with full force. In 1823, the British government instituted a committee on Public Instruction at Calcutta to investigate the best mode of imparting

22. Charles Grant, Observation on the State of Society among the Asiatic Subjects of Great Britain, Parliamentary Papers. House of Commons. East India Affairs, 15 June 1813, reprinted in Mahmood, Syed (1895), A History of English Education: Extracts from Parliamentary Papers, Official Reports, Authoritative Despatches, Minutes and Writings of Statesmen, Resoulution of the Government etc. M. A. O. College, Aligarh, p. 17, cited in Baber (1996), p. 191.
23. Appendix "A" to John Bebb's letter to the Court of Directors, Parliamentary Papers, House of Commons, Papers Relating to the Affairs of the East India Company, 15 June 1813:8, cited in Baber (1996), pp. 192-3.

instruction. The committee consisted of members of the colonial administration who held diverse opinions about the direction public education under state patronage ought to take. The two dominant views were later crystallized into the "Orientalist" and "Anglicist" factions; the former arguing for the establishment of institutions on the model of madāris and *vidyalayas*, where instructions should be imparted in the "vernacular", the latter supporting instruction in English and the withdrawal of any state patronage for Sanskrit, Persian and Arabic. These debates would later lead to the infamous "Minute on Education" by Thomas Babington MacCaulay and to the collapse of traditional institutions which is simultaneously associated with the rise of a new kind of institutional structure that would produce the first crop of "educated" Indians who looked down at their own tradition, history and civilization. Then they took lead and established a number of colleges to promote instruction in English language, literature and Western science.

Extensive inland trade by the Company had intertwined its fortunes with the interest of a small segment of Indian merchants who had been facilitated by many policies of the Company, most of all through the Cornwallis' Permanent Settlement which provided opportunities for large-scale purchase of cheap land by a handful of Indian merchants. This new elite, *bhadralok,* had emerged through a fundamental structural transformation of the India society. Most of the members of this elite had enormously benefited from the depopulation of Bengal in the wake of the 1770 famine when traditional tillers of land were forced to sell their land to this elite because they could not pay taxes to the Company. Many members of the new urban elite also sought employment in the rapidly expanding British administration and thus acquired a social prestige and power by associating with the rulers, however remote that association might have been.

It was the representatives of the *bhadralok* in Bengal who first established colleges in Bengal for teaching English language, literature and Western science. The Calcutta Hindu College, or *vidyalaya*, was founded in 1816 by the Indian merchants with funds donated by this elite class and augmented by the Company. It was managed by a joint committee of Indians and Englishmen. In July 1818, another college was established in Benares through funds donated by one Joynarain Ghossal and a number of other colleges emerged in the Bombay Presidency between 1821 and 1823. In 1821, H. H. Wilson, acting on the earlier "Minute on Education" by Lord Minto established the Hindu Sanskrit College at Calcutta on the pattern of the Benares Hindu College with the hope of using the agency of Brahmans to impart the education of modern science and technology. Lord Minto in his "Minute of 1811" had pointed out that "the prevalence of the crimes of perjury and forgery...is in a great measure ascribable, both in the Mahomedans and Hindus, to the want of due instruction in the moral and religious tenets of their respective faiths," and Wilson's move to establish a Sanskrit college represented, in part, an attempt to fulfill those aims. But Raja Ram Mohun Roy, a representative of the rising *bhadralok* of Calcutta, opposed it. He had hoped that through this seminary [the Sanskrit school], the "natives of India [will receive instructions] in mathematics, natural philosophy, chemistry, anatomy, and other useful sciences." He said that, "We already offered our thanks to Providence for inspiring the most generous and enlightened nations of the West with the glorious ambition of planting in Asia the arts and sciences of modern Europe." But now he was disappointed because the Benares Hindu College was going to impart education in Sanskrit, "the Sangscrit language, so difficult that almost a lifetime is necessary for its acquisition, is well known to have been for ages a lamentable check on the diffusion of knowledge...[T]he Sangscrit system of education would be the best calculated to keep this country in darkness..."[24] This new and rising class of Indians looked at their culture and tradition through the eyes of the colonizers and it had been mentally colonized.

Nevertheless, the Company itself introduced various educational institutions to fulfill its needs. For instance, a "Minute by Lord Auckland", written on October 1, 1839, states: "A native medical staff would be very useful for department duty. The state would obtain a cheap class of well-educated natives on whom the climate would make no impression."[25]

Muslims were not far behind in this race. But because the British had wrested the control of India mostly through active battles with Muslims, it was natural for them to consider Muslims of India as potentially more hostile to them than Hindus whom they started to favor in various administrative jobs. Initially, Muslims had kept aloof from the new English schools. Their own languages, Arabic, Persian, and Urdu, along with

24. Quotation from "Lord Minto's Minute" is cited by Mahmood, Syed (1895), p. 20; excerpt of Raja Roy's criticism has been cited in Sharpe, H. (ed. 1920), *Selections from Education Records;* both references are cited from Baber (1996), pp. 196-97.
25. Quoted from Sangwan, Satpal (1991), *Science, Technology and Colonisation: An Indian Experience (1757-1857)*, Anamika Prakashan, Delhi, p. 64.

centuries of traditional learning, had been rendered obsolete in a matter of a few years, through fundamental restructuring of the society and its institutions. Telling signs of the general atmosphere at this time in history are demonstrated in proverbs like the famous, *Parhey Fārsī béche tél,* which stated, in essence, that the only possible utility left for those who study Persian is to be the small time neighborhood grocer who sells oil.

In 1858, when India was placed under direct Crown rule, a number of administrative and structural changes were made, including restructuring of the armed forces. The role of private companies was minimized and the Crown took direct control of many private enterprises, such as the railway that was initiated previously under private companies. Because the Muslim soldiers were perceived to be the major instigators of the 1857 effort to gain independence, the British wrath fell on them with extreme severity. Established families were uprooted, the remaining members of the Tīmūrī royal family were killed or exiled and cities like Delhi and Agra were desecrated. In a report entitled "Our Indian Musalmans: Are They Bound in Conscience to Rebel Against the Queen?", W. W. Hunter had argued that "the Mohammadans have now sunk so low that, even when qualified for Government employment, they are studiously kept out of it by Government notifications."[26] The Company government therefore, earnestly desired to "induce youths of respectability and superior attainments to attach them to the study of medical sciences".[27]

Gradually, the new situation forced some Muslims to come forward and advocate active participation by their fellow Muslims in the new administrative and educational system that had come into existence in the post-1858 Indian subcontinent. The most important representative of this group was Sayyid Ahmad Khan (1817-1898), who would be knighted as the Knight Commander of the Star of India in 1888. Ahmad Khan established the Aligarh Scientific Society in 1864 with the goal of "causing the blessed morning of civilization to dawn on the night of ignorance and darkness which for ages has retarded the advance of this country." This goal resonates with the views of Charles Grant and James Mill, whose *Elements of Political Economy* was translated by the Aligarh Scientific Society into Urdu. But we will have more to say about this in the following section.

---

26. Hunter, William (1872), *The Indian Musulmans,* Trubner, London, quoted in Reetz, Dietrich (1988), "Enlightenment and Islam: Sayyid Ahmad Khan's Plea to Indian Muslims for Reason", *Indian Historical Review,* vol. 14, pp. 206-18, cited in Baber (1996), p. 226.
27. Ibid.

When Lord George Curzon, who has been called "the last of the British Mughals",[28] arrived in India in 1898, in the aftermath of yet another spell of devastating famines, he was determined to transform the administrative structure of India that governed science and technology, along with its educational institutions. On the very first opportunity that came his way, he called the educational system set up by his predecessors "faulty but not rotten".[29] Ironically, long before his pronouncement on the system, many Indians had begun to look askance at the rapid westernization of their youth and the value of British-controlled education. The system that had been established with great zeal had certain fundamental flaws so that the universities had been reduced to being little more than a collection of lecture rooms where students crammed to fill their minds with texts in order to pass the examination and get a job. The constitution and composition of the senates and the syndicates which governed the newly established universities at Allahabad, Madras, Bombay, Calcutta and Lahore had often been filled with men whose interests were hardly educational and some of whom could not even sign their names. Curzon knew this state of affairs and so did some of the educated Indians who were beginning to stand up for their rights. But when Curzon convened the Educational Conference, not a single Hindu was invited to participate in the deliberations concerning their future and only a handful of handpicked Muslims were present. When this fact became public, the Viceroy was "pleased to invite" Sir Gurudas Banerjee, as an afterthought. When the new Education Bill was finally passed on March 21, 1904, hundreds of students came out on the streets to protest against the overweening British lord who had taken it upon himself to reform the "natives". But this was merely the beginning of the grand design which Curzon had for his new empire.

In 1902, he set up a Board of Scientific Advice (BSA) to coordinate all scientific research in India. From now on, India was to emulate the scientific organizations of England; BSA being a replica of "Scientific Advisory Council" which was proposed for Britain three decades earlier by Alexander Strange and Norman Lockyer but which had never been established. Sir Norman Lockyer, an influential scientist and editor of *Nature*, expressed enthusiasm over the creation of BSA that was supposed to coordinate research in India with the assistance of the Royal Society. But

---

28. Goradia, Nayana (1993), *Lord Curzon: The Last of the British Moghuls*, Oxford University Press, Delhi.
29. Goradia (1993), p. 178.

over time, BSA and the Royal Society developed differences over the nature of research to be carried out in India. The basic issue revolved around "fundamental" versus "applied" research and the ability of Indian scientists to perform "pure" scientific research. The experience of BSA, however, served as a model for the establishment of a number of other scientific organizations both in Britain as well as in India. In India, the new institutions included the Committee of Civil Research (1925); the Economic Advisory Council (1930); the Scientific Advisory Committee (1940-45). In 1923, BSA was dissolved as part of a temporary economic measure but in its stead a number of other organizations were established in the following years. These were the Indian Science Congress (1924), the National Institute of Science (1935), and the Indian Academy of Sciences (1924). Eventually the Council for Scientific and Industrial Research (CSIR), established in 1934, succeeded BSA. In 1947, when the British left and the Indian subcontinent was divided into two nation states, Pakistan and India, this institutional structure had firmly taken hold in the administrative realm and it was retained by both states with only slight modifications. In Pakistan, CSIR is called PCSIR and the Academy of Science was renamed as the Pakistan Academy of Sciences; both institutions still exist.

Other Regions

We have outlined the emergence of modern science in the Indian Tīmūrī empire in some detail to provide a model. Similar developments can be traced in other Muslim lands. This background is essential to understand the new dimensions of the Islam and science discourse because these new facets of the discourse emerged out of the historical situation which was characterized by political, economic and intellectual colonization of the Muslim world at a time marked by internal strife and upheavals.

The situation in other regions of the Muslim world was different from India only in its particulars. In general, the ultimate result of the process of colonization was the same: the replacement of older institutions with Western institutions, the creation of a small elite that eagerly followed the lifestyles, aspirations and worldviews of the colonizers. We will not go into the details of this history as it is readily available in numerous sources. But by way of a summary, let us note that during the eighteenth century, except for Morocco and Yemen, the entire contemporary twenty-two sovereign Arab states—which are now members of the Arab League—were under the Ottoman rule. During the course of the century, this vast geographical area, which had always been the heartland of Islam, broke away from the center. The dynamics of global politics and economics, built on the new science, forced a new organization of societies, a new configuration of entities that made up nation states.

In the course of the next century, a century known to the Arab historians as the century of Christian missions, the Ottoman authority dwindled in its eastern provinces. Syria, which included the present-day Palestine, Israel, Lebanon, Jordan and present-day Syria, played a leading role in the emergence of a new social order. It had long acted as a cultural and commercial link between the Arab world and the West. Syrian and Lebanese merchants had maintained active contacts with West, long before the French invasion of Egypt in 1798. For example, during 1613-18, the Lebanese Amīr Fakhr al-Dīn al-Manī allied with the Medici Court in Italy and invited Italian technologists to develop the mountainous land in Lebanon. Soon after Napolean's invasion, the *Institut d'Egypt* was established in 1798.

When Muḥammad ʿAlī came to power in 1805, he realized that his administrative structure as well as army was inferior to the European forces in its training, equipment and techniques. He started to import European teachers to set up new institutions. The adoption of western models of governance simultaneously brought the western educational system to the Muslim lands, from primary level right up to universities. And as the traditional religious schools receded into the backwaters, institutions that provided western education flourished in the main cities, offering the only alternative to a populace that was increasingly becoming aware of its intellectual as well as material poverty compared to European civilization. It was this sense of inferiority that was at work when Muḥammad ʿAlī sent 400 students to Europe to study all branches of science. Intense translation activity followed.[30] More than 200 books were translated during Muḥammad ʿAlī's rule. When he died in 1849, many schools were closed and under the rule of Khedive ʿAbbās and Khedive Saʿīd, a reaction set in. However, with Khedive Ismaʿīl's coming to power in 1863, schools were re-opened and he sent another 120 students to Europe. Egyptian rule over Syria and Lebanon (1831-1841) heralded the return of Muḥammad ʿAlī's philosophy and his son, Ibrahīm Pāsha, encouraged modern western

30. Good sources on the translations movement are Abu-Lughod, Ibrahim (1963), *Arab Rediscovery of Europe*, Princeton University Press, Princeton; al-Shayyal, J. (1951), *Ta'rīkh al-Tarjama fī ʿAṣr Muḥammad Ali*, Cairo, cited in Ziadat, Adel A. (1986), *Western Science in the Arab World*, Macmillan Press, London, p. 4.

education. Following the English occupation, Egyptian schools switched to English as the language of instruction in 1887; this had tremendous impact on the pace of westernization. Even the Syrian Protestant College (SPC), which had taught all subjects in Arabic for sixteen years, switched to English in 1882. The role of missionary colleges in spreading western science in the Arab world has been the focus of many recent studies.[31]

The history of the emergence of the learned societies in the Arab world follows a pattern similar to the one in the Indian subcontinent. The Society of Arts and Science, founded by Protestant American missionaries and a few Christian Arab intellectuals in Beirut in 1847, only lasted five years and had no Muslim participation.[32] The Jesuits followed the Protestant example by founding the Oriental Society in 1850 at the initiative of a French priest Deprunières (1821-1872). It was also dominated by Christians, whether Arab or European and it collapsed after two years. In 1882, the Syrian Scientific Society reopened for the third time under the name of Eastern Scientific Society with the express goal of advancement of applied science.[33]

The arrival of the printing press in the Fertile Crescent in 1733 also helped to generate interest in modern education. In fact, Arab scientific journalism predates the appearance of modern Arab universities and specialized education. The periodicals that helped in the dissemination of modern knowledge, at a time when books on Western science were rare, include *al-Waqāʾiʿi,* first appearing in 1828 and *Ḥadīqat al-Akhbār* (The Garden of News), published from Beirut by al-Khuri in 1857. In 1865, the first scientific journal, *Yacoup al-Ṭib,* (*Medical Review*) was established in Cairo and was followed by *al-Muqtaṭaf,* founded by Sarruf and Nimr in Beirut in 1876 and moved to Egypt in 1885. *Al-Muqtaṭaf* played a leading role in the transmission of scientific ideas to the Arab world.[34] In 1834, the

31. Ziadat, Adel A. (1986) is a good source for works dealing with the question of modernization of the Arab world. The sources cited by him include, among others, Tibawi, A. L. (1969), *A Modern History of Syria,* Edinburgh University Press, Edinburgh; Jessup, H. (1910), *Fifty-three Years in Syria,* 2 vols., New York; Hanna, Faith, (1979), *The Story of the American University of Beirut,* Alphabet Press, Boston; Sami, A. (1917), *al-Taʿlīm fī Miṣr* (*Education in Egypt),* Cairo; Aḥmed, Seraj al-Din, (1966), "*al-Ḥaraka al-tarbawiyya fī Lubnan wa Sūriyya,*" ("Educational Movements in Lebanon and Syria," in *al-Abḥāth,* vol. 19 (1966), pp. 330-40.
32. Ziadat (1986), p. 10.
33. Ziadat (1986), p. 11.
34. Ziadat (1986), p. 13.

American Protestant missionaries transferred their operations and press from Malta to Beirut. It was followed by a Jesuit press in 1847. By 1875, there were eleven printing presses in Beirut alone, four in Damascus and three in Aleppo.[35] Egypt acquired its first printing press, the Bulaq Press in Cairo, in 1821; by 1850, it had published 81 Arabic works on various sciences. In Beirut alone, seven new periodicals were founded in 1870.

In Turkey, the Young Ottomans Movement (later to be called Young Turk Movement) was the result of a similar process of modernization. In its earliest conception, the most influential theorist of the movement, Ziya Gökalp, the author of *Türkçügün Esaslari* (*The Essence of Turkism*), saw the revival in terms of Islam and its motto was "Turkify, Islamize and Modernise".[36] But this movement was to take a secular turn with the arrival of Mustafa Kemal on the scene, who saw Islam as the main obstacle in the modernization of Turkey.

Gasparali (1851-1914), a Crimean Tatar who had been educated in Europe and who had worked in Istanbul and Paris, opened his first *uṣul al-Jadīd* (New Method) school in 1884 with the aim of improving the standard of education of teachers and to create a literary language that could be understood by every Turk, from those living "along the shores of the Bosporus to those living in Kashgar". He also argued that Muslims must borrow from the West to revitalize their intellectual and social lives. Ottoman Reform laws of 1846 and 1869 brought new curricula for all levels of education (primary, secondary and higher); schools were removed from the supervision of local religious communities and they were opened to all children, irrespective of religion. The laws of 1869 provided for a minimum compulsory education of four years. At the secondary level, mathematics, biology and chemistry were introduced. Many Turks were sent to Europe. Among them was Yirmisekiz Mehmet Çelebi (Chalabi) who arrived in Paris as the Ottoman ambassador in 1720 and became one of the first Ottomans to give a first-hand report of modern Europe, especially France. When compared with the accounts of earlier Muslim travelers to Europe, such as that of Evliya Çelebi, his reports and letters show in an unequivocal way the psychology of the eighteenth century: a proud Muslim soul torn between the glory of his history and the mind-boggling

35. Ziadat (1986), p. 2.
36. Cornell, Svante and Svanberg, Igvar (1999), "Turkey" in Westerlund, David and Svanberg, Ingvar (eds.), *Islam Outside the Arab World*, Curzon, Surrey, p. 128.

advancement of the Aafranjī, the infidels of Europe. Mehmet Çelebi's reports published under the title of *Sefāretnāme* became a small genre of its own to be followed by later Ottoman envoys to Europe.[37]

Let us also note that the general decline of intellectual activity in the Muslim world was not as widespread in Iran as elsewhere. The Iranian religious and philosophical scholars remained deeply entrenched in the traditional sciences and the educational system continued to use resources of Islamic tradition during the sixteenth and the seventeenth centuries. Qum, Mashhad, Iṣfaḥān and Tabrīz remained major centers of Islamic philosophy. In recent years, this tradition has been strengthened through the celebration of centenaries of Muslim philosophers. These occasions have created an important intellectual platform through international conferences and meetings which are instrumental in dissemination of philosophical works.[38] But during the sixteenth and the seventeenth centuries, most intellectual activity in Iran was limited to philosophical and religious disciplines; it did not include natural sciences. The Islamic scientific tradition had already been weakened during the Ṣafavīd period and the Qajārs did little to revive it.

Major Transformations

The process of inner struggle and reform which had emerged in the Muslim world during the late seventeenth and early eighteenth centuries

---

37. His *Sefāretnāme* was translated into French in 1757 by Julien Galland as *Relation de l'embassade de Mehmet Effendi a la cour de France en 1721 ecrite par lui meme et traduit par Julien Galland*, Constantinople and Paris. For a brief but hostile account on Mehmet Çelebi in English, see Lewis, Bernard (1982), *The Muslim Discovery of Europe*, W. W. Norton & Company, New York, pp. 114-16. On the relationship between the Muslim world and Europe, see Gibb, H. A. R. and Bowen, Harold (eds., 1957), *Islamic Society and the West: A Study of the Impact of Western Civilization on Moslem Culture in the Near East*, Oxford University Press, Oxford; and Grunebaum, Von G. E. (1962), *Modern Islam: The Search for Cultural Identity*, Greenwood Press, Connecticut.
38. For example, the millinery of Ibn Sīnā held at the Tehran University in 1951 during which many of his works as well as works on him were republished, the seven hundredth anniversary of Nasīr al-Dīn al-Ṭūsī, the four hundredth anniversary of Mullā Ṣadrā (1961) which triggered a series of publications on him, the eleven hundredth anniversary of Muḥammad ibn Zakariyyā al-Rāzi (1965), the hundredth anniversary celebration of the death of Ḥājjī Mullā Hādī Sabzwārī (organized by the Mashhad University in 1969) and the millinery of Shaykh Muḥammad al-Ṭūsī (Mashhad University, 1970).

was terminated by the invasion and colonization of these societies by the European powers. The Russians and the Chinese absorbed Inner Asia; the British claimed India, Malaya, parts of the Middle East, East Africa, Nigeria and other parts of West Africa; France seized North Africa, much of West Africa and parts of the Middle East; and the Dutch occupied Indonesia. Thus at the dawn of the twentieth century, independent Muslim states existed only in Central Arabia, Iran, Turkey and Afghanistan and they too were weak and under the influence of the European powers.

This brief survey brings us to the threshold of the modern period which came into existence on the basis of a redrawn map of the world. By then, the colonization of the Muslim societies had not only cut short the process of inner evolution, change and revival of these societies, it had also produced a startling transformation of the most basic institutions, completely changing the nature of the relationship between Islam and science.

This fundamental transformation of the Muslim societies through the replacement of their basic institutions, models, ideology and in most cases, language of learning was achieved through certain methods that were uniformly applied to all Muslim societies. Following the conquest, assimilation or annexation, the colonized societies were subjected to a reign of terror. Old and established families were uprooted. Leading figures were executed or exiled, ruling classes and people of wealth and fame were made targets of special retribution. The continuity of institutions was disrupted and in many cases, they were destroyed in both the physical and the functional sense.

After this period, which varied in length in different societies, new institutions were planted, a new administrative system was designed, and in time a new elite was created. This elite group was more than willing to cooperate with the colonial rulers. Products of the new educational system, these people had little or no knowledge of their own history and heritage. Intoxicated by the life-style of their rulers, men and women of this elite group considered it an unbounded honor to speak the language of their colonial masters and think and act like them. They accepted the ideas presented to them by their Western mentors without any critical analysis. Their personalities and worldviews were shaped by the teachings of Western philosophers, and religion had little importance for them. The members of this elite group slowly became the leading figures in the colonized societies and the masses started to look toward them as their models.

The third phase of this process started with the second generation of the elite group, raised in luxury and comfort and twice removed from the traditional sources. They were also removed from the period of terror and violence and could aspire to seek equality with the Western rulers. Many went to Europe for education and their experiences in the West contributed toward the development of a sense of dignity and equality. When they returned to their respective countries, they started to demand greater power and influence in the affairs of their country. As a result, independence movements were born.

Within this broad framework, the transformation of Muslim societies took various forms in different countries, as discussed in the previous chapter. The four fundamental changes were (i) the political transformation, (ii) the change in the status of Arabic language, (iii) the replacement of the education system, and (iv) the establishment of Western institutions. These developments pushed the Islamic tradition of learning into the background through violent political, economic and social changes.

This does not mean that the representatives of this tradition silently accepted the verdict of the colonial rulers; there was a sustained effort to dislodge the new rulers as well as their institutions. But all that these efforts could do was to establish a secure, albeit non-transforming, niche for the religious institutions. The magnitude of the transformation of the social, political and economic structures of the Islamic civilization can be judged from the prestige and status of these institutions and all those who belonged to them. Whereas in the pre-colonial era, the madrasa was the institution par excellence in the Islamic civilization and those who held teaching posts in these institutions or those who studied there were looked upon as the real leaders of the community. In the colonial era, these institutions became the haunts of the dispossessed. The rising urban elite had no interest in these institutions, except for the ceremonial and ritual needs for which they utterly depended on them, because having lost even the most elementary knowledge of religion, they could not perform the rites of birth, marriage and death. But in general, the madāris supported the orphans, the poor, the needy and the old. Those who studied in these institutions, which had once produced al-Ghazālīs, could barely sustain themselves against the onslaught of a new social order. Ironically, the deep sense of inferiority toward western civilization and its products from which the urban elite and the graduates of the newly established western educational institutions suffered, would, in time, also creep into the psyche of those who populated the traditional schools, of course with notable exceptions.

This situation intensified the consciousness that something had gone wrong and reform was desperately needed. In various Muslim regions, different reform patterns emerged but in almost all cases, the traditional institutions of learning were compared with the western institutions and, in many cases, the reform of these traditional institutions meant introduction of those subjects that formed the regular curriculum of western style education. Instead of solving the problem, this compounded it by creating a parallel curriculum. The institutions where allegedly modern curriculum was not introduced eventually became the harbingers of a truncated version of traditional Muslim education which could produce neither al-Ghazālīs nor Newtons, but which could, at least, keep the glow of the old tradition alive along with a profound sense of loss.

A detailed discussion of these responses will take us too far afield. Suffice it to say that, in addition to the heightened consciousness of the need to reform these institutions precipitated by the encounter with the West, Islam's inherent mechanism of reform and revival (*iṣlāḥ wa tajdīd*)—which has always remained operative in the Islamic civilization ever since its birth—was also at work. There is enough historical evidence to support the conclusion reached by numerous scholars that a general revival was building up in the Muslim societies during the seventeenth century and it had taken a definite shape in by the early decades of the eighteenth century.[39] It was the inherent mechanism of reform that had produced movements such as the one started by Shaykh Aḥmad Sirhindī (d. 1034/1624), Shāh ʿAbd al-Raḥīm (d. 1131/1719), Sayyid Aḥmad Shahīd (d. 1246/1831), and Shāh Walī Allāh (1114-1176/1703-1762). These reform movements, which were present in all parts of the Muslim world, were aiming to produce a comprehensive change in the society by addressing the spiritual, cultural and intellectual malaise.[40] For instance, the Farāʾiḍī Movement in Bengal, started by Ḥājjī Sharīʿat Allāh (b. *ca*. 1178/1764), who had gone for pilgrimage in 1196/1782 and had stayed in Makkah until 1217/1802, not only wanted to reform the society, it also aimed at waging

39. For a general survey, see Rahman, Fazlur (1979, 1996), *Islam,* University of Chicago Press, Chicago; especially chapter 12, "Pre-Modern Reform Movements", pp. 193-211.

40. A recent useful study on Shāh Walī Allāh is al-Ghazali, Muhammad (2001), *The Socio-political Thought of Shāh Walī Allāh,* International Institute of Islamic Thought and Islamic Research Institute, Islamabad.

an armed struggle against the colonial power.[41] The Farā'iḍī Movement declared that (i) India had become *Dār al-Ḥarb* (Abode of War) and this meant that an armed struggle against the British had become obligatory on all Muslims; (ii) it advocated a social-economic reform, directed against the rich landlords; and (iii) it strove to purify Muslim religious practices that had become corrupt under the influence of Hinduism. The movement continued after the death of Ḥājjī Sharī'at Allāh by his son, Dūdhū Miyān (d. 1281/1864); the followers of this movement are still present in Bengal.

The history of other equally important reform movements in various parts of the Muslim world which sprang from this inner mechanism provides a rare opportunity to study the dynamics of Muslim societies at this stage of history. Although these movements have been studied under the new discipline of Islam and modernity, their impact on the revival of Islamic scholarship, social structure of the societies and on major institutions is still not clear. Many movements and works remain unstudied or partially studied. For example, the work of two Yemenite scholars, Muḥammad al-Murtaḍā (d. 1204/1790) and Muḥammad ibn 'Alī al-Shawkānī (1172-1250/1759-1834), who attempted to reform their societies, needs more attention. Al-Murtaḍā's response was to reassert a Ghazālian solution while al-Shawkānī rejected the idea of simple acceptance of authority (*taqlīd*) and called for fresh thinking (*ijtihād*) to find solutions to contemporary problems.

Some movements were extreme in their corrective methodology. For example, the puritan Wahhābī movement, which was originally inspired by the teachings of Ibn Taymiyya (d. 728/1328), violently rebelled against the Ottoman rulers. Its leader, Muḥammad ibn 'Abd al-Wahhāb (1115-1206/1703-92) found the moral laxity of his brethren in faith anathematic. But the mechanism of correction he and his movement used was equally disruptive. He found a local chieftain, ibn Sa'ūd (d. 1178/1765), in Dar'iyya who brought his considerable military force to expand the puritan movement from its original center in Najd to Hijāz and, later, to encompass the sacred cities of Makkah and Madinah. In doing so, al-Wahhāb and his forces created a deep rift in the Muslim community.

41. Both Makkah and Madinah still played the role of major guiding cities for the entire Muslim world. The example of Ḥājji Sharī'at Allāh, who returned to India to start a reform movement, is not an isolated incident. Sayyid Aḥmad Shahīd as well as Shāh Walī Allāh had also gone to Ḥijāz where they met various Muslim scholars who discussed the state of Muslim societies and proposed solutions.

Ironically, a cardinal criticism of Ibn ʿAbd al-Wahhāb was the disunity of the Muslim community! Thus, it was perhaps the failure to develop a strategy of reform and revival in the changed circumstances that caused the ultimate deluge.[42]

In any case, these inner mechanisms of reform were not allowed to play their rightful role because of the European intervention. The colonizers often pitted one segment of society against the other. In the course of the nineteenth century, they were able to subjugate almost all parts of the Muslim world. This was a powerful blow from which the Muslim world has still not recovered. The colonization of the Muslim world shattered the inner fabric of the Islamic tradition and brought it face to face with a foreign civilization at a time when it was at its weakest state. Thus, the western civilization managed to carve a portion of Islamic space as its own territory. This produced a small Muslim elite within these societies that turned its face away from the Islamic tradition and looked toward the Western civilization for intellectual nourishment. But no matter how intensely it attached itself to the Western civilization, as long as it kept its faith, it had to return to the sources of spiritual guidance and solace that have always been the focus of the faithful. This created an inner tension that still reverberates in the social, political, and intellectual struggles.

Needless to say, the Islam and science discourse was deeply affected by all of this. This was the beginning of a new kind of discourse between Islam and science in which science was no more the integral unit of the Islamic tradition but a science of the brave new world, a science that had broken away from all traditions and was an autonomous and powerful entity, independently and defiantly charting its own course, complete with a theology of nature and a worldview competing against other worldviews.

---

42. The Wahhābis were militarily defeated by Muḥammad ʿAlī of Egypt under the orders of the Ottoman government. They found refuge in Kuwait for eleven years and then re-emerged in Najd. In January 1901, ʿAbd al-ʿAzīz ibn ʿAbd al-Raḥmān was able to re-establish his rule in Riyāḍ and by 1904, he had re-conquered all provinces previously ruled by his grandfather from Najd. By 1924, the clan had established its rule over the entire territory now known as 'Saudi Arabia', the 'Arabia of the Saʿūdīs'. For a brief critical study of the Wahhābi Movement and its founder, see Algar, Hamid (2002), *Wahhabism: A Critical Essay*, iPi, New York.

CHAPTER NINE

The Colonized Discourse

The new Islam and science discourse that emerged from the ruins of the old tradition during the nineteenth century is a "colonized discourse", steeped in the great chasm that separates our contemporary world from the traditional Islamic universe and the science it inspired and cultivated for almost eight centuries. The modern Muslim scientist is unlikely to find any resonance with his peers in that universe of discourse not because modern science has discovered some new facts about nature that are fundamentally different from the scientific data of Ibn Sīnā and al-Bīrūnī. It is not the scientific content that is of importance in this widening breach that separates the contemporary Muslim scientist from the Islamic scientific tradition. Had it been the scientific content, the Newtonian and the quantum physics could not have shared a common universe in which they remain rooted in spite of their vast divergence; both are constructs of a concept of reality formulated *within* the metaphysical and philosophical worldview of the modern Western civilization. Thus, it is neither the heliocentricity nor the contemporary atomic theory of matter that has rent asunder the traditional universe of Islam and science discourse; it is the foundational philosophy of modern science that stands as an unbridgeable chasm between modern science and the Islamic scientific tradition. This great chasm between the pre-colonial Islam and science nexus and its post-colonial caricature is not the result of any specific theory of science, but that of a radical recasting of the foundations of science since the seventeenth century.

It was during the colonial era that the Islam and science discourse accumulated a heavy overlay of extraneous issues which had never been part of the traditional discourse. There are three important facets of this new discourse that keep it hostage to the legacy of the colonial era: it is inextricably linked to a feverish demand for the acquisition of Western science—which, in turn, is laden with a whole range of issues in the realms of education and modernity; its apologetics; and a deep layer that is the product of the cultural schizophrenia which characterizes the post-colonial Muslim world. Hundreds of works deal with the issues related to various aspects of Islam in the modern world. In almost all cases, these works posit the challenge of modernity within a social and cultural context and invariably find the question of Islam and science as an integral part of the discourse on modernity.

This has led to the emergence of the new Islam and science discourse in a realm that is not its own.[1] These three facets cast such a deep shadow on the new discourse that it is almost impossible to separate it from this burden. This heavy overlay expresses itself in various attempts to "Islamize" modern science and in the extensive literature that attempts to prove the existence of various modern theories in the Qur'ān. Among its other formulations are (i) the Arab *Nahda* (renaissance, rebirth) movement of the nineteenth century which focuses on the works of Muslim reformers and thinkers such as Jamal al-Din Afghani, Rifāʿah al-Ṭahṭāwī, and Muḥammad ʿAbduh; (ii) a typically Orientalist reconstruction of the problem of decline, formulated by Hamilton Gibb, Gustave von Grunebaum, Louis Gardet, Robert Brunschvig and others, finding expression in various works on Islam and modernity; (iii) the discourse shaped by various secular responses, such as nationalism and Marxism which emerged in the Muslim world as part of its efforts to dislodge the colonial yoke but which also affected educational, scientific and social institutions; and (iv) formulations which posit the religious response to modernity in the context of a "static" tradition that had been conquered by the "mobile" and "energetic" West.[2]

---

1. Two useful works dealing with the challenges of modernity are: Nasr, Seyyed Hossein (1981), *Traditional Islam in the Modern World,* KPI, London and Nasr, Seyyed Hossein (1975), *Islam and the Plight of Modern Man,* Longman, London. Also see Rahman, Fazlur (1982, 1984), *Islam and Modernity: Transformation of an Intellectual Tradition,* The University of Chicago Press, Chicago, London; von Grunebaum, G. E. (1962), *Modern Islam: The Search for Cultural Identity*, Greenwood Press, Westport; for a post-modern perspective, see Majid, Anouar (2000), *Unveiling Traditions: Postcolonial Islam in a Polycentric World,* Duke University Press, Durham & London; for a post-modern analysis of the impact of Mustafa Kemal's policies on Turkey, see Sayyid, Bobby, S. (1997), *A Fundamental Fear: Eurocentrism and Emergence of Islamism,* Zed Books Ltd., London, New York. For a case study of Turkey, see Mardin, Şerif (2000), *The Genesis of Young Ottoman Thought: A Study in the Modernization of Turkish Political Ideas*, Syracuse University Press, Syracuse, first published in 1962. Other useful references are: Hourani, Albert (1962, reprnt. 1983), *Arabic Thought in the Liberal Age: 1798-1939,* Cambridge University Press, Cambridge; Sharabi, Hisham (1970), *Arab Intellectuals and the West: The Formative Years 1875-1941,* The Johns Hopkins Press, Washington DC.
2. For various formulations of reform movements, see Enayat, Hamid (1982), *Modern Islamic Political Thought,* The University of Texas Press, Austin; Gibb, H. A. R. (1947), *Modern Trends in Islam,* Chicago

It was also amidst these various patterns of response that there appeared a persistent rhetoric calling for acquisition of modern science. This need seems to have dawned upon all proponents of mutually exclusive response-patterns as well as upon many reformers of the nineteenth century with such great urgency that it became the battle cry for all groups, except for a small segment of traditional 'ulamā' who called for a revival of the Islamic spiritual and ethical norms, rather than acquisition of Western science, as a cure. As a result of these developments, it is impossible to extricate the discourse on Islam and science from the burden it has accumulated in the past two centuries.

Unlike the Islam and science nexus that had developed naturally in the eighth century and which grew in various schools of thought and produced a vast corpus of literature, the new discourse is strained, labored and carries the burden assigned to Islam in the discourse: the legitimization of the modernists' agenda. It is also important to note that most of the champions of the new discourse were neither scientists nor 'ulamā', but reformers, who wanted Muslims, especially the young Muslim students, to acquire Western science. But because this realization was simultaneously attached to the Western cultural baggage which the religious scholars deemed to be a threat to the Islamic way of life, many reformers found themselves pitched against the traditional 'ulamā'; this is how Goldziher's ill-conceived notion of an Islamic "orthodoxy against foreign sciences" finally arrived in the Islamic polity. The battle-lines were sharply drawn and they covered the entire Muslim world with only minor local variations.

The overlay of other issues makes it difficult to explore the new discourse without simultaneously discussing the accumulated themes of modernity, development, education, progress and a host of other issues intertwined in the discourse. Yet, following the threads of these issues is not the focus of this study; hence the need to draw a fine line between totally ignoring the related issues and delving too deeply in them at the cost of losing focus.

University Press, Chicago; Siddiqi, Mazheruddin (1982), *Modern Reformist Thought in the Muslim World*, Islamic Research Institute, Islamabad; von Grunebaum, Gustave (1982), *Islam: Essay in the Nature and Growth of a Cultural Tradition,* Greenwood Publishing Group, Westport; and Smith, W. Cantwell (1957), *Islam in Modern History*, Princeton University Press, Princeton.

The Reformers' Discourse

Formulated in terms of mutual complementarity of the "Work of God" (nature) and the "Word of God" (the Qur'ān), the reformers' discourse on Islam and science was marked by their desire to show that modern science had nothing against Islam and its sacred text and to entice Muslims to acquire modern science. Hidden in this two-fold agenda was a desire to bring the Muslim world out of its sorry state; the path was the acquisition of modern science. Almost all reformers translated the Arabic word *ʿilm* (knowledge) as "science" (meaning modern science) and framed their discourse on the necessity to acquire knowledge upon which the Qur'ān insists and which has been made obligatory for all Muslims by the Prophet. This reduction of the word *ʿilm* was conveniently used to produce a new strand of Islam and science discourse.

In the Indian subcontinent Sayyid Ahmad Khan (1817-1898) and his followers were the first champions of this reform agenda. Born in the twilight of the Indian Tīmūrī era to a distinguished family, Sayyid Ahmad Khan was involved in a wide range of activities—from politics to education. He was to leave a deep mark on the new Islam and science discourse through his writings and by influencing at least two generations of Muslims who studied at the educational institutions he founded.[3]

It was during the decade of 1860s, that Ahmad Khan developed his ideas of a "modern Islam" and a Muslim polity living under the British rule. During this time, he wrote *Tārīkh Sarkashī'ī Zilʿa Bijnore* (*A History of Insurrection in Bijnor District*) and *Asbāb-i Baghāwat-i Hind* (*The Causes of Indian Mutiny*). He sent 500 copies of the latter book to the India Office of the British Government in London and a personal copy to Lord Canning in Calcutta. The book was translated into English by Colonel Graham and Sir Auckland Colvin and published in Benares. In 1860-1861, he published another tract, *Risālah Khair Khawahān Musalmanān: An Account of the Loyal Mahomdans of India*, in which he claimed that the Indian Muslims were the most loyal subjects of the British Raj because of their kindred disposition and because of the principles of their religion. He also wrote a commentary on the Old and the New Testament, *Tabīyān al-Kalām fī Tafsīr al-Tawrā wa'l Injīl ʿalā Millat al-Islām* (*The Mahomedan Commentary on the Bible*). He attached a *fatwā* (religious decree) by Jamāl ibn al-ʿAbd Allāh ʿUmar al-

3. Notably the Aligarh College, established in 1881, which became a university in 1920 and which remained the mainstay of Muslim education in the Indian subcontinent until 1947.

Ḥanafī, the Mufti of Makkah, at the end of the book. This *fatwā* stated, "as long as some of the peculiar observances of Islam prevailed in [India], it is *Dār al-Islam* (Land of Islam)." This was to counter the religious decrees that had been issued by many Indian ʿulamāʾ, stating that the Indian subcontinent had become a *Dār al-Ḥarb,* the land of war. This political overture was favorably received in the ruling circles.

The first two decades after 1857 witnessed Sayyid Ahmad Khan's increasing preoccupation with the prevailing conditions of Muslims in India. He perceived Muslims as backward and in need of education. This period also saw an increasing degree of public involvement in educational and social arenas. On January 9, 1864, he convened the first meeting of the Scientific Society at Ghazipur. The meeting was attended, among others, by Ahmad Khan's future biographer, Colonel Graham, who was convinced that India could benefit from England's technological wealth. The Society was established with two clear objectives; two more objectives were added in 1867. Thus the goals of the Society were:

> (i) to translate into such languages as may be in common use among the people those works on arts and sciences which, being in English or other European languages, are not intelligible to the natives; (ii) to search for and publish rare and valuable oriental works (no religious work will come under the notice of the Society); (iii) to publish, when the Society thinks it desirable, any [periodical] which may be calculated to improve the native mind; (iv) to have delivered in their meetings lectures on scientific or other useful subjects, illustrated, when possible, by scientific instruments.[4]

Ahmad Khan and the Society moved to Aligarh in 1867 where he was able to procure a piece of land from the government for experimental farming. The Duke of Argyll, who was also the Secretary of State for India, became the Patron of the Society and Lt. Governor of the N.W. Province its Vice-Patron. Ahmad Khan was the secretary of the Society as well as member of the Directing Council and the Executive Council. In a memorandum of the Society to its President, Ahmad Khan wrote, in May 24, 1877, that for several years "the Society has cultivated wheat and barley according to the methods prescribed in Scot Burn's book on modern

4. "Proceedings of the First Meeting of the Scientific Society", Ghazipur, January 9, 1864, published in *Fikr-o-Naẓar,* April (1963), Aligarh, pp. 8-11.

farming and showed the results to *Talukdars* (estate holders) of Aligarh; new instruments were used to cultivate corn by Burn's methods; several vegetables were grown from newly developed European seeds and their seeds were distributed to farmers; the Society cultivated American cotton seeds, and demonstrated their superior product."[5]

Ahmad Khan now devoted all his energies and a portion of his personal income to the Society. He was also able to receive small sums from various Muslim and non-Muslim philanthropists. Ahmad Khan realized that the political realities of India dictated that Muslims should establish their own organizations. On May 10, 1866, he established The Aligarh British Indian Association. The inaugural session was held at the Aligarh office of the Scientific Society in the presence of a sizeable number of local landowners and a few European officers. The Association failed to achieve any degree of impact on the decisions of the government and, one after the other, its plans were aborted. Ahmad Khan wanted to establish a "vernacular university" for the N.W. Provinces but he was discouraged by the champions of Hindi who wanted such a university to teach in Hindi, rather than Urdu. In 1868, the Association announced assistance for persons traveling to Europe for educational and scientific purposes but at that time, most Muslims of northern India considered social contacts with Englishmen undesirable for their moral and religious integrity. Ahmad Khan had been elected an honorary Fellow of the Royal Asiatic Society of London in 1864 and he decided to go to England himself to see the ways of the British in their homeland.

On April 1, 1869, Ahmad Khan, his two sons, Sayyid Hamid and Sayyid Mahmud, a younger friend, Mirza Khuda Dad Beg, and a servant known only by the affectionate name of Chachu left Benaras and arrived in London on May 4, 1869 after spending five days in Marseilles and Paris.[6] To pay for his trip, Ahmad Khan had to mortgage his ancestral house in Delhi and borrow 10,000 rupees from a moneylender at 14 percent interest rate for the first 5,000 rupees and at 8 percent for the rest. He had also

5. Malik, Hafeez (1980), *Sir Sayyid Ahmad Khan and Muslim Modernism in India and Pakistan,* Columbia University Press, New York, pp. 88-9.
6. Pānipatī, Shaikh Muḥammad Ismā'īl (1976), *Maktubāt-e Sir Sayyid,*(*Letters of Sir Sayyid Ahmad,* henceforth *Letters*), 2 vols., Majlis-e Taraqi-e Adab, Lahore, vol. 1, p. 413. Ahmad Khan's letters to Nawab Mohsin al-Mulk, and Mawlavi Mahdi Ali Khan, written from England, were first published in Sir Sayyid's journal *Tahdhīb al-Ikhlāq,* under the general title of *Safar Namah-i Musāfrān-i London.*

availed the opportunity created by the Government Resolution of the 30th June 1868, which had founded nine scholarships for the Indian Youth for their education in England and applied for a scholarship for his son, Sayyid Mahmud, who was then a student at the Calcutta University.[7]

Ahmad Khan lived in rented houses in London. His seventeen-month stay (from May 4, 1869 to October 2, 1870) in England was full of social and literary activity as well as political activity. He was "in the society of lords and dukes at dinners and evening parties", he saw "artisans and the common working-man in great numbers", he was awarded the title of the Companion of the Star of India by none other than the Queen herself; this "elevated" him so that henceforth he would call himself Sir Sayyid Ahmad Khan Bahadur, C.S.I.; he dined with the Secretary of State for India and though he was beset with economic problems, he fulfilled the protocol by hiring private horse carriages for his visits which drained his purse.[8]

His visit to England convinced him of the superiority of the British. "Without flattering the English," he wrote, "I can truly say that the natives of India, high and low, merchants and petty shopkeepers, educated and illiterate, when contrasted with the English in education, manners, and uprightness, are like a dirty animal is to an able and handsome man."[9] Ahmad counted himself among the "animals" and felt the pain and anguish of being part of a degenerated culture.

While in England, Khan read William Muir's biography of the Prophet Muhammad, which "burned his heart", and its "bigotry and injustice cut his heart to pieces". He resolved to write a full-length biography of the Prophet as a refutation "even if its preparation would turn him into a

---

7. Ahmad Khan's letter of July 28, 1869, to the Secretary of State (George Douglas Campbell, the Eighth Duke of Argyll, 1823-1900), in Pānipatī, Shaikh Muḥammad Ismā'īl (ed., 1993) *Letters to and from Sir Syed Ahmad Khan,* Board for Advancement of Literature, Lahore, pp. 3-5.
8. "One can easily live here in one hundred and fifty rupees per month, except when one has to go for visits. It costs four hundred rupees a month just for the coaches! And this will only fetch a one-horse carriage with occasional two horse carriages. Last night Mahmud was invited to the house of an Englishman, he spent two hours there, he went there in a pathetic horse carriage, the like of which one can fetch in Benaras for two or three annas (one rupee had sixteen annas); it cost seven shillings, i.e. seven and a half rupees..." Ahmad Khan's letter of June 18, 1869 to Nawab Mahdi. *Letters, op. cit,* vol. 1, pp. 421-22, my translation.
9. Pānīpatī, Shaikh Muḥammad Ismā'īl (ed. 1961), *Musāfrān-i London,* Majlis Taraqi-e Adab, Lahore, p. 184.

pauper and a beggar for on the Day of Judgment, it would be said, 'Bring forth the one who died penniless for the sake of his grandfather Muhammad!'"[10] From the moment he started to read Muir's book in August 1869, until he finished its refutation in February 1870, Ahmad Khan could do nothing but think about the rejoinder he wished to write. He wrote letters to friends in India, soliciting books, references and money for his rejoinder. Because his own English was inadequate, he had to hire an Englishman for polishing his draft which he wrote until his back ached. He also had to pay for the translation of Latin, German, and French material he used in his book. But when he finally published the refutation, it was merely *A Series of Essays on the Life of Mohammad*;[11] he hoped to write the second volume but he was exhausted and penniless.

After finishing the book, Ahmad Khan was eager to return to India. During his stay in England, he had visited universities of Oxford and Cambridge and certain private schools, including Eaton and Harrow; these would serve as models for his own Muhammadan Anglo-Oriental College. Ahmad Khan returned home on October 2,1870.

After his return to India, Ahmad Khan started a periodical *Tahdhīb al-Akhlāq* to "educate and civilize" Indian Muslims. He remained in the judicial service until his early retirement in July 1876. After that, he settled in Aligarh where he established the Muhammadan Anglo-Oriental College in 1877. In 1920, the College would become Aligarh Muslim University, an institution that would have a decisive impact on the course of Islamic polity in India as well as on the history of India. In 1886, he instituted "The

10. *Letters, op. cit.* vol. 1, p. 431.
11. Published by Trubner & Co., 1870. In London, Khan had to borrow Rs. 3,000; the book cost him Rs. 3,948; the sale of 20 copies and donations from friends in India brought back Rs. 1,691. (*Letters, op. cit.*) Ahmad Khan's book was a fitting rejoinder to Muir's outburst against the Prophet of Islam. He undertook a point-by-point refutation of the main arguments in twelve essays which start with the "Historical Geography of Arabia" and end with "On the Birth and Childhood of Mohammed". Interestingly, Ahmad Khan produced his own genealogy on the back of the large size sheet which contains the genealogy of the Prophet, tracing it back to the Prophet of Islam through his daughter Fāṭima. This book has been reprinted many times. The one I have used was reprinted by Premier Book House in 1968 in Lahore. The title page states that the "original English text of these essays has been revised and corrected by a friend" and author's name is given as Syed Ahmed Khan Bahador, C.S.I. The Urdu version was published in 1887 as *Khuṭbāt al- Aḥmdiyya fi'l Arab wa al-Sīrat al-Muḥammadiyya*, Aligarh.

Muhammadan Educational Conference" which held annual meetings in various Indian cities.

In his drive for modernization, Ahmad Khan wanted to re-interpret Islam. "We need a modern *ʿilm al-Kalām,"* he said in a speech delivered at Lahore in 1884, "by which we should either refute the doctrines of modern sciences or show that they are in conformity with the articles of Islamic faith." But what became apparent in the subsequent writings was the fact that Ahmad Khan was not really interested (or qualified) to refute any modern scientific doctrine; all he could do was to re-interpret Islam to show that the "work of God (nature and its laws) was in conformity with the Word of God (the Qurʾān)", an adage that earned him the title of *Néchari.*

In his attempts to re-interpret Islam to accommodate modern Western science, Ahmad Khan exposed his weaknesses in both domains of knowledge. He was severely criticized by the ʿulamāʾ for the lack of qualifications to interpret the Qurʾān and Ḥadīth and the shallowness of his knowledge of Western science and its philosophical underpinnings was apparent from his own writings. He had no training in any natural science or in philosophy of science and he had never finished his traditional education. Yet, he tried to demythologize the Qurʾān and its teachings. His interpretation of various fundamental aspects of Islamic teachings which could not be proved by modern scientific methods, such as the nature of supplication *(duʿāʾ),* which he thought was merely psychological rather than real, met fierce resistance from the traditional scholars but in spite of this, he gained widespread popularity among the ruling elite and in the early 1880s, he became the acknowledged leader of the Muslim community. He was loyal to the British Raj, but he fought various legal and constitutional battles with the British administrators in order to secure fundamental rights for the Muslim community. He was rewarded by the British in many ways. In 1878, he was nominated as a member of the Vice Regal Legislative Council; in 1888, he was knighted as the Knight Commander of the Star of India; in 1889, he received an honorary degree from the University of Edinburgh. In spite of his life-long interest in educational matters, Ahmad Khan did not produce any new theory of education; he was merely interested in promoting western education without reservation.

Like many other Muslim thinkers of the nineteenth century, Ahmad Khan was convinced that Muslims need to acquire Western science and he attempted to show that modern science is in perfect harmony with Islam. Not only that, he went as far as proclaiming that the Qurʾānic invitation to ponder and reflect on the perfect system of nature was, in fact, a call to

Muslims to excel in science—an argument that gained currency with time and is still used by many thinkers and rulers who want Muslims to acquire Western science.

Others who advocated similar ideas during the nineteenth century include Khayr al-Dīn al-Tūnisī (d. 1889), Rifā'ah al-Ṭaḥṭāwī (d. 1871), Jamal al-Din al-Afghani (d. 1897) and Muḥammad 'Abduh (d. 1905). This trend also gave birth to modern scientific exegesis (*tafsīr 'ilmī*) of the Qur'ān. In 1880, an Egyptian physician, Muḥammad ibn Aḥmad al-Iskandrānī, published one such *tafsīr*[12] in Cairo. This was followed by another work of the same kind, though not a *tafsīr*.[13] It is not clear whether Ahmad Khan knew about these publications or not. But in 1879, he wrote,

> Now that *Ghadar* is over,[14] and whatever had to pass for the Muslims has passed, I am worried about improvement of our nation. I pondered hard and after a long reflection came to the conclusion that it is not possible to improve their lot unless they attain modern knowledge and technologies that are a matter of honor for other nations in the language of those who, through the Will of Allāh, rule over us.[15]

To help his mission, Khan decided to write a *tafsīr* because in all previous *tafsīr* literature, he "could only find grammatical and lexicographical niceties, statements concerning the place and time of revelation and descriptions of previous *tafāsīr*."[16] In the preface to the first partial edition of his work, he wrote,

> When I tried to educate Muslims in modern sciences and English, I wondered whether these are, in fact,

12. Iskandarānī, Muḥammad b. Aḥmad (1297/1880), Kash al-Asrār 'an al-Nūrāniyya al-Qur'āniyya fī-mā yata 'allaqu bi'l-Ajrām al-Samāwiyya wa'l-Arḍiyya wa'l-Ḥaywanāt wa'l-Nabāt wa'l-Jawāhir al-Ma'ādaniyya, 3 vols. Cairo.
13. Al-Iskandarānī, Muḥammad b. Aḥmad (13001883), Tibyān al-Asrār al-Rabbāniyya fī'l-Nabāt wa'l-Ma'ādin wa'l-Khawāṣ al-Ḥaywāniyya, Damascus.
14. The 1857 effort to gain independence from the British rule was called "mutiny" by the British; its Urdu equivalent, *Ghadar*, was used by some pro-British writers for this heroic effort which failed due to many reasons, including treason by Muslims and Hindus loyal to the British.
15. See Pānipatī, Maulānā Muḥammad lsmā'īl (ed., 1963), *Maqalāt-i Sir Sayyid,* 16 vols., Majlis-eTaraqqi-'i Adab, Lahore, [henceforth *Maqālāt*], vol. 2, pp. 199-200.
16. Ibid.

> against Islam as it is often claimed. I studied *tafsīr*, according to my abilities, and except for the literary matters, found in them nothing but rubbish and worthless (*fazūl*) discussions, mostly based on baseless and unauthentic traditions and fables (*mamlū bar riwāyāt ḍaʿif wa mawḍūʿ aur qaṣaṣ bé saropā*) which were often taken from the Jewish sources. Then I studied books of the principles of *tafsīr* according to my ability with the hope that they would definitely provide clues to the principles of the Qurʾānic interpretation based on the Qurʾān itself or which would be otherwise so sound that no one could object to them but in them I found nothing but statements that the Qurʾān contains knowledge of such and such nature...then I pondered over the Qurʾān itself to understand the foundational principles of its composition and as far as I could grasp, I found no contradiction between these principles and the modern knowledge...then I decided to write a *tafsīr* of the Qurʾān which is now complete up to *Sūrat al-Naḥl*."[17]

Ahmad Khan's *tafsīr* was published as it was being written. The work began in 1879 and was left unfinished at the time of his death in 1898. This *tafsīr* faced fierce resistance not only from ʿulamā but also from Ahmad Khan's staunch admirers and friends. One of his friends, Nawāb Muhsin al-Mulk wrote to him two long letters expressing his anguish at Ahmad Khan's radical interpretation of certain verses of the Qur'ān. In response, Ahmad Khan composed a short treatise to explain the principles of his *tafsīr*. This was published in 1892 as *Taḥrīr fī uṣūl al-tafsīr*.[18]

Ahmad Khan declared that nature is the "Work of God" and the Qur'ān is the "Word of God" and there could be no contradiction between the two. But in his efforts to prove that there is no contradiction between the Qur'ān and the modern scientific knowledge, Ahmad Khan denied all miracles and insisted on bending the Word of God to suit his understanding of His Works. In the Ninth Principle of his *tafsīr*, he stated that:

> there could be nothing in the Qurʾān that is against the principles on which nature works...as far as the supernatural is concerned, I state it clearly that they

17. Ibid.
18. For a discussion on Ahmad Khan's reinterpretations, see Troll, C. W. (1979), *Sayyid Ahmad Khan: A Reinterpretation of Muslim Theology*, Oxford University Press, Karachi.

> are impossible, just like it is impossible for the Word of God to be false...I know that some of my brothers would be angry to [read this] and they would present verses of the Qur'ān that mention miracles and supernatural events but we will listen to them without annoyance and ask: could there be another meaning of these verses that is consonant with the Arabic idiom and the Qur'ānic usage? And if they could prove that it is not possible, then we will accept that our principle is wrong...but until they do so, we will insist that God does not do anything that is against the principles of nature that He has Himself established.[19]

When he died in 1898, he was mourned by thousands. He had made effective contributions to take the despairing Muslims out of their unhappy lot after the demise of the Indian Tīmūrī era in the Indian subcontinent but in doing so, he also embarked them upon a path that made no sense of their history and heritage and that led to the eclipse of the tradition of learning and excellence that had been the hallmark of Islamic civilization for more than a millennium.

Ahmad Khan's followers, derogatorily called "the Nécharīs", were opposed by the religious scholars on the grounds that they transgressed the bounds of religion by veneration of the regularities of nature and by their belief that nature is a self-sustaining entity requiring no other agency for its existence and maintenance. These ideas had appeared in a society that still had traditional values and a thin layer of traditional educational institutions, though these had become dysfunctional. The new Niẓāmī curriculum (*Dars-i Niẓāmī*), introduced by Mullā Niẓām al-Dīn (d. 1747) of the Firangī Maḥal madrasa in the eighteenth century, had sixteen different subjects and some eighty-three works. The subjects included Arabic grammar, rhetoric, prosody, logic, philosophy, Arabic literature, Kalām, history of Islam, medicine, astronomy, geometry, art of disputation, principles of Ḥadīth, principles of Qur'ān interpretation and Qur'ān commentaries.[20] In comparison, the *Dār al-ʿUlūm* of Deoband in the Saharanpur district of Uttar Pradesh, founded by Ḥājjī Muḥammad ʿĀbid Ḥusayn with the active support of Mawlawī Muḥammad Qāsim, who was appointed its patron-principal in 1867, attempted a synthesis of various

19. *Maqālāt*, vol. 2, pp. 239-40, my translation.
20. Aḥmad, N. (1972), *Jā'izah Madāris-i ʿArabiyya Islamiyya Maghribi Pakistān* (*A Survey of Arabic Madāris of West Pakistan*), Muslim Academy, Lahore, p. 587.

educational reforms that had been undertaken in the Indian subcontinent, though its mainstay was on the work of Shāh Walī Allāh and his Dihlī school of *muḥaddithīn*. Now an international seat of Islamic learning, it provided an alternate to the westernization as well as generations of Islamic scholars who were influential in resisting Ahmad Khan's attempts to secularize education. Ahmad Khan himself was not happy with the product of his educational policy and he described the early products of Aligarh as "satans". These became the notorious *maghrib zadah* (the West-stricken) who were ridiculed by Ḥālī, Shiblī Nuʿmānī, and later, by Muhammad Iqbal; they could neither be Muslim scholars with strong roots in their own tradition, nor British; these young men were, indeed, a sad generation; many of them "could be seen in, say, Lahore with the M. A. degrees, shining shoes on the steps of a petty shop."[21] Dissatisfied by the Aligarh experiment, Shiblī Nuʿmānī left Ahmad Khan and in 1894 helped to establish the *Nadwat al-ʿUlamāʾ* (The Assembly of Islamic Scholars) in Lucknow. The Nadwa, whose graduates have influenced Islamic thought in the subcontinent perhaps second only to Deoband, was not interested in producing graduates of modern secular learning but sought a *via media* between Deoband and Firangī Maḥal on the one hand and Aligarh on the other. But the most important contribution of Nadwa is its emphasis on Arabic which made it possible for its faculty and students to establish connections with the contemporary Arab world and the vast heritage of Islamic learning. This made it possible for the Nadwa students to benefit from the traditional literature on the Qurʾān and Ḥadīth and formulate a refreshing outlook toward the contemporary situation. Nevertheless, it was, and is, an institution that competes with the secular institutions and remains incomplete in the sense that it does not offer instruction in modern science. Another institution, *Madrasat al-Iṣlāḥ* (Madrasa for Reform), established at Sarāʾi Mīr, U. P., under the leadership of Ḥamīd al-Dīn al-Farāhī, an important Qurʾān commentator, attempted to bring together different schools of ʿulamāʾ. In an attempt to combine modern education with the traditional, the Jāmiʿa Milliyya Islāmiyya (The Islamic University), established in 1920 near Delhi, experimented with teaching both the modern sciences and traditional Islamic subjects but its Islamic character was never strong and it remains a futile experiment.

Outside the Indian subcontinent, the pressure of Western civilization produced similar responses. The ʿulāmāʾ of these regions found themselves

21. Rahman (1982, 1984), p. 72.

in more or less the same predicament of fighting a lost battle against western education. But some of them sought to reform the Islamic educational institutions by advocating the inclusion of modern Western science in the curriculum of these institutions. Perhaps one of the first to call for these reforms was Rifāʿa al-Ṭaḥṭāwī, who had spent several years in Paris. Upon his return to Egypt, he opened a college of languages and translated the French constitution and French civil law into Arabic. He called for introduction of modern sciences in the al-Azhar curriculum. But these reforms were always caught in the same dilemma: how much of modern science can be taught without importing secularism? And no one had an answer to this dilemma. In the absence of a clear path, the process was always sidetracked, often ending in personal disputes. Nonetheless, the reforms did go through and when al-Azhar became a state institution, it lost its former prestige as an independent Islamic educational institution and became an organ for the propagation of state policies. The most radical of the new changes were brought about in the 1960s. A new law was enacted in 1961, which paved the way for the establishment of a school of medicine and a school of agriculture; in 1962 a women's college was also established, which has now become a university within the al-Azhar complex.

A similar process of struggle is observable in Turkey where Islam was officially abolished as state religion by Mustafa Kemal but where a remarkable new growth of Islamic educational institutions during the last decades of the twentieth century has established a new effort to find a way out of the predicament. Likewise, Iran has seen several new developments aimed at finding a way of modernization without losing that distinct Islamic characteristic that defines the Islamic way of life for the individual as well as for the society as a whole.

In Search of a *Modus Vivendi*

The search for a *modus vivendi* is not an easy task. And the dilemmas are nowhere more apparent than in the life and work of Sayyid Jamal al-Din Muhammad b. Safdar al-Afghani (1838/39-1897), who represents an important link in the changes that took place in the Islam and science discourse during the colonial era. Like Sayyid Ahmad Khan in India, he is important both for his own work, as well as because of his impact on a large number of influential thinkers. Afghani stands alone in the recent Islamic history, a dim light, urging Muslims to cast away the colonial yoke. His call assumes an enormously different dimension when seen in the historical background of his time. Arising from an uncertain place, he rose to traverse a large area under colonial rule, stirring dull souls. His birthplace has remained a source of controversy among scholars and he is said to have received his early education in religious schools near Kabul (Afghanistan), Qazwin or Tehran (Iran).[22] But we know for sure that he went to India in 1855/6, shortly before the great uprising of 1857. We do not know the exact duration of his stay in India but his encounter with the British rule before he was twenty left a deep mark on him; this first hand experience may have been the basis for his life-long opposition to the British imperial rule of Muslim lands. After spending some time in India,[23] he left for a long trip that culminated in Makkah, where he performed Ḥajj. He returned to Afghanistan in 1861[24] by way of Iraq and Iran where he became an advisor to Amīr Dūst Muḥammad Khān. He came back to India toward the end of 1879 and stayed for three years.[25] It was during this stay, primarily in the princely state of Hyderabad in south India which had become the cultural center of Indian Muslims, that he wrote his famous *The Truth About the Neichari Sect and an Explanation of the Neicharis* in Persian,[26] in rejection of

---

22. See the Master's thesis of Sharīf al-Mujāhid (1954), "Sayyid Jamāl al-Dīn al-Afghānī: His Role in the Nineteenth Century Muslim Awakening", McGill University, Canada; also Keddie, Nikki R. (1972), *Sayyid Jamāl ad-Dīn "al-Afghānī": A Political Biography,* University of California, Berkeley; Keddie, Nikki, R, (1968), *An Islamic Response to Imperialism,* University of California Press, Berkeley; Badawi, Zaki, M. A. (1976, 1978), *The Reformers of Egypt,* Croom Helm, London; Kedourie, Elie (1966), *Afghani and 'Abduh: An Essay on Religious Unbelief and Political Activism in Modern Islam,* Frank Cass & Co. Ltd., London; and Qudsi-Zadah, Albert (1970), *Sayyid Jamal al-Din al-Afghani: An Annotated Bibliography,* E. J. Brill, Leiden.
23. Estimates vary from just over a year to several years.
24. According to Mujāhid (1954), p. 17, but in December 1866, according to Keddie (1972), p. 37.
25. During the intervening years, he was in Afghanistan, which he left in December 1868. From Afghanistan, he went to Bombay, where he stayed for two months (March-April 1869), and then to Egypt where he delivered lectures at al-Azhar. From Egypt, he went to Istanbul where he stayed for almost two years (1869-71); he returned to Egypt in 1871 for a fruitful eight-year stay during which he gained tremendous popularity among the young intellectuals of Egypt who were beginning to realize the dangers of Khedive's complaisance toward the French and British. In September 1879, Afghani was expelled from Egypt; he was put on a boat destined for Karachi; thus he returned to India.
26. *Ḥaqīqat-i Madhhab-i Néchari wa Bayān-i Ḥāl-i Néchariyyān* (*The Truth of the Néchari Religion and the True State of the Néchariīs*), first published in 1881 in Hyderabad. It was translated into Arabic by one of Afghani's Egyptian students and reformer, Muḥammad 'Abduh and Abū Turāb,

the views of Sayyid Ahmad Khan and his followers.

Afghani left India in late 1882 and arrived in Paris at the beginning of 1883 after a short stay in London.[27] His arrival in Paris coincided with the defeat of the ʿUrābī movement[28] in Egypt by the British and the beginning of the supposedly temporary British occupation of Egypt.[29] This resulted in the arrest or exile of many young men who had been influenced by Afghani; Muḥammad ʿAbduh, who had been exiled to Beirut, was invited by Afghani to join him in Paris, which he did. Together, they launched their most important joint venture in 1884 from Paris: the publication of the newspaper, *al-ʿUrwa al-Wuthqā* (*The Firmest Bond*).[30] Between March and October 1884, eighteen issues of *al-ʿUrwa* were published. But then its publication ceased because of a number of reasons, including financial and political. In Paris, Afghani also wrote his now famous "Answer to Renan" on

---

who shortened the title to *ar-Radd ʿala ad-Dahriyyīn* (*Refutation of the Materialists*), Beirut, 1886; English translation by Keddie, Nikki, R. in Keddie (1968), *op. cit.* pp. 130-174. The original Persian was reprinted in the year of its publication (1298/1881) from Bombay. There was also an Urdu translation, under its original Persian title, dated Calcutta, 1883. Sayyid ʿAbd al-Ghafūr Shahbāz, who translated the *Refutation* into Urdu, also published twelve other Persian articles by Afghanī under the title *Maqālāt-i Jamāliyya,* Calcutta, 1884; six of these had been previously published in the Hyderabad periodical, *Muʿallim-i Shafiq,* a journal edited by Muḥibb Husain which began publication late in 1880.

27. According to the report by the Government of India's Thagi and Dakaiti Department (Department of Fraud and Dacoity), Afghani left India in November 1882, via the S. S. India, *cf.* F.O. 60/594, "Memorandum" by A. S. Lethbridge, General Superintendent, Thagi and Dakaiti Department, 1896, cited in Keddie (1972), p. 182, n.1. During his entire stay in India, he was under constant secret service surveillance.

28. Headed by Colonel Aḥmad ʿUrābī, who was influenced by Afghani's pan-Islamic activities in Egypt, this movement was successful in establishing its control over Egypt beginning in 1880; by 1882, this small group of revolutionary young men had become de facto rulers of Egypt but in September 1882, the British invaded Egypt with full force and crushed the movement.

29. During Afghani's brief stay in London, Louis Ṣābunjī's London newspaper, *an-Naḥla,* published an article, "English Policy in Eastern Countries" written by Afghani. In this article, Afghani attacked the British policy, stating that the reason for this hostile policy was that the British knew that Sultan ʿAbd al-Ḥamīd was succeeding in his effort to have all Muslims adhere to the firm bond, *al-ʿurwa al-wuthqā,* of the caliphate.

30. This phrase occurs in the Qurʾān (Q. 2:256): *Whoever believes in Allah, has grasped the firmest bond.*

May 18, 1883, in response to a lecture by Ernest Renan on "Islam and Science," first given at the Sorbonne and published on March 29, 1883 in the *Journal des Débats*.[31] Renan had repeated the usual orientalist claim that "early Islam and the Arabs who professed it were hostile to the scientific and philosophic spirit and that science and philosophy had entered the Islamic world only from non-Arab sources."[32]

During his stay in Paris, Afghani was looked upon as the Muslim spokesman by a large number of liberal and left-wing politicians. He was approached by the British to intervene in the situation in Sudan where Mahdi had captured Khartoum along with the British General Gordon in 1885. Afghani sought freedom of Egypt in return. Nothing came out of these negotiations. Afghani was disgusted by the intrigues of the British foreign office and in 1886, he went to Moscow and later to St. Petersburg, where he tried to make an alliance between Russia, Turkey and Afghanistan against the British. He was given a warm reception and he was able to convince the Czar to permit Muslims to print the Qur'ān and other religious books.[33] After almost a year's stay in Russia, Afghani was invited by Shah Naṣīr al-Dīn to Iran and offered the position of special adviser to the Shah, which he accepted. Afghani, however, was critical of the Shah's policies on the question of political participation and he wanted to bring about far-reaching reforms which the Shah did not support. This difference of opinion forced Afghani to leave Iran for Russia in 1887 where he stayed until 1889. In 1889 on his way to Paris, Afghani met Shah Naṣīr al-Dīn in Munich who persuaded him to return to Iran. But the intrigues at the Court and Afghani's unabated criticisms of the rule and conduct of the Shah led to his eventual deportation from Iran in the winter of 1891. Afghani spent the last part of his life (1891-97) in Istanbul where he cooperated with Sultan ʿAbd al-Ḥamīd II for the implementation of his political program of pan-Islamic unity (*ittiḥad-i Islam*). He wrote numerous letters in Arabic, Persian, Turkish and Urdu to the leaders of public opinion and ʿulamāʾ for this purpose. But eventually, Afghani realized that the Sultan was more interested in strengthening his own power than promoting Islamic unity. ʿAbd al-Ḥamīd, on his part, was led by his advisors to distrust Afghani. Eventually, Afghani's movements were restricted and he spent the

31. Ernest Renan (1947), *Oeuvres Complètes,* vol. 1, Paris, p. 961, cited in Keddie (1972), p. 189, n. 18.
32. Keddie (1972), pp. 189-90.
33. Al-Mujahid, Sharīf (1954), p. 27.

last months of his life under virtual house arrest. Afghani died on March 9, 1897 and was quietly and hurriedly buried in Istanbul, which gave rise to suspicions of poisoning.

Afghani's life, struggles and ideas bring into sharp relief the dilemmas of the nineteenth century Muslim reformers who tried to find a *modus vivendi* between the Islamic tradition and the challenges of modernity, which were forced on the Muslim world with full thrust. In response, many ʿulamāʾ rejected all things western, others, like Sayyid Ahmad Khan, chose the opposite and a few, like Afghani, took the middle position, seeking the acquisition of the Western science within the larger Islamic framework of reform and renewal (*iṣlāḥ wa tajdīd*). Afghani, who had a sound understanding of the traditional Islamic philosophy (*ḥikma*), produced a scathing criticism of the naturalist and materialist position from the scientific, philosophical, ethical, and social perspectives. In order to refute the doctrines of the nineteenth century *Nécharīs,* Afghani placed their philosophy in the general history of philosophy. He divided philosophers into two groups: the theists (*mutaʾallihūn*) who "believed that behind sensate beings and beyond material creations there are beings devoid of matter and duration...free from the inseparable attributes and the accidental attributes of bodies, and pure of the defects of corporeal objects."[34] Afghani counted Pythagoras, Socrates, Plato, and Aristotle among the theists. "The other group believed that nothing exists except *matiére,*" Afghani wrote,

> meaning matter and material objects that are perceived by one of the five senses. This group was called materialists. When they were asked the cause of the various effects and properties of different materials, the most ancient representatives of that group answered that they all arise from the nature of matter. Nature in the French language is "nātūr," and in English it is "neicher." Therefore this group also became known as naturalists; naturalist (*ṭabīʿī*) in

34. All quotations from Afghani's text are from the English translation of the Hyderabad edition of 1298/1880-81, which was published using al-Ḥusainī, as appellation for Jamal al-Din Afghani, indicating his descent from Ḥusain, the grandson of the Prophet of Islam; the original text was published as, Jamāl Ad-Dīn al-Ḥusainī, *The Truth about the Neicheri Sect*; English translation by Nikki R. Keddie in Keddie (1968), pp. 130-174; [henceforth *Refutation*], pp. 132-3. A French translation by A. M. Goichon, from the Arabic version, was published in 1942: Jamāl ad-dīn al-Afghānī, *Refutation des Matérialistes,* tr. by A. M. Goichon, Paul Geuthner, Paris.

> French is "naturalisme," and materialists (*mādī*) is "matérialisme".[35]

Afghani traced the origin of this belief to Democritus. He also elaborated on the variations in this belief, pointing out that there were those "who believed that the heavens and earth have existed in their present form from eternity, and that they will always be so, and that the chain of species of plants and animals has no beginning. In every seed a plant is enclosed, and in every one of these enclosed plants seeds are hidden, and so forth."[36] In addition, there was a small group who believed that "species of plants and animals with the passage of time changed from one form to another until they reached their present form. This supposition appeared with Epicurus, one of the followers of Diogenes the Cynic."[37] Afghani then traced the emergence of Darwin's theory and went on to refute it on philosophical grounds. "If one asked him why the fish of Lake Aral and the Caspian Sea, although they share the same food and drink and compete in the same arena, have developed different forms—what answer could he give except to bite his tongue...only the imperfect resemblance between man and monkey has cast this unfortunate man into the desert of fantasies?"[38] Afghani also rejected the ideas of those materialists who attributed the cause of all changes in the composition of the heavens and earth to "matter, force and intelligence." He went on to "expose the corruption that has come into the sphere of civilization from the materialists or *neicheri* sect, and the harm that has resulted in the social order from their teachings, and to explain and elucidate the virtues, advantages, and benefits of religions, especially the Islamic religion."[39] He accused the materialists of undermining the very foundations of human society by destroying the "castle of happiness" based on the three religious beliefs and three qualities:

> The first of these great beliefs is [that] there is a terrestrial angel (man), and that he is the noblest of creatures. [Second] is the certainty that his community is the noblest one, and that all outside his community are in error and deviation. The third is the firm belief

35. *Refutation,* p. 133, Keddie notes that Afghani's argument comes, in part, from al-Ghazālī's *al-Munqidh min al-Ḍalāl.*
36. *Refutation,* pp. 133-4.
37. Ibid.
38. *Refutation,* p. 136.
39. *Refutation,* p. 140.

> that man has come into the world in order to acquire accomplishments worthy of transferring him to a world more excellent, higher, vaster, and more perfect than this narrow and dark world that really deserves the name of the Abode of Sorrows.[40]

The three qualities, "that have been produced in peoples and nations from the most ancient times because of religion" are:

> *modesty* (*ḥayā*ʾ), that is, the modesty of the soul at committing acts that would cause foulness and disgrace, and its reluctance to acquire qualities that violate the world of humanity...this quality is attached to the nobility of the soul...[which is] the basis of good order in human relations, the foundation of truthfulness in promises and firmness in treaties, and the cause of man's trustworthiness in words and deeds...this quality, that is modesty, is the bond of human alliances, associations, and societies...it is this quality that adorns man with good manners, separates him from the obscene acts of animals, and calls him to straightforwardness and righteousness in what he does or refrains from doing.... The second quality is *trustworthiness*. It is clear to everyone that the survival of the human race and its life in this world is dependent on dealings and reciprocal relations, and the life and the soul of all dealings and reciprocal relations is trustworthiness...[The third] of those qualities is *truthfulness* and honesty...The quality of truthfulness is the firmest pillar of the survival of the human race, and the strong bond of the social order of nations. No society can come into being without it—neither the society of a home nor that of a civilization.[41]

Having built his "foundation of the stability of human existence" on the basis of this "six-sided castle of human happiness that is built on those three noble beliefs and three great qualities", Afghani described how "these deniers of divinity, the *neicheris,* in whatever age they showed themselves and among whatever people they appeared" tried to destroy this foundation:

> ...they said that man is like other animals, and has no distinction over the beasts...with this belief, they

40. *Refutation,* p. 141.
41. *Refutation,* p. 146-7; translation emended.

> opened the gates of bestiality...and facilitated for man the perpetration of shameful deeds and offensive acts, and removed the stigma from savagery and ferocity. Then they explained that there is no life aside from this life, and that man is like a plant that grows in spring and dries up in the summer, returning to the soil...because of this false opinion, they gave currency to misfortunes of perfidy, treachery, deception, and dishonesty; they exhorted men to mean and vicious acts; and prevented men from discovering truths and traveling toward perfection.[42]

Afghani said that trustworthiness and truthfulness spring from the belief in the Day of Judgment and from the innate quality of modesty that humans are endowed with—and he accused the *nécharīs* of destroying these two beliefs. He invoked history, giving examples of those materialists who undermined the great nations of the past. Thus, according to Afghani, Epicurus, the naturalist and Epicureans, "who called themselves sages" and who were later known as Cynics,[43] were responsible for the disappearance of Greek glory. The Persians lost their nobility and civilization due to Mazdak, the *nécharī,* and Muslims lost their glory due to the appearance of those who held ideas like those of the *Baṭinīs,*[44] "one of [whom] found an opportunity to declare publicly to the world these corrupt, harmful beliefs from the *minbar* at Alamūṭ. He said: 'At the time of the Resurrection there will be no duties incumbent upon mankind, neither external nor internal ones. The Resurrection consists of the rising of the True Redeemer, and I am the True Redeemer. After [my arrival], let everyone do whatever he wants, since obligations have been removed.'"[45] Afghani counted the *Bābīs,* who had appeared in Iran shortly before his time, among the *nécharīs*. He also denouced Rousseau and Voltaire, who claimed, "to remove superstitions and enlighten minds" and who "considered manners and customs superstitions, and religions the inventions of men of deficient

---

42. *Refutation*, p. 148; translation emended.
43. Interestingly, the Arabs translated "Cynic" literally from the Greek word for cynic, which is an attributive adjective or noun from the word for "dog" [*kyôn,* stem *kyn*]; in Arabic, the Greek word for cynic was translated as *kalbī,* "like a dog". This has been noted by Keddie.
44. An extreme sect of the Ismāʿilīs, who, among other things, claimed that the truest interpretation of Islamic law and the Qurʾān was an esoteric, or *bāṭinī,* interpretation, rather than literal. See "Bāṭiniyya," *EI,* vol. i, pp. 1098-1100.
45. *Refutation,* p. 157; translation emended.

reason," and who "caused the corruption". Afghani held that it is the appearance of the *nécharīs* among the Ottoman that is the cause of their "present sad state". He said that the "*socialistes, communists,* and *nihilists* (*ijitimā'iyyīn, ishtirākiyyīn,*and *'adamīyyīn*), are all three followers of this path."

In the last part of his *Refutation,* Afghani extolled the virtues of religions because "of the two firm pillars—belief in a Creator and faith in rewards and punishments—and because of the six principles that are enshrined in religions."[46] And among the religions, he said, "we will find no religion resting on such firm and sure foundations as the religion of Islam...The first pillar of Islam is *tawḥīd,* [which] purifies and cleans off the rust of superstition, the turbidity of fantasies, and the contamination of imagination."[47] Anticipating an objection to his elucidation, he closed his treatise by saying: "If someone says: If Islam is as you say, then why are the Muslims in such a sad condition? I will answer: When they were [truly] Muslims, they were what they were and the world bears witness to their excellence. As for the present, I will content myself with this sacred text: *Verily, God does not change the state of a people until they change themselves inwardly.*"[48]

Afghani's main target in the *Refutation* was Sayyid Ahmad Khan and his followers in India. Afghani's treatise, with its lavish use of polemics, attempted to draw the attention of the Muslim intellectuals to the religious, philosophical and ethical challenges of the modern Weltanschauung. But when he wrote his famous response to Ernest Renan, whose quasi-racist lecture, *l'Islamisme et la science* ("Islam and Science"), given at Sorbonne and published in the *Journal des Débats* on March 29, 1883, had sought to prove that there was something inherently wrong with Islam and Arabs in reference to cultivation of science, Afghani's language remains apologetic throughout his letter of response.[49] He constructs a case of "warfare" between religion and philosophy and blames all religions for being intolerant and being an obstacle for the development of science and philosophy, thus agreeing with Renan. But he rejected Renan's racial

46. *Refutation,* p. 168.
47. *Refutation,* p. 169-70.
48. *Refutation,* p. 173.
49. Perhaps first written in Arabic and then translated into French, the "Answer to Renan" was published in *Journal des Débats* on May 18, 1883; it has been republished as an "Annex" to the aforementioned *Refutation des Matérialistes,* tr. by A. M. Goichon, Paul Geuthner, Paris (1942), pp. 174-85; English translation by Keddie can be found in *Response, op.cit,* pp. 181-7, [henceforth "Answer"].

arguments and, in their place, constructed an evolutionary developmental view of people and societies:

> ...I will say that no nation at its origin is capable of letting itself be guided by pure reason...And, since humanity, at its origin, did not know the causes of the events that passed under its eyes and the secrets of things, it was perforce led to follow the advice of its teachers and the orders they gave. This obedience was imposed in the name of the Supreme Being to whom the educators attributed all events, without permitting men to discuss its utility or its disadvantages. This is no doubt for man one of the heaviest and most humiliating yokes, as I recognize; but one cannot deny that it is by this religious education, whether, it be Muslim, Christian, or pagan, that all nations have emerged from barbarism and marched toward a more advanced civilization If it is true that Muslim religion is an obstacle to the development of sciences, can one affirm that this obstacle will not disappear someday? How does the Muslim religion differ on this point from other religions? All religions are intolerant, each one in its way...

Afghani then makes a strange turn and agrees with Renan on a critical point:

> In truth, the Muslim religion has tried to stifle science and stop its progress. It has succeeded in halting the philosophical or intellectual movement and in turning minds from the search for scientific truth. A similar attempt, if I am not mistaken, was made by the Christian religion, and the venerated leaders of the Catholic Church have not yet disarmed so far as I know. They continue to fight energetically against what they call the spirit of vertigo and error. I know all the difficulties that the Muslims will have to surmount to achieve the same degree of civilization, access to the truth with the help of philosophic and scientific methods being forbidden them...but I know equally that this Muslim and Arab child whose portrait M. Renan traces in such vigorous terms and who, at a later age, became "a fanatic, full of foolish pride in possessing what he believes to be absolute truth," belongs to a race that has marked its passage in the world, not only by fire and blood, but by brilliant sciences, including philosophy (with which, I must

recognize, it was unable to live happily for long).[50]

Here Afghani seems to forgo the essential distinction between revelation and its unfolding in history, that is, the distinction between Islam and Muslims and concludes his letter by creating a very sharp contrast between religion and philosophy:

> Whenever the religion will have an upper hand, it will eliminate philosophy; and the contrary happens when it is philosophy that reigns as sovereign mistress. So long as humanity exists, the struggle will not cease between dogma and free investigation, between religion and philosophy; a desperate struggle in which, I fear, the triumph will not be for free thought, because the masses dislike reason, and its teachings are only understood by some intelligences of the elite, and because, also, science, however beautiful it is, does not completely satisfy humanity, which thirsts for the ideal and which likes to exist in dark and distant regions that the philosophers and scholars can neither perceive nor explore.[51]

This somewhat abrupt and surprising conclusion leaves many issues unresolved: What was Afghani's position in reference to revelation and the normative tradition of Islamic learning? What was his opinion about the relationship between Islam and the scientific tradition it had inspired? But Afghani is not alone in this respect. There is a general trend among many Muslim intellectuals of the colonial period; they show unrestrained admiration for modern science. This is understandable given the political and social conditions in which they lived and worked. Afghani had a first hand experience of the power of modern science through his travels in the Western world and perhaps more than others, he was deeply conscious of the domination of the Western powers in world affairs. Afghani was a charismatic man of action; more than his writings, it was his "presence", his message of hope and his personal influence that helped to loose some of the mental shackles in which the Muslim intellectuals of the colonial era had found themselves.[52]

---

50. "Answer", pp. 182-4.
51. "Answer", pp. 187.
52. Some of Afghani's own works were collected and published in 1968 from Cairo; these include: *al-Taʿliqāt ʿalā Sharḥ al-Dawwānī li'l-ʿAqā'id al-ʿAḍudiyya*; in this Afghani glosses over Dawwānī's commentary on the famous Kalām book of ʿAḍud al-Dīn al-ʿĪjī, called *al-ʿAqā'id al-*

Renan's condescending rejoinder to Afghānī, published in the *Journal des Débats* on May 19, 1883, stated that "there was nothing more instructive than studying the ideas of an enlightened Asiatic in their original and sincere form." He found in them a rationalism, which gave him hope that "if religions divide men, Reason brings them together; and that there is only one Reason."[53] He reiterated his racial views, even in praising Afghani: "Sheikh Jemmal-Eddin is an Afghan entirely divorced from the prejudices of Islam; he belongs to those energetic races of Iran, near India, where the Aryan spirit lives still energetically under the superficial layer of official Islam."[54] Renan then admits "he may have appeared unjust to the Sheikh" in singling out Islam for his attack by stating that "Christianity in this respect is not superior to Islam. This is beyond doubt. Galileo was no better treated by Catholicism than Averroes by Islam."[55] Renan concludes his rejoinder by stating that Afghani had "brought considerable arguments for *his* fundamental theses: during the first half of its existence Islam did not stop the scientific movement from existing in Muslim lands; in the second half, it stifled in its breast the scientific movement, and that to its grief."[56]

Sayyid Ahmad Khan and Afghani, though poles apart in their background, training, religious and intellectual perspectives, nevertheless agreed on the need for acquisition of Western science to stop further decline and disintegration of the *dār al-islām*. They also saw little in Western science that was not just science; they perceived no implicit worldview, philosophy and metaphysical assumptions in science. For them, science ruled the world. "There was, is, and will be no ruler in the world but science," Afghani had declared in a lecture in 1882,

> ...it is evident that all wealth and riches are the result of science. There are no riches in the world without

---

'Aḍudiyya; *Risālat al-Wāridat fi Sirr al-Tajalliyāt*; Afghani had dictated this work to his student Muḥammad 'Abduh when he was in Egypt; in addition, see his *Tatimmat al-Bayan*, published in 1879 at Cairo, which is a political, social and cultural history of Afghanistan; and *Khāṭirāt Jamāl al-Dīn al-Afghānī al-Ḥusayni*, Beirut, 1931. This is a book compiled by the Lebanese journalist Muhammad Pasha al-Mahzūmī who participated in most of Afghani's talks during the last years of his life and developed his conversations with Afghani into the present book. The book contains important information about Afghani's life and ideas.

53. Reproduced in Keddie (1972), *Sayyid Jamāl ad-Dīn, op. cit.* p. 196.
54. Ibid.
55. Idem., p. 197
56. Ibid., emphasis added.

> science. In sum, the whole world of humanity is an industrial world, meaning that the world is a world of science. If science were removed from the human sphere, no man would continue to remain in the world.[57]

This erroneous view—which is still held by many Muslims—was based on the presumed objectivity of modern physical sciences. However, Afghani was not completely blind to the presence of some philosophical underpinnings in science. But he viewed these as "philosophic spirit" which was a praiseworthy quality. He was dismayed that his contemporary ʿulamāʾ

> have divided science into two parts. One they call Muslim science, and one European science. Because of this they forbid others to teach some of the useful sciences. They have not understood that science is that noble thing that has no connection with any nation, and is not distinguished by anything but itself. Rather, everything that is known is known by science, and every nation that becomes renowned becomes renowned through science. Men must be related to science, not science to men.
>
> How strange it is that the Muslims study those sciences that are ascribed to Aristotle with the greatest delight, as if Aristotle were one of the pillars of the Muslims. However, if the discussion relates to Galileo, Newton, and Kepler, they consider them infidels. The father and mother of science is proof, and proof is neither Aristotle nor Galileo. The truth is where there is proof, and those who forbid science and knowledge in the belief that they are safeguarding the Islamic religion are really the enemies of that religion. The Islamic religion is the closest of religions to science and knowledge, and there is no incompatibility between science and knowledge and the foundation of Islamic faith.[58]

Afghani also sought al-Ghazālī's help in bringing home his point that Islam is not incompatible with "geometric proofs, philosophical demonstrations, and the laws of nature" and "any one who claimed so was an ignorant friend of Islam. The harm of this ignorant friend to Islam is

57. "Lecture on Teaching and Learning" [henceforth "Lecture"], in Keddie (1968), *Response*, pp. 102-3.
58. "Lecture", pp. 104-7.

greater than the harm of the heretics and enemies of Islam."[59] He failed to realize the distinction between the metaphysical underpinning of the sciences to which al-Ghazālī's was referring and those of modern science. This rhetoric found new expressions in the next generation of Muslim intellectuals, many of whom were deeply influenced by Afghani, though each in his own way and not without significant departures from Afghani's courageous stand against colonization. Among them are Muḥammad ʿAbduh (*ca.* 1850-1905) and Rashīd Riḍā (1865-1935) in Egypt, Badiuzzeman Said Nursi (1877-1960), and Namik Kemal (1840-1888) in Turkey.[60] Kemal had also written a response to Renan's views which focused on the scientific achievements of the Muslims.[61] Namik Kemal, Said Nursi, and to a lesser extent, Muhammad Iqbal (d. 1938) also wrote on the topic of agreement between modern science and Islam as if it were a logical necessity. They did not see science as being culture-specific. They believed that modern science can be, rather should be, learned and it can be learned without adopting Western values. The underlying assumption was that the secular worldview of the modern West had no inroads into the philosophy, structure, operation and results of the natural sciences. They thought modern science can be imported without any ethical components of Western culture. Because they did not see any incongruity between modern science and Islam, some of them tried to create a semantic bridge by consciously employing the language used in natural sciences in their works on the Qur'ān. They also gave birth to a rationalistic discourse that had a strong overlay of modern science.

---

59. "Lecture", pp. 107-8.

60. Born to a distinguished family, whose roots go back to Shehīd Ṭopal ʿOthmān Pasha of Mora, who had been Ṣadr-e Aʿẓam in the eighteenth century and was famous for his acts of heroism, Meḥmed Kemāl Nāmiq (generally known as Namik Kemal), received spiritual training through his grandfather who lived near a Mawlawī *zāviyya* in Afyon. He also attended *Dār al-Maʿārif* in Istanbul between the age of 12 and 13 for about a year and a half where he is likely to have studied the works of Muḥyī'l-Dīn Ibn al-ʿArabī. He also studied Turkish *dīvān* poets with the famous *muderris*-poet Sayyid Meḥmed Ḥāmid (1779?-1854), who guided him through the *Mathnawī*.

61. This was *Rènan Mudāfaʿa-Nāmesi* (*The Defense against Rènan*), which he finished at Mytilene in September 1883; it has been published many times in Turkish. For a brief account of his life and works, see *EI*, vol. vi, pp. 875-79. For his political thought in general, see Mardin, Ṣerif (2000), *The Genesis of Young Ottoman Thought: A Study in the Modernization of Turkish Political Ideas*, Syracuse University Press, Syracuse; originally published in 1962.

The Case of Turkey

It is important to remember that this new discourse was not being pursued in isolation from other events that were making and unmaking traditions and customs in the Muslim world. These were times of quantum changes in the Muslim world and many forces were operative. Islam was generally seen as a spent force not only by non-Muslims but also by a small but powerful group of Muslim elite. In Turkey, for instance, the abolition of the caliphate in March 1924, marked the end of a struggle in which all other possibilities of constructing a new political order (pan-Islamism, pan-Ottomanism) were finally suppressed in favor of Turkish nationalism. Further, it was the sign of the ultimate fragmentation of Muslim communities. In Turkey, it ushered in a new era of secularism in which attempt was made to force the Islamic presence out of the public life.

The abolition of Caliphate necessitated the formulation of a new ideology on which a new Turkish political identity could be based. This ideology, sometimes called Kemalism, employed four strategies: secularization, nationalism, modernization and westernization. Mustafa Kemal saw these interwoven concepts as the foundation of his vision of a new Turkey. Secularization, for him, was a process that involved not just the separation of the state from the institutions of Islam but also the liberation of the individual mind from the traditional Islamic concepts and practices. Thus Turkey became a country rooted in contradiction of terms: a secular Muslim state, a state whose constitution forbade religious laws from having any role in the state and society (Article 2 of the Turkish Constitution, revised in 1982). During the initial fervor of Kemalism, the ruling group purged all expression of religion from public life: Arabic alphabet was replaced with Roman alphabet, Islam and its study was taken out of the educational curriculum, ritual prayer was not held in Arabic, but in Turkish, religious education in traditional *ṭaruq* and *zāviyās* was banned, a new legal system based on the European model was adopted and most important for our study, the theory of evolution was introduced as an important part of biology curriculum. By the time Mustapha Kemal died in 1938, Turkey had been transformed into a secular state run by men and women who called themselves Muslims but who were fiercely against Islam as a way of life.

While Islam remained the religion of the majority of Turks, the country was now ruled by a small elite who fought an unending battle with its own nation. They purged Islam from public sphere, forced women to take off their scarves, banned Islamic studies from school and university curricula, forbade traditional modes of dress, practices and norms of the society that had evolved over centuries. By brute force of arms, this ruling elite made it increasingly difficult for the adherents of Islam to articulate a worldview based on their faith. The center-stage was held by secularists who considered everything coming from the West a divine writ. The Kemalists saw the Western model of nation state to be the only legitimate and scientific form of a political community. Turkey under the influence of Kemalism became a repressive state which regularly imprisoned and tortured ʿulamāʾ, closed Islamic educational institutions and controlled mosques. Anyone who spoke of Islam publicly had to risk life and possessions. Islam was equated with backwardness.

The work of Said Nursi, the founder of the Nurcu movement in Turkey, who was exiled to western Anatolia in 1925 along with hundreds of other Muslims, has to be seen in this historical situation. He spent twenty-five years in exile, sometimes in prisons, but always under harsh conditions. Left without books, without his home and family, and restricted to a remote region of the country, Said Nursi was to make a remarkable impact on the lives of thousands of Turkish men and women through his powerful writings and he continues to be a revered figure in Turkey and other Muslim lands. His works, now collectively called *Risāle-i Nūr*, were clandestinely circulated. They were copied by hand; the figure given for the hand-written copies is 600,000. Nursi and his work is an excellent example of the conditions in which the discourse on Islam and science progressed in Turkey during the early decades of the twentieth century and how politics and faith were intertwined in the discourse. His movement spread quietly until 1950 despite all efforts to crush it and then entered a new phase in which a great number of young Turks, who had gone through the state-run secular institutions of the Republic, openly responded to his call. Toward the end of his life, Nursi's influence spread beyond Turkey. Today, there are several offshoots of this movement, some of which have become rather profane.

Said Nursi had considerable knowledge of modern science and he attempted to integrate it within a theistic perspective. For him, the Qurʾān and modern physical sciences had no dissonance; rather, relating the truth of the Qurʾān to modern men and women was even easier. Written during his exile, *Risāle-i Nūr* was later described as "a *mānevī tefsīr*, or commentary which expounds the truths of the Qurʾān."[62] In the course of his expressive

62. Nursi, Said Bediuzzaman (1998), *The Words*, being the English

prose, which pulsates with energy, Nursi substantiates Islamic faith on the basis of the certainties of modern physical sciences and reads the cosmic verses of the Qur'ān in the light of modern science. As a religious scholar well grounded in traditional Islamic sciences, Nursi was aware of the apparent discrepancy between traditional cosmology articulated by Muslim philosophers and Sufis, and the Newtonian worldview, but instead of rejecting the mechanistic view of the universe presented by Newtonian science, he tried to appropriate it by appealing to the classical arguments from design. He saw no contradiction between the order and harmony of the universe and Newtonian determinism. Rather, through a radical recasting of God as the Divine artisan, he found support for the mechanistic view of the universe. He thought of the universe as a machine or clock, just like the nineteenth century deists, but he transformed this enduring symbol of the European tradition to lend support to the theistic claims of creation. For him, the Qur'ānic themes of the regularity and harmony of the natural order, when combined with the predictability of Newtonian physics, disproved the triumph of the secularists and positivists of the nineteenth century and provided a solid rock on which to construct a new understanding of the message of the Qur'ān.

Nursi's approach to modern science needs to be interpreted with due consideration of the social and political conditions in which it was written; unlike many other reformers of the nineteenth century, there is an additional element here: the need to survive in an environment dominated by state sponsored harassment. Perhaps this is the reason for the emergence of a number of conflicting ways in which Nursi's work has been judged; some take the work as if it was a scholar's commentary on the Qur'ān; others read it with due regard to the life of the writer and his social and historical conditions. There are those who take his work to be an attempt to deconstruct metaphysical claims of modern science by using the language of Newtonian physics, chemistry, and astronomy. And there are those who emphasize the influence of modern science and positivism on Nursi. In addition, the work itself is not a smooth and calm exposition and many additions have been made to it. Originally, it was not even written; it was "dictated at speed to a scribe, who would write down the piece in question with equal speed" and these handwritten copies would circulate clandestinely. There were no books for references. The *Risāle-i Nūr*

translation of the Turkish *Sözler,* new revised edition, Sözler Neşriyat Ticaret ve Sanayi, Istanbul, p. 806.

collection is, in essence, a collection of dictations of an inspired mind, secretly written, for all religious teaching was forbidden. As such, Nursi's work does not fall in the category of so-called *al-tafsīr al-ʿilmī* (scientific commentary); rather, in its style and purpose, the collection now known as *Risāle-i Nūr* is a collection of sermons—a title that is used for one of the "Words", "The Damascus Sermon", which was delivered at the historic Umayyad Mosque in early 1911 to a gathering "of ten thousand, including one hundred scholars...the text was afterwards printed twice in one week,".[63] "The Damascus Sermon" is a sermon on hope, a commentary on Q. 39:53: *Do not despair of God's mercy*, a diagnosis of the maladies that had afflicted Muslims and an impassionate appeal to act resolutely to change the conditions.

As we have seen in other cases, a heavy overlay of political and social conditions defined Nursi's discourse. In order to appeal to an audience under the spell of rationalism, Nursi himself adopts a rationalistic style in many cases, but then the burden of his arguments makes it totally irrational, bordering on the ridiculous. For example, the verse *...and We have created for them similar [vessels] on which they ride,*[64] points to the railway and the "Light Verse" alludes to electricity, as well as to numerous other lights and mysteries.[65] And the verse: *To Solomon [We made] the wind [obedient]: its early morning [stride] was a month's [journey], and its evening [stride] was a month's [journey],*[66]

> suggests that the road is open for man to cover such a distance in the air. In which case, O man! since the road is open to you, reach this level! And in meaning Almighty God is saying through the tongue of this verse: "O man! I mounted one of my servants on the air because he gave up the desires of his soul. If you too give up laziness, which comes from the soul, and benefit thoroughly from certain of my laws in the cosmos, you too may mount it..." the verse specified final points far ahead of today's aeroplanes.[67]

---

63. As stated in the Publisher's Preface to the second revised English translation, see Nursi, Bediuzzaman Said (1989), *The Damascus Sermon*, tr. from the Turkish by Şükran Vahide, Sözler Neşriyat ve Sanayi A. Ş, Istanbul.
64. Q. 36: 42.
65. Nursi (1998), p. 261.
66. Q. 34:12.
67. Nursi (1998), pp. 262-3.

And the miracle of Prophet Moses' staff mentioned in the Qur'ān (Q. 2:60), predicts the development of modern drilling techniques to dig out such indispensable substances of modern industry as oil, mineral water, and natural gas. The mention of iron in the Qur'ān (Q. 34:10), which had been "softened for David", becomes a sign of the future significance of iron and steel for modern industry. In its popular and cruder version, Said Nursi's encounter with modern science has led his followers to establish one-to-one correspondences between new scientific findings and Qur'ānic verses. His practice of using science as the decoder of the sacred language of nature has influenced numerous Turkish students, professionals, and lay persons who are making similar attempts. Nursi's followers try to show the miracle of creation through comparisons between the cosmological verses of the Qur'ān and new scientific discoveries. Every new scientific discovery is quickly adopted as yet another proof for the miraculous nature of the Qur'ān. This has led to a gross profanation of the text of the Qur'ān and a great injustice to the scientific data. These trends also gave birth to formal works of Qur'ān interpretation in which modern science appears as the most important subject matter. Some of these works are examined in chapter ten.

Nursi was followed by a large number of young people who were seeking spiritual fulfillment in a society where religion had been under attack. This characteristic Turkish dilemma has given birth to a society which is divided and at war with itself. Thus the Islam and science discourse in Turkey is not a calm academic discourse; it is a matter of life and death. The inner tensions became apparent during the last decade of the twentieth century. In the course of events, the Science Research Foundation (established in 1991 and known in Turkey with its Turkish initials as BAV) and pro-evolutionists were locked in a deadly campaign against each other. Tens of local meetings and rallies for and against evolution were held. Pro-evolutionists have depicted BAV as a "fundamentalist organization". They have claimed that the most prominent anti-evolutionist writer Adnan Oktar (whose penname is Harun Yahya), is actually a group of writers supported by BAV.[68] At other times, they have

68. The website of Adnan Oktar/Harun Yahya, www.harunyahya.org, states that "he has devoted his life to explaining the existence and unity of Allāh". The biographical note also states that he is the author of over 100 books. Among his works are *The Evolutionary Deceit*, Okur Publishing, Istanbul and *The Disasters Darwinism Brought to Humanity* tr. by Carl Rossini, Vural Yayincilik, Istanbul, both published in 2000.

claimed that Harun Yahya is actually Necmettin Erbakan, the leader of an Islamic political party.[69] The opponents of BAV also accuse the organization of having an alliance with the Institute of Creation Research (ICR) in the United States. They trace the history of these links and of the establishment of BAV to the report on Darwinism that was commissioned by the Minister of Education, Vehbi Dinçerler, in 1985. Adem Tatli wrote the report and it was distributed to various educational institutions as a "working paper".

These Turkish debates have assumed a new dimension through the publication of an article by Arthur M. Shapiro, Professor of Evolution and Ecology at the University of California, Davis and a member of National Center for Science Education (NCSE) who has accused Vehbi of making a phone call to ICR in San Diego, expressly requesting material on creationism that would be suitable "for translation and distribution in Turkey".[70] He also wrote that the report by Tatli "reproduced the ICR's arguments, but omitted all Christian fundamentalist hobbyhorses about the age of the earth. Predictably, it concluded that evolution had been falsified by scientists and was still being taught only because of its ideological value to Marxists. Soon afterwards, Tatli's effort was amplified into a booklet called "Evolution: a Bankrupt Theory" and was widely distributed by the political Islamists."[71] Shapiro also noted that BAV conferences held in 1998 and 1999 had "star speakers recruited from ICR and other American sources... between August 1998 and May 1999, BAV staged local meetings and rallies in some 60 Turkish cities."[72]

In response to the activities of BAV, the Turkish Academy of Sciences (TUBA) issued a declaration on September 17, 1998.[73] It opens with a quotation from Mustafa Kemal, which states: "I do not leave any scripture, any dogma, any frozen and ossified rule as my legacy in ideas. My legacy is science and reason." This declaration provides an insight into the complex nature of various currents that have become entwined in the discourse on Islam and science. "Science is the most successful enterprise developed by

69. Ümit Sayin and Aykut Kence, "Islamic Scientific Creationism: A New Challenge in Turkey" in *Reports of the National Center for Science Education*, vol. 19 (1999), no. 6, pp. 18-29. This issue of the *Reports* has extensive coverage on the fierce battle being fought in Turkey between the proponents and foes of evolution.

70. *Reports, op. cit.* p. 16.

71. Ibid.

72. Ibid.

73. The complete text of the declaration is available at the website of the Academy: www.geocities.com/Athens/Cyprus/8732/tubabildiri.html.

mankind in order to understand and explain the universe and nature we live in, by way of observation, experiment, and testing." The declaration further states:

> For centuries scientists have not submitted [to] oppression and obstruction, defending the supremacy of man's reasoning and intellect, and its ability to attain the truth against prejudiced ideas and traditions. Today science is the greatest and most reliable pathfinder for human civilization's goals of investigating nature and magnifying and advancing the happiness of societies.

The declaration also expresses unqualified support for the theory of evolution and claims it to be a fundamental concept. "Today the theory of evolution is a fundamental concept that brings clarity to many problems concerning life; it finds very widespread acceptance in the world of science and it is strongly supported by reputable scientists and scientific organizations." The declaration equates the opposition to theory of evolution with opposition to science:

> The true purpose of these attacks on accumulated scientific tradition, which is centuries old, is to bring up unthinking, unquestioning and uncritical individuals who do not test ideas and who accept dogmatic and incorrect information exactly as they are given to them. It is obvious that those circles who conduct an open or covert war against secular government, freedom in education, and advancement in science and technology in our country do not desire independent-thinking civilized people.

Finally, the declaration ends with a call to eliminate all "non-scientific elements" from the educational system to bring up a "democratic and secular generation", imbibed with "free thought, free knowledge and free conscience":

> The Turkish Academy of Sciences (TUBA) believes that science is the correct path and approach to understanding the universe in which people and societies live, defining nature and determining its laws, and progressing in social, economic and cultural platforms. The citizens of our country have the right and responsibility not only to consume the products of science reflected in technology, but to learn the methods and ways of thought of science and contribute

> to its progress. Therefore we consider it our duty to warn and inform the public on the matters of eliminating the non-scientific elements of our educational system, installing modern methods of scientific thought and its products in our educational curricula, and taking necessary precautions to ensure that as we hail the twenty-first century a democratic and secular generation with "free thought, free knowledge, and free conscience" is brought up.

To be sure, this declaration does not mark the contemporary battle lines in the Islam and science discourse; it remains an extreme position. Most Muslim scholars and organizations are more likely to call for "Islamization" of modern science without, however, realizing the impossibility of such a task.

Scientific Journalism

Let us conclude this chapter with a brief note on the role of Arab scientific journalism that also contributed significantly to the developments in the discourse on Islam and science. In addition to *al-Manār*, edited by Rashīd Riḍā, two other scientific journals of the nineteenth century led the way: *al-Muqtaṭaf, al-Hilāl* and *al-Mashriq*.[74] These journals regularly published articles that discussed the relationship between science and religion. The writers of these articles were Muslims as well as Christians. Some of the prominent Arab Christian writers of late nineteenth and early twentieth centuries, such as Jurjī Zaydān (d. 1914), Shiblī al-Shumayyil (d. 1916), Faraḥ Anṭūn (d. 1922), and Ya'qūb Ṣarrūf (d. 1927), advocated the secular outlook of modern science as a way of joining the European path of modernization.[75] Others used a mixture of secular and religious

---

74. Rashīd Riḍā and *al-Manār* are discussed separately in chapter ten. For a survey of Arabic periodicals see Hartmann, Martin (1899), *The Arabic Press in Egypt*, London, cited in Ziadat, Adel A. (1986), *Western Science in the Arab World: The Impact of Darwinism, 1860-1930*, Macmillan, Houndmills and London, p. 12 and notes 51-3. The first of these three, *al-Muqtaṭaf*, started in Beirut in 1876, *al-Hilāl* was founded by Jurjī Zaydān (1861-1914), a Lebanese Christian, in Cairo in 1892 and *al-Mashriq* was launched by Father Louis Cheikho, S. J., an Arab Christian, in 1898 and it lasted until 1971.
75. For Shumayyil and Anṭūn, see Hourani, Albert (1993), *Arabic Thought in the Liberal Age: 1798-1939*, Cambridge University Press, Cambridge, pp. 245-59; also see, Sharabi, Hisham (1970), *Arab Intellectuals and the West: The Formative Years 1875-1941*, The Johns Hopkins Press,

formulations but most agreed that Arabs need to adopt modern science. It was through these journals that the science and religion dialogue first addressed specific issues—such as Darwinism—that dominated the discourse during this era.

Among the prominent Muslim writers of this era who wrote on the relationship between Islam and science are Ḥusayn al-Jisr (1845-1909), a Lebanese Shīʿī scholar, and Ismāʿīl Maẓhar (1891-1962) who was born in Egypt, the editor of several short-lived periodicals and the translator of Darwin's *The Origin of Species*. Ḥusayn al-Jisr wrote more than twenty-five books, including *al-Risāla al-Ḥamīdiyya fī Ḥaqīqat al-Diyāna al-Islāmiyya wa Ḥaqīqat al-Sharīʿa al-Muḥammadiyya* (*Ḥamīdian Essay on the Truthfulness of Islamic Religion and the Truthfulness of Islamic Law*).[76] Al-Jisr was also the teacher of influential Arab scholars, including Rashīd Riḍā. Both al-Jisr and Maẓhar wrote on Darwin's theory. Al-Jisr attempted to refute it but he formulated his response in the context of western materialism and made an attempt at an empirical interpretation of the Qur'ān. In order to reconcile the theory of evolution with the Qur'ānic teachings, he quoted several Qur'ānic verses, especially the verse: *We made every living thing from water. Will they not then believe?* and then agreed with the theory of evolution.[77] Al-Jisr argued that this verse proved that life originated in water and the other verses appear to denote special creation for every species but, in fact, "there is no further evidence in the Quran (*sic*) to suggest whether all species, each of which exists by the grace of God, were created all at once or gradually.... Al-Jisr explained the role of natural selection and survival of the fittest as mechanisms of variations leading to the emergence of new species; he was reluctant to accept them before conclusive intellectual evidence (*dalil aqli qati*) (*sic.*) established their validity. When that happened, he was willing to interpret the Quran (*sic.*) to accommodate the new evidence."[78] This epistemological shift in the Qur'ān interpretation, from the Qur'ān itself to modern science, was to open floodgates of another kind: each and every new scientific discovery would, henceforth, bring a shift in the rules of the interpretation.

Washington DC.

76. Al-Jisr, Husayn (1887), Beirut; Ḥamīd in the title refers to al-Jisr's patron Sultan ʿAbd al-Ḥamīd.
77. Q. 21:30; he also quotes Q. 24:45, 23:12-14, and 53:45-46. Al-Jisr, *Risāla*, p. 298, cited from Ziadat (1986), p. 94-5.
78. Ibid.

Al-Jisr's attempts at reconciling modern scientific theories with Islam found a fuller expression in the works of many other writers of the era. In particular, Abū al-Mājid Muḥammad Riḍā al-Iṣfahānī, a Shīʿī scholar of Karbala, Iraq, wrote a book in two parts, *Naqd Falsafa Darwin* (*Critque of Darwin's Philosophy*) in which he defended all religions against the "non-religion" and attempted to produce a theistic version of the theory of evolution.[79] He counted Wallace, Lamarck, Huxley, Spencer and Darwin among those who believed in God. He referred to *Kitāb al-Tawḥīd* of Imām Jaʿfar al-Ṣādiq as well as to the works of Ikhwān al-Ṣafā' to point out that the question of anatomical similarities found in Man and apes had already been discussed by these writers in far more detail than what has been provided by Darwin. He affirmed that the structural unity of living organisms was a result of heavenly wisdom and not a consequence of blind chance in nature; he also asserted that "man is human by reason of his soul; it is not his physical structuring which makes him human."[80]

When Haeckel's work on evolution was translated into Arabic by Ḥassan Ḥusayn, an Egyptian Muslim scholar, it further intensified the discussion.[81] In his seventy-two page introduction, Ḥussein agreed with some scientific ideas propagated by Haeckel but he refuted all ideas against religion, though he tried to reconcile Islam and science. He insisted that there was no contradiction between divine laws (*al-Sharīʿa*) and reason and argued for a non-literal reading of the Qur'ānic verses referring to "creation in six days". He also tried to equate Darwin's theory with the works of Ikhwān and claimed that what Darwin was saying had already been written by the Ikhwān under the title of heavenly wisdom (*Ḥikma Ilāhiyya*).[82]

Four years after the publication of Ḥusayn's book, Ismāʿīl Maẓhar translated the first five chapters of Darwin's *Origin of Species* into Arabic, adding four more chapters in 1928. The complete translation was published in 1964. He advocated adoption of the scientific method not only in education but also in all aspects of life. He published a journal, *al-ʿUṣūr* (*The Ages*), which had, as its motto, the phrase *Ḥarrīr fikrak,* "Liberate your thought". He saw nothing worthwhile in the Islamic civilization. For him, religion had to be a personal relationship between a human being and

79. First published in 1914 from Baghdad, quoted from Ziadat (1986), p. 95.
80. Cited from Ziadat (1986), p. 99.
81. Translated as *Faṣal al-Maqāl fī'l-Falsafa al-Nushū wa'l-Irtiqā'* (*On the Philosophy of Evolution and Progress*), Cairo, 1924, cited by Ziadat (1986), p. 110.
82. Ziadat (1986), p. 114.

God but even in this formulation, it was a natural impulse of humanity in its early stage. He advocated that the Islamic laws were only suitable for the time when they were first formulated and that they were totally incompatible with the modern times. He associated Darwin's theory with the notion of progress and wrote a book on the theory of evolution in 1924.[83]

These examples do not cover all aspects of the new discourse but they provide a general survey of various trends. They show that during the colonial era, the discourse on Islam and science became hostage to numerous extraneous considerations. Economics, local and international politics, individual influences, education, state power and many other factors continue to influence the direction of this discourse. Another facet of this colonized discourse emerged in the form of the scientific exegesis of the Qur'ān. This genre made its appearance toward the end of the nineteenth century, spread rapidly and then waned in the final decades of the twentieth century, leaving behind residual secondary works. The next chapter is devoted to an exploration of this genre.

---

83. Maẓhar, Isma'īl, *Maqāla al-Sabīl fi'l-Madhhab al-Nushū wa'l-Irtiqā'*, Cairo, 1926, quoted by Ziadat (1986), p. 114.

CHAPTER TEN

The Scientific Exegesis

The colonized Islam and science discourse that emerged in the nineteenth century made its most daring attempt to securely lodge itself in the Islamic tradition by finding a niche in the very heart of the tradition: the Qur'ānic exegesis. Perhaps it was in the very nature of things that instead of seeking roots in the Islamic scientific tradition, the proponents of the new discourse sought legitimacy and sanction for their program in the Qur'ān; for they would have found nothing in the Islamic scientific tradition that could justify their agenda. As we have seen in chapter 4, and throughout this book, the Islamic scientific tradition had never sought legitimacy for science by directly invoking the Qur'ānic text in support of its various findings; it operated within the metaphysical and ethical universe of Islam and within a hierarchy of knowledge wherein it had a legitimate place as a birthright. It was linked to all other branches of knowledge that had emerged within the Islamic civilization through an organic relationship that had evolved over time. Most of all, it was linked to the central vertical axis of the Islamic civilization which held all of its diverse manifestations in historical time with a reality that was atemporal and transcendental.

It is because of this secure and natural linkage that we do not find Muslim scientists who practiced science in the framework of inquiry that was anchored in the Qur'ānic metaphysics seeking support for their science in the text of Qur'ānic, or worse, attempting to "prove" the divine origin of the Qur'ān through science; both of these phenomena only emerged in the final decades of the nineteenth century when the Islamic scientific tradition had already withered. Almost all scientific works of the pre-seventeenth century Muslim scientists start with an invocation to God, followed by salutations to the Prophet as was the customary and most natural practice of Muslims who always sought God's help and assistance in their tasks. And then they proceed directly to the subject matter. The absence of direct use of the Qur'ānic text in support of scientific data was a natural consequence of the metaphysical underpinnings of the Islamic scientific tradition which linked it to the central doctrines of Islam. The most important and powerful of these doctrines is *Tawḥīd,* the Unicity of God. It was this uncompromising monotheism that shaped and defined all things Islamic.

The Qur'ān itself had made it easier for the faithful to establish a nexus between faith and science because it forged a seamless linkage between the transcendental and the historical—that is, "between that which exists in an intelligible world beyond space and time, and that which is bounded by and lies within the real spatio-temporal world with a finite beginning and an end."[1] The Qur'ān neither draws a clear line of demarcation between various realms of existence nor admits any multiplicity in their ontological status; all things exist in an inalienable relationship to each other and in a sublime ontological dependence on God, who is *al-Muḥīṭ* ("All-Encompassing"). *And He has encompassed all things*, the Qur'ān declares in an unequivocal manner.[2] "To remember God as *al-Muḥīṭ* is to remain aware of the sacred quality of nature," Nasr wrote in a doctrinal exposition of this concept, "the reality of natural phenomena as signs (*ayāt*) of God and the presence of the natural environment as an ambience permeated by the Divine Presence of that Reality which alone is the ultimate 'environment' from which we issue and to which we return."[3]

Thus, because the Islamic scientific tradition was naturally rooted in the Qur'ānic worldview and because it shared a common universe of discourse with the divine revelation, there was never any need to read back into the "Word of God" any scientific discovery or explanation of the "Work of God"; the emergence of these two entities in the Islamic tradition was purely under an influence which came from external sources. And this happened only when that traditional universe of discourse had been rent asunder and when Muslims found themselves overwhelmed by the power of modern science. It was precisely at that time in their history that Muslims sought such consonances. And ironically, those who pursued this new agenda were neither scientists nor exegetes with formal training in the long-established tradition of Qur'ānic exegesis (*tafsīr*, pl. *tafāsīr*),[4] at least not initially. It was only after a number of reformers had written scientific exegesis of the Qur'ān, *al-tafsīr al-ʿilmī,* with the sole aim of finding sanctity for the modern science in the Qur'ān in order to encourage Muslims to acquire it, that the discourse gained popularity among some scientists and religious scholars. Nevertheless, beginning in 1880, when an Egyptian

1. Haq, Nomanul S. (2001), "Islam" in Jamieson, Dale (ed.), *A Companion to Environmental Philosophy,* Blackwell Publishers, Malden, p. 113.
2. Q. 4:126.
3. Nasr, Seyyed Hossein (1993), *The Need for a Sacred Science,* State University of New York Press, Albany, p. 131.
4. *Tafsīr*, pl. *tafāsīr*, exegesis; *mufassasir*, pl. *musfassirūn*, exegetes.

physician Muḥammad ibn Aḥmad al-Iskandarānī published his book, *The unveiling of the luminous secrets of the Qur'ān in which are discussed celestial bodies, the earth, animals, plants and minerals,*[5] a new vista was opened for those modernist thinkers who were interested in justifying an agenda of reform, predominantly based on urging Muslims to acquire modern science. After this publication, the trend of writing scientific exegeses of the Noble Qur'ān gained momentum. Al-Iskandrānī published another book in 1883 that dealt with the "Divine Secrets in the world of vegetation and minerals and in the characteristics of animals".[6] Al-Iskandrānī repeatedly construed his explanations of the Qur'ānic verses to prove the presence of specific European inventions and discoveries in the verses of the Qur'ān.[7]

In the Indian subcontinent, Sayyid Ahmad Khan had begun his *tafsīr* in 1879; it was left unfinished at the time of his death in 1898. This was not yet a full expression, for Khan was restricted in his knowledge of western science to identify specific discoveries and inventions but, nevertheless, his main intent was to motivate Muslims to acquire modern science.[8] But soon scientific exegesis became a fully differentiated discipline to the extent that subsequent books on Qur'ānic exegesis have devoted special attention to this genre. Thus, al-Dhahabī, whose seminal work, *Tafsīr wa'l-Mufasirūn* (*Exegesis and Exegetes*), is one of the most important twentieth century surveys of the field, devotes a full chapter to *al-tafsīr al-ʿilmī* (scientific exegesis).[9] In addition, Muḥammad ʿIffat

5. Al-Iskandarānī, Muḥammad b. Aḥmad (1297/1880), *Kashf al-Asrār ʿan al-Nūrāniyya al-Qur'āniyya fi-mā yataʿallaqu bi'l-Ajrām as-Samāwiyya wa'l-Arḍiyya wa'l-Ḥaywanāt wa'l-Nabāt wa'l-Jawāhir al-Maʿdaniyya,* 3 vols. Maktabat al-Wahba, Cairo.
6. Al-Iskandarānī, Muhammad b. Ahmad (1300/1883), *Tibyān al-Asrār al-Rabbāniyya fi'l-Nabāt wa'l Maʿādin wa'l-Khawāṣṣ al-Haywaniyya* (*The Demonstration of Divine Secrets in the Vegetation and Minerals and in the Characteristics of Animals*), n.p., Damascus. The word *tibyān* (explanation) in the title is taken from Q. 16:89: *And We have sent down to thee the Book, explaining all things—a guide, a mercy and glad tidings for Muslims.*
7. For example, al-Iskandarānī (1883), *Tibyān,* p. 5, 29, 132, etc.
8. Khan's exegesis has been discussed in the previous chapter.
9. Al-Dhahabī, Muḥammad Ḥusayn (1985), *al-Tafsīr wa'l-Mufassirūn,* 2 vols., 4th ed., Maktabat al-Wahba, Cairo. This work has been posthumously reprinted in three volumes by Shirkah Dār Arqam bin abī al-Arqam, n.d.; in a short note at the beginning of the third volume, the publisher states that this volume is based upon al-Dhahabī's lectures which he delivered at the University of Baghdad between 1960-63 and they are like a prologue to many discussions of *al-Tafsīr wa'l-*

al-Sharqāwī,[10] J. J. G. Jansen,[11] and J. M. S. Baljon[12] have all paid attention to this genre. In the Arab world, in addition to al-Iskandarānī, early partisans of scientific exegesis include ʿAbd Allāh Bāshā Fikrī, Sayyid ʿAbd al-Raḥmān al-Kawkabī, and physician Muḥammad Tawfīq Ṣidqī, all of whom either wrote exegesis or works supporting scientific explanation of the verses of the Qur'ān.[13] By the end of the nineteenth century, scientific exegesis had established itself as an independent discipline, though it still lacked general acceptance granted to other kinds of exegesis, such as *tafsīr fiqhī* and *tafsīr lughāwī*.[14]

The twentieth century saw a steady stream of such works in several languages. One of the first was that of Muhammad ʿAbduh (*ca.* 1850-1905),[15] based on a series of lectures he gave during 1900/01; these became the influential *Tafsīr al-Manār*, which has gone through several editions in the twentieth century.[16] This trend reached a high point in 1931 with the

---

Mufassirūn. All references are from this expanded edition [henceforth al-Dhahabī (new edition)].

10. Al-Sharqāwī, Muḥammad ʿIffat (1972), *Ittijāhāt al-Tafsīr fi Miṣr fil-ʿAṣr al-ḥadīth*, Maṭbaʿat al-Kīlānī, Cairo.
11. Jansen, J. J. G. (1974), *The Interpretation of the Koran in Modern Egypt*, E. J. Brill, Leiden.
12. Baljon, J. M. S. (1961), *Modern Muslim Koran Interpretation, 1880-1960*, E. J. Brill, Leiden.
13. Al-Dhahabī (new edition), vol. 2, p. 348.
14. That is, juristic and linguistic exegeses, so called because of their stress on the juristic or linguistic aspects of the Qur'ān; other distinct categories of traditional *tafsīr* include: *tafsīr riwā'ī*, which makes transmitted report (*riwāya*) as its main stay; *tafsīr kalāmī*, which focuses on theological issues; *tafsīr naḥwī*, which discusses issues of grammar; and *tafsīr adabī*, which treats matters of language and style. In many *tafāsīr*, aspects mentioned above are often combined.
15. For useful biographical information on ʿAbduh, see Badawi, M. A. Zaki (1976, 1978), *The Reformers of Egypt*, Croom Helm, London, pp. 35-95; also see Kedourie, Elie (1966), *Afghani and ʿAbduh: An Essay on Religious Unbelief and Political Activism in Modern Islam*, Frank Cass & Co. Ltd. London which mostly deals with Afhani's influence on ʿAbduh.
16. ʿAbduh gave a series of lectures on the Qur'ān and his Syrian student, Muḥammad Rashīd Riḍā took notes which he later expanded. The enlarged work was shown to ʿAbduh who approved and corrected, as needed. These lectures appeared in the periodical *Al-Manār*, vol. iii, 1900, as *Tafsīr Manār* of ʿAbduh. After the death of ʿAbduh in 1905, Rashīd Riḍā continued *Tafsīr al-Manār*, from Q. 4:125 to Q. 12:107, indicating those parts (in these posthumous portions) which were the result of ʿAbduh's lectures and his own additions. Eventually, *Tafsīr Manār* was published in 12 volumes in 1927; a later edition with indices is *Tafsīr al-Qur'ān al-Ḥakīm al-Mustahir bi Tafsīr al-Manār*, 12

publication of the twenty-six volume *tafsīr* of Ṭanṭawī Jawharī (1870-1940), *al-Jawāhir fī Tafsīr al-Qur'ān al-Karīm,* illustrated with drawings, photographs and tables.[17] This is one of the earliest comprehensive scientific exegesis in which the author expressly states that he prayed to God to enable him to interpret the Qur'ān in a way that includes all the sciences that were attained by humans so that Muslims could understand the cosmic sciences; the author also believed that the Sūras of the Qur'ān complement things that were discovered by modern science. Scientific *tafsīr* was also, sometimes, integrated into the general *tafsīr* literature. A work of this kind is Farīd Wajdī's *Ṣafwat al-ʿIrfān* (*The Best Part of Cognition*), a Qur'ān commentary with an elaborate introduction, now commonly known as *al-Muṣḥaf al-Mufassar* (*The Qur'ān Interpreted*).[18] This commentary, printed in the margin of the text of the Qur'ān, is divided into two parts. The first part, *Tafsīr al-Alfāẓ* (*Explanation of Words*) explains difficult and rare words; the second, *Tafsīr al-Maʿānī* (*Explanation of Meaning*) "translates" the text of the Qur'ān in contemporary Arabic with remarks spread throughout the translation. It is in these remarks that Wajdī inserts his scientific explanations, often with exclamations placed in parentheses: "you read in this verse an unambiguous prediction of things invented in the nineteenth and the twentieth centuries"; or "modern science confirms this literally".[19] Unlike many other works, Wajdī's commentary is not exclusively devoted to the scientific explanations. But there are many other works which have been primarily written for this purpose.[20] In their zeal to

---

published, in his own life time, *Tafsīr Juz' ʿAmmā,* al-Maṭb. al-Amīriyya, Cairo, 1322/1904; *Tafsīr Sūrat al-ʿAṣr,* Cairo, 1903; [*Tafsīr al-Fātiḥa*], *Fātiḥat al-Kitāb, Tafsīr al-Ustādh al-Imām...,* Kitāb al-Taḥrīr, Cairo, 1382; and his lectures on the Qur'ān were edited and published by Tahir al-Tanakhi as *Durūs min al-Qur'ān al-Karīm,* Dār al-Ḥilāl, Cairo, n.d.

17. Jawharī, Ṭanṭawī (1931), *al-Jawāhir fī Tafsīr al-Qur'ān al-Karīm al-Mushtamil ʿalā ʿAjā'ib,* 26 vols., Muṣtafa al-Bābī al-Ḥalabi, Cairo.
18. Wajdī, Muḥammad Farīd (n.d.), *Al-Muṣḥaf al-Mufassar,* Cairo.
19. Wajdi (n.d.), p. 346 and 423.
20. For instance, the 1954 work of Ḥanafī Aḥmad, *Muʿjizāt al-Qur'ān fī Wasf al-Kā'ināt,* which was reprinted in 1960 and 1968 as *al-Tafsīr al-ʿIlmī lī Āyāt al-Kawniyya* (*Scientific Exegesis of the Cosmic Verses*); Ismāʿīl, ʿAbd ʿAzīz (1938), *al-Islām wa'l-ṭibb al-Ḥadītha* (*Islam and the Modern Medicine*), Maṭb. al-Iʿtimād, Cairo; al-Harāwī, Ḥusain (1361/1942), *al-Naẓariyyā al-ʿIlmiyya fī'l-Qur'ān* (*Scientific Theories in the Qur'ān*) Cairo; ʿAtiyyah, Ḥasan Ḥāmid (1992), *Khalq al-Samāwatī wa'l-Arḍ fī Sittati Ayyāmin fī'l-ʿIlm wa'l-Qur'ān* (*Creation of the Heavens and the Earth in Six Days in Science and in the Qur'ān*), Nashr wa-Tawzīʿ Mu'assasā ʿAbd al-

prove the existence of modern science in the Qur'ān, some exegetes have gone to the extent of formulating their theories on the foundation of classical exegeses of the Qur'ān. In doing so, they primarily borrow the concepts which have been dealt in the vast *tafsīr* literature. One such concept is the concept of *'ijāz*, the inimitability of the Qur'ān. For example, this classical theme was "misappropriated" by Muḥammad Kāmil, for his claim that "the scientific miracle [of the Qur'ān] is greater than the miracle of its matchless eloquence."[21] By now, the genre seems to have exhausted all verses of the Qur'ān that can be shown to contain specific information and knowledge of a scientific nature. This voluminous *tafsīr* literature has also given birth to a large amount of secondary literature, books, articles, television productions, audiovisual and web-based material. Some authors have produced lists of all "scientific verses"; others have classified these verses according to their applicability to various branches of modern science, such as physics, oceanography, geology, cosmology.[22] According to Ṭanṭawī Jawharī, the number of such verses is 750, out of a total of some 6616 that make up the Qur'ān.[23] In addition to his *tafsīr*, he also published

Karīm b. 'Abd Allāh, Tunis; al-Khatīb, Mūsā (1415/1994), *Min Dalā'il al-I'jaz al-'Ilmi fi'l-Qur'ān wa'l-Sunna al-Nabawiyya* (*Signs of the Scientific Miracles of the Qur'ān and the Prophetic Sunna*), Mu'assasāt al-Khalīj al-'Arabī li'l al-Ṭiba'a wa'l-Nashr, Cairo; Nawfal, 'Abd al-Razzāq (1409/1989), *Min al-Āyāt al-'ilmiyya* (*On the Scientific Verses*), Dār al-Shurūq, Cairo and Beirut; and Shāhīn, 'Abd al-Raḥmān (1369/1950), *I'jāz al-Qur'ān wa'l-iktishāfāt al-Ḥadītha* (*The Inimitability of the Qur'ān and Modern Discoveries*), Cairo.

21. Kāmil, Muḥammad (1955), *Al-Qur'ān al-Karīm wa'l-'Ulūm al-Ḥadītha* (*The Noble Qur'ān and the Modern Sciences*), Dār al-Fikr al-Ḥadīth, Cairo, p. 15 wherein he states: "*fihi min i'jāz 'ilmī fawq mā fihi min i'jāz balāghi.*"
22. Qurashi, M. M.; Bhutta, S. M.; and Jafar, S. M. (1987), *Quranic Ayaat Containing References to Science and Technology*, Sh. Sirri Welfare & Cultural Trust and Pakistan Science Foundation, Islamabad; Nurbakī, Halūk (1993), *Verses from the Glorious Koran and the Scientific Facts*, 3rd edition, Türkiye Diyanet Vakfi, Ankara.
23. This is a highly problematic number. The end of a Qur'ānic verse (*āya*) is generally marked by a small circle. This convention is, however, a later development. Early Qur'ān exegetes had precisely defined *āya* in its technical sense and numerous books exist on this subject. Jalāl uddīn al-Sayūṭī (849-911/1445-1505), mentions various such works in his *al-Itqān fi 'Ulūm al-Qur'ān*, 2 vols., Maṭb'a Amīr, Cairo, 1967, pp. 225-43. Depending on the technical definition of *āya* employed to count the total number of verses of the Qur'ān, they are said to be 6000, 6616, or 6216; the total number of letters that make up the Qur'ān is 323,671. But the classification of verses into legal or scientific is not a simple matter as many verses address more than one topic. Jawharī also uses a

a book in 1925, *al-Qur'ān wa'l-'Ulūm al-'Aṣriyya* (*The Qur'ān and the Modern Sciences*), in which he prescribed two remedies for freedom from foreign rule: unity and scientific development.

While the trend of writing scientific *tafsīr* seems to have abated, publication of secondary literature on the Qur'ān and modern science is on the rise.[24] In addition to proving the existence of specific scientific knowledge in the Qur'ān, some of these works have also created a sub-branch of the scientific exegesis, *al-i'jāz al-'ilmi*, the scientific miracle, which treats its subject on the same lines as those on which the classical *tafsīr* literature dealt with the theme of the inimitability of the Qur'ān (*i'jāz al-Qur'ān*),[25] which had originated on the basis of the Qur'ānic challenge to the unbelievers to produce a sūra like it.[26] This theme, repeated in the Qur'ān in various forms,[27] had given rise to a fully differentiated branch of exegesis which explored and defined, in precise terms, what is meant by the inimitability of the Qur'ān, examined various aspects of the challenge, and explored the spiritual and linguistic aspects of this concept. In an effort to gain legitimacy, the new scientific exegesis was grafted onto this coherent body of classical tradition; thus in addition to the classical form of *i'jāz* (inimitability), a new category was invented.[28]

During the last three decades of the twentieth century, a number of social, political and economic factors contributed to the spread and popularity of this literature. Various state-sponsored institutions organized

---

very loose definition of the word "science".

24. This literature is being produced in all languages and from all countries. A few examples of such works are: Al-Bārr, Muḥammad 'Alī (1986), *Khalq al-Insān bayn al-Ṭibb wa'l-Qur'ān* (*The Creation of Human Being in Medicine and the Qur'ān*), al-Dār al-Sa'ūdiyyah, Jeddah; Barq, Ghulam Jilani (n.d.), *Dô Qur'ān* (*Two Qur'āns*), Shaykh Ghulam Ali, Lahore; Mahmood, S. Bashir ud-Din (1991), *Doomsday and Life After Death*, Holy Qur'ān Research Foundation, Islamabad; Naqvi, Syed Sibte Nabi (1973), *Islam and Contemporary Science*, World Federation of Islamic Missions, Karachi; El-Naggar, Z. R. (1991), *Sources of Scientific Knowledge. The Geological Concept of Mountains in the Qur'ān*, The Association of Muslim Scientists and Engineers and The International Institute of Islamic Thought, Herndon.
25. The word *i'jāz*, from the root *'JZ*, has various meanings, including, "to disable, to incapacitate, to be impossible, to be inimitable", see Lane (1984), *op. cit.* vol. 2, pp. 1959-62.
26. Q. 10:38.
27. For example, Q. 2:23-24, Q. 11:16, and Q. 17:90.
28. Many books have been written on this aspect. See, for example, Muslim, Muṣṭafā (1999), *Mabāḥith fī I'jāz al-Qur'ān*, Dār al-Qalam, Damascus.

conferences and seminars in which scientists linked specific verses of the Qur'ān to specific data and theories of modern science to prove (i) that the Qur'ān is really a book of God, revealed to the Prophet of Islam because such specific scientific information was unknown during his life and (ii) that the Qur'ān contains all scientific knowledge and it is for science and scientists to discover this knowledge. This approach is encumbered with an emotional, psychological, even political, baggage and has been opposed and challenged by serious scholarship. But its mass popularity remains uncontestable. This has given rise to mountains of apologetic literature which ranges from the enormously popular book of the French Muslim Maurice Bucaille, *The Bible, the Qur'an and Science*—first published as *La Bible, le Coran et la science*[29] in 1976 and since then translated into every language spoken in the Muslim world—to hundreds of websites which attempt to prove that the Qur'ān is, in fact, the word of God because it contains scientific theories and facts which modern science has only recently discovered. The rise, popularity and mass distribution of this literature also owes its existence to the oil-boom and politics of the late 1970s and early 1980s. It was during this time that the rulers of Arabia established a "Commission for Scientific Miracles of Qur'ān and Sunna" (*Hai't al Iʿjāz al-ʿilmī fī'l-Qur'ān wa'l-Sunna*), at Makkah, under the aegis of the World Muslim League (*Rābiṭa al-āʿlam al-islāmī*) with six goals and objectives.[30] In 1992, the Commission published a booklet which contains

29. Bucaille, Maurice (1976), *La Bible, le Coran et la science: les Écritures saintes examinées à la lumière des connaissances modernes,* Seghers, Paris, translated by Alastair D. Pannell and the author as *The Bible, the Qur'an and Science*. The English translation was first published in 1978 by the North American Trust Publications, Indianapolis, and has since been published in hundreds of pirated local editions all over the Muslim world.

30. These "Aims and Objectives" appear in many publications of the Commission; the following verbatim quotation is from the inner back title of the booklet entitled, *Proposed Medical Research Projects Derived from the Qur'an and Sunnah*, "prepared" by Abdul-Jawwad M. As-Sawi, M.D. and published by the Commission in 1992: "(i) To lay down governing rules for and methods of signs in the Scientific signs in the Holy Qur'an and Sunnah; (ii) To train a leading group of scientists and scholars to consider the scientific phenomena and the cosmic facts in the light of the Holy Qur'an and Sunnah; (iii) To give an Islamic Character to the physical sciences through introugcing the conclusion of approved researches into the curricula of the various stages of education; (iv) To explain, without constraint, the accurate meanings of the Quranic verses and the Prophet's Traditions relating to Cosmic

seventeen research projects in therapeutic medicine and nineteen in preventive medicine. The Commission has published about twenty books dealing with the "scientific miracles" of the Qur'ān in various fields such as embryology, botany, geology, astronomy and cosmology. Five international conferences have been organized by the Commission between 1987 and 2000 in various countries. These conferences have a set pattern: the organizers invite scientists,[31] especially non-Muslim scientists,[32] and ask them to relate their scientific research to specific verses of the Qur'ān or to the traditions of the Prophet of Islam which they receive in translation much before the conference. The proceedings of the conferences are videotaped and then these tapes are widely distributed throughout the world.[33]

This profanation of the religious texts, patronized by powerful state institutions, has received little opposition from the religious quarters, which is a sign of a deep-rooted malaise of the contemporary Islamic

---

Sciences, in the light of modern scientific finds, linguistic analysis and purpose of Shari'ah; (v) To provide Muslim missionaries and mass-media with Da'wah; (vi) To publicize the accepted researches in simplified forms to suit the various academic levels and to translate those papers into languages of the Muslim world and the other living languages."

31. Notable among the Muslim scholars who have been associated with the Commission are Sheikh Abdul Majeed Zindanni, its founder and first secretary-general and Zaghloul El-Naggar, an Egyptian geologist.

32. Among the non-Muslim scholars who have participated in these conferences are gynecologist Joe Leigh Simpson, marine scientist William Hay, and Keith Moore, the author of a widely used embryology textbook, *The Developing Human,* which was published by the Commission with "Islamic Additions: Correlation Studies with Qur'ān and Ḥadīth" by Abdul Majeed A. Azzindani, and who wrote in the "Foreword" of this edition: "I was astonished by the accuracy of the statements that were recorded in the 7th century AD, before the science of embryology was established. Although I was aware of the glorious history of Muslim scientists in the 10th century AD and of some of their contributions to medicine, I knew nothing about the religious facts and beliefs contained in the Qur'ān and Sunnah. It is important for Islamic and other students to understand the meaning of these Qur'ānic statements about human development, based on current scientific knowledge." Moore, Keith L. (1982), *The Developing Human: With Islamic Additions,* Commission. He also published, *Qur'ān and Modern Science: Correlation Studies,* Islamic Academy for Scientific Research, Jeddah, 1993.

33. The first international Conference, organized by the Commission was held in Islamabad, Pakistan in 1987; the fifth in Beirut in 2000.

scholarship. But this large-scale misguided exercise has not been totally ignored. Following the 1987 conference of the Commission, held in Islamabad under the direct patronage of the then military ruler of Pakistan, General Muhammad Zia-ul Haq, Pervez Hoodbhoy produced a scathing criticism of the whole project.[34] This angry response to an ill-conceived plan which was being orchestrated by the Commission with the help of a small number of mostly old and retired Muslim scientists and an equally small number of Western scientists who had been lured into the plan by offers of attractive financial rewards and an opportunity to rub shoulders with the rulers, mercilessly exposed this profanely executed endeavor. But, it is, in itself, equally flawed because of its own agenda which was to support, reiterate and re-establish the "religious orthodoxy versus foreign sciences" thesis of Ignaz Goldziher discussed in chapter 5. Hoodbhoy finds nothing worthwhile in the Islamic scientific tradition, except "five great 'herectics' (al-Kindī, Muḥammad ibn Zakariya al-Rāzī, Ibn Sīnā, Ibn Rushd and Ibn Khaldūn, see chapter 10 of his book); he accepts the discredited periodization in which Islamic scientific tradition is said to have withered by the thirteenth century, with its so-called "golden age" being in the eleventh century. In his "Why Didn't the Scientific Revolution Happen in Islam?" (chapter 11), he reproduces a caricature of the arguments used by Orientalists: the role of Muslim law, autonomous institutions, political factors, especially the 1258 sacking of Baghdad, and, of course, al-Ghazālī, who "routed the rationalists".[35]

The appearance of the scientific exegesis of the Qur'ān at a time when most of the Muslim world was under colonial rule, its linkage with the agenda of the reformers with their insistent demands for the acquisition of modern science and technology and the historical absence of a differentiated field of *tafsīr 'ilmī* cast suspicion on the genre. But all of these can be, and have been, set aside. For example, the historical absence can be discarded as an obstacle because after all, all other genres of *tafsīr* made

34. Hoodbhoy, Pervez (1991), *Islam and Science: Religious Orthodoxy and the Battle for Rationality*, Zed Books Ltd., London and New Jersey.
35. We have examined all of these factors in chapter 5. But the most important aspect of Hoodbhoy's work is not the reproduction of old, discredited theories, based on a scholarship that took no note of the discoveries of Islamic scientific texts after 1960s, but its disparaging attitude toward the Islamic tradition and its unqualified awe of modern science, without any recognition of the metaphysical and philosophical underpinnings, which are necessarily part of all scientific endeavors in all civilizations.

their appearance in historical time. *Tafsīr Kalāmī*, for instance, arose when Kalām tradition had matured and overshadowed many other aspects of Islamic intellectual tradition. Likewise, the mystical interpretation arose in its own historical time. The proponents of this genre argue that the Qur'ān has always been looked upon as a book of guidance and knowledge and that there is no reason not to extend the range of Qur'ānic guidance and knowledge to modern science. An often cited verse in support of finding contemporary scientific data in the Qur'ān is: *We have ignored nothing in the Book.*[36] But their most basic justification rests on the presence of a large number of verses, though not 750, which draw attention to a variety of natural phenomena. For instance, the Qur'ān refers to the order and balance that characterizes the universe (Q. 25:2; 55:5-7; 67:3), it mentions the harmonious interdependency of various parts of the physical world, and it describes regularities of celestial movements. At times, the Qur'ānic details are rather specific, such as when it refers to the various stages through which the fetus develops (Q. 22:5; 23:12-14; 40:67). Similarly, the Qur'ānic concept of pairs (Q. 13:3; 36:36; 53:45; 55:52), which refers to the principle of the complementarity of opposites seems to characterize a large part of the physical world. For these reasons—and the list is not exhaustive—the case for the scientific exegesis of the Qur'ān has been supported by many exegetes.

The scientific exegesis of the Qur'ān has not been without opposition. It is interesting to note that this criticism is built upon *uṣūl al-fiqh* (the principles of jurisprudence), the queen of Islamic sciences. Many scholars base their criticism of modern scientific exegesis on the work of eminent *uṣūlī* scholar, al-Shāṭibī,[37] who had dealt with the question of *bidā* (innovation) in his *Kitāb al-Iʿtiṣām*,[38] and in his doctrinal work, *al-Muwāfaqāt fī Uṣūl al-Sharīʿa*,[39] in a general way. "And among them are those who

36. Q. 6:38: *mā farraṭnā fi'l-kitābi min shay'in*; the word *farraṭā*, used here in the negative case, literally means "to neglect, to overlook, to leave out of calculation"; sometimes part of 16:89, *We have sent down to thee the Book, explaining all things*, is also used.

37. Abū Isḥāq Ibrāhīm bin Mūsā al-Shāṭibī al-Andulasī (d. 790/1388), the *uṣūlī* scholar from al-Andalus, not to be confused with Abū'l Qāsim b. Firruh b. Khalaf b. Aḥmad al-Ruʿaynī (538-590/1144-1194), eminent Qur'ānic scholar from al-Andalus, famous for his mnemonic techniques in the discipline of Qur'ānic recitation, *qirā'a*.

38. Edited by Rashīd Riḍā in his influential periodical *al-Manār*, xvii (1333/1913), reprinted several times.

39. First published from Tunis 1302/1884, and later from Cairo 1341/1923;

transgress the bounds in their claims about the Qur'ān by saying that the Qur'ān contains all knowledge of the ancients and the moderns in branches [such as] physics, geometry, mathematics, logic, and linguistics."[40] These critics point out that the Qur'ān is not a compendium of medicine, astronomy, geometry, chemistry, or necromancy, but a book of guidance, sent down by God to bring humanity out of darkness and usher it into light. They criticize the use of the Qur'ānic verses, such as *We have ignored nothing in the Book*, by pointing out that though the word *farraṭa* in the verse literally means "to neglect, to overlook, to leave out of calculation", it should not be interpreted to mean that the Qur'ān contains detailed knowledge of all things, but only that it contains general principles of all those matters that are important for human beings to know so that they can act in order to reach physical and spiritual perfection; it leaves the door open for human beings to figure out and elucidate, to the extent possible in a given age, details of different disciplines of knowledge. This is the position taken by al-Dhahabī. He also lists other scholars who have rejected scientific exegesis; they include such authorities as Maḥmūd Shaltūt, Muḥammad Mustafa al-Marāghī, and Amīn al-Khūlī.

But it is to al-Khūlī that we credit a detailed and systematic modern refutation of the scientific exegesis.[41] Al-Khūlī divided his major arguments under various headings; these include: (i) Lexicological: The Qur'ānic words do not bear a correspondence with the terms and vocabulary of modern sciences; (ii) Philological: The scientific exegesis is philologically unsound because the Qur'ān was first addressed to the contemporaries of the Prophet and cannot contain anything that they did not understand; (iii)

---

for a contemporary study of his life and thought, see Masud, Muhammad Khalid (1977), *Islamic Legal Philosophy: A Study of Abū Iṣḥāq al-Shāṭibī's Life and Thought*, Islamic Research Institute, Islamabad, repr. with additions (1995) as *Shāṭibī's Philosophy of Islamic Law*, Islamic Research Institute, Islamabad.

40. Quoted in al-Dhahabī (new edition), vol. 2, p. 342, *al-Muwāfqāt*, vol. 2, p. 79.

41. Amīn al-Khūlī taught Qur'ān exegesis at the Egyptian University at Giza. He never published a commentary but his various works on the relationship between philology and Qur'ān exegesis have been influential in setting the principles of modern Qur'ān interpretation. A collection of his previously published articles appeared in 1961: al-Khūlī, Amīn (1961), *Manāḥij Tajdīd fi'l-Naḥw wa'l-Balāgha wa'l-Tafsīr wa'l-Adab*, Dār al-Maʿrifa, Cairo; also important in this respect is his 1944 work: *al-Tafsīr: Maʿālim Ḥayāti Minhaj al-Yawm*, Dār al-Maʿrifa Cairo.

Theological: It is theologically unsound because the main intent of the Qur'ān is guidance and it does so by establishing a worldview based on certain doctrines, not scientific principles; and (vi) Logical: It is logically absurd to assume that the finite quantity of Qur'ānic text should contain ever-changing views of the nineteenth and twentieth century scientists.

A similar critique was written in the Indian subcontinent by Maulānā Ashraf 'Alī Thanvī (d. 1943), who pointed out various errors involved in subjecting the Qur'ānic verses to scientific interpretation. "As soon as people hear or see any new finding of science by the Europeans," he wrote, "they try in one way or the other to posit such finding as a connotation of some verse of the Qur'ān. They reckon this as a great service to Islam, a cause of pride for the Qur'ān, and a sign of their own ingenuity."[42]

In sum, there are numerous objections against the very concept of *tafsīr al-'ilmi*. It is vulnerable on the ground that science is changeable, and that it is wrong to interpret the Qur'ān in the light of a knowledge that is always changing.[43] It is an unsound enterprise because in spite of the voluminous literature so far produced in the name of *tafsīr al-'ilmī*, nothing has been shown to be rooted in the centuries of scholarship that has existed in the Islamic tradition. This literature is filled with attempts to show that everything in the contemporary world—from microbes to telegraphs—can be shown to originate in the verses of the Qur'ān. Likewise, it reads all major scientific theories—from Big Bang to theories of evolution—in the text of the Noble Qur'ān. It also attempts to build a case for the origin of all contemporary sciences in the Qur'ān. Thus, it finds the origins of modern astronomy, physics, chemistry, botany, zoology, geology, geography, anthropology, sociology, economics, and psychology in the Qur'ān. It is motivated by a wish to demonstrate compatibility (*muwāfaqa*) between the Qur'ān and modern Western science.[44] We have already

42. This quotation from *al-Intibāt al-Mufīdah 'an al-Ishtibāhāt al-Jadīda* of Maulānā Thānvī is cited from a book review of Maurice Bucaille's *The Bible, the Qur'ān and Science* by Muhammad al-Ghazali; see *Islamic Studies*, vol. 40 (2001), no. 2, pp. 333-4.

43. It is important to note that almost all literature supporting scientific exegesis discreetly avoids citing older scientific findings which have become obsolete. What would be the value of the works which cite contemporary theories when these theories will be discarded by science?

44. A parallel may be drawn between this and the attempts to show the existence of an essential harmony between revelation and reason, though the two attempts differ from each other in many respects.

pointed out that during the era when the Islamic scientific tradition was the most powerful scientific tradition anywhere in the world, all major Qur'ān commentaries generally remained free of direct references to science. Its recent appearance is, therefore, somewhat puzzling. The scientific exegesis is also unsound on the grounds that it is not consistent with the treatment of the rest of the Qur'ānic data. For instance, the Qur'ān makes a very specific prediction in the opening verses of Chapter 30, *The Romans*. It states that the Romans, who had been defeated by the Iranians, would turn the tables on Iran within three to nine years. This prediction was fulfilled but no one claimed that the Qur'ān contains specific and detailed knowledge of all historical events. It was understood that the fact that the Qur'ān made *a* specific prediction does not imply that it contains information about *all* future events. Thus, this would not be a possible basis for claiming that the Qur'ān also makes reference to Ṭāriq bin Ziyād's invasion of Spain in 711, or the Iranian Revolution of 1979. After all, if the Qur'ān is said to contain the knowledge of the ancients and those who came in the latter times (*'ilm al-awwalīn wa'l-akhirīn*), then this should be true of history no less than of science. But if it cannot be claimed that the Qur'ān is a repository of all events that would ever happen in historical time, it can also not be claimed to be a repository of all the scientific inventions and discoveries that would ever be made.[45]

The discourse on Islam and science has not remained colonized; it did find liberators who have produced a small body of literature that is free from the colonial trappings. Their work forms the basis of a new nexus—an emerging and developing nexus to be sure, but the one that can eloquently express perspectives rooted in the Islamic tradition.

Nevertheless, there exists in Islam a well-established tradition of scholarship in this field including works by Fakhr al-Dīn al-Rāzi, al-Ghazālī, Ibn Taymīyya, and Ibn Rushd. This subject has also received substantial attention by many later scholars of the Indian subcontinent, such as Shaykh Aḥmad Sirhindī (d. 1034/1624), Shāh Walī Allāh (d. 1176/1762), Maulānā Fazl-i Ḥaq Khayrābādī (d. 1278/1861), Mawlānā Muḥammad Qāsim Nānautvī (d. 1297/1880), and Maulānā Ashraf 'Alī Thānvī (d. 1362/1943).

45. This last argument has been made in an as yet unpublished conference paper: Mir, Mustansir (2001), "Scientific Exegesis of the Qur'ān—A Viable Project?", presented at the International Conference on "Science in the Islamic Civilization", Kuala Lumpur, Malaysia, November 2-5, 2001.

CHAPTER ELEVEN

The New Nexus

We live in a world that has been transformed by a unique event: the spread of modern science and its various extensions to all parts of the globe. This singular phenomenon is not merely characterized by the visible changes in lifestyles and modes of communication, travel and production that are apparent, it also has many not-so-apparent aspects which affect the most fundamental beliefs about God, life and the cosmos. These more subtle aspects of modern science have given birth to contemporary religion and science discourse. It would not be wrong to say that in this discourse between modern science and religion, science has been the driving force. Whether it is the question of the age of the earth or ethical, moral and religious issues arising out of stem cell research or neuroscience, it is science that defines the contours of the discourse; religion is forced to respond. Through its powerful discoveries, science pushes the boundaries, religion limps along. The self-propagating mechanism of science generates its own agenda, religion tries to catch up. It is also important to recognize that modern science is not a static entity; its essence is defined by an onward march that virtually knows no limits. Religion, on the other hand, is rooted in certain fundamentals that can neither evolve, nor change; these can only be reiterated in different forms which have to always remain perpetually connected to the veritable central axis, if they are to remain true. These and many other factors have inundated the contemporary discourse between modern science and religion with many mutually incongruous typologies, all of which attempt to define a complex relationship that remains an evolving and, for some, an elusive process.

As far as Islam is concerned, a *sine qua non* for any genuine discourse is that the "and" in the phrase "Islam and science" must always remain a unitive and never become a connector.[1] This essential pre-requisite of the

---

1. This essential aspect of the discourse has been alluded to in previous chapters, especially in the "Introduction" and chapter four. In another context, this concept has been used to describe Seyyed Hossein Nasr's book *Religion and the Order of Nature*. See Saran, A. K. (2001), "A Nasr Sentence: Some Comments" in Hahn, Lewis Edwin, Auxier, Randalle E., and Stone, Lucian W. Jr. (eds.), *The Philosophy of Seyyed Hossein Nasr*, Open Court, Chicago and La Salle, p. 429; also see Nasr's reply in

discourse stems from the fact that it is inconceivable to think of an Islamic discourse in which there exist two orders of reality or two completely independent paths to Reality. This is not to say that there cannot be more than one expression of Reality or many paths to it. What is being said is that all expressions of Reality and all paths to it must remain connected to each other through a central nexus which is the unitive function. This unique aspect of the Islamic perspective on modern science renders many contemporary typologies irrelevant to the discourse.[2] Needless to say, most of these typologies were first formulated to describe the relationship between modern science and Christianity and were not even necessarily meant to be applicable to the non-Christian traditions. It has also been recognized by many perceptive minds in the West that modern science is not merely limited to a study of nature; it is a way of thinking and, consequently, a way of life. Already in the middle of the twentieth century, Werner Heisenberg (1901-1976)—the celebrated physicist whose 1927 uncertainty (or indeterminacy) principle had turned the laws of physics into statements about relative, not absolute, certainties—had recognized that as compared to the West, modern science was going to have a very different kind of impact on the rest of the world. "One has to remember that every tool carries with it the spirit by which it has been created," he wrote in 1958:

> ...In those parts of the world in which modern science has been developed, the primary interest has been directed for a long time toward practical activity, industry and engineering combined with a rational analysis of the outer and inner conditions for such activity. Such people will find it rather easy to cope with the new ideas since they have had time for a slow and gradual adjustment to the modern scientific methods of thinking. In other parts of the world these

---

which he calls it "a very perceptive comment" and a "profound observation" (p. 441).

2. These contemporary typologies include Ian Barbour's four types of relations, each with subtypes: conflict (scientific materialism, biblical literalism); independence (contrasting methods, differing languages); dialogue (boundary questions, methodological parallels); and integration (natural theology, theology of nature, systematic synthesis), see Barbour, Ian (1988), "Ways of relating science and theology" in Russell, Robert John; Stoeger, S. J. William R.; and Coyne, S. J. George V. (eds.), *Physics, Philosophy and Theology: A Common Quest for Understanding*, Harper & Row, San Francisco, pp. 21-48.

> ideas would be confronted with the religious and philosophical foundations of native culture. Since it is true that the results of modern physics do touch such fundamental concepts as reality, space and time, the confrontation may lead to entirely new developments which cannot be foreseen. One characteristic feature of this meeting between modern science and the older methods of thinking will be its complete internationality. In this exchange of thoughts the one side, the old tradition, will be different in different parts of the world, but the other side will be the same everywhere and therefore the results of this exchange will be spread over all areas in which the discussions take place.[3]

Let us note that for the non-Western cultures, it is not entirely a question of not "having had enough time for a slow and gradual adjustment"; their encounter with Western science is rooted in much deeper soil and it is not a question of adjusting to the "modern scientific methods of thinking" but of fundamental consequences for their very existence. The brevity of Heisenberg's remark should not be misleading however, for he does note elsewhere in the same book that "such remarks should not be misunderstood as an underestimation of the damage that may be done or has been done to old cultural traditions by the impact of technical progress. But since this whole development has for a long time passed far beyond any control by human forces, we have to accept it as one of the most essential features of our time and must try to connect it as much as possible with the human values that have been the aim of the older cultural and religious traditions."[4]

This leads us to another aspect of modern science: What avenues are open for non-Western cultures to preserve their cultural and spiritual values in the face of a rapid penetration of an alien tradition through modern science? This is the question that is especially important for the Muslim societies and the one that has vexed several generations of scholars, thinkers, reformers and politicians. It is frequently assumed by a majority of reformers and politicians, and even by some scholars, that the Muslim societies can overcome their economic, political and social problems by importing Western science and technology without importing

3. Heisenberg, Werner (1958, 1999), *Physics and Philosophy: The Revolution in Modern Science*, Prometheus Books, New York, pp. 27-28.
4. Ibid. pp. 202-3.

any of the philosophical and ethical values that lie behind this science and its products. This facile assumption is based on another assumption: the supposed objectivity and neutrality of modern science—a Newtonian legacy which has been shattered by developments within science itself. Newton had left the impression that there are no assumptions in his physics which are not necessitated by the experimental data. By the end of the nineteenth century, it had become apparent that this assumption was not valid. Expressed positively, this means that the scientific theories are neither a mere description of experimental facts nor something deducible from such a description; in stead, facts are theory laden and theories are formulated on the basis of certain philosophical assumptions. These developments in modern science, especially in quantum physics, have been instrumental in shaking the hold of scientism and many Western philosophers of science have written about various kinds of reductionisms that underlie scientific methodology.

These efforts have not only yielded a clearer understanding of various types of reductionism—such as the methodological, espistemological, and ontological[5]—but have also produced works that underscore the limits of modern science.[6] Within the science and Christianity discourse, many scholars have tried to counter this by establishing non-reducible hierarchies of sciences. Arthur Peacocke, for instance, has developed such a hierarchy in two dimensions: vertically it contains levels of increasing complexity (the physical world, living organisms, their behavior, and human culture), horizontally, it orders systems by part-to-whole hierarchies. In biology, for example, the hierarchy emerges in this order: macromolecules, organelles, cells, organs, individual organisms, populations, ecosystems. Arthur Peacocke places theology at the top of the hierarchy as an integrating discipline and Nancey Murphy and George Ellis have argued that in this role, theology can provide answers to all fundamental questions raised at

---

5. See Ayala, Francisco (1974), "Introduction" in Ayala, Francisco and Dobzhansky, Theodosius (eds.), *Studies in the Philosophy of Biology: Reduction and Related Problems*, University of California Press, Berkeley.
6. See, for instance, Ratzsch Del (2000), *Science and its Limits*, InterVarsity Press, Downers Grove and Leicester, England; and Smith, Wolfgang (1984), *Cosmos & Transcendence: Breaking Through the Barrier of Scientistic Belief*, Sherwood Sugden & Company, Peru, Ill. For a radical new approach to the physical universe and the corporeal world, see Smith, Wolfgang (1995), *The Quantum Enigma: Finding the Hidden Key*, Sherwood Sugden & Company, Peru.

lower levels.[7] Various scholars in Christian theology and science have endorsed different combinations of epistemological and ontological schemes; others continue to support epistemic and ontological dualism.[8] There are also many Christian scientists who view science and religion as two non-overlapping zones, others find them in eternal conflict and then there are those who defend epistemic reductionism and reductive materialism. In the early 1990s, William Dembski and a small number of other scientists and philosophers challenged the "modernist monopoly on science" by outlining a research program based on Intelligent Design.[9]

In case of Islam, as we have previously mentioned, Islamic theology cannot be expected to play the same role as Christian theology does in its discourse with science. It is critical to understand that just as there are no councils, synods, or ecclesiastical institutions in Islam, Islam has no theology as the term is understood in the Western religious tradition. The representatives of the Islamic tradition have always preferred another

---

7. Peacocke, Arthur (1979), *Creation and the World of Science*, Clarendon Press, Oxford; Murphy, Nancey and Ellis, George (1996), *On the Moral Nature of the Universe: Theology, Cosmology, and Ethics*, Fortress Press, Minneapolis, ch. 4.
8. For example, Aurther Peacocke, Ian Barbour, and John Polkinghorne accept the hierarchy of the sciences but differ over its ontological implications. Robert John Russell works with non-foundationalist epistemology and favors ontological emergence whereas Nancey Murphy tends to favor emergent monism. Richard Swinburne and Sir John Eccles support epistemic and ontological dualism. For this summary, I have relied on a conference paper by Robert John Russell, "Theology and Science: Current Issues and Future Directions". Also see Barbour, Ian (1997), *Religion and Science: Historical and Contemporary Issues*, revised and expanded edition, HarperCollins, San Francisco.
9. I have taken the phrase "modernist monopoly on science" from Phillip Johnson's article "The Intelligent Design Movement" which bears this subtitle; see Dembski, William A. and Kushiner, James M. (2001), *Signs of Intelligence*, Brazos Press, Grand Rapids, pp. 25-41. Also see Behe, Michael, J. (1996), *Darwin's Black Box*, Simon & Schuster; Dembski, William (2001), *No Free Lunch*, Rowman Littlefield Publishers, Blue Ridge Summit, PA and his (1998), *The Design Inference*, Cambridge University Press, New York; (1999), *Intelligent Design The Bridge Between Science and Theology*, InterVarsity Press. For those who advocate conflict or non-overlapping hypothesis, see Gould, Stephen J. (1999), *Rocks of Ages: Science and Religion in the Fullness of Life*, Ballantine Publications Group, New York; also see Dawkins, Richard (1995), *The Blind Watchmaker*, Oxford University Press, Oxford; also his (1976), *The Selfish Gene*, Oxford University Press, Oxford.

name for their "theology": *uṣūl al-dīn,* "the principles or foundations of religion". In doing so, they also established an analogy with the term *uṣūl al-fiqh,* "the principles or foundations of jurisprudence". Thus, for a creative exploration of the relationship between Islam and modern science, one needs to examine modern science from the perspective of the Islamic concept of nature taken as a whole and within its own matrix. These essential pre-requisites have not been totally ignored and there exists a small body of literature that has examined the relationship between Islam and modern science in the light of these concepts. This small body of literature has produced a solid foundation for future scholarship. It ranges from a critique of modern science from various perspectives—ethical, epistemological, and philosophical—to suggesting alternatives.[10]

These alternatives are sometimes misunderstood as attempts to revert science back to its pre-modern state. The critics of this approach do not see this effort as an attempt to restore a tradition in which science had not divested nature of its essential sacredness, but as an attempt to restore the pre-modern science as such. Nothing can be as absurd as this, yet the contemporary Islam and science discourse is often construed in terms of these two opposing trends, one calling for an all-out embrace of modern science by imparting upon it a universality by superimposing claims of it being a value-free, objective and beneficial enterprise, even an integral constituent of progress and an essential need for survival. The other trend emphasizes the philosophical underlay of modern science and seeks to show the damaging effect of this worldview not only for the Islamic way of life but for the whole human habitat, which is already suffering from a colossal and irreversible environmental devastation. The former attempts to sanctify its agenda through the agency of religion by appealing to the religious duty to acquire knowledge from whichever source it comes, the latter seeks nothing short of a total re-structuring of science in an effort to re-establish its severed ties to Ultimate Reality from which all existent things come and to which they return.

10. For a general survey of some of the contemporary views on science, see Stenberg, Leif (1996), *The Islamization of Science: Four Muslim Positions Developing an Islamic Modernity*, Lund Studies in History of Religion, Lund; also see my review of this book in *Islamic Studies*, vol. 36 (1997), no. 3, pp. 663-8.

Liberating the Discourse

Perhaps nothing could have been so helpful in liberating the discourse and shaking off the hold of positivism and physical materialism as developments within science such as quantum physics. Likewise, the emergence of certain new aspects of philosophy of science which deal with the criteria for establishing truth claims of science have been helpful in the emergence of a clear break from the colonized discourse with which we dealt in the previous chapter. In addition, the theory-observation dichotomy, fact-value distinction, and related issues dealing with the very notion of scientific community, history and sociology of science have opened many new avenues for the discourse.

But at the same time, these new avenues of philosophical discourse have produced certain constraints and misplaced importance on certain aspects of modern science. Thus, it is not uncommon to run into "Islamic" critiques of modern science—based primarily on the work of Thomas Kuhn, Karl Popper, or Paul Feyerabend—which attempt to produce an "epistemic correction" in order to "Islamize" modern science. These attempts share a common notion that science is primarily an epistemic enterprise that attempts to explain the order of physical reality within the exclusive framework of the scientific method. In the wake of an oil-boom that produced great wealth in some Muslim countries and in the heady days of the dawn of the fifteenth Muslim century, this gave rise to a new movement that originated from this deep concern with the epistemology of modern knowledge. Its foremost advocate, Ismail al-Faruqi (1921-1986), conceived the concept of "Islamization of knowledge". Al-Faruqi realized that the "epitome of Muslim decline" was the "educational system, bifurcated as it is into two subsystems, one 'Modern' and the other 'Islāmic'."[11] And he sought to redress this "malaise" by discarding the methods used by the reformers. "In the past," he wrote,

> many great Muslims have attempted to 'reform' Islāmic education by adding to its curriculum subjects constitutive of the alien view. Sayyid Aḥmad Khān and Muḥammad ʿAbduh were champions of this cause.

---

11. Al-Fārūqī, Ismāʿīl, R. (1982), *Islāmization of Knowledge: General Principles and Work Plan* [henceforth *Islamization*], International Institute of Islāmic Thought, Washington DC. 1982, p. viii. This book has been republished in a revised and enlarged edition by a group of scholars associated with the International Institute of Islamic Thought. The Institute also publishes a quarterly *Journal of Islamic Social Sciences*.

> Jamāl ʿAbd al-Nāṣir brought its strategy to completion in 1961 when Al Azhar, the greatest fortress of Islāmic education, was turned into a "modern university". All their efforts, and those of millions like them, rest on the assumption that the so-called "modern" subjects are harmless and can only lend strength to the Muslims. Little did they realize that the alien humanities, social sciences, and indeed the natural sciences as well were facets of an integral view of reality, of life and the world, and of a history that is equally alien to that of Islām. Little did they know of the fine and yet necessary relation which binds the methodologies of these disciplines, their notions of truth and knowledge, to the value system of an alien world. That is why their reforms bore no fruit.[12]

The solution to this "Malaise of the Ummah", according to al-Faruqi, was a two fold plan that would (i) unite the two educational systems and (ii) Islamize Knowledge. "The Islāmic system of education," he argued, "consisting of elementary and secondary *madrasahs* (*sic*) as well as of college level *kulliyyahs* or *jāmiʿahs* ought to be united with the secular system of public schools and universities. The union should bring to the new, unified system the advantages of both, the financial resources of the state and the commitment to the vision of Islām."[13] The task of "Islamization of knowledge" was perceived "in concrete terms, to Islāmize the disciplines, or better, to produce university level textbooks recasting some twenty disciplines in accordance wit[h] the Islāmic vision".[14] This idea led to the establishment of the International Institute of Islamic Thought (IIIT), which continues to pursue al-Faruqi's vision. However, the exclusion of natural sciences from this plan has not only been a major handicap to this whole effort, it has also produced the illusion that natural sciences create knowledge in the epistemological framework established by the social scientists; this equates the very concept of knowledge (*al-ʿilm*) with social sciences. This has also excluded all possibilities of eventually proposing any solutions for the manifold impact of the encounter of the contemporary Muslim societies with modern science.

A second response that seeks to place modern science within a social framework arose from the work of Ziauddin Sardar and a few closely

---

12. Ibid.
13. *Islamization*, p. 9.
14. *Islamization*, p. 14.

associated scholars who once called themselves "Ijmalis". Sardar and his associates contributed to the liberation of the colonized discourse by forcefully articulating that all knowledge, including natural sciences, is socially constructed and is instrumental. Arising in the background of the beginning of the fifteenth century of Islam, with its typical feeling of an upsurge and emphasis on a global dimension of Islam, Sardar's major work, *Explorations in Islamic Science*, is based on the main assumption,

> that the "purpose" of science is not to discover some great objective truth; indeed, reality, whatever it may be and however one perceives it, is too complex, too interwoven, too multidimensional to be discovered as a single truth. The purpose of science, apart from advancing knowledge within ethical bounds, is to solve problems and relieve misery and hardship and improve the physical, material, cultural and spiritual lot of mankind. The altruistic pursuit of pure knowledge for the sake of 'truth' is a con-trick. An associated assumption is that modern science is distinctively Western. All over the globe all significant science is Western in style and method, whatever the pigmentation or language of the scientist.
>
> My second assumption follows from this: Western science is only a science of nature and not *the* science. It is a science making certain assumptions about reality, man, the man-nature relationship, the universe, time, space and so on. It is an embodiment of Western ethos and has its foundation in Western intellectual culture.[15]

But by situating science within the social realm, and insisting on its utilitarian aspect, Sardar reduces all aspects of philosophy of science to sociology of science and, though it produces one strand of criticism of modern Western science, it leaves out many other aspects. In this culture-specific construction, Sardar and others have built a case for each civilization producing its own specific kind of science within its own worldview but their formulations are not without serious problems which stem from the very assumptions on which their case rests.

---

15. Sardar, Ziauddin (1989), *Explorations in Islamic Science*, Mansell Publishing Ltd. London, p. 6; also see Sardar, Ziauddin (1985), *Islamic Futures*, Mansell Publishing Ltd., London; Sardar, Ziauddin (ed., 1984), *The Touch of Midas: Science, Values and the Environment in Islam and the West*, University of Manchester, Manchester.

For instance, their reductive approach to science which constructs it as a social enterprise leaves out the ontological and metaphysical considerations from their discourse. They build an epistemology of science without any philosophy and ontology. The Ijmalis have also produced a rather excessively violent critique of Bucaillism, modern science and the position of those who build their discourse on a metaphysics that is rooted in the traditional beliefs—a position discussed in the following section. But, surprisingly, Sardar has also equated the Ijmali position with that of al-Ghazālī against the *falāsifa*:

> The Ijmali position is similar to that of al-Ghazzali. The propagandists for science, just like the propagandists for Greek philosophers, have attributed to science things which are beyond its abilities and scope. While we do not, indeed cannot, deny the solid achievements of modern science, we emphasize the "repulsive façade" of its metaphysical trappings, the arrogance and violence inherent in its methodology, and the ideology of domination and control which has become its hall mark.[16]

Perhaps anticipating an argument against their position, Sardar makes a pre-emptive statement by declaring that

> it would be wrong to assume from this that the Ijmalis are simply Kuhnian; we neither sanction the extreme relativism of Kuhn, nor the anarchistic epistemology of Feyerabend; neither do we support the class-based science of radical Marxists, or a science based on "evolutionary epistemologies" of the new schools—we do, however, appreciate the positive contribution of each and learn from their expositions, just as we have learned from the positivist interpretation of science. But we do, even though we have only just begun, have a unique position of our own which is derived solely from the ethical, value (*sic*) and conceptual parameters of Islam. The essence of Ijmali thought is *reconstruction, complexity* and *interconnection*, or what Riaz Kirmani has called complementarity.[17]

16. Sardar (1989), p. 155.
17. Ibid. Emphasis is in the original text.

The Ijmali position, which seemed quite important during its heyday, did not take roots in the discourse on Islam and science. Its proponents were freelancers who could not sustain their discourse.[18]

These developments in the discourse on Islam and science had their roots in the political and economic climate of the late 1970s and early 1980s. Then, it seemed that the Muslim world was in the initial phase of a great reawakening. The discourse among various groups was intense and so were the bonds and enmities. But within a short time, all of this was lost. The fervor of Islamic revival lost its ideological components to a great extent and the various Islamic institutions established in the initial rush of oil money either disintegrated or became mere skeletons with no intellectual output. A new generation of oil-rich urban Arab elite emerged on the scene in pursuit of a decadent life based on Hollywood ideas of what life is in the West. The oil money produced neither Islamic nor Western science in the Muslim world. All it could do was to produce a caricature of Western educational institutions and enact a modern communication and transport infrastructure in some countries—a growth that remains perpetually in conflict with the centuries-old pattern of life.

The appearance of supersonic jets, satellite phones, and a vast network of freeways within one generation has not only destroyed traditional patterns of life in these countries, it has also given birth to numerous cultural, social and environmental problems which are multiplying at a dangerous rate. Signs of collapse of traditional societies are apparent throughout the Muslim world, especially in countries where modern science and technology has made inroads: A hospital in Jeddah, solely dedicated to the treatment of drug addicts; the unusual high divorce rate in Malaysia (which suddenly astonished everyone after a decade of fast

18. For a representative sampling of the work of two other members of this group, Pervez S. Manzoor and Munawwar Anees, see Anees, M. A., "Islamic Science—an antidote to reductionism" in *Afkar*/Inquiry, 1 (1984) 2, p. 49; "Laying the foundations of Islamic science" in *Inquiry*, 2 (1985) 11, pp. 36-43; "What Islamic science is not" in *J. Islamic Sc.* 2(1986) 1, pp. 9-20; and "Islamic values and Western science: a case study of reproductive biology" in Sardar, Ziauddin (ed., 1984), *Touch of Midas, op. cit.* Although the *Journal of Islamic Science*, which originally published many writings of this group, still makes an irregular appearance and the two organizations in India, the Muslim Association for the Advancement of Science and Centre for Studies on Science, are still somewhat active, their contribution to the discourse has been marginal.

modernization and technical progress) along with the breakdown of traditional values and the appearance of millions of drug addicts; and the transformation of the states in the Persian Gulf into a vast luxury resort, complete with casinos, bars and dysfunctional families, are merely a few outward signs of the calamity that is still engulfing the Muslim world in the wake of its encounter with modernity. One can expand this list to include all regions of the Muslim world. An early morning walk through the streets of Samarqand or Bukhāra—once great centers of Islamic learning—or a bus ride through the countryside of this land which had once produced some of the greatest scholars of Islam, is enough to know what is meant by hollowing out of a tradition. And yet, it is neither the sickening sight of drunken men and women on the streets of Tashkent, nor the stinking hog farms that fill the countryside that tell the story; it is the complete abasement of all that was held most valuable in the Islamic civilization that shows the extent of the calamity. We cannot go into the details of this catastrophe because it will take us away from our focus. But this brief narrative description should not be construed as a shallow linkage between modern science and the breakdown of traditional patterns of life in the Muslim world. There are definite direct as well as indirect ways in which the Muslim encounter with modernity has been greatly affected by modern science and its products. These range from the devastation caused by the loss of traditional ways of rural life to the emergence of large, overpopulated and polluted cities with unmanageable chaos. It shows itself in the incongruous buildup of modern weapons in certain countries where most of the population remains in a perpetual state of poverty because the small ruling elite plunders all national resources in the name of buying security through the build up of arms.

The invasion of modern technology in the Muslim world has not only destroyed traditional lifestyles, it has also obliterated that enchanting "Islamic space" that once filled the ancient places of worship, homes, shrines and madāris; this rude intrusion is nowhere as painful as in the most sacred mosque of Islam where many pilgrims can now be seen carrying their cellular phones while making their rounds around the ancient House of God, the Kaʿba.

The incessant desire to prove the divine origin of the Qurʾān through modern science is still another aspect of this asynergy that has spread all across the traditional Muslim lands. Heisenberg's perceptive remark that every tool carries with it the spirit by which it has been created has yet another facet to it: tools created in one culture can also have a totally different, and often perverted, function in another. This is so painfully apparent in the contemporary Muslim world where the imported tools, created by the applications of modern science, play a role that is often totally out of place with their original goal and usage in the culture of their birth. But this is not surprising; after all, these tools have little affinity with the cultural practices of the society which has imported them. All of these elements constitute the broad picture of the impact of modern science on the Muslim societies and, in turn, these myriad effects filter into the making of various strands of the discourse on Islam and science. Most notable in this category is, of course, the insatiable desire to find every fact and theory of modern science in the Qur'ān. But let us leave these shallow waters and move toward the final aspect of the contemporary discourse which will lead us to the conclusion of this chapter (and the book).

The Metaphysical Dimension

Seen from the perspective of traditional Islam, and set in the niche of its spirituality, this last strand of the contemporary Islamic discourse on science has emerged through the work of a handful of scholars who have all imbibed from the fountain of metaphysical truths in search of a beatific serenity, each in his own way. Their view of science, indeed of all human expressions and endeavors, is placed within a metaphysical framework which derives its principles from the immutable teachings of divine revelation. In contrast to philosophical and sociological views of science, this metaphysical view of science imparts to the traditional science a sacredness that arises from the essential and inalienable sacredness of nature itself which, in turn, derives its own sacred quality from the revelation which construes nature in terms of it being a Sign (*āya*) of the Creator. Thus it is the application of metaphysical principles to various domains of contingency that gives birth to cosmological and traditional sciences.

The origin of this aspect of the discourse can be traced back to the French Muslim traditionalist René Guénon ('Abdul Wāḥid Yaḥya, d. 1951), whose work has been defined by Frithjof Schuon (1907-98),[19] another member of the group, by four words: "intellectuality, universality, tradition,

19. Schuon, whose Islamic name is Shaykh 'Īsā Nūr al-Dīn Aḥmad al-Shādhilī al-Darqāwī al-'Alawī al-Maryamī, died in May 1998 in Bloomington, Indiana, USA. For brief life sketches and short notes on his work see *Sophia* 4 (1998) 2, which is dedicated to his memory.

theory".[20] In addition to Guénon and Schuon, other Muslim scholars whose work has been instrumental in illuminating this aspect of the discourse include Titus Ibrāhīm Burckhardt (d. 1984), Martin Lings (Abū Bakr Sirāj al-Dīn, b. 1909)[21] and Charles Le Gai Eaton (b. 1921).[22] But the most representative voice of this position is that of Seyyed Hossein Nasr (b. 1933), who has tirelessly explained various aspects of this particular view of science since the early 1960s.[23] At a different level and in their own way, Syed Muhammad Naquib al-Attas (b. 1931), Mehdi Golshani (b. 1940), and Alparslan Açikgenç (1952) have also contributed to the discourse.

The most fundamental aspect of this view of science is that it sees science in relation to nature and cosmology within which it functions. The traditional natural sciences, these traditionalists argue, derived their metaphysical and ontological principles from the divine revelation because they were rooted in a conception of knowledge according to which the knowledge of the world acquired by man and the sacred knowledge revealed by God were seen as a single unity. Needless to say that the methodologies of these sciences also traced their roots to the same source. Thus elevated above the historical and geographical planes, this view of science links all sciences which were cultivated in the traditional societies to their metaphysical principles. Guénon wrote about the general principles of sacred science, the science of symbolism and on mathematics, Schuon was especially interested in anthropology as understood in a traditional way, Burchkardt was mostly interested in cosmological sciences, and

20. Schuon, Frithjof, "René Guénon: Definitions" in *Sophia* 1 (1995) 2, p. 5. It must be pointed out that these terms are used by Schuon in their traditional meaning. The article has been translated from the French by Daphne Beaucroy.

21. See *Sophia* 5 (1999) 2, dedicated to Martin Lings and Titus Burckhardt, for brief biographical sketches and some reviews on their works.

22. Born in Switzerland and educated at Charterhouse and King's College, Cambridge, Gai Eaton worked for many years in Jamaica and Egypt, where he embraced Islam in 1951; later he joined British Diplomatic Service and is now consultant to the Islamic Cultural Centre, London. See Eaton, Charles Le Gai (1986), *Islam and the Destiny of Man*, State University of New York Press, Albany and (1990), *King of the Castle*, Islamic Text Society, Cambridge.

23. For a comprehensive view of Nasr's life and works in one volume, see *The Philosophy of Seyyed Hossein Nasr, op. cit.*; this Library of Living Philosophers vol. xxviii, contains an 82 page "Intellectual Autobiography" by Nasr, 29 critical essays about his work and Nasr's replies to his critics along with the most comprehensive bibliography of his works.

though Martin Lings has not written specifically about the place of natural sciences in the larger context of Islamic tradition, his short book, *The Eleventh Hour*,[24] contains a profound critique of Darwinism.

According to this view, the cosmos is teleological and displays a remarkable degree of order and purpose. This *telos* is, moreover, built into the very nature of cosmos and is not something that is imparted to it by the observer. This view also holds that it should be the metaphysical knowledge that is used to interpret knowledge gained by specific physical sciences not the other way around. Furthermore, the knowledge gained from the specific physical sciences should be integrated into the framework provided by *sophia perennis* (perennial philosophy), rather than by Cartesian bifurcation and quantitative reductionism. "By *Philosophia Perennis*—to which should be added the adjective *universalis*—is meant a knowledge which has always been and will always be and which is of the universal character both in the sense of existing among peoples of different climes and epochs and of dealing with universal principles," wrote Nasr in his 1993 work, *The Need For a Sacred Science*:

> This knowledge which is available to the intellect, is, moreover, contained in the heart of all religions or traditions, and its realization and attainment is possible only through those traditions and by means of methods, rites, symbols, images and other means sanctified by the message from heaven or the Divine which gives birth to each other. The epistemology provided by *sophia perennis* covers incomparably greater range of possibilities since it opens the way for relating all acts of knowing to the intellect and, finally, to the Divine.[25]

This metaphysical view of science, thus, restores to the contemporary discourse on Islam and science a perspective that goes back to the revealed sources of knowledge, the Qur'ān and the Sunna, and brings the Islamic scientific tradition into the discourse through its exposition of sciences of nature which admits no reductionism and uses a language of discourse that has affinity to key traditional concepts such as hierarchy, interconnectedness, isomorphism, and unity—qualities built into the very structure and methodology of traditional sciences of nature. As opposed to

24. Lings, Martin (1986), *The Eleventh Hour*, Kazi Publications, Chicago.
25. Nasr, S. H. (1993), *The Need for a Sacred Science*, State University of New York Press, Albany, pp. 53-4.

various attempts to graft Islamic ethics and epistemology on to modern science through artificial means, this approach attempts to (i) re-establish the deeper metaphysical framework of inquiry, (ii) constructs a concept of nature according to these metaphysical principles, and (iii) explains the contours of sciences of nature within this framework.

The philosophical underpinnings of this view are clearly derived from the metaphysical principles of Islam. The most important concept in this construction is none other than the central notion of *Tawḥīd*, the Unicity of God, to which we have referred throughout this work. There are two aspects of this concept. First of all, it construes nature as a single unity with all of its parts interconnected. Secondly, nature is not merely a huge collection of purposeless matter that has somehow appeared on the cosmic plane; it is a sacred entity meant to lead the one who studies it to the One who created it, through a process of intellection, when the word intellect is understood in its traditional sense of contemplation and not in the modern sense of analytical function of the mind. Thus philosophy plays a crucial role in the sciences of nature but it always functions within a definite framework of ontology and cosmology. Moreover, philosophical considerations in this view are not merely restricted to ethics. In short, this view constructs its foundations on the basis of a clearly defined metaphysics in which nature possesses a spiritual significance which should not be equated with any nebulous nature mysticism.

Seen from this perspective, modern science is obviously an anti-thesis of all that is sacred in nature. Thus, it is not surprising that the rise of modern science is seen by Nasr and others who hold this perspective as a phenomenon accompanied by a major break with the spiritual realm and hence something that is hurling humanity into an abyss. They believe that this fundamental severance has secularized nature, leaving no room for the Divine in the order of nature. It is no wonder that Nasr's writings on science contain a relentless exposition of havocs caused by modern science, may they be environmental or intellectual. Throughout his work, one detects an undercurrent of a profound sense of loss, both for the Muslim world and for humanity in general. This sense of loss comes from a realization of the great calamity that has brought modern world to the brink of a cataclysmic disaster. Yet, there is no sense of defeat; in fact, his work is permeated with an untiring effort to express the alternatives which may still prevent the final apocalypse. This hope, combined with the realization of what has been lost, form the two basic strands of Nasr's work. Perhaps this hope is not vain. In recent times, certain developments within modern science have opened a niche for understanding its own limitations and perhaps the day is not far when those who pursue knowledge of the unseen realm will not be seen as quaint relics of a lost world.

The New Nexus

It has been shown throughout this book that the discourse on Islam and science is not merely an academic exercise for the Muslims. More than a century has passed since the early nineteenth century reformers chose a doomed path for the resurrection of Islamic civilization. A century is a sufficient time to learn. Heisenberg's perceptive remark at the beginning of this chapter is not only an axiom, it is an experiential truth for the Muslim world. One cannot resurrect a dead tradition by infusing alien blood into it. By now, it has become exceedingly apparent to a large number of Muslim scholars that the malaise from which the Muslim world is suffering cannot be cured by merely importing Western science and its products; on the contrary, this has only aggravated the situation by creating numerous new problems. So, what is the solution? What are the ways open to more than one billion Muslims who live on this planet to find their rightful place in a world dominated by modern science and its numerous products without losing all sight of their spiritual tradition? How should Islam be related to modern science? What are the new modes through which one can find an expression of this discourse that is intelligible to even those who are not open to the spiritual truths in which such a discourse has to be rooted by necessity?

These questions, which have run their course for more than a century, have remained the most fundamental concern of all Muslim thinkers since the nineteenth century. They do not admit a simple answer; in fact, any simplistic treatment leads to false solutions which, in turn, cause further clouding of the discourse. However inadequate and tentative, certain answers have been provided and they form the foundation of further analysis. The least that can be said about this situation is that a century of reflection, false starts, wrong diagnoses and the terrible price paid for pursuing wrong paths has produced enough clarity, at least for a small group in the vanguard, to clearly understand the malaise; this is not a small step. According to all traditional wisdom, diagnosis of the disease is half the cure.

What has become abundantly clear is that Islamic perspectives on modern science have to be rooted in the spiritual and intellectual universe of Islam; any attempt to formulate this discourse outside this universe will be anything but Islamic. With this fundamental premise clearly understood, it should also be clear that this does not mean that this discourse is a nostalgic attempt to resurrect a body of scientific literature that has been superceded by new discoveries. Nothing can be more absurd than this. When al-Bīrūnī had asked Ibn Sīnā "if things expand through heating and contract through cooling, then why does a [sealed] flask full of water break when the water within freezes?", Ibn Sīnā had responded by stating that it was not due to the expansion of water that the flask breaks but due to the contraction of the air in the flask that creates a vacuum, causing the flask to break. Al-Bīrūnī was not satisfied. He said, "your answer would have admitted no doubts had the flask collapsed inward, but the matter in reality is exactly the opposite; the flask bursts outwardly, as if it can no longer hold its contents."[26] This dissatisfaction with the answer of the man, who was then the acknowledged master of medicine, philosophy and various other sciences, was not only a reflection of al-Bīrūnī's penetrating intelligence and boundless quest for the nature of things as they really are, it also shows that such a body of factual knowledge always remains under scrutiny without being any threat to any faith. Thus, it is not the replacement of such facts, which were once believed to be true in the Islamic scientific tradition, which is the issue here; it is what lies beneath the facts. Seeing an ice crystal under a powerful microscope, one is not only dazzled by the fact that each molecule of water has formed hydrogen bonds to four, and only four, neighboring molecules at the corners of a tetrahedron around it, and that this tetrahedral arrangement has produced wonderfully arranged puckered hexagonal rings which join side by side to form puckered hexagonal layers which lie perpendicular to the hexagonal axis but also—and more importantly—by the fact that this unique property of water arising out of its ability to form hydrogen bonds leads to some of the most fundamental conditions for life to exist. And yet, modern science can only tell us that this wonderful structure is formed at this precise angle because of hydrogen bonding but tells us nothing about why hydrogen

26. Al-Bīrūnī and Ibn Sīnā (repr. 1995), *Al-As'ilah wa'l-Ajwibah*, edited with an English and Persian introduction by Seyyed Hossein Nasr and Mehdi Mohaghegh, International Institute of Islamic Thought and Civilization (ISTAC), Kuala Lumpur. Al-Bīrūnī asks ten questions pertaining to Aristotle's *De Caelo* and eight other questions which were not related to Aristotle; this is the seventh of the latter questions. His eighth question was: "Why does ice float on water while its earthly parts are more than water and it is therefore heavier than water?" To this Ibn Sīnā responded briefly: "Upon freezing, ice preserves in its internal spaces and lattices airy parts which prevent it from sinking in water." pp. 48-50.

atoms have this innate ability to form hydrogen bonds; it can only *explain* these bonds. And this is not a unique case; in fact, the ultimate limit of science is precisely this: its ability to explain—however precisely or inaccurately—what exists, and that too, in a rather limited realm.

But for a believing chemist, it remains a point of reflection that it is hydrogen, the most basic of all atoms, that combines with oxygen, the most essential element for all living organisms, to form water, which has this unique hydrogen bonding that holds its molecules at a certain angle so that, unlike many other solids, when water freezes, its density decreases, allowing ice to float over water, thus ensuring that a vast range of life will continue to exist in oceans and rivers, in all seasons, even in climes like the one in Antarctica. This is not merely an allusion to yet another argument from design; what is being said is much more fundamental. *And We have created all living things from water*, the Qur'ān asserts with its characteristic brevity.[27] Why? One may ask, why does science stop at mere explanation? What defines the new nexus between Islam and science is not a mere facile correspondence between *explanations* of science and the Qur'ānic verses; it is an effort to first of all understand the metaphysical truths of the revealed text and then examine modern science in the light of this knowledge which cannot be merely a knowledge obtained and contained through the dissection of the text; by necessity, it has to be a knowledge that has been interiorized and that remains perpetually connected to its source, without such a living connection that constantly shines forth through the intellect, this knowledge cannot be called a true knowledge and the state of those who carry such knowledge is like that of a donkey that carries learned books, as the Qur'ān so poignantly tell us.[28]

Another aspect of the discourse that has become apparent is that modern science cannot be "Islamized" by sprinkling Qur'ānic verses over its theories. This realization has fundamental implications for the Islam and science discourse as well as for the Muslim world in its search for a *modus vivendi*. It is true that at the practical level, it has become impossible for any civilization to remain unaffected by modern science and the force and extent of penetration of modern science into other cultures will continue to increase. But it is also true that in spite of the loss that such an infusion entails, it is still possible for the representatives of traditional civilizations to fortify their civilizations by recourse to the primary sources.

27. Q. 21:30.
28. Q. 62:5.

In practical terms, this involves the training and nurturing of a large number of young men and women in the perennial truths of the tradition. Once a critical mass has been attained, this will have a major impact on the future direction of these societies. Fortunately for Muslims, this is not an impossible task because the primary sources of Islam remain intact, both in content and message, both in their outward (*al-ẓāhir*) as well as inward (*al-bāṭin*) aspects. And at a certain level, this process has already begun and while in the immediate future, Muslim societies will continue to drift away from the traditional patterns of life, this centrifugal drift is bound to come to a halt through this effort which is now firmly established. What is needed is not the solution prescribed by the colonized minds of the nineteenth and the early decades of the twentieth century, but a true revival of the Islamic tradition of learning which will then give birth to a process of appropriation of modern science, something akin to what was accomplished during the eighth to eleventh centuries, though the new methods of appropriation, transformation and naturalization will be, by necessity, different from the one which had emerged in the previous case.

Although it is not within the framework of this inquiry to discuss the details of this new process of appropriation, it is important to state that this new process is integrally linked to the Islam and science discourse. It is through this discourse that a clearer understanding of the philosophical underpinnings of modern science are being realized. It is also the rightful function of this discourse to cull, out of the contemporary issues, enough material to formulate general as well specific Islamic perspectives on those aspects of contemporary scientific discoveries in various disciplines which have direct bearing on our notions of life, God and the cosmos. These perspectives need to be articulated vigorously and with integrity, always remaining true to the fundamental truths of the Islamic tradition. With a persistent effort at different levels—ranging from limited exploratory interactions between scholars to public forums—the new nexus will become central in the discourse and the profane efforts to prove the revealed text by modern science or to find one to one correspondence between the two will disappear.

Likewise, the revival of the severed ties with the Islamic tradition is a *sine qua non* for understanding the relationship between Islam and modern science. Without these ties re-established at the most fundamental level, nothing can be achieved. It is this re-established nexus that will help to make the discourse a vibrant and living entity, capable of sorting and processing material as well as having enough force to destroy the colonial legacy by liberating hearts and minds. This does not mean a resuscitation of the glories of the achievements of the Muslim scientists as a nostalgic exhibit of a heritage that can be displayed in museums and enacted in scholarly texts; it means a wholesale reorientation of the society away from the colonized mindset, with a conscious centripetal move toward the living fountain of the tradition that would transform both the inward and the outward aspects of contemporary Muslim societies. Given the enormous impact of modern science already apparent, it may seem like an impossibility, yet this is the only option; all other paths lead to the perpetuation of the same doomed patterns that have emerged during the last hundred years. This effort should not be understood as any idealized call back to nature or yet another slogan for escape into some nebulous realm. This is not even a call to shun modern science and its products and seek refuge in some esoteric truth. It is precisely the opposite. It is an effort to seek, understand and interiorize the metaphysical truths of the tradition and then apply the wisdom gained from this process to contemporary realities with full vigor, force, persistence and clarity. It is the process of return in a certain way, but not of retreat.

Although it is still too early to articulate the exact paths through which modern science will be appropriated and naturalized within a renewed Islamic understanding, it is important to point out two major aspects. First, this process will take place within a more general process of revival of Islamic tradition of learning which is integrally linked to the revival of the Arabic language. Throughout this book, and especially in the second and the fourth chapters, we have discussed certain inalienable links between various expressions of the Islamic civilization (including its scientific tradition) and the language of revelation. For a revival of the Islamic tradition of learning, these links need to be re-established. This is only possible through a large-scale effort to re-educate Muslims in the various sciences that deal with the language of revelation. Without this grounding, nothing can be accomplished that can have any significant impact on the general process of revival. The self-evident proof of this fundamental requirement is that those regions of the traditional Muslim world from where Arabic has disappeared during the course of the last two centuries have become intellectual wastelands and even in the Arab world, masterpieces of Islamic scholarship remain buried in libraries because of a certain corruption of the language that has made this vast corpus inaccessible to many. The need to revive the tradition of Arabic teaching at a very young age has already been understood by a large number of

Muslims and the large-scale revival of Arabic language now apparent in Turkey, Pakistan and many other countries points to its becoming a generally accepted norm.

The second aspect is related to the Qurʾān and science. The language of the Qurʾān does not allow a semantic transference to the language of modern science. Thus, it is futile, rather absurd, to find telephones, microbes and the Big Bang in the text of the Qurʾān. What is relevant, however, is the metaphysical teachings of the revealed Book which remain, by their very nature, ahistorical, timeless and forever true. It is this metaphysical framework that needs to be applied to modern science, and indeed, to all knowledge, whatever its source. This is neither a simple process, nor should this be the case.

This is also not a task that everyone can undertake. It requires institutions where a small number of scholars can be trained who are rooted in the spiritual universe of the tradition but who are also intellectually equipped to understand specific branches of modern science. Fortunately, there is already a large number of Muslim scientists now living in the West and working in some of the most advanced laboratories of the world; they are well suited to undertake this task, provided they receive formal training in Islamic sciences with the understanding that their education of modern Western science is both an asset and an impediment. It is an impediment because their formal training and personal experiences of a life lived in a non-traditional environment have created numerous cognitive patterns, peculiar habits of mind and a certain clouding of the intellect that act as blackholes. But, we affirm that a mirror remains a mirror, no matter how much dust may have settled on it, for a well-scrubbed mirror holds back nothing. Likewise, a new generation of ʿulāmāʾ with enough understanding of modern science is emerging on the scene; the future of the discourse will be determined by these two groups. In general, the Qurʾānic doctrine, *and you will journey on from stage to stage,*[29] is true for both individuals as well as for societies and civilizations and Allah knows best.

29. Q. 84:19.

Bibliography

ʿAbduh, Muḥammad and Riḍā, Rashīd (1927), *Tafsīr Manār*, (reprn., 1954-61) as *Tafsīr al-Qurʾān al-Ḥakīm al-Mustahir bi Tafsīr al-Manār*, 12 vols. al-Maṭb. al-Amīriyya, Cairo.

Abdul Mabud, Shaikh (1991), *Theory of Evolution: An Assessment from the Islamic Point of View*, The Islamic Academy, Cambridge and The Islamic Academy of Science, Kuala Lumpur.

Abu-Lughod, Ibrahim (1963), *Arab Rediscovery of Europe*, Princeton University Press, Princeton.

Açıkgenç, Alparslan (1993), *Being and Existence in Ṣadrā and Heidegger*, International Institute of Islamic Thought and Civilization, Kuala Lumpur.

Açıkgenç, Alparslan (1996), *Islamic Science: Towards a Definition*, International Institute of Islamic Thought and Civilization, Kuala Lumpur.

al-Afghani, Jamal ad-din, tr. by A. M. Goichon (1942), as *Réfutation des Matérialistes*, Paul Geunther, Paris.

Afnan, Soheil (1964), *Philosophical Terminology in Arabic and Persian*, E. J. Brill, Leiden.

Ahmed, Akbar S. and Donnan, Hastings (eds., 1994), *Islam, Globalization and Postmodernity*, Routledge, London.

Amitai-Preiss, Reuven and Morgan, David, O. (eds., 1999), *The Mongol Empire and Its Legacy*, E. J. Brill, Leiden

al-Andalusī, Ṣāʿid, *Ṭabaqāt al-Umam* (tr., 1991), by Semaʿan I. Salem and Alok Kumar as *Science in the Medieval World, Book of the Categories of Nations*, University of Texas Press, Austin.

Aquinas, Thomas, *De Unitate Intellectus Contra Averroistas* (tr., 1968), by Beatrice H. Zedler as *On the Unity of The Intellect Against the Averroists*, Marquette University Press, Milwaukee.

Arberry, A. J. (1964), *Aspects of Islamic Civilization*, A. S. Barnes and Co. Inc., New York.

Ashis Nandy (1980), *Alternative Sciences: Creativity and Authenticity in Two Indian Scientists*, Allied Publishers Private Limited, New Delhi.

Athearn, Daniel (1994), *Scientific Nihilism*, State University of New York Press, Albany.

ʿAṭiyyah, Ḥasan Ḥāmid (1992), *Khalaq al-Samāwati waʾl-Arḍ fī Sittati Ayyāmin fīʾl-ʿIlm waʾl-Qurʾān (Creation of the Heavens and the Earth in Six Days in Science and in the Qurʾān)*, Muʾassasāt ʿAbd al-Karīm b. ʿAbd Allāh, Tunis.

al-Attas, Syed Muhammad Naquib (1991), *The Concept of Education in Islām*, International Institute of Islamic Thought and Civilization, Kuala Lumpur.

al-Attas, Syed Muhammad Naquib (1993), *Islām and Secularism*, International Institute of Islamic Thought and Civilization, Kuala Lumpur.

Avicenna, *Danesh-Nāme Ilāhi* (tr., 1971), by Farhang Zabeeh as *Avicenna's Treatise on Logic*, Marinus Nijhoff, The Hague.

Ayala, Francisco and Dobzhansky, Theodosius (eds., 1974), *Studies in the Philosophy of Biology: Reduction and Related Problems*, University of California Press, Berkeley.

Azmi, Mohammad Mustafa (1978), *Studies in Early Hadith Literature*, American Trust Publications, Indianapolis.

Azmi, Muhammad Mustafa (1985), *On Schacht's Origins of Muhammadan Jurisprudence,* King Saud University, Riyad and John Wiley, Chichester.

Baber, Zaheer (1996), *The Science of Empire,* State University of New York Press, Albany.

Bacon, Francis, ed. by John M. Robertson (1905), *The Philosophical Works of Francis Bacon*, Routledge and Sons Ltd., London.

Bacon, Francis, ed. by Sidney Warhaft (1965), *Francis Bacon, A Selection of His Works*, Macmillan, Toronto.

Badawi, M. A. Zaki (1976, 1978), *The Reformers of Egypt: A Critique of al-Afghani, Abduh and Ridha,* Croom Helm, London.

Bakr, Osman (1991), *Tawhid and Science: Essays on the History and Philosophy of Islamic Science*, Secretariat for Islamic Philosophy and Science, Kuala Lumpur.

Bakr, Osman (1992), *Classification of Knowledge in Islam*, Institute for Policy Research, Kuala Lumpur.

Baljon, J. M. S. (1961), *Modern Muslim Koran Interpretation (1880-1960)*, E. J. Brill, Leiden.

Barbour, Ian (1990), *Religion in an Age of Science: The Gifford Lectures*, vol. 1, Harper, San Francisco.

Barbour, Ian (1993), *Ethics in an Age of Technology: The Gifford Lectures,* vol. 2, Harper, San Francisco.

Barbour, Ian (1996), *Issues in Science and Religion*, Prentice-Hall, Englewood Cliffs.

Barbour, Ian (1997), *Religion and Science: Historical and Contemporary Issues*, HarperCollins, San Francisco.

Barq, Ghulam Jilani (n.d.), *Do Qur'ān (Two Qur'āns)*, Shaykh Ghulam Ali, Lahore.

al-Bārr, Muhammad ʿAlī (1986), *Khalq al-Insān bayn al-Ṭibb wa al-Qurʾān (The Creation of Human Being in Medicine and the Qurʾān)*, al-Dār al-Saʿūdiyya, Jeddah.

Behe, Michael, J. (1996), *Darwin's Black Box*, Simon & Schuster, New York.

Ben-David, Joseph (1971), *The Scientist's Role in Society*, Prentice-Hall, Englewood Cliffs.

al-Bīrūnī, Abū Rayḥān (ed., 1937), by A. Zeki Valīdī Togan as *Beruni's Picture of the World*, Archeological Survey of India, Delhi.

al-Bīrūnī, Abū Rayḥān, *Kitāb al-Jamahir fī Maʿrifat al-Jawāhir* (tr., 1989), by Hakim Mohammad Said as *The Most Comprehensive Book on the Knowledge of Precious Stones*, Pakistan Hijrah Council, Islamabad.

Böwering, Gerhard (1980), *The Mystical Vision of Existence in Classical Islam*, Walter De Gruyter, Berlin.

Brockelmann, Carl (1898, reprn., 1996), *Geschichte der Arabischen Litteratur*, A New Edition, with a Preface by Jan Just Witkam, E. J. Brill, Leiden.

Brooke, J. H. (1991), *Science and Religion: Some Historical Perspectives*, Cambridge University Press, Cambridge.

Bucaille, Maurice (1976), *La Bible, le Coran et la science: les Écritures saintes examinées à la lumière des connaissances modernes*, Seghers, Paris.

Bucaille, Maurice and Pannell, Alastair D. (tr., 1978), *The Bible, the Qur'an and Science*. North American Trust Publications, Indianapolis.

Burchardt, Titus (1987), *Mirror of the Intellect: Essays on Traditional Science and Sacred Art*, Quinta Essentia, Cambridge.

Burchardt, Titus (1995), *Alchemy, Science of the Cosmos, Science of the Soul*, Quinta Essentia, Cambridge.

Burchardt, Titus (1999), *Moorish Culture in Spain*, tr. by Alisa Jaffa and William Stoddart, Fons Vitae, Louisville.

Ceylan, Yasin, (1996), *Theology and Tafsīr in the Major Works of Fakhr al-Dīn al-Rāzī*, International Institute of Islamic Thought and Civilization, Kuala Lumpur.

Chelkowski, Peter J. (ed., 1975), *The Scholar and the Saint: Studies in Commemoration of Abuʾl-Rayhan al-Bīrūnī and Jalal al-Din al-Rūmī*, New York University Press, New York.

Chittick, William (1989), *The Sufi Path of Knowledge: Ibn al-Arabi's Metaphysics of Imagination*, State University of New York Press, Albany.

Chittick, William (1998), *The Self-Disclosure of God: Principles of Ibn al-ʿArabī's Cosmology*, State University of New York Press, Albany.

Cook, M.A. (ed., 1970), *Studies in the Economic History of the Middle East*, Oxford University Press, London.

Corbin, Henry (1977), *Spiritual Body and Celestial Earth*, ed. and tr. by Nancy Pearson, Princeton University Press, Princeton.

Corbin, Henry (1969, 1997), *Alone with the Alone: Creative Imagination in the Sūfism of Ibn ʿArabī*, Princeton University Press, Princeton.
Corey, M. A. (1993), *God and the New Cosmology: The Anthropic Design Argument*, Powman and Lettlefield, Lanham.
Corlett, William and Moore, John (1980), *The Islamic Space*, Bradbury Press, Scarsdale, N. Y.
Craig, William Lane (1979), *The Kalām Cosmological Argument*, Macmillan Press Ltd., London.
Craig, William Lane (1980), *The Cosmological Argument from Plato to Leibniz*, Macmillan Press Ltd., London.
Craig, William Lane and Smith, Quentin (1993), *Theism, Atheism, and Big Bang Cosmology*, Clarendon Press, Oxford.
Crombie, A. C. (1995), *The History of Science: From Augustine to Galileo*, Dover Publications, Mineola, N.Y.
Dahiyat, Ismail M. (1974), *Avicenna's Commentary on the Poetics of Aristotle*, E. J. Brill, Leiden.
Davidson, Herbert A. (1987), *Proofs for Eternity, Creation and the Existence of God in Medieval Islamic and Jewish Philosophy*, Oxford University Press, New York.
Davidson, Herbert A. (1992), *Alfarabi, Avicenna, and Averroes on Intellect*, Oxford University Press, New York.
Dawkins, Richard (1976), *The Selfish Gene*, Oxford University Press, Oxford.
Dawkins, Richard (1995), *The Blind Watchmaker*, Oxford University Press, Oxford.
DBS: *Dictionary of Scientific Biography* (1970-80), 16 vols., Charles Scribner's Sons, New York.
Dembski, William (1998), *The Design Inference*, Cambridge University Press, New York.
Dembski, William (1999), *Intelligent Design: The Bridge Between Science and Theology*, InterVarsity Press.
Dembski, William (2001), *No Free Lunch*, Rowman Littlefield Publishers, Blue Ridge Summit.
Dembski, William A. and Kushiner, James M. (2001), *Signs of Intelligence*, Brazos Press, Grand Rapids.
al-Dhahabī, Muḥammad Ḥusayn (1985), *al-Tafsīr wa'l-Mufassirūn*, 2 vols., 4th ed., al-Maktaba al-Wahbiyya, (reprn., n.d.) in 3 vols. Dār al-arqam, Beirut.
Dhanani, Alnoor, (1994), *The Physical Theory of Kalam: Atoms, Space, and Void in Basrian Muʿtazili Cosmology*, E. J. Brill, Leiden.
Draper, John William (1926), *History of the Conflict between Religion and Science*, Vanguard Press, New York.
Duhem, Pierre (1913–1959), *Le Système du Monde*, 10 vols. Hermann, Paris.

Eamon, William (1994), *Science and the Secrets of Nature*, Princeton University Press, Princeton.

Eaton, Charles Le Gai (1985), *Islam and the Destiny of Man*, G. Allen and Unwin, London.

Eaton, Charles Le Gai (1990), *King of the Castle*, Islamic Text Society, Cambridge.

Eaton, Charles Le Gai (2000), *Remembering God: Reflections on Islam,* Kazi Publications, Chicago.

EI: *The Encyclopaedia of Islam* (1986—), new edn. 11 vols., E. J. Brill, Leiden.

El-Naggar, Z. R. (1991), *Sources of Scientific Knowledge: The Geological Concept of Mountains in the Qur'ān,* Association of Muslim Scientists and Engineers and International Institute of Islamic Thought, Herndon.

Enayat, Hamid (1982), *Modern Islamic Political Thought,* University of Texas Press, Austin.

Fakhry, Majid (1970 and 1983), *A History of Islamic Philosophy*, Columbia University Press, Cambridge.

al-Fārābī, Abū Naṣr, *Iḥṣā' al-'ulūm,* (ed., 1947), by 'Uthmān Amīn, Dār al-Fikr al-'Arabī, Cairo.

al-Fārābī, Abū Naṣr (tr., 1962), by Muhsin Mahdi as *Philosophy of Plato and Aristotle*, The Free Press of Glencoe, New York.

al-Fārābī, Abū Naṣr, *Mabādi' Ārā' ahl al-Madīna al-Fāḍila* (tr., 1985), by Richard Walzer as *al-Farabi on The Perfect State*, Clarendon Press, Oxford.

al-Fārūqī, Ismā'īl, R. (1982), *Islāmization of Knowledge: General Principles and Work Plan,* International Institute of Islamic Thought, Washington DC.

Ferber, Stanley (ed., 1975), *Islam and the Medieval West*, State University of New York, Binghamton.

Fihrist: See Ibn al-Nadīm (reprn., 1994).

Frank, Richard M. (1966), *The Metaphysics of Created Being According to Abu'l Hudhayl al-'Allaf,* Nederlands Historisch-Archaeologish Institute in Het Nabije Oosten, Istanbul.

GAL: See Brockelmann, Carl.

GAS: See Sezgin, Fuat.

Gascoigne, John (1998), *Science in the Service of the Empire*, Cambridge University Press, Cambridge.

al-Ghazālī, Abū Ḥāmid Muḥammad b. Muḥammad, *Mishkat al-Anwār* (tr., 1952), by W. H. T. Gardiner as *The Niche for Lights*, Sh. Muhammad Ashraf, Lahore.

al-Ghazālī, Abū Ḥāmid Muḥammad b. Muḥammad, *al-Iqtiṣād fi'l-'Itiqād* (tr., 1970), by Abdur-Rahman Abu Zayd as *al-Ghazzali on Divine Predicates and their Properties*, Sh. Muhammad Ashraf, Lahore.

al-Ghazālī, Abū Ḥāmid Muḥammad b. Muḥammad, *Iḥyā' 'Ulūm al-Dīn*, selections (tr., 1977), by Edwin Elliot Calverley as *The Mysteries of Worship in Islam,* Sh. Muhammad Ashraf, Lahore.

al-Ghazālī, Abū Ḥāmid Muḥammad b. Muḥammad, *Mukāshfat al-Qulūb* (Urdu tr., 1399/1978), by Mawlana Qari Muḥammad 'Aṭā'llāh (1399/1978), Makataba-i Islāmīyyāt, Lahore.

al-Ghazālī, Abū Ḥāmid Muḥammad b. Muḥammad, *al-Munqidh min al-Ḍalāl* (tr., 1980), by Richard Joseph McCarthy as *Deliverance From Error and other Relevant Works of al-Ghazālī,* Twayne Publishers, Boston.

al-Ghazālī, Abū Ḥāmid Muḥammad b. Muḥammad, *Kitāb Jawāhir al-Qur'ān* (tr., 1983), by Muhammad Abul Quasem as *The Jewels of the Qur'ān,* Kegan Paul International, London.

al-Ghazālī, Abū Ḥāmid Muḥammad b. Muḥammad, *Rasā'il Imām Ghazālī,* (reprn., 1990); a collection of fifteen works by al-Ghazālī, translated into Urdu by various translators, Dār al-Ishā'at, Karachi.

al-Ghazālī, Abū Ḥāmid Muḥammad b. Muḥammad (reprn., 1411/1991), *al-Munqidh min al-Ḍalāl,* Mu'assat al-Kutub al-Thaqāfiyya, Beirut.

al-Ghazālī, Abū Ḥāmid Muḥammad b. Muḥammad, *al-Maqṣad al-Aṣnā fī Sharḥ Asmā' Allāh al-Ḥusnā* (tr., 1992), by David B. Burrell and Nazih Daher as *The Ninety-Nine Beautiful Names of God,* Islamic Texts Society, Cambridge.

al-Ghazālī, Abū Ḥāmid Muḥammad b. Muḥammad, *Iḥyā' 'Ulūm al-Dīn* (tr., 1993), by Fazlul Karim as *Revival of Religious Learnings*, 4 vols. in 2, Darul Ishaat, Karachi.

al-Ghazālī, Abū Ḥāmid Muḥammad b. Muḥammad, *Iḥyā' 'Ulūm al-Dīn*, Book XL, *Kitāb Dhikr al-Mawt wa-mā Ba'dahu* (tr., 1995), by T. J. Winter as *The Remembrance of Death and the Afterlife*, Islamic Texts Society, Cambridge.

al-Ghazālī, Abū Ḥāmid Muḥammad b. Muḥammad (reprn., 1417/1996), *Iḥyā' 'Ulūm al-Dīn,* 5 vols., Maktaba al-'Aṣrīyya, Beirut.

al-Ghazālī, Abū Ḥāmid Muḥammad b. Muḥammad, *Tahāfut al-Falāsifah, A Parallel English-Arabic Text* (tr., 2000), by Michael E. Marmura as *The Incoherence of the Philosophers*, Brigham Young University Press, Provo, Utah.

al-Ghazālī, Abū Ḥāmid Muḥammad b. Muḥammad, *Iḥyā' 'Ulūm al-Dīn*, Book XXXV, *Kitāb al-Tawḥīd wa'l-Tawakkul* (tr., 2001), by David B. Burrell as *Faith in Divine Unity & Trust in Divine Providence*, Fons Vitae, Louisville.

al-Ghazālī, Abū Ḥāmid Muḥammad b. Muḥammad, *Kīmīyā-i Sa'ādat*, (Urdu tr., n.d.), by Muḥammad Sa'īd al-Raḥmān 'Alawī, Maktaba Raḥmāniyya, Lahore.

al-Ghazālī, Abū Ḥāmid Muḥammad b. Muḥammad (reprn., n.d.), *Mukāshfat al-Qulūb,* Dār al-Qalam, Beirut.

al-Ghazali, Muhammad (2001), *The Socio-political Thought of Shāh Walī Allāh*, International Institute of Islamic Thought and Islamic Research Institute, Islamabad.

Gibb, H. A. R. (1947), *Modern Trends in Islam*, Chicago University Press, Chicago.

Gibb, H. A. R. and Bowen, Harold (eds., 1957), *Islamic Society and the West: A Study of the Impact of Western Civilization on Moslem Culture in the Near East*, Oxford University Press, Oxford.

Gohlman, William, E. (1974), *The Life of Ibn Sina: A Critical Edition and Annotated Translation*, State University of New York Press, Albany.

Goldstein, Bernard R. (1971), *al-Biṭrūjī: On the Principles of Astronomy*, Variorum Reprints, London.

Goldstein, Bernard R. (1985), *Theory and Observation in Ancient and Medieval Astronomy*, Variorum Reprints, London.

Goldziher, Ignaz (1915), "Stellung der alten islamischen Orthodoxie zu den antiken Wissenschaften," *Abhandl. Der Preuss. Akad. D. Wiss. (Philos.-hist. Kl.)* Vol. 8, pp. 3-46; English translation as "The Attitude of Orthodox Islam Toward the 'Ancient Sciences'" in Swartz, Merlin L. (ed., 1981), *Studies on Islam*, Oxford University Press, New York, pp. 185-215.

Goradia, Nayana (1993), *Lord Curzon: The Last of the British Moghuls*, Oxford University Press, Delhi.

Gould, Stephen J. (1999), *Rocks of Ages: Science and Religion in the Fullness of Life*, Ballantine Publications Group, New York.

Grant, Edward (1966), *The Foundations of Modern Science in the Middle Ages*, Cambridge University Press, Cambridge.

Greaves, Richard L. (1969), *The Puritan Revolution and Educational Thought*, Rutgers University Press, New Brunswick.

Guenon, René (1941), *East and West*, tr. by Lord Northbourne, Luzac and Co., London.

Guenon, René (1942), *The Crisis of the Modern World*, tr. by Arthur Osbourne, Luzac and Co., London.

Guenon, René, (1953), *The Reign of Quantity and the Signs of the Times*, tr. by Lord Northbourne, Luzac and Co., London.

Gutas, Dimitri (1998a), *Greek Thought, Arabic Culture*, Routledge, London and New York.

Gutas, Dimitri (1998b), *Avicenna and Aristotle*, Brill Academic Publishers, Leiden.

Gutas, Dimitri (2000), *Greek Philosophers in the Arabic Tradition*, Ashgate, Aldershot.

Hafez, Kai (ed., 2000), tr. by Mary Ann Kenny, *The Islamic World and the West*, E. J. Brill, Leiden.

Hahn, Lewis Edwin; Auxier, Randalle E. and Stone, Lucian E. Jr. (2001), *The Philosophy of Seyyed Hossein Nasr*, Open Court, Chicago.
Hall, Rupert, A. (1983), *The Revolution in Science 1500–1750*, Longman, London.
Hamidullah, Muhammad (1988), *The Prophet's Establishing a State and His Succession*, Pakistan Hijra Council, Islamabad.
Hammond, Robert (1947), *The Philosophy of Alfarabi and Its Influence on Medieval Thought*, Hobson Book Press, New York.
Hanna, Faith (1979), *The Story of the American University of Beirut*, Alphabet Press, Boston.
Haq, Syed Nomanul (1994), *Names, Nature and Things*, Kluwer Academic Publishers, Dordrecht, Boston, London.
al-Harawī, Ḥusayn (1942), *al-Naẓariyyāt al-ʿIlmiyya fi'l-Qur'ān* (*Scientific Theories in the Qur'ān*), n.p., Cairo.
Hartmann, Martin (1899), *The Arabic Press in Egypt*, London.
Hartner, W. (1975), "The Islamic Astronomical Background to Nicholas Copernicus", in *Ossolineum, Colloquia Copernica* III, Nadbitka, 7-16.
Haskins, Charles Homer (1924), *Studies in the History of Mediaeval Science*, Harvard University Press, Cambridge.
Hasse, Dag Nikolaus (2000), *Avicenna's De Anima in the Latin West*, The Warburg Institute, London.
Hawking, Stephen W. (1987), *A Brief History of Time*, Bantam Press, London.
Hefner, Robert and Horvatich, Patricia (eds., 1997), *Islam in an Era of Nation-States*, University of Hawaii Press, Honolulu.
Heisenberg, Werner (1958, 1999), *Physics and Philosophy: The Revolution in Modern Science*, Prometheus Books, New York.
Hempel, Carl (1966), *Philosophy of Natural Science*, Prentice-Hall, New York.
Hicks, R. D. (tr. 1907), *Aristotle De Anima*, University Press, Cambridge.
Hodgson, Marshall, G. S. (1974), *The Venture of Islam*, 3 vols. University of Chicago Press, Chicago.
Hoodbhoy, Pervez (1991), *Islam and Science: Religious Orthodoxy and the Battle for Rationality*, Zed Books Ltd., London and New Jersey.
Hourani, Albert (1993), *Arabic Thought in the Liberal Age: 1798-1939*, Cambridge University Press, Cambridge.
Hourani, George F. (ed., 1975), *Essays in Islamic Philosophy and Science*, State University of New York Press, Albany.
Huchingson, James E. (ed., 1993), *Religion and the Natural Sciences: The Range of Engagement*, Harcourt-Brace, London.
Huff, Toby E. (1993), *The Rise of Early Modern Science: Islam, China and the West*, University of Cambridge, Cambridge.
Humphreys, R. Stephen (1991), *Islamic History: A Framework for Inquiry*, Princeton University Press, Princeton.

Ibn al-Haytham (rprn., 1971), *al-Shukūk ʿalā Baṭlamyūs (Dubitationes in Ptolemaeum)*, ed., by A. Sabra N. Shehaby, National Library Press, Cairo.

Ibn Khaldūn, ʿAbd al-Raḥmān Abū Zayd ibn Muḥammad, *Muqaddima*, (reprn., 1413/1992), Dār al-Qalam, Beirut.

Ibn Khaldūn, ʿAbd al-Raḥmān Abū Zayd ibn Muḥammad, *Muqaddima* (tr., 1967), by Franz Rosenthal as *The Muqaddima*, Princeton University Press, Princeton.

Ibn Khallikān, Abū al-ʿAbbās Shams al-Dīn Aḥmad b. Muḥmmad ibn Abī Bakr (ed. Iḥsān ʿAbbās, edition 1994), *Wafayāt al-Aʿyān wa Anbāʾ Abnāʾ al-Zamān*, 8 vols., Dār Ṣādir, Beirut. English translation by B[N] MacGuckin de Slane (1842-71, reprn., 1961), as *Ibn Khallikan's Biographical Dictionary*, 4 vols., facsimile reprint by Johnson Reprint Corporation, New York and London.

Ibn al-Nadīm, *al-Fihrist* (tr., 1970), by Bayard Dodge as *The Fihrist*, Columbia University Press, Cambridge.

Ibn al-Nadīm, *al-Fihrist* (reprn. 1994), ed.by al-Shaikh Ibrāhīm Ramadān, Dār El-Marefah, Beirut.

Ibn Rushd, *Tahafut al-Tahafut* (tr., 1954), by Simon Van Den Berghn as *The Incoherence of the Incoherence*, 2 vols. University Press, Oxford.

Ibn Saʿd, Abū ʿAbd Allāh Muḥammad b. Saʿd (reprn., 1418/1998), *al-Ṭabqāt al-Kubrā*, 8 vols., Dār Ṣādir, Beirut.

Ibn Sīnā, *Kitāb al-Shifāʾ* (reprn., 1959), ed. by F. Rahman, Oxford University Press, London.

Ibn Sīnā, *al-Shifāʾ: al-Ilāhiyyāt* (rprn., 1960), ed. G. C. Anawati, Mohammad Mousa Yousef, Solayman Dunya, and Saʿid Zayed, Cairo.

Ibn Sīnā, *Dānish Nāma-i ʿalāʾī* (tr., 1973), by Parviz Morewedge as *The Metaphysica of Avicenna*, Routledge and Kegan Paul, London.

Ibn Sīnā, *al-Qānūn fiʾl-Ṭibb* (reprn., 1420/1999), Dār al-Fikr, Beirut.

Iḥyāʾ: See al-Ghazālī, Abū Ḥāmid Muḥammad b. Muḥammad (reprn., 1417/1996).

al-Irāqī, Abūʾl Qāsim Muḥammad ibn Aḥmad, *Kitab al-ʿIlm al-Maktasab fi Zirāʿat adh-Dhahab* (tr., 1923), by E. J. Holmyard as *Book of Knowledge Acquired Concerning the Cultivation of Gold*, n.p., Paris.

al-Iskandarānī, Muhammad b. Ahmad (1880), *Kashf al-Asrār ʿan al-Nūrāniyya al-Qurʾāniyya fi-mā yataʿallaqu bi al-Ajrām as-Samāwiyya wa al-Arḍiyya wa al-Ḥaywanāt wa al-Nabāt wa al-Jawāhir al-Maʿādaniyya (The unveiling of the luminous secrets of the Qurʾān in which are discussed celestial bodies, the earth, animals, plants and minerals)*, 3 vols. n.p., Cairo.

al-Iskandarānī, Muhammad b. Ahmad (1883), *Tibyān al-Asrār al-Rabbāniyya fiʾl-Nabāt waʾl Maʿādin waʾl-Khawāṣṣ al-Haywaniyya*, n.p., Damascus.

Ismāʿīl, ʿAbd ʿAzīz (1938), *al-Islām wa al-Ṭibb al-Ḥadīth* (*Islam and the Modern Medicine*), Maṭbʿat al-Iʿtimād, Cairo.

Iztutsu, Toshikiko (1964), *God and Man in the Koran: Semantics of the Koranic Weltanschauung,* Keio Institute of Cultural and Linguistic Studies, Tokyo.

Jacob, Margaret C. (1997), *Scientific Culture and the Making of the Industrial West,* Oxford University Press, New York.

Jāmī, ʿAbd al-Raḥmān, *Lawaʾih* (tr., 1914), by E. H. Whinfield and M. M. Kazvini as *Flashes of Light: A Treatise on Sufism,* Royal Asiatic Society, London.

Jamieson, Dale (ed.), *A Companion to Environmental Philosophy,* Blackwell Publishers, Malden.

Jansen, J. J. G. (1974), *The Interpretation of the Koran in Modern Egypt,* E. J. Brill, Leiden.

Jawharī, Ṭanṭawī (1931), *al-Jawāhir fī Tafsīr al-Qurʾān al-Karīm al-Mushtamil ʿalā al-ʿAjāʾb,* 26 vols., Mustafa al-Babi al-Halabi, Cairo.

Jayyusi, Salma Khadra (ed., 1994), *The Legacy of Muslim Spain,* 2 vols. E. J. Brill, Leiden.

Kamal, Mohammad (1993), *Heterodoxy in Islam: A Philosophical Study,* Royal Book Company, Karachi.

al-Kāshī, Jamshīd ibn Masʿūd ibn Maḥmūd Ghiyāth al-Dīn (or Kāshānī), *Nuzhat al-Ḥadāʾiq* (tr., 1960), from a Persian version by E. S. Kennedy as *The Planetary Equatorium,* Princeton University Press, Princeton.

Keddie, Nikki, R. (1968), *An Islamic Response to Imperialism, Politcal and Religious Writings of Sayyid Jamāl ad-Dīn "al-Afghānī",* University of California Press, Berkeley.

Keddie, Nikki R. (1972), *Sayyid Jamāl ad-Dīn "al-Afghānī": A Political Biography,* University of California, Berkeley.

Kedourie, Elie (1966), *Afghani and ʿAbduh: An Essay on Religious Unbelief and Political Activism in Modern Islam,* Frank Cass and Co., London.

Kennedy, E. S. (1973), *A Commentary upon Biruni's Kitab Tahdid al-Amakin,* American University of Beirut, Beirut.

Kennedy, Edward S. and Ghanem, Imad (1976), *The Life and Works of Ibn al-Shāṭir,* Aleppo University, Aleppo.

Kennedy, E. S. and Pingree, David (1971), *The Astrological History of Māshā ʾallāh,* Harvard University Press, Cambridge, Mass.

Kennedy, E. S. et al. (1983), *Studies in the Islamic Exact Sciences,* American University, Beirut.

Khālid b. Yazīd b. Muʿāwiyah, *Morieni Romani, Quondam Eremitae Hierosolymitani, de transfiguratione metallorum, & occulta, summaque antiquorum Philosophorum medicina, Libellus, nusquam hactenus in lucem editus. Paris, apud Gulielmum Guillard, in via Iacobaea, sub diuae*

Barbarae signo, translated from the 1559 Latin by Lee Stavenhagen (1974), as *A Testament of Alchemy*, The University Press of New England, Hanover, New Hampshire.

Khan, Sayyid Ahmad, *Musāfrān-i London*, (ed., 1961), by Shaikh Muḥammad Ismā'īl Pānīpatī, Majlis-ī Taraqqi-ī Adab, Lahore.

Khan, Sayyid Ahmad, *Maqālāt-i Sir Sayyid*, (ed., 1963), by Shaikh Muḥammad Ismā'īl Pānīpatī, 16 vols., Majlis-ī Taraqqi-ī Adab, Lahore.

Khan, Sayyid Ahmad, *Maktūbāt-ī Sir Sayyid (Letters of Sir Sayyid Ahmad)* (ed., 1976), Shaikh Muḥammad Ismā'īl Pānīpatī, 2 vols., Majlis-ī Taraqqi-ī Adab, Lahore.

al-Khaṭīb, Mūsā (1994), *Min Dala'il al-I'jāz al-'Ilmī fi'l-Qur'ān wa'l-Sunna al-Nabawiyya*, Mu'assasāt al-Khalīj al-'Arabī li'l-Ṭab'a wa'l-Nashr, Cairo.

al-Khūlī, Amīn (1944), *al-Tafsīr: Ma'ālim Ḥayātī-Minhaju al-Yawm*, Dār al-Ma'rifa, Cairo.

al-Khūlī, Amīn (1961), *Manāhij Tajdīd fi'l-Naḥw wa'l-Balāgha wa'l-Tafsīr wa'l-Adab*, Dār al-Ma'rifa, Cairo.

al-Khwārazmī, Abū Ja'far Muḥammad bin Mūsā, *Kitāb al-Mukhtaṣir fi'l Ḥisāb al-Jabr wa'l Muqābala* (tr., 1989), by Frederic Rosen as *Algebra*, Pakistan Hijrah Council, Islamabad.

King, David (1986), *Islamic Mathematical Astronomy*, Variorum Reprints, London.

King, David (1987), *Islamic Astronomical Instruments*, Variorum Reprints, London.

King, David (1999), *World Maps for Finding the Direction and Distance to Mecca*, E. J. Brill, Leiden.

Koyré, Alexandre (1968), *Metaphysics and Measurement: Essays in the Scientific Revolution*, Chapman and Hall, London.

Kuhn, Thomas (1962), *The Structure of Scientific Revolutions*, University of Chicago Press, Chicago.

Lane, Edward W. (1877, reprn., 1984), *An Arabic-English Lexicon*, Islamic Texts Society, Cambridge.

Lapidus, Ira M. (1988), *A History of Islamic Societies*, Cambridge University Press, Cambridge.

Lattin, Harriet Pratt (tr. 1961), *The Letters of Gilbert with His Papal Privileges as Sylvester II*, Columbia University Press, New York.

Leaman, Oliver (1988), *Averroes and His Philosophy*, Clarendon Press, Oxford.

Leaman, Oliver and Nasr, Seyyed Hossain (1996), *Routledge History of World Philosophies*, 2 vols. Routledge, London.

Lecomte, G. (1965), *Ibn Qutaiba, L'homme, son oeuvre ses ides*, Publications de l'Institute Français de Damas, Damascus.

Levtzion, N. (ed., 1987), *Eighteenth Century Renewal and Reform in Islam,* Syracuse University Press, Syracuse.
Lewis, Bernard (ed., 1976), *Islam and the Arab World,* Knopf, New York.
Lewis, Bernard (1982), *The Muslim Discovery of Europe,* W. W. Norton and Company, New York.
Lindberg, David, C. (1976), *Theories of Vision: From al-Kindi to Kepler,* The University of Chicago Press, Chicago.
Lindberg, David C. (1992), *The Beginnings of Western Science,* The University of Chicago Press, Chicago and London.
Lindberg, David C. and Numbers, Ronald L. (1986), *God and Nature: Historical Essays on the Encounter between Christianity and Science,* University of California Press, Berkeley.
Lings, Martin (1986), *The Eleventh Hour,* Kazi Publications, Chicago.
Lings, Martin (1999), *The Book of Certainty,* Suhail Academy, Lahore.
Maddison, Francis; Pelling, Margaret and Webster, Charles (eds., 1977), *Linacre Studies: Essays on the Life and Works of Thomas Linacre c. 1460-1525,* Clarendon Press, Oxford.
Mahmood, S. Bashir ud-Din (1991), *Doomsday and Life After Death,* Holy Qur'ān Research Foundation, Islamabad.
Maier, Anneliese (1949-1958), *Studien zur Naturphilosophie der Spätscholstik* (*Studies on late scholastic natural philosophy*), 5 vols. Edizioni di Storia e Letteratura, Rome.
Maier, Anneliese (1964, 1967 and 1977), *Ausgehendes Mittelalter,* Collective Essays on Fourteenth-Century Intellectual History, 3 vols. Edinioni di Storia e Letteratura, Rome.
Maier, Anneliese (1966), *Storia e Letteratura,* 9 vols. Edizioni di Storia e Letteratura, Rome.
Maier, Anneliese (1982), *On the Threshold of Exact Science: Selected Writings of Anneliese Maier on Late Medieval Natural Philosophy,* selected and translated with an introduction by Steven D. Sargent, University of Pennsylvania Press, Philadelphia.
Maierù, A. and Bagliani, A. Paravicini (1981), *Studi sul XIV secolo in Memoria di Anneliese Maier,* Edizioni di Storia e Letteratura, Rome.
Majid, Anouar (2000), *Unveiling Traditions: Postcolonial Islam in a Polycentric World,* Duke University Press, Durham and London.
Makdisi, George (1981), *The Rise of Colleges: Institutions of Learning in Islam and the West,* Edinburgh University Press, Edinburgh.
Makdisi, George (1991), *Religion, Law and Learning in Classical Islam,* Variorum, Hampshire.
Malik, Hafeez (1980), *Sir Sayyid Ahmad Khan and Muslim Modernism in India and Pakistan,* Columbia University Press, New York.

Mardin, Şerif (2000), *The Genesis of Young Ottoman Thought: A Study in the Modernization of Turkish Political Ideas*, Syracuse University Press, Syracuse.

Marmura, Michael E. (ed., 1984), *Islamic Theology and Philosophy, Studies in Honor of George F. Hourani*, State University of New York Press, Albany.

Martin, R. N. D. (1991), *Pierre Duhem, Philosophy and History in the Work of a Believing Physicist*, Open Court, LaSalle, Illinois.

Mason, Herbert (1986), *A Legend of Alexander and the Merchant and the Parrot,* University of Notre Dame Press, Notre Dame.

Massignon, Louis (1982), *The Passion of al-Hallāj*, 4 vols., Princeton University Press, Princeton.

Masud, Muhammad Khalid (1977), *Islamic Legal Philosophy. A study of Abū Isḥāq al-Shāṭibī's life and thought*, Islamic Research Institute, Islamabad.

Masud, Muhammad Khalid (1995), *Shāṭibī's Philosophy of Islamic Law*, Islamic Research Institute, Islamabad.

McEvoy, James (1982), *The Philosophy of Robert Grosseteste*, Clarendon Press, Oxford.

Melville, Charles (ed. 1996), *Safavid Persia*, I. B. Tauris & Co Ltd, London, New York.

Mendelsohn Everett (ed., 1984), *Transformation and Tradition in the Sciences: Essays in Honor of I. Bernard Cohen,* Cambridge University Press, Cambridge.

Mendelsohn, Everett and Elkana, Yehuda (eds., 1981), *Sciences and Cultures*, E. Reidel Publishing Co., Dordrecht.

Merton, Robert K. (1970), *Science, Technology and Society in Seventeenth-Century England,* Harper and Row, New York.

Meynell, Hugo A. (1982), *The Intelligible Universe: A Cosmological Argument*, Macmillan Press Ltd., London.

Moore, Keith L. (1982), *The Developing Human: With Islamic Additions*, Commission on the Scientific Miracles of the Qur'ān and Sunna, Jeddah.

Moore, Keith L. (1993), *Qur'ān and Modern Science: Correlation Studies*, Islamic Academy for Scientific Research, Jeddah.

Morewedge, Parviz (ed., 1979), *Islamic Philosophical Theology*, State University of New York Press, Albany.

Morewedge, Parviz (ed., 1992), *Neoplatonism and Islamic Thought*, State University of New York Press, Albany.

al-Mujahid, Sharif (1954), *Sayyid Jamal al-Din al-Afghani: His Role in the Nineteenth Century Muslim Awakening*, Master's Thesis, McGill University, Montreal.

Murphy, Nancey and Ellis, George (1996), *On the Moral Nature of the Universe: Theology, Cosmology, and Ethics*, Fortress Press, Minneapolis.

Murata, Sachiko and Chittick, William (1995), *The Vision of Islam*, State University of New York.

Muslim, Mustafa (1999), *Mabāḥith fi'l-i'jāz al-Qur'ān*, Dār al-Qalam, Damascus.

Nadhr, Aḥmad (1972), *Jā'izah-i Madāris-I 'Arabiyya Islāmiyya Maghribī Pakistān* (*A Survey of Arabic Madāris of West Pakistan*), Muslim Academy, Lahore.

Naqvi, Syed Sibte Nabi (1973), *Islam and Contemporary Science*, World Federation of Islamic Missions, Karachi.

Nasr, Seyyed Hossein (1964), *An Introduction to Islamic Cosmological Doctrines*, Belknap Press of Harvard University Press, Cambridge, reprn., (1993), State University Press of New York, Albany.

Nasr, Seyyed Hossein (1968), *Science and Civilization in Islam*, Harvard University Press, Cambridge.

Nasr, Seyyed Hossein (1975a), *Islam and the Plight of Modern Man*, Longman, London.

Nasr, Seyyed Hossein (1975b), *The Philosophy of Mulla Ṣadra*, Albany: State University of New York Press, Albany.

Nasr, Seyyed Hossein (1981a), *Islamic Life and Thought*, State Univeristy of New York Press, Albany.

Nasr, Seyyed Hossein (1981b), *Knowledge and the Sacred*, Edinburgh University Press, Edinburgh.

Nasr, Seyyed Hossein (1981c), *Traditional Islam in the Modern World*, KPI, London.

Nasr, Seyyed Hossein (1987), *Islamic Art and Spirituality*, State University of New York Press, Albany.

Nasr, Seyyed Hossein (1993), *The Need for a Sacred Science*, State University of New York Press, Albany.

Nasr, Seyyed Hossein (1996a), *The Islamic Intellectual Tradition in Persia*, Curzon Press, Surrey.

Nasr, Seyyed Hossein (1996b), *Religion and the Order of Nature*, Oxford University Press, Oxford.

Nasr, Seyyed Hossein and Chittick, William C. (eds., 1975-91), *An Annotated Bibliography of Islamic Science*, Cultural Studies and Research Institute, Tehran.

Nasr, S. H. and Leaman, O. (eds., 1996), *A History of Islamic Philosophy*, 2 vols., Routledge, London.

Nasr, Seyyed Hossein and Mohaghegh, Mehdi (eds., 1995), *al-As'ilah wa'l-Ajwibah*, International Institute of Islamic Thought and Civilization (ISTAC), Kuala Lumpur.

Nawfal, 'Abd al-Razzāq (1989), *Min al-Āyāt al-ʿIlmiyya* (*About the Scientific Verses*), Dār al-Shurūq, Cairo and Beirut.

Needham, Joseph (1954—), *Science and Civilization in China,* 7 vols. Cambridge University Press, Cambridge.

Netton, Ian Richard (1989), *Allāh Transcendent*, Curzon Press, Surrey.

Neugebauer, O. (1957), *The Exact Sciences in Antiquity,* Brown University Press, Providence; all references are to the 1969 reprint, Dover Publications Inc. New York.

Neugebauer, O. (1975), *A History of Ancient Mathematical Astronomy,* Springer-Verlag, New York.

Northbourne, Lord (1970), *Looking Back on Progress,* Perennial Books, London.

Nurbakī, Halūk (1993), *Verses from the Glorious Koran and the Scientific Facts,* 3rd edition, Türkiye Diyanet Vakfi, Ankara.

Nursi, Said Bediuzzaman (reprn. 1998), *The Damascus Sermon,* Sözler Neşriyat ve Sanayi A. Ş, Istanbul.

Nursi, Said Bediuzzaman, *Sözler* (tr., 1998), as *The Words,* Sözler Neşriyat Ticaret ve Sanayi A. Ş, Istanbul.

Nyazee, Imran Ahsan Khan (2000), *Islamic Jurisprudence,* Islamic Research Institute, Islamabad.

Ormsby, Eric L. (1984), *Theodicy in Islamic Thought,* Princeton University Press, Princeton.

Osler, Margaret and Farber, Paul L. (1985), *Religion, Science, and Worldview, Essays in Honor of Richard S. Westfall,* Cambridge University Press, Cambridge.

Pailin, D. (1994), *Probing the Foundations: A Study in Theistic Reconstruction,* Pharos, Kampen, The Netherlands.

Pānīpatī, Shaikh Muḥammad Ismāʿīl (ed., 1993), *Letters to and from Sir Syed Ahmad Khan,* Board for Advancement of Literature, Lahore.

Peacocke, Arthur (1979), *Creation and the World of Science,* Clarendon Press, Oxford.

Peacocke, Arthur (1990), *Theology for a Scientific Age*, Blackwell, Oxford.

Pedersen, Johannes (reprn. 1984), *The Arabic Book,* tr. by Geoffrey French with an introduction by Robert Hillenbrand, Princeton University Press, Princeton.

Peters, F. E. (1968), *Aristotle and the Arabs: The Aristotelian Tradition in Islam,* New York University Press, New York.

Peters, Ted; Iqbal, Muzaffar and Haq, Nomanul S. (eds., 2002), *God, Life and the Cosmos: Christian and Islamic Perspectives,* Ashgate, Aldershot.

Petry, Carl F. (1981), *The Civilian Elite of Cairo in the Later Middle Ages,* Princeton University Press, Princeton.

Piamenta, M. (1983), *The Muslim Conception of God and Human Welfare,* E. J. Brill, Leiden.

Pines, Shlomo (1986), *Studies in Arabic Versions of Greek Texts and in Medieval Science,* The Magnes Press, Hebrew University, Jerusalem.

Qudsi-zadah, Albert (1970), *Sayyid Jamal al-Din al-Afghani: An Annotated Bibliography*, E. J. Brill, Leiden.

Qurashi, M. M.; Bhutta, S. M. and Jafar, S. M. (1987), *Quranic Ayaat Containing References to Science and Technology*, Sh. Sirri Welfare & Cultural Trust and Pakistan Science Foundation, Islamabad.

Ragep, Jamil F. and Ragep, Sally P. (eds., 1996), *Tradition, Transmission, Transformation,* E. J. Brill, Leiden,

Rahbar, Daud (1960), *God of Justice: A Study in the Ethical Doctrine of the Qur'ān*, E. J. Brill, Leiden.

Rahman, Fazlur (1965), *Islamic Methodology in History*, Islamic Research Institute, Islamabad.

Rahman, Fazlur (1966), *Islam,* Weidenfeld and Nicolson, London.

Rahman, Fazlur (1980), *Major Themes in the Qur'ān*, Bibliotheca Islamica, Minneapolis.

Rahman, Fazlur (1982, 1984), *Islam and Modernity: Transformation of an Intellectual Tradition,* The University of Chicago Press, Chicago, London.

Rahman, Fazlur, ed., by Ebrahim Moosa (2000), *Revival and Reform in Islam: A Study of Islamic Fundamentalism*, Oneworld Publications, Oxford.

Raschid, M. S. (1981), *Iqbal's Concept of God*, Kegan Paul International, London.

Rashed, Roshdi (ed., 1996), *Encyclopedia of the History of Arabic Science*, Routledge, London.

Ratzsch, Del (2000), *Science and its Limits*, InterVarsity Press, Downers Grove and Leicester.

Rescher, Nicholas (1966), *Studies in Arabic Philosophy*, University of Pittsburgh Press, Pittsburgh.

Rosenthal, Franz (1990a), *Greek Philosophy in the Arab World*, Variorum, Aldershot.

Rosenthal, Franz (1990b), *Muslim Intellectual and Social History*, Variorum, Aldershot.

Russell, Robert; Murphy, Nancey and Isham, C. J. (eds., 1993), *Quantum Cosmology and the Laws of Nature: Scientific Perspectives on Divine Action*, Vatican Observatory Foundation, Vatican City State.

Russell, Robert; Stoeger, S. J. William R. and Coyne, S. J. George V. (eds., 1988), *Physics, Philosophy and Theology: A Common Quest for Understanding*, Harper and Row, San Francisco.

Sabra, A. I. (1994), *Optics, Astronomy and Logic: Studies in Arabic Science and Philosophy*, Variorum, Aldershot.

Ṣadrā, Mullā (reprn. 1968), *al-Asfār al-Araba'a al-'qliyyah* ed. by Allama Muḥammad Ḥasayn Ṭabātabā'ī, Fourth Book, Qom.

Ṣadrā, Mullā (reprn., 1981a), *al-Ḥikmat al Muta'liyya*, 9 vols. Dār Iḥyā' al-Turāth al-'Arabī, Beirut.

Ṣadrā, Mullā, *al-Mabdā' wa'l-Ma'ād* (tr., 1981b), by James Morris as *The Beginning and End,* Princeton University Press, Princeton.

Ṣadrā, Mullā, *al-Ḥikmat al-'arshiyya* (tr.. 1981c), by James Morris as *The Wisdom from the Divine Throne,* Princeton University Press, Princeton.

Saliba, George (1994), A *History of Arabic Astronomy: Planetary Theories during the Golden Age of Islam,* New York University Press, New York.

Sangwan, Satpal (1991), *Science, Technology and Colonisation: An Indian Experience (1757-1857)*, Anamika Prakashan, Delhi.

Sardar, Ziauddin (ed., 1984), *The Touch of Midas: Science, Values and the Environment in Islam and the West,* University of Manchester, Manchester.

Sardar, Ziauddin (1985), *Islamic Futures*, Mansell Publishing Ltd., London.

Sardar, Ziauddin (1989), *Explorations in Islamic Science*, Mansell Publishing Ltd., London.

Sarton, George (1931-48), *Introduction to the History of Science*, 3 vols., published for the Carnegie Institute of Washington by The Williams and Wilking Company, Baltimore.

Saud, Muhammad (1986), *Islam and Evolution of Science*, Islamic Research Institute, Islamabad.

Sayili, Aydin (1960), *The Observatory in Islam,* Publications of the Turkish Historical Society, Series VII, No. 38, Türk Tarih Kurumu Basimevi, Ankara, (reprn., 1981), Arno Press, New York.

al-Sayūṭī, Jalāl al-Dīn (reprn., 1967), *al-Itqān fī 'Ulūm al-Qur'ān*, 2 vols., Maṭb'a Amīr, Cairo, 1967.

Sayyid, Bobby, S. (1997), *A Fundamental Fear: Eurocentrism and Emergence of Islamism,* Zed Books Ltd., London, New York.

Schact, J. (1950), *The Origins of Muhammadan Jurisprudence,* Oxford University Press, Oxford.

Schact, J. (1964), *An Introduction to Islamic Law,* Oxford University Press, Oxford.

al-Sharastanī, Abī al-Fatḥ 'Abd al-Karīm, *Kitāb al-Milal wa'l-Niḥal* (reprn., 1964), Maktabat al-Mathnā, Baghdad.

al-Sharqāwī, Muḥammad 'Iffat (reprn., 1972), *Ittijāhāt al-Tafsīr fī Miṣr al-'Aṣr al-Ḥadīth*, Maṭba'at al-Kīlānī, Cairo.

Schuon, Frithjof, (1965), *Light on the Ancient Worlds*, tr. by Lord Northbourne, Perennial Books, London.

Schuon, Frithjof (1966), *Dimensions of Islam*, tr. by P. N. Townsend, Allen and Unwin, London.

Schuon, Frithjof (1966), *Understanding Islam*, tr. by Lord Northbourne, Allen and Unwin, London.

Sezgin, Fuat (1966—), *Geschichte des arabischen Schrifttums*, 9 vols., E. J. Brill, Leiden.

Shah-Kazemi, Reza (ed., 1997), *Algeria Revolution Revisited*, Islamic World Report, London.

Sharabi, Hisham (1970), *Arab Intellectuals and the West: The Formative Years 1875-1941*, Johns Hopkins Press, Washington DC.

Sharif, M. M. (1963, reprn., 1983), *A History of Muslim Philosophy*, 2 vols. Pakistan Philosophical Congress, Karachi.

Shehadi, Fadlou (1982), *Metaphysics in Islamic Philosophy*, Caravan Books, New York.

Siddiqi, Mazheruddin (1982), *Modern Reformist Thought in the Muslim World*, Islamic Research Institute, Islamabad.

Smith, Huston (2001), *Why Religion Matters*, HarperCollins, New York.

Smith, W. Cantwell (1957), *Islam in Modern History*, Princeton University Press, Princeton.

Smith, Wolfgang (1984), *Cosmos & Transcendence: Breaking Through the Barrier of Scientistic Belief*, Sherwood Sugden & Company, Peru.

Smith, Wolfgang (1995), *The Quantum Enigma: Finding the Hidden Key*, Sherwood Sugden & Company, Peru.

Stahl, William H. (1962), *Roman Science: Origins, Development and Influence to the Later Middle Ages*, University of Madison Press, Madison.

Stenberg, Leif (1996), *The Islamization of Science: Four Muslim Positions, Developing an Islamic Modernity*, Lund Studies in History of Religions, Ludwig.

Stephenson, Bruce; Bolt, Marvin and Friedman, Anna F. (2000), *The Universe Unveiled, Instruments and Images Through History*, Cambridge University Press, Cambridge.

Storer, Norman (ed., 1973), *The Sociology of Science: Theoretical and Empirical Investigations*, University of Chicago Press, Chicago.

Stroumsa, Sarah (1999), *Freethinkers of Medieval Islam*, E. J. Brill, Leiden.

Stuewer, Roger H. (ed., 1970), *Historical and Philosophical Perspectives of Science*, Gordon and Breach, New York.

Swartz, Merlin L. (ed., tr., 1981), *Studies on Islam*, Oxford University Press, New York.

Swerdlow, N. M. and Neugebauer, O. (1984), *Mathematical Astronomy in Copernicus's De Revolutionibus*, Springer, New York.

Taub, Liba Chaia (1993), *Ptolomy's Universe, The Natural Philosophical and Ethical Foundations of Ptolomy's Astronomy*, Open Court, Chicago.

Thānvī, Maulānā Ahsraf ʿAlī (1994), *Islam awr ʿaqliyyāt*, ed. by Muhammad Mustafa Bijnauri, Idāra Islamyāt, Lahore.

Thorndike, Lynn (1944), *Science and Thought in the Fifteenth Century*, Columbia University Press, New York.

Thorpe, W. H. (1965), *Science, Man and Morals*, Methuen and Co. Ltd. London.

Tibawi, A. L. (1969), *A Modern History of Syria*, Edinburgh University Press, Edinburgh.

Tipler, Frank J. (1994), *The Physics of Immortality*, Doubleday, New York.

Toledano, Ehud R. (1990), *State and Society in Mid-Nineteenth Century Egypt*, Cambridge University Press, Cambridge.

Toomer, Gerald, J. (1990), *Apollonius Conics Books V to VII: The Arabic Translation of the Lost Greek Original in the Version of the Banū Mūsā*, 2 vols. Sources in History of Mathematics and Physical Sciences 9, Springer-Verlag, New York.

Toomer, Gerald (1995), *The Study of Arabic in England During the Seventeenth Century*, Oxford University Press, Oxford.

Troll, C. W. (1979), *Sayyid Ahmad Khan: A Reinterpretation of Muslim Theology*, Oxford University Press, Karachi.

Turner, Howard R. (1995), *Science in Medieval Islam*, University of Texas Press, Austin.

al-Ṭūsī, Naṣīr al-Dīn, *al-Tadhkira fī 'Ilm al-Hay'a* (tr., 1993), by F. J. Ragep as *Naṣīr al-Dīn Ṭūsī's Memoir on Astronomy*, 2 vols. Springer-Verlag, New York.

al-Ṭūsī, Naṣīr al-Dīn, *Sayr wa Sulūk* (tr., 1998), by S. J. Badakhchani as *Contemplation and Action: The Spiritual Autobiography of a Muslim Scholar*, I. B. Tauris, London.

Tyacke, Nicholas (ed.), *The History of the University of Oxford*, Oxford University Press, Oxford.

Van Cittert, P. H. (1954), *Astrolabes*, E. J. Brill, Leiden.

Van Steenberghen, Fernand (1955), *Aristotle in the West*, tr. by Leonard Johnston, Nauwelaerts, Louvian.

Von Grunebaum, G. E. (1962), *Modern Islam: The Search for Cultural Identity*, Greenwood Press, Connecticut.

Von Grunebaum, G. E. (1982), *Islam: Essay in the Nature and Growth of a Cultural Tradition*, Greenwood Publishing Group, Connecticut.

Wafayāt: See Ibn Khallikān.

Walzer, Richard (1962), *Greek into Arabic, Essays on Islamic Philosophy*, Harvard University Press, Cambridge.

Watt, Montgomery W. (1973), *The Formative Period of Islamic Thought*, Edinburgh University Press, Edinburgh.

Watt, Montgomery W. (1985), *Islamic Philosophy and Theology*, Edinburgh University Press, Edinburgh.

Weber, Max (1949), *The Methodology of the Social Sciences*, Free Press, New York.

Westerlund, David and Svanberg, Ingvar (eds., 1999), *Islam Outside the Arab World,* Curzon Press, Surrey.

Westfall, Richard S. (1971, 1977), *The Construction of Modern Science: Mechanisms and Mechanics*, Cambridge University Press, Cambridge.

Whitall, Perry N. (1995), *The Widening Breach: Evolutionism in the Mirror of Cosmology*, Quinta Essentia, Cambridge.

Wotton, William (1694, reprn., 1968), *Reflections upon Ancient and Modern Learning*, Georg Olms Verlagsbuchhandlung, Hildesheim.

Yahya, Harun (2000a), *The Disasters Darwinism Brought to Humanity* tr. by Carl Rossini, Vural Yayincilik, Istanbul.

Yaḥyā, Harun (2000b), *The Evolutionary Deceit*, Okur Publishing, Istanbul.

Yaḥyā, O. (1964), *Historie et classification de l'oeuvre d'Ibn ʿArabī,* Publications de l'Institute Français de Damas, Damascus.

Yaqūt, Shihāb al-Dīn Abī ʿAbd Allāh (reprn., 1993, 1995), *Muʿjam al-Buldān*, Dār Ṣadar, Beirut.

Yazdi, Mehdi Hairi (1992), *The Principles of Epistemology in Islamic Philosophy*, State University of New York Press, Albany.

Ziadat, Adel A. (1986), *Western Science in the Arab World,* Macmillan Press, London.

Index

ʿAbbās, Iḥsān, 152
ʿAbduh, Muḥammad, 242, 250, 256, 267, 282, 299
al-Abharī, Athīr al-Dīn, 132
Abū Bakr, 11, 18, 62, 178-9, 306
Abū Ḥanīfa, 10, 133, 147
Abu-Lughod, Ibrahim, 232
Abū Maʿshar, 62
Abū Qurra, Thodore, 43
Abū Turāb, 255
Abū Yūsuf, Qāḍī, 17
Abulfeda, 196, 199
Abū'l Jaʿfar, 16
Açıkgenç, Alparslan, 98
Adelard of Bath, 179
Aeneas, 197
Afghani, Jamal al-Din, 242, 258
Afghanistan, 71, 236, 255, 257, 265
Afghans, 206
Aḥmad b. Ḥanbal, 10
Aḥmad, Nadhr, 252
Aḥmed, Seraj al-Din, 233
Akbar, 167
Alcuin, 172
Aleppo, 63, 66, 114, 234
Alfred of Sareshel, 179
Algar, Hamid, 240
Algebra, 37, 72, 177, 180
Alhazen, 58, 199
Alhazen problem, 199
Aligarh British Indian Association, 246
Aligarh College, 244
Aligarh Muslim University, 248
Aligarh Scientific Society, 229
Allah, 26, 30, 32, 34, 72, 79, 110, 113, 115, 119, 256, 314
Allahabad, 230
Almagest, 24, 53, 61, 62, 64, 88, 160, 177, 180, 198
al-Āmilī, Bahā' al-Dīn Muḥammad, 95
Amulī, S., 95
Anawati, G.C., 73
al-Andalus, 16, 63, 68, 99, 162-3, 289
Anees, Munawwar, 303
Anglicist, 227
Antioch, 41, 99
Anṭūn, Faraḥ, 275
Anwā', 24, 62, 84
Apollonius, 26, 53
Apologetic Literature, xix, 203, 286
Appropriation, xvi, xx, 44-5, 82-3, 139, 171, 186, 213, 312
Aquinas, Thomas, 90, 183
Arab League, 231
Arab scientific journalism, 233, 275
Arabesque, 205
Arabists, 199
Architecture, 123, 205
Aristotle, 26-7, 40, 42-3, 50, 52, 55, 64-5, 73-4, 82, 84-5, 87, 91-3, 96, 105, 107, 112, 153, 172, 179-84, 190, 197-8, 258, 266, 310
Ark, 34
Arkwright, Richard, 215
al-Aṣamm, 20
Asfār, 94, 95
Aṣḥāb al-Ṣuffa, 156
Ashaʿrites, 47, 98-9
Asiatic Researches, 217, 219
Asiatic Society of Bengal, 217
Asmā', 35, 36, 111
As-Sawi, Abdul-Jawwad M., 286
Association of Muslim Scientists and Engineers, 285

Asṭarābadī, Sayyid Bāqir Muḥammad, 94
Astronomy, 2, 23-4, 27, 31, 52, 57-9, 61, 63-4, 68, 70, 77, 88, 102, 135-6, 145, 169, 173, 177-8, 185, 195, 218, 225, 252, 270, 287, 290-1
Athens, 40-1, 182, 273
al-Attas, Syed Muhammad Naquib, 306
Atto, the bishop of Vich, 173
Augustine, xvii, 59, 139
Aurangzeb, 167
Authority, 11-12, 18, 25, 31, 51-2, 78, 130, 140, 143-4, 154, 162, 166-7, 182, 196, 204, 232, 239
Auxier, Randalle E., 293
Averroes, 68, 107, 151, 191, 265
Ayala, Francisco, 296
al-Azhar, 207
Azmi, Mohammad Mustafa, 13, 14, 81, 147, 156
Azzindani, Abdul Majeed A., 287

Baalbek, 39, 41
Baber, Zaheer, 215-21, 223-6, 228-9
Bach, Johann Sebastian, 201
Bacon, Francis, 163, 188, 195, 197
Badawi, Zaki, M. A., 73, 255
Baer, Gabriel, 144
Baghdad, xviii, 16-18, 23-4, 41, 53, 104, 128, 136, 157-9, 164-6, 168, 177, 277, 281, 288
al-Baghdādī, al-Khatīb, 157
Bainbridge, John, 195
Bakhtīshū' family, 41
Balance of Letters, 28
Balīnās, 26
Baljon, J. M. S., 282
Banū Mūsā, 53, 54
Barbour, Ian, 294, 297
Barq, Ghulam Jilani, 285
al-Bārr, Muḥammad 'Alī, 285
Baṣra, xviii, 7, 11, 47, 116, 168
Bāṭinite, 99
al-Bāṭiniyya, 100
al-Battānī, 88, 195
Bayt al-Ḥikma, 43
Beaucroy, Daphne, 306
Behe, Michael, J., 297
Benares Hindu College, 228
Bengal, 215-19, 221, 225, 227, 239
Bengal Atlas, 217
Berggren, J. L., 53, 77, 137
Bhadralok, 227
Bhutta, S. M., 284
Big Bang, 291, 314
Bihzād, 167
al-Bīrūnī, Abū Rayḥān, 37, 42, 55-6, 61, 88, 118, 142-3, 179, 241, 310
al-Biṭrūjī, 64, 68, 151, 154
Board of Scientific Advice, 230
Boethius of Dacia, 184
Bologna, 174-5, 181
Bombay, 221, 224, 227, 230, 255-6
Bonaventure, 90, 182
Botanical Gardens, 214, 220, 223
Bowen, Harold, 235
Boyle, Robert, 190, 199
Brahe, Tycho, 195
Brahmans, 228
Bramah, Joseph, 201
Brethren of Purity, 25, 116
British Empire, 221
Brockelmann, Carl, 126
Bruno, 190
Brunschvig, Robert, 242
Bucaille, Maurice, 286
Bucaillism, 302
Bukhāra, 9, 84, 160-1, 304
Bulaq Press, 234
Burchardt, Titus, 123-4
Burchhardt, Jacob, 188
Buridan, Jean, 188
Burn, Scot, 245
Burrow, Reuben, 217
Burzōe, 40

Caesar, 144, 197
Cairo, 7, 15, 61, 73-4, 165, 168, 232-3, 250, 264, 275, 277-8, 281-4, 289-90
Calcutta, 217, 220-1, 223, 227, 230, 244, 247, 256
Calico Craze, 215
Caliphate, 16, 42, 208, 268
Canon of Medicine, 177, 180
Carolingian Empire, 172
Carra De Vaux, 66
Casaubon, Isaac, 194
Catching-up Syndrome, xv, xix, 203
Causality, 96, 98, 104, 109-10, 186, 191
Çelebi (Chalabi), Yirmisekiz Mehmet, 234
Çelebi, Evliya, 235
Ceylon, 216, 220, 223
Chaghatay Turks, 163
Chain of Being, 94, 96, 98, 118
Charlemagne, 172-3
Charles the Bald, 173
Chaucer, Geoffrey, 193
China, 39, 59, 125, 140-41, 164-5, 221-2
Chittick, William C., 56
Chosroes Anūshriwān, 40
Christian missions, 232
Christianity, xvii, xx, xxi, 41, 130, 181, 185-6, 226, 265
Chrysippus, 113
Cicero, 112-3, 115, 197
Cinchona, 221-3
Clagett, Marshall, 188
Clive, Robert, 217
Colonel Graham, 244-5
Colonization, xviii, xix, 76, 206-8, 210, 213, 216, 231, 236, 240, 267
Commission for Scientific Miracles of Qur'ān and Sunna, 286
Condorcet, 188
Constantine, 166, 176, 183
Constantine the African, 176, 183
Constantinople, 41, 69, 166, 235
Continuity Debate, 187, 189
Contreni, John J., 174
Cook, M.A., 144
Copernicus, 58, 65-6, 68-70, 154, 188
Córdoba, 9, 16, 123-4, 152, 176
Cornell, Svante, 234
Cosmology, xvii, xxi, 24, 39, 89-91, 93-5, 111, 153, 182, 270, 284, 287, 306, 308
Cotton, 9, 215, 246
Council for Scientific and Industrial Research, 231
Coyne, S. J. George V., 294
Creatio ex nihilo, 32
Creation of Earth, 5, 19, 27, 29, 31-5, 48-9, 89-90, 93-6, 98, 106, 108, 114-16, 118-19, 146, 153, 182, 184, 186, 191, 210, 216, 231, 270, 272, 276-7
Crombie, A. C., 59, 139, 179, 189
Crompton, Samuel, 215
Cross, Robert, 223
Crusades, 99
Curzon, George, 230

Dā'irat al-Wujūd, 94
d'Alembert, Jean le Rond, 202
Damascus, 7, 10, 12, 43, 65, 100, 121, 127, 144, 154, 163, 165, 234, 250, 271, 281, 285
Dānish Nāma'i 'Alā'ī, 73, 92
Dante Alighieri, 197
Dār al-Ḥarb, 239
Darwin, 117-8, 210, 259, 276, 277, 297
Darwinism, 118, 272-3, 275-6, 307
Davidson, Herbert A., 112
Davis, Samuel, 217
Dawkins, Richard, 297
de Boer, Tj., 117

De Natura Deorum, 112, 114-5
De Partibus Animalium, 112
De Usu Partium, 112
de Vaux, Carra, 66, 117
Del, Ratzsch, 296
Delhi, xviii, 165-6, 169, 206, 224-5, 228-30, 246, 253
Dembski, William A., 297
Deprunières, 233
Descartes, Rene, 22, 188, 190
al-Dhahabī, Muḥammad Ḥusayn, 281
Dhanani, Alnoor, 20-22, 98
Di Bona, Joseph, 224
Diderot, 202
Dieterici, 117
Dinçerler, Vehbi, 273
Dobzhansky, Theodosius, 296
Doestoyevsky, 76
Dominicus Gundissalinus, 179
Duhem, Pierre, 188
Dundas, Henry, 220
Dunya, Solayman, 73
Dutch, 196, 214, 216, 220, 236

East India Company, 214, 217, 222, 225-6
Eastern Scientific Society, 233
Eaton, Charles Le Gai, 122, 306
Eccles, Sir John, 297
Ecclesiastical History of the English People, 172
Edessa, 39-41
Edward III, 193
Egypt, 7, 9, 14, 33, 40, 165, 202, 205, 207, 232-4, 240, 254-7, 265, 267, 275-6, 282, 306
Einstein, 154
Electra, 197
Elements of Political Economy, 230
Ellis, George, 296
El-Naggar, Zaghloul, 285, 287
Emanationists, 37
Empedocles, 78
Enayat, Hamid, 242
Erbakan, Necmettin, 273
Erpenius, Thomas, 194
Etienne Tempier, 184
Euclid, 53, 55, 70, 81, 85, 177, 180, 183, 199
Evolution, xvii, 46, 61, 89, 117, 211, 236, 268, 272-4, 276-8, 291
Exegesis, 2, 4, 38, 96, 250, 278-81, 283, 285, 288-92

Faḍl Allāh, Rashīd al-Dīn, 165
Fakhry, Majid, 49, 107
al-Falak, 28
Falāsifa, xxi, 22, 103-4, 302
Falsafa, xxi, 52, 167
Famine, 219, 227
al-Fārābī, Abū Naṣr, 37, 73-4, 84-5, 103, 105, 142
Farā'iḍī Movement, 239
al-Faruqi, Ismail, 299
al-Fazārī, 24, 62
Feingold, Mordechai, 193, 195
Feyerabend, Paul, 299
Fez, 121, 144
al-Fihrist, 3, 6, 15, 26, 39, 43, 48, 53, 126
Fiqh, 2, 84, 99, 147, 282
Fī Ẓilāl al-Qur'ān, 212
Firangī Maḥal Madrasa, 252
Fleisch, H., 159
Fortune, Robert, 221
French Revolution, 202
French, Geoffrey, 161
Frithjof Schuon, 305
Fuchs, Leonhart, 199
al-Fusṭāṭ, 7

Gabrieli, G., 177
Galen, 43, 81, 85, 105, 112, 176, 198
Galileo, Galilei, 59, 139, 142, 188, 190, 265-6

Galland, Julien, 235
Gardet, Louis, 242
Gasparali, 234
Gassendi, 190
al-Ghazālī, Abū Ḥāmid Muḥammad b. Muḥammad, 18, 35, 38, 75, 80-82, 90, 93, 99-101, 103-15, 120, 136, 237-8, 259, 266-7, 288, 292, 302
al-Ghazali, Muhammad, 238
Gerard of Cremona, 176, 179
Gerbert, 173, 176
Ghazan, 165
Gibb, Hamilton, 114, 235, 242
God, xvii, xix, xxii, 1, 11-13, 19-20, 22-23, 27, 29-39, 46-49, 51, 72, 78-80, 83, 90, 92, 96, 98, 102-6, 108-9, 111-122, 124, 129, 144, 147, 150, 153, 156, 161, 185-6, 191-2, 197, 210-11, 244, 249, 251-2, 262, 270-1, 276-80, 283, 286, 290, 293, 304, 306, 308, 312
Gohlman, W. E., 160
Goichon, A. M., 258, 262
Goldziher, Ignaz, 76-8, 80, 114, 130, 137-40, 142, 243, 288
Goldziherism, 76-7
Golshani, Mehdi, 306
Goradia, Nayana, 230
Gould, Stephen J., 297
Grant, Charles, 226, 229
Grant, Edward, 139
Greaves, John, 196
Greaves, Richard, L., 198
Gregory, 172
Griffith, William, 222
Grunebaum, Von G. E., 235
Guénon, René, 305-6
Guilds, 121-2, 143-4, 148, 174-5
Guillame, A., 148
Gutas, Dimitri, 77, 139-40

Haeckel, 277
Hahn, Lewis Edwin, 293
Ḥājjī Khalīfa, 126
al-Ḥakam II, 123
Hall, A. Rupert, 189-90
Ḥāmid, Sayyid Meḥmed, 267
Hamidullah, Muhammad, 148
al-Ḥanafī, Jamāl ibn al-ʿAbd Allāh ʿUmar, 245
Ḥanafi, 146
Ḥanbali, 140, 146
Hanna, Faith, 233
Haq, Muhammad Zia-ul, 288
Haq, Syed Nomanul, 25-28, 153, 280
Hargreaves, James, 215
Harrānians, 37
Hartmann, Martin, 275
al-Harāwī, Ḥusain, 283
Haskins, Charles Homer, 188
Hastings, Warren, 217, 219
Hay, William, 287
Hay'a, 24, 61-3
Hayūlā', 116
Heinen, A., 77, 80
Heisenberg, Werner, 294
Henry IV, 193
Henry Corbin, 25, 73
Herlihy, David, 174
Hermann the Dalmatian, 176
Hermeneutics, 96
al-Ḥikmat al-ʿarshiyya, 95
al-Hilāl, 275
Hillenbrand, Robert, 161
Hindu, xvi, 78, 89, 118, 227, 230
Hippocrates, 176
Hitu, Muḥammad Hasan, 100
Hodgson, Marshall G. S., 131, 163
Homs, 39, 41
Hoodbhoy, Pervez, 288
Hourani, Albert, 242, 275
Huff, Toby E., 59, 77, 140-46, 148-51, 155
Hugh of Santalla, 176
Hülegü, 164, 165

Human being, xvi, 9, 33, 35, 38, 46, 83, 102, 118-19, 162, 277, 290
Humanists, 194, 199
Hume, David, 202
Hunter, W. W., 219, 229
Husain, Muḥibb, 256
Hyde, Thomas, 199

Ibn Abī Uṣaybiʿa, 42
Ibn ʿAqīl, 127-8
Ibn ʿAṭā, 48
Ibn Bābak, Ardashīr, 39
Ibn Bāja, 64
Ibn Biṭrīq, Yuḥannā, 43, 50
Ibn al-Haytham, 58, 61, 63, 67, 70, 87, 154, 179-80, 199
Ibn Ḥazm, 118-19, 152
Ibn Isḥāq, 148
Ibn al-Jawzī, 157
Ibn Jundab, Abū Isḥāq Ibrāhīm ibn Ḥabīb ibn Sulaimān ibn Samura, 18
Ibn Khaldūn, 75, 76, 168, 288
Ibn Khallikān, 26
Ibn al-Muqaffaʿ, 40
Ibn al-Nadīm, 15, 26, 39, 48, 53, 62, 126
Ibn al-Nafīs, 132
Ibn Nāʿima, 43
Ibn Nawbakht, Abū Sahl al-Faḍl, 39
Ibn Qanbar, Abū Bishr (or Abū'l Ḥasan) ʿAmr ibn ʿUthmān, 17
Ibn Qutaiba, 127
Ibn Rushd, 50, 64, 87, 90, 120, 141, 142, 179, 181, 183, 190, 197, 288, 292
Ibn Sallām, 156
Ibn Saʿūd, 239
Ibn al-Shāṭir, 58, 65-7, 69, 132, 141, 53-4, 163
Ibn Sīnā, 37-8, 52, 55-6, 61, 66, 73, 75, 82, 87, 91-5, 97, 103-5, 108-9, 142, 160, 178, 198, 235, 241, 288, 310
Ibn Taymiyya, 239
Ibn Ṭufayl, 64
Ibrāhīm, Qāsim b., 116
Ifrād al-Maqāl, 88
Iḥṣā' al-ʿulūm, 73-4
Iḥyā' ūlūm al-Dīn, 35, 95, 99, 102, 109, 111
al-'ijāz al-ʿilmī fi'l-Qur'ān, 213
Ijāza, 51, 149
Ijmalis, 301, 302
Ijtihād, 208, 239
Ikhwān al-Ṣafā', 116, 277
Ilāhiyyāt, 73, 94
al-ʿilm al-ṭabīʿī, 73
Imāmite, 12, 35
Independence Movements, 211, 237
Indian Academy of Sciences, 231
Indian Science Congress, 231
Indian Timūrī empire, 165, 167, 214, 221
Indonesia, 236
Insān, 35, 83, 84, 103
Institut d'Egypt, 232
Intellectual Sciences, 51, 96
International Institute of Islamic Thought, 55, 238, 285, 299, 300, 310
Iqbal, Muhammad, 253, 267
Iqbal, Muzaffar, 153
al-Iqtiṣād fi'l-Iʿtiqād, 109
Iranian Revolution, 211, 292
Iṣfahān, xviii, 121, 144, 164, 166-7, 169, 206, 235
al-Iṣfahānī, Abū al-Mājid Muḥammad Riḍā, 277
al-Isharāt, 94
Isidore of Seville, 171
Iṣlāḥ wa Tajdīd, 238, 258
Islam and Science, xix, xxi-ii, 70-72, 76, 84, 89, 94, 99, 103, 121, 125, 130, 170-71, 201-3, 207, 210,

212-4, 224, 231, 236, 240-44, 254, 269, 272-3, 275-9, 292-3, 298, 303, 305, 307, 309, 311-2
Islamic Art, 122-4
Islamic Astronomy, 24, 45, 58, 61, 66, 70
Islamic educational institutions, 254, 269
Islamic Orthodoxy, 130, 136, 139-40
Islamic Science, xvi, xxii, 2, 8, 19, 45, 67, 77-8, 101, 121, 124, 131, 134-5, 137-8, 142, 173, 270, 289, 303, 314
Islamic Scientific Tradition, xvi, xviii-xix, xxi, 1-8, 10, 13, 16, 18, 23-4, 29, 38-40, 44, 46, 49, 54-7, 59-60, 65-7, 70-71, 77, 83-7, 89-90, 113, 121, 124-8, 130, 135-6, 142, 145, 149-52, 155, 158-9, 162-3, 165-6, 169-71, 173, 177-9, 185, 187, 191-2, 195, 201, 203, 213, 235, 241, 279-80, 288, 292, 307, 310
Islamization, 38, 60, 82, 275, 298-300
Islamization of Knowledge, 299-300
Islamize, 234, 242, 299-300
Ismāʿīl, ʿAbd ʿAzīz, 283
Ismāʿilīs, 118, 261
Istanbul, xviii, 55, 73, 126, 166, 169, 234, 255, 257, 267, 270-2
Istiḥsān, 10
Iʿtibār, 87, 88

Jābir ibn Aflaḥ, 195
Jābir ibn Ḥayyān, 6, 15, 25-8, 179
Jabrites, 19, 46, 48
Jafar, S. M., 284
Jāʿfar al-Ṣādiq, 6
Jaffa, Alisa, 123
Jahāngīr, 167, 214
al-Jāḥiẓ, 114, 127
Jahm b. Ṣafwān, 19, 20, 48
Jālūt, 34, 165
James I, 214
Jāmiʿa Milliyya Islāmiyya, 253
Jansen, J. J. G., 282
Jawāhir, 38, 80, 102-3, 120, 250, 281, 283
Jawhar, 21, 74, 92, 96-97
Jawharī, Ṭantāwī, 31, 283-4
Jayyusi, Salma Khadra, 16, 162
al-Jazārī, 132
Jessup, H., 233
Jesuits, 233
Jism, 35, 92, 116
John Duns Scotus, 184
John of Seville, 176, 179
John Scotus Eriugena, 172
Johnson, Phillip, 297
Johnston, Leonard, 180
Jones, William, 217-8
Joseph R. Straye, 174
Joseph the Spaniard, 173
Journal of Islamic Social Sciences, 137, 299
Journal of the Asiatic Society, 219
Jundishāpūr, 40-1
al-Jūzjānī, 66-7, 160

Kaʿba, 121, 304
Kalām, 84, 282
Kalām Physical Theory, 20
Kalin, Ibrahim, 95
Kāmil, Muḥammad, 284
Kant, Immanuel, 202
Karīm Khān Zand, 206
Kashf al-Ẓunūn, 120
al-Kāshī, Jamshīd Ghiyāth al-Dīn, 57, 132
Kātib Çelebī, 169
al-Kawkabī, Sayyid ʿAbd al-Raḥmān, 282
Kazvini, M. M., 80
Keddie, Nikki R., 255
Kedourie, Elie, 255, 282
Kemal, Namik, 267

Kemalism, 268-9
Kence, Aykut, 273
Kennedy, E.S., 24, 45, 57, 65-8, 133
Kepler, 86-7, 195, 266
Khālid b. Yazīd, 14
Khalīfa, Hājjī, 126
Khalīl, 50, 164
Khān, Amīr Dūst Muḥammad, 255
Khān, Nādir, 206
Khān, Riḍā, 207
Khan, Sayyid Ahmad, 229, 244-7, 251, 254, 258, 262, 265, 281
Khāqānī Zīj, 132
Khārijites, 12, 19
Khārijites, 46-7
al-Khatīb, Mūsā, 284
Khawārij, 12
Khayāl, 34
Khayrābādī, Maulānā Fazl-i Ḥaq, 292
al-Khāzin, 55, 88
Khedive ʿAbbās, 232
Khedive Ismaʿīl, 232
Khedive Saʿīd, 232
Kheirandish, Elaheh, 86
al-Khūlī, Amīn, 290
Khurāsān, 8, 26, 165, 168
Khūzistān, 40
Khwājawī, Muḥammad, 95
Khwārazm, 37, 72, 164
al-Khwārazmī, 37, 72, 152
al-Kindī, Yaʿqūb ibn Isḥāq, 22, 86, 142, 178, 288
King, David, 45, 133
Kirmani, Riaz, 302
Kirsten, Peter, 194
Kitāb al-Dalāʾil, 115
Kitāb al-Funūn, 128
Kitāb al-Ḥurūf, 74
Kitāb Jawāhir al-Qurʾān, 80, 101, 119-20
Kitāb al-Kharāj, 17
Kitāb al-Manāẓir, 58, 87
Kitāb al-Mashāʿir, 95
Kitāb al-Tawḥīd, 116, 277
Klaproth, M. H., 202
Kochu Bey, 204
Koenig, Johan Gerard, 218
Koyré, Alexandre, 188, 190
Kraus, Paul, 25
Krisciunas, Kevin, 133
Kūfa, 3, 7, 15-16, 26, 47, 168
al-Kūhī, Abū Sahl, 53
Kuhn, Thomas, 141, 299
Kumūn, 37, 49
Kushiner, James M., 297
Kyd, Robert, 220-1

Lahore, 230, 246-50, 252-3, 285
Langbaine, Gerard, 195
Lapidus, Ira M., 131
Latin, 14, 16, 37, 58, 68, 127, 138, 173-82, 196, 201, 248
Lattin, Harriet Pratt, 173
Laud, William, 195
Lavoisier, Antoine, 202
League of Nations, 211
Leaman, O., 98
Leibniz, Gottfried Wilhelm, 202
Leonardo da Vinci, 188
Levtzion, N., 208
Lewis, Bernard, 131, 235
Lindberg, David, 86, 137, 187, 189, 191
Lings, Martin, 306-7
Lingua franca, 1, 209
Lockyer, Norman, 230
Logic, xxi, 49, 85, 94, 108, 132, 160, 172, 177, 252, 290
Lord Minto, 228
Luptins, 173

Macarthy, R. J., 100, 127
MacCaulay, Thomas Babington, 227
Mackay, David, 22-1
Madāris, 47, 155, 157-9, 225, 227, 237, 304

Mādda, 74
Maddison, Francis, 199
Madinah, 3, 8, 10, 13-15, 17, 148, 156, 207-8, 239-40
Madrasa, 57, 133, 155, 158, 162, 237
Madrasat al-Iṣlāh, 253
Magyar, 173
Māhiya, 19-20, 47-8, 91-3, 96, 104-5, 108, 191, 229, 271, 293, 302
al-Māhānī, 54-5
Mahmood, S. Bashir ud-Din, 285
Mahmood, Syed, 226, 228
al-Mahzūmī, Muhammad Pasha, 265
Maier, Anneliese, 188-90
Maimonides, 90
Majid, Anouar, 242
Majlis, 156
Makdisi, George, 127-8, 130, 139-40, 156
Makkah, xvi, 57, 121, 134, 207-8, 239-40, 245, 255, 286
Malaya, 236
Malik, Hafeez, 246
Mālik b. Anas, 10
Maliki, 146
Mamlūks, 165, 205
al-Mā'mūn, 43, 88
al-Manār, 275, 282, 289
Māshāllāh, 16
al-Manṣūr, 41, 62
al-Manī, Fakhr al-Dīn, 232
Manzoor, Pervez S., 303
Map of Hindoostan, 217
al-Maqṣad al-Asnā fī Sharaḥ Asma' Allah al-Ḥusnā, 111
Marāgha, 57, 66-9, 164
al-Marāghī, Muḥammad Mustafa, 290
Mardin, Şerif, 242
Mark of Toledo, 176
Markham, Clements, 217, 223
Marmura, Michael E., 103
Marx, Karl, 215
Marxism, 242
Mashhad, 235
al-Mashriq, 275
Mason, Herbert, 162
Massie, J. W., 225
Massignon, Louis, 35, 37, 157
Masud, Muhammad Khalid, 290
al-Ma'ṣūmī, 55
Mathematics, 23-4, 31, 52, 54, 57, 70, 73, 77, 90, 94, 101, 123, 132, 134, 136-7, 145, 162, 177, 180, 228, 234, 290, 307
al-Mātuīdī, 116
Mawjūd, 74
Maẓhar, Ismā'īl, 276-7
McEvoy, James, 182
McVaugh, Michael, 176
Meḥmed 'Alī Pasha, 205
Medici Court, 232
Medicine, xvii, 2, 14, 17, 23-4, 26-7, 42, 52, 77, 101-2, 132, 145, 153, 160, 172, 177-8, 180, 185, 199, 252, 254, 287, 290, 310
Melikian-Chirvani, Assadullah Souren, 134
Melville, Herman, 77
Mendelsohn, Everett, 125, 151
Merton, Robert K., 141
Merv, 9, 15, 161
Metaphysica, 50, 73, 92, 93
Metaphysics, xxi, 5, 22, 73-4, 85, 95-6, 100, 104, 150, 190-91, 279, 302, 308
Meteorology, 180
Miḥna, 88
Micheal Scot, 179
Mill, James, 229
Minute on Education, 227-8
Mīr Damād, 94, 167
Mir, Mustansir, 292
Miracle, 185, 272, 284-5
Missionary Colleges, 233
Mithāq, 35

Miyān, Dūdhū, 239
Mi'yār al-'ilm, 104
Modern science, xv-xvii, xix-xxii, 38, 54, 71, 90, 124, 126-8, 138, 141-2, 144-5, 162, 170, 178, 187, 189, 192, 196, 203, 206, 210, 213, 216, 224, 228, 231, 241-4, 249-50, 253-4, 264, 267, 269-70, 272, 275-6, 280-81, 283, 285-6, 288, 290, 293-6, 298-304, 308-9, 311-14
Modernity, 190, 239, 241, 242-3, 258, 304
Mohaghegh, Mehdi, 310
Moin, M., 73
Monastery, 171, 172, 174, 176
Mongol, xviii, 136, 164, 165, 166
Monopsychism, 183
Moore, Keith, 287
Morris, James Winston, 95
Moses Farachi, 179
Mousa, Mohammad Yousef, 73
Mozarabs, 176
Mozart, Wolfgang Amadeus, 201
Muḥāsbī, 115
Muḥammad, 1, 7, 11, 18, 22, 53-4, 57, 62, 72, 95, 100, 147, 165, 197, 205-6, 232-3, 235, 239-40, 242, 247-8, 250, 252, 255-6, 265, 267, 276, 281-4, 288, 290, 299
Muḥammad 'Alī, 205-6, 240
Muḥammad Shāh, 206
al-Mujāhid, Sharīf, 255
Mu'jizāt, 110
al-Mulk, Nawāb Muhsin, 251
al-Munqidh min al-Ḍalāl, 100, 259
al-Muqtaṭaf, 233, 275
Mu'tazila, 19, 48-9
Mu'tazilites, 47, 99
Mueller, M., 120
Mughal Empire, 163
Muhammadan Anglo-Oriental College, 248
Muir, William, 247
Mujarradāt, 92
Mullā Niẓām al-Dīn, 252
Mumkin, 91-2
Mumtani', 91
Munro, Thomas, 224
Murji'a, 12
Murji'ites, 46, 47
Murphy, Nancey, 296-7
al-Murtaḍā, Muḥammad, 239
Musa, Mark, 197
Muslim, Muṣtafā, 285
Muslim traditionalist, 305
Musnad of Aḥmad, 78
Mustafa Kemal, 234, 242, 254, 268, 273
Mustafa Naima, 204
Muta'allihūn, 258
Mutakallimūn, xxi, 6, 13, 19-21, 23, 36, 82, 143
Mu'tazila, 19
Mu'āwiya, 12, 14
Muḥaddithūn, 13
al-Muzaffar, Raḍā, 95

Nadwat al-'Ulamā', 253
Nahda, 242
al-Najjār, al-Ḥusayn, 20
Nānautvī, Mawlānā Muḥammad Qāsim, 292
Napoleon, 145, 202, 205
Naqvi, Syed Sibte Nabi, 285
Nasr, Seyyed Hossein, 29, 32, 55-7, 91, 93-5, 98, 116-8, 123, 192, 242, 280, 293, 306-8, 310
al-Nātilī, Abū 'Abd Allāh, 160
National Institute of Science, 231
Nationalism, 209, 242, 268
al-Naubakht, 16
Nawfal, 'Abd al-Razzāq, 284
al-Naẓẓām, Ibrāhīm ibn Sayyār, 20
Necessary Being, 91-3, 96
Nécharīs, 252, 255, 258

Needham, Joseph, 125, 141
Neoplatonism, 55
Nestorius, 41
Neugebauer, O., 65-7, 69-70
Neuroscience, xvii, xxii, 293
Newton, Isaac, xvii, 190, 201, 266, 296
Nizzāmiyya Madrasa, 104
Nicole Oresme, 188
Nigeria, 236
Nisibis, 39, 41
Novum Organum, 197
Nūḥ ibn Manṣūr, 161
Nurbakī, Halūk, 284
Nurcu Movement, 269
Nursi, Badiuzzeman Said, 267
Nyazee, Imran Ahsan Khan, 147

Oktar, Adnan, 272
On the Nature of Things, 172
On the Unicity of the Intellect, Against the Averroists, 183
Ontology, 95-6, 302, 308
Optics, 86, 145, 177, 180
Organon, 42, 91
Oriental Society, 233
Orme, Nicholas, 174
Orpheus, 197
Otto, 176
Ottoman, xviii, 135, 140, 163, 165, 167, 169, 204-7, 232, 234, 239-40, 242, 262, 267
Ottoman Empire, 135, 167
Oxford, 29, 48, 76, 107, 112, 128, 144, 146, 148, 174-5, 181-2, 195, 199, 230, 235, 248, 251, 297
Ozbegs, 166

Pagel, Walter, 199
Pahlavī, 40, 43, 50, 71, 207
Pahlavī Dynasty, 207
Pakistan Academy of Sciences, 231
Panchiat System, 225
Pānipatī, Shaikh Muḥammad Ismāʿīl, 246-7
Pan-Islamic, 211, 256-7
Paris, 14-15, 17, 25, 62, 66, 87, 127, 174-5, 180, 183-4, 188, 196, 234-5, 246, 254, 256-8, 262, 286
Parviz Morewedge, 73, 92-3
Pāsha, Ibrahīm, 205, 233
Pathshalas, 225
Peacocke, Arthur, 296
Pedersen, Johannes, 161
Pellat, Ch., 127
Pelling, Margaret, 199
Perennial Philosophy, 307
Peripatetics, 97
Permanent Settlement, 216, 220, 227
Peter the Hermit, 99
Peters, Ted, 153
Philoponus, 107
Philosophy of science, 249, 299, 301
Physica, 107, 190
Pines, Shlomo, 22, 45
Pingree, David, 24, 45, 62
Planck, 154
Plato, 81, 105, 153, 176, 180, 183, 197, 258
Plato of Tivoli, 176
Plotinus, 37, 50
Pococke, Edward, 195
Polkinghorne, John, 297
Pope, Alexander, 202
Pope John XXII, 184
Pope Sylvester II, 173
Popper, Karl, 299
Portuguese, 214
Posterior Analytics, 182
Precursorism, 45
Prideaux, Humphrey, 196
Priestley, Joseph, 202
Principia, 201
Prophet of Islam, xx, xxi, 1, 4, 6, 76, 78-9, 129, 148-9, 248, 258, 286
Ptolemaic Models, 64, 154

Ptolemy, 40, 53, 58, 61, 65, 68-9, 81, 85, 88, 177, 180

Qabasāt Ḥaqq al-Yaqīn fī Ḥudūth al-ʿālam, 94
al-Qānūn fi'l-Ṭibb, 179
Qābīl, 33
Qajār, 94, 206, 235
Qalb, 35
Qiyās, 10, 147
Quantum Physics, xvii, 241, 296, 299
Quasem, Muhammad Abul, 120
Queen of Sheba, 33
Quinine, 221, 223
Qum, 95, 136, 235
Qur'ān, xix-xx, xxii, 2-5, 11-12, 20, 29, 30-39, 44, 46-9, 51-2, 62, 72-3, 75-6, 79-81, 83-5, 88-96, 101-3, 110, 113-15, 119-20, 123-4, 132, 143, 147-9, 156, 196, 203, 212-13, 242, 244, 249-53, 256-7, 261, 267, 269-70, 272, 276-92, 304-5, 307, 311, 314
Qur'ānic Cosmology, 62, 84, 90
Qur'ānic metaphysics, 30
Qur'ānic Order of Nature, 5
Qur'ānic Sciences, 2, 5
Qur'ānic Universe, 31
Qur'ānic Worldview, xxii, 37-8, 85, 280
Qurashi, M. M., 284
Qusṭā b. Lūqā, 62
Quṭb, Sayyed, 212

Ragep, Jamil, 20, 54, 57, 67, 77, 82, 86, 137, 193
Raḥla fi'l ʿilm, 208
Rahman, Fazlur, 98, 238, 242
Raïnow, T. I., 118
Raja Ram Mohun Roy, 228
Rasā'il, 25, 55, 116-17
al-Rashid, Hārūn, 17, 53, 169
Ray, 9, 55, 179
al-Rāzī, Abū Bakr Muḥammad b. Zakariyyā, 18, 22-3, 62, 85, 142-3, 153, 288
al-Rāzī, Fakhr al-Dīn, 56
Reductionism, 45
Reductionist approach, 213
Renaissance, 123, 138, 188, 191, 194, 196, 199
Renan, Ernest, 257, 262
Rennell, James, 216
Revelation, 1, 5, 31, 33, 36, 39, 44, 51, 79, 129, 209, 250, 264, 280, 291, 305-6, 313
Richard II, 193
Riḍā, Rashīd, 267, 275-6, 282, 289
al-Risāla al-Qudssiya, 119
Risalāt al-Ḥashr, 95
al-Risālat al-Kālīyya, 133
Risale, 204
Riyāḍiyyāt, 94
Robert de Courçon, 180
Robert Grosseteste, 182
Robert of Chester, 176, 179
Robert of Ketton, 196
Robertson, John M., 197
Roe, Thomas, 214
Roger Bacon, 182
Roman Empire, 41, 172
Rosen, Frederic, 37, 72
Rosetta Stone, 202
Rossini, Carl, 272
Rousseau, Jean-Jacques, 202
Royal Asiatic Society of London, 246
Royal Society of London, 217
al-Ruʿaynī, Abū'l Qāsim b. Firruh b. Khalaf b. Aḥmad, 289
Ruḥ, 35
Ruska, Julius, 15, 37
Russell, Robert John, 294
Rutherford, Daniel, 202

Saadia, 90
al-Ṣābī, Abū Isḥāq, 53

Sabra, A. I., 45-6, 58, 61, 68, 70, 82, 87-8, 129, 139, 151-2, 154, 199
Sabziwārī, Ḥājī Mullā Hadī, 94
al-Ṣādiq, Imām Jaʿfar, 277
al-Ṣafadī, 50-1
Sago Palm, 220-1
Saliba, George, 24-5, 61-2, 64-9, 131-2, 154
Salīm III, 205
Samarqand, 8, 9, 57, 132-3, 158, 164, 304
Sami, A., 233
Sangwan, Satpal, 228
Sanskrit, 23, 40, 43, 62, 227-8
Saqīfā Banū Sāʿda, 11
Saran, A. K., 293
Sardar, Ziauddin, 301, 303
Sargent, Steven D., 189
Ṣarrūf, Yaʿqūb, 275
Sarton, George, 17, 127
Sassanian Dynasty, 39
Savile, Henry, 195
Sayf al-Dawla, 64
Sayili, Aydin, 37, 57
Sayin, Ümit, 273
al-Sayūṭī, Jalāl uddīn, 284
Sayyid Ahmad Khan, 229, 244-7, 251, 254, 258, 262, 265, 281
Sayyid, Bobby, S., 242
Scaliger, Joseph, 194
Schacht, Joseph, 146
School of Illumination, 94
Schweigger, Solomon, 196
Science and Christianity, xvii, xx, 294, 296
Science and Religion, xvii-xviii, 180, 275, 293, 297
Science of Balance, 26-8
Science of Nature, 73, 301
Science Research Foundation, 272
Scientific Advisory Committee, 231
scientific journals, 275
Scientific Revolution, 125-6, 136, 141, 152, 154, 189, 191-2, 288
Scientism, 296
Sefāretnāme, 235
Selden, John, 195
al-Shāfiʿī, 146, 148
Shāh ʿAbbās, 164, 167
Shāh ʿAbd al-Raḥīm, 238
Shāh Jahān, 167
Shah Naṣīr al-Dīn, 257
Shāh Rūkh, 164
Shahbāz, Sayyid ʿAbd al-Ghafūr, 256
Shahīd, Sayyid Aḥmad, 238, 239
Shāhīn, ʿAbd al-Raḥmān, 284
Shaltūt, Maḥmūd, 290
Shapiro, Arthur M., 273
Sharīʿa, 276, 277, 289
Sharabi, Hisham, 242, 275
al-Shāṭibī, Abū Isḥāq Ibrāhīm bin Mūsā al-Andulasī, 289
al-Shawāhid al-rububiyya, 95
al-Shawkānī, Muḥammad ibn ʿAlī, 239
Shaykh Aḥmad of Massina, 207
al-Shayyal, J., 232
Shīʿa, 12
Shiblī Nuʿmānī, 253
Shihāb al-Dīn, Yāqūt bin ʿAbd Allāh, 161
Shīʿites, 99
al-Shirāzī, Quṭb al-Dīn, 67-8, 132
al-Shukūk ʿalā Baṭlīmūs, 61, 88
Shukūk Literature, 61, 63, 64
al-Shumayyil, Shiblī, 275
Siddiqi, Mazheruddin, 243
Ṣidqī, Muḥammad Tawfīq, 282
Siger of Brabant, 184
Simplicius, 107
Simpson, Joe Leigh, 287
Sir Henry Savile, 195
Sir Joseph Banks, 220
Sīrat Rasūl Allāh, 148
Sirhindī, Shaykh Aḥmad, 238, 292

Smith, W. Cantwell, 243
Smith, Wolfgang, 296
Socialism, 211
Society of Arts and Science, 233
Spain, 8, 15-16, 71, 84, 123, 145, 162, 173, 176-7, 179, 292
Spices, 215, 220
St. Benedict, 171
Stahl, William H., 171
Starkey, George, 198
Stenberg, Leif, 298
Stoddart, William, 123
Stoeger, S. J. William R., 294
Stone, Lucian W. Jr., 293
Storer, Norman, 145
Strange, Alexander, 230
Strohmaier, G., 177
Stroumsa, Sarah, 153
Sudan, 206, 257
Sufis, 48, 270
Suleymān, 167
Sullam al-Samā', 132
Sultan ʿAbd al-Ḥamīd II, 257
Sunna, xx-xxi, 13, 47, 76, 147-8, 203, 210, 213, 284, 286, 307
Sunnīs, 99
Supreme Principle, 28
Sūra, 6, 32, 285
Svanberg, Igvar, 234
Swartz, Merlin L., 128
Swinburne, Richard, 297
Syria, 39, 42, 53, 232-3
Syrian Protestant College, 233
Syrian Scientific Society, 233

Ṭabāṭabā'ī, M., 95
Tabrīz, 165-6, 235
Tadbīr, 114
Tafsīr al-ʿilmī, 38, 280-1
Tafsīr, 2, 4, 250-1, 281
Tahāfut al-Tahāfut, 107
Tahdhīb al-Akhlāq, 248
al-Ṭahṭāwī, Rifāʿah, 242
Tāj Mahal, 167
Tajriba, 87
al-Tanakhi, Tahir, 283
Taqdīr, 114
Taqlīd, 239
al-Tawḍīḥ fī Ḥall Jawāmid al-Tanqīḥ, 147
Tawḥīd, 27, 29, 36, 72, 116, 129, 262, 279, 308
Tea, 221-2
Teleology, xvii, 89, 191
Thābit ibn Qurrah, 43
Thamūd, 33
Thanvī, Maulānā Ashraf ʿAlī, 291
The Letters of Gerbert, 173
Theology, xvi, xviii, xx-xxii, 91, 94, 172, 182-4, 240, 294, 296-7
Theology of Nature, xvi, 240, 294
Theon of Alexandria, 85
Thomas Aquinas, 183-4
Thorndike, Lynn, 188
Tibawi, A. L., 119, 233
Timaeus, 82, 180
Timūr, xviii, 163-7, 169, 206, 214
Timūrī Empire, 163
Tīpū Sultān, 216
Toledo, 176-7, 179
Toomer, Gerald, 53, 195
Translation Movement, 41
Transmitted Sciences, 51, 96, 113
Transoxania, 164, 168
Tulip Age, 205-6
Türkçügün Esaslari, 234
Turkey, 204, 234, 236, 242, 254, 257, 267-9, 272-3, 314
Turkic Bulghārs, 164
Turkish Academy of Sciences, 273-4,
al-Ṭūsī, Nasīr al-Dīn, 235

Ulugh Beg, 57, 132-3, 158, 163-4
al-ʿulūm al-ʿaqliyya, 51, 96
al-ʿulūm al-naqliyya, 51, 96
Umayyads, 15-16

Umma, 11, 208-9, 211
United Nations, 211
Unmoved Mover, 50
ʿUrābī, Colonel Aḥmad, 256
al-ʿUrḍī, Mu'ayyad al-Dīn, 132
al-ʿurwa al-wuthqā, 256
Uṣūl al-Dīn, xx, 298
Uṣūl al-Fiqh, xx, 289, 298
Uṣul al-Jadīd School, 234
Usher, James, 195

Van Den Bergh, Simon, 107
Van Steenberghen, Fernand, 180
Vauquelin, L. N., 202
Venerable Bede, 171
Vidyalayas, 227
Viking, 173
Voll, John, O., 208
Voltaire, 188, 202, 261
von Grunebaum, Gustave, 242
von Linné, Carl, 202
Vossius, G. J., 194

Wafayāt al-Aʿyān wa Anbā' Abnā'a al-Zamān, 3, 26, 51
al-Wahhāb, Muḥammad ibnʿAbd, 239
Wahhābī Movement, 239
Wahhābīs, 140, 206
Wāhima, 34
Wajdī, Muḥammad Farīd, 283
Wājib al-Wujūd, 91
Walī Allāh, Shāh, 207, 238-9, 253, 292
Wallis, John, 199
al-Waqā'ʿi, 233
Waqf, 149, 158
Watt, James, 201
Watt, Montgomery, 19, 48, 156
Watton, William, 198
Weber, Max, 140
Webster, Charles, 199
Westerlund, David, 234
Westernization, 230, 233, 253, 268
Whinfield, E. H., 80
Wilczynski, Jan Z., 118
William of Moerbeke, 178
William of Ockham, 184
Wilson, H. H., 228
World Muslim League, 286
Wujūd, 29, 74, 84, 91, 95-6

Xenophon, 112, 115

Yacoup al-Ṭib, 233
Yahya, Harun, 272
Yaḥyā ibn Khālid ibn Barmak, 53
Yaḥyā, O., 127
Yaʿqūb b. Ṭāriq, 24, 62
Yathrib, 10
Yazdajird III, 40
Yazdī, Muḥammad Bāqir ibn Zayn al-ʿĀbidīn, 57
Young Turk Movement, 234

Zaman, Iftikhar, 81
Zaydān, Jurjī, 275
Zayed, Saʿid, 73
Ziadat, Adel A., 232-3, 275
Zīj, 63, 65, 69, 88, 132
Zīj al-Mumtaḥan, 88
Zindanni, Sheikh Abdul Majeed, 287
Ziya Gökalp, 234
Zoroastrians, 8